CHAUCER, LANGLAND, ARTHUR

CHAUCER, LANGLAND, ARTHUR:

Essays in
Middle English Literature

by

Alfred L. Kellogg

RUTGERS UNIVERSITY PRESS

New Brunswick, New Jersey

Copyright © 1972 by Rutgers University,
The State University of New Jersey

Library of Congress Cataloging in Publication Data

Kellogg, Alfred Latimer, 1915–
    Chaucer, Langland, Arthur: essays in Middle English lit-
erature.

    Includes bibliographical references.
    CONTENTS: Brityna, a new character in Geoffrey of Mon-
mouth's British book (with R. A. Caldwell)—The location of
the Green Chapel in Sir Gawain and the Green Knight.—Malory
and color symbolism: two notes on his translation of the Queste
del St. Graal. [etc.]
    1. Chaucer, Geoffrey, d. 1400—Criticism and interpretation.
2. Langland, William, 1330?–1400? 3. Arthur, King. I. Title.

PR1924.K4   821'.1'09   74–138423
            ISBN 0–8135–0683–2

MANUFACTURED IN THE UNITED STATES OF AMERICA
BY RAE PUBLISHING COMPANY, INC., CEDAR GROVE, NEW JERSEY

ACKNOWLEDGMENTS

Permission to reprint essays by Alfred L. Kellogg is acknowledged as follows:

From the American Philosophical Society for "The Location of the Green Chapel in *Sir Gawain and the Green Knight*," published as a Report in the *Year Book* for 1966

Fordham University Press for "Langland and Two Scriptural Texts" from *Traditio*, XIV, 1958

The Mediaeval Academy of America for "An Augustinian Interpretation of Chaucer's Pardoner," "Satan, Langland, and the North," and "Susannah and the 'Merchant's Tale'" from *Speculum*, XXVI, 1951; XXIV, 1949; and XXXV, 1960; respectively

Medium Aevum for "Chaucer's Self-Portrait and Dante's," Vol. XXIX, 1960

Modern Language Association of America for "Chaucer's Satire of the Pardoner" from *PMLA*, LXVI, 1951

Notes and Queries for "The 'Friar's Tale,' Line 1314" from Vol. CCIV, 1959

Pontifical Institute of Medieval Studies for "On the Tradition of Troilus's Vision of the Little Earth" from *Medieval Studies*, XXII, 1960

Revue Belge de Philologie et d'Histoire for " 'Seith Moyses by the Devel': A Problem in the 'Parson's Tale,' " XXXI, 1953

Rutgers University, The State University of New Jersey, for "Langland's 'Canes Muti': The Paradox of Reform" from *Essays in Literary History*, ed. Rudolf Kirk and C. F. Main

Scriptorium for "The Fraternal Kiss in Chaucer's 'Summoner's Tale,' " VII, 1953

Permission to reprint from "To an Athlete Dying Young," in A. E. Housman, *Collected Poems*, has been granted by Holt, Rinehart and Winston, Inc., and The Society of Authors as the literary representative of the Estate of A. E. Housman and Jonathan Cape Ltd.; and from "Among School Children," in the *Collected Poems of W. B. Yeats*, by Mr. M. B. Yeats, Macmillan & Co. Ltd., and the Macmillan Co. of Canada

For Ellen

Contents

List of Illustrations

List of Abbreviations

Preface

It is hoped that the present collection of essays may be of use to anyone interested in medieval literature. It is intended principally for the nonspecialist, although—again it is hoped—there is something of value for the professional scholar. If there is a philosophy behind the collection, its expression is dual. On the one hand, it seeks to avoid the scholarly agon, at the expense perhaps of due recognition of scholarly achievement; for this pardon is besought. On the other hand, it seeks to stress original sources, and the opportunity for enjoyment which original sources offer alike to undergraduate and to graduate of indeterminate vintage.

The present collection of notes and essays has been produced over an extensive period of years, and the accrued indebtedness is, in consequence, very considerable. For financial assistance, I am indebted (chronologically) to the Ford Foundation, the John Simon Guggenheim Foundation, the American Philosophical Society, and the Rutgers Research Council, which has continuously supported my research for a period longer than I should wish to remember. For scholarly assistance, I should like to thank Professors Robert A. Pratt and Ruth J. Dean, the University of Pennsylvania; Professor B. J. Whiting, Harvard University; Miss Beryl Smalley, retired Vice-Principal of St. Hilda's College, Oxford; Dr. Richard Hunt, Keeper of Western Manuscripts, the Bodleian Library, Oxford; the Rev. Leonard E. Boyle, O.P., the Pontifical Institute of Medieval Studies, Toronto; the Rev. James A. Weisheipl, O.P., the Dominican House of Studies, River Forest; Professors Morton W. Bloomfield, Harvard University; John Conley, University of Illinois at Chicago Circle; E. Talbot Donaldson, Yale University; Robert A. Kaske, Cornell University.

I am throughout indebted to Professor Alfred L. Foulet of Princeton University, whose constant assistance has been both a support and an inspiration.

CHAUCER, LANGLAND, ARTHUR

1

"Brityna": A New Character in Geoffrey of Monmouth's British Book

I N THE *Register* of Godstow Nunnery appears the following entry, dated *ca.* 1140:

A Charter of Walter, Archedekon of Oxenford, for the lond of Shillyngford the which Brytyn his leman held, I-made to the mynchons of Godestowe. The sentence of this evidence is, that Walter, Archedekon of Oxenford, shewyng that he made the chirche of Seynt Iohn Baptist of Godestowe heire of the lond of Shillyngford, the which Brytyn his leman held by right heritage, and wherof she made hym heire. These beyng witnesse, & cetera.

The editor of the *Register*, Andrew Clark, adds the following note:

The Latin is "hereditavi ecclesiam de Godstow de terra de Schillingford quam Brityna amica mea hereditario jure tenuit et inde ipsa hereditavit me."[1]

The name "Brityna" is apparently rare,[2] but however rare, it inevitably suggests Breton or Welsh connections. This in turn brings to mind the book "in the British tongue, the very old book,"[3] which Geoffrey of Monmouth, as he himself informs us, translated into Latin. This book, which contained precisely what Geoffrey had been looking for, the missing *History of the Kings of Britain,* was obtained for Geoffrey by Walter, Archdeacon of

Oxford, an erudite man and one learned in little-known history.[4] So much we learn at the very beginning of the *Historia*. At the very end, in Geoffrey's valedictory, we learn that Walter had in fact brought the venerable history "ex Britannia."[5] The confusion in the terms "Britannia" and "Brito" are numerically endless, but in the Arthurian controversy they are in fact limited to Wales and Britanny. One view, or more appropriately conviction, has been that Walter conveyed the book out of Wales, the other holds that it was brought out of Britanny. "Brityna" may suggest either.[6]

Brityna's gift, since it ultimately became the property of Godstow Nunnery,[7] brings us into another set of connections involving Walter, Archdeacon of Oxford, and his friend Geoffrey.[8] The dedication of the church of Godstow was carried out by Alexander, Bishop of Lincoln, at whose request Geoffrey laid aside the *Historia* to write the *Prophecies of Merlin*.[9] At this ceremony Walter, Archdeacon of Oxford, not only was present, but made a gift of the tithe of his land of Cutslow, "and put hit vpon the auter in the dedicacion of the chirche, afore Alisaundir bisshop of lincolne and other bisshoppes, the which halowed hit & cetera."[10]

Here we are in a company of familiars. Brityna is, therefore, not simply a name snatched "out of Fairye," but a name existing in an established context. It is rather clear that Brityna is to be accepted as a lady of wealth and family. As such, could not Brityna have been an interested party in the unknown transactions responsible for the appearance of the work which made the fame of the Britons celebrated throughout the world? If we accept the possibility of her Breton or Welsh connections, may she not have bestowed upon Walter a book—of whatever origins—as readily as a parcel of land?[11]

NOTES

1. *The English Register of Godstow Nunnery, near Oxford,* ed. Andrew Clark (London, 1905–1906), II, 535. *EETS O.S.* Nos. 129–130.
2. Dr. Alan Orrick was kind enough to look into this problem some years ago, but did not consider his results conclusive.
3. "quendam britannici sermonis librum vetustissimum" (*Historia regum*

Britanniae, ed. Acton Griscom [London, 1929], p. 219). Lack of the references to Geoffrey as writer, to Walter, and to the British Book is a characteristic of the variant text (Geoffrey of Monmouth, *Historia regum Britanniae,* ed. Jacob Hammer [Cambridge, 1951], pp. 22, 250, 264). Hammer worked from a photostat, seems not to have examined the Exeter manuscript (E) itself. His account (p. 6) of this manuscript is not altogether correct. The matter is too complicated for full discussion here, but the entire prologue does occur in E, separated from the variant text following it in such a way as to indicate that it is not to be taken as part of that text. The absence of these references is, of course, one of the reasons for the suggestion made in note 11 below.

4. "vir in oratoria arte. atque in exoticis hystoriis eruditus" (Griscom, *Historia,* p. 219).

5. *Ibid.,* p. 536.

6. John J. Parry and Robert A. Caldwell, "Geoffrey of Monmouth," in *Arthurian Literature in the Middle Ages,* ed. R. S. Loomis (Oxford, 1959), p. 81, note 1. Cited hereafter as *ALMA.*

7. More properly, the tithe rather than the land was the gift to Godstow.

8. For relationship between them, see *ALMA,* p. 73.

9. *Godstow Register,* p. 28. The dedication occurred in 1138/9.

10. *Godstow Register,* p. 321.

11. It is possible to go further than a completely undefined book and to suggest that Walter's book is in fact the "variant version" which in the opinion of the present writers was earlier than the Vulgate; i.e., that edited by Griscom. In the introduction to his edition (cited above, note 3), Hammer did not discuss the order of the two versions, although he wrote in a way suggesting that he considered the variant to be derived from the Vulgate (see, e.g., pp. 17, 19). In conversation with one of the writers, he gave the impression that he believed the variant to be the earlier. This is not, however, within the province of the present note.

2

The Identity of the Green Chapel in "Sir Gawain and the Green Knight"

THE PROBLEM OF THE LOCATION of the Green Chapel, which Sir Gawain must, according to his oath, seek out through all the hardships of winter, although his reward is to be the somewhat questionable pleasure of having his head removed by a gigantic Green Knight, is a difficult and perennially appealing one.[1] Quite apart from the nature of the reward Gawain is to receive for his efforts, he has not the slightest idea where the Green Chapel is (1053)—yet he must, to preserve his honor and the honor of the Round Table, arrive there on the first of the year. At the beginning, his route is reasonably clear. From southern Camelot (Winchester? Cadbury?), he proceeds generally north until he enters the wilderness of Wirral in Cheshire (701). After this, however, no further locations are forthcoming. It is nevertheless clear that Gawain is to be understood as having traversed a very considerable distance after Wirral, since his most harrowing adventures are reserved for the period after Wirral. More than a century ago, Sir Frederic Madden suggested that the Green Chapel to which Sir Gawain went was the "Chapel of the Grune," which he had seen "on older maps of Cumberland."[2] However, Sir Frederic's remarks about the Chapel of the Grune

Reprinted, with slight revisions, from *Year Book* of the American Philosophical Society (1966), pp. 652–654.

are quite tentative, since, as he said, "its history I have in vain searched for in various topographical works."[3] Since Sir Frederic's suggestion was, for reasons to be mentioned later, more appealing to me than recent inquiries which place the Green Chapel to the east in Staffordshire or Derbyshire, it seemed worthwhile to take the chance of discovering something about the "Chapel of the Grune" at Skinburness, which lies at the exact northwest corner of England, at the base of the Grune, or "hog's snout," which juts out into Solway Firth.

The first discovery one makes about Skinburness is that, aside from a pleasant vacation hotel, it is simply nonexistent. The Grune also has become merely the surroundings of a path, which vacationers from Carlisle ritually walk. However, at Carlisle is Tullie House, and in Carlisle Castle the newly established County Record Office, both research libraries for Cumberland history and antiquities. At Tullie House, I was kindly provided with several volumes of not particularly antique clippings, which appeared to be the collected works of one "W. T. M.," all published in the "Odds and Ends" column of the *Cumberland News.* "W. T. M.," however, turned out to be Walter Travers McIntire, former director of Tullie House and former editor of the *Cumberland and Westmorland Antiquarian and Archaeological Society.*[4] What the volumes furnished me contained was precisely what Sir Frederic Madden had lacked—an overwhelming array of information concerning everything Cumbrian: folklore, family histories, castles, and—most important—towns. In the article "Skinburness" (November 27, 1931), there appeared the following statement:

> From the details of the service of patrols or coastguards organised in 1552 by Thomas, Lord Wharton, and given by Nicolson and Burn, it appears that "Skinburneyes and Pellathow [Pelutho]" had to keep watch from the "Estcote to *St. John's of the Green [Grune].*"

The quotation from Nicolson and Burn, *History of Westmorland and Cumberland,* proved discoverable and exact.[5] What Madden had conjectured was in fact true. "Grune" was understood to mean "green." Hence at Skinburness there was a "Green Chapel."

This may seem a very facile solution, but there is considerable evidence to support it. First, that furnished by what might be called religious folklore. In medieval direction symbolism, left, "sinister," is always evil: right is always good. In exactly the same way, east and south are invariably good, and west and north invariably bad. As regards north, Satan is so constantly associated with this direction, especially as the green-garbed hunter after souls, that the green-north idea could be relied on by Chaucer to serve as the central point to his *Friar's Tale*.[6] To medieval man, north or northwest was symbolically the land of evil and of Satan. From Langland's *Piers Plowman*, one learns that "northern men" did not find this idea particularly gratifying.[7]

The words "Grune" and "Skinburness" would convey to a non-northern man much of this same feeling of the desolate and demonic. "Grune" in the sense of "hog's snout" is known only in the extreme north. In Lancashire, for instance, it has the usual form derived from Old French "groyne."[8] However, "grune," also spelled "gren" or "grene," did have a generally recognized meaning, namely a "trap for catching birds or animals," with equal frequency used metaphorically as temptation, or trap of the Devil: "Tyl he (Satan) had us caught . . . in our owne *gren*."[9] Secondly, "Skinburness" has approximately the same connotations as those of "grune." According to the *English Place Name Society* in its "*Cumberland*" volumes, the meaning of "Skinburness" is "demon or spectre haunted stronghold."[10]

Finally, the history of the Chapel of the Grune, and to a lesser extent, Holm Cultram, the abbey to which it was attached, reinforces these same suggestions. Holm Cultram was a Cistercian abbey, founded in 1150 as a dependency of Melrose. Its early history was one of great affluence, and it is said to have been the richest house of the Border area. Founded when Cumberland was placed under the rule of Scotland by Stephen as a means of gaining Scottish support, Holm Cultram received large land grants and also large donations. When Cumberland was reconquered, Holm Cultram was the recipient of large English bequests. When about 1300 Edward decided to use Skinburness, then located on the Grune itself, as a western naval base, the abbey's prosperity increased to the point that it gained permission to build a chapel, dedicated to St. John, at Skinburness, since no parish church was near. The chapel must have risen rapidly, since it serves as a landmark on virtually all early maps; but between 1301 and 1304, the whole of Skinburness disappeared into the Solway, leaving only the chapel.[11] Storms of such destructiveness were attributed to divine judgment, but more often to diabolic forces operating in conjunction with necromancers. Here again the suggestion of evil is borne out. Wulsty Castle ("wolf-path"), which was both treasury and fortress for the monks of Holm Cultram, was believed to have had as a tenant Michael Scot, whose distinction in the occult arts was sufficiently great to be noticed by both Dante and Boccaccio. After his death his books were believed to be stored there.[12]

The identity of the Green Chapel is of some importance in that *Sir Gawain and the Green Knight* is a story of temptation as well as of chivalric adventure. If the attempted proof of Sir Frederic Madden's conjecture is valid, the identity of the chapel would conform to the evil connotations of the northwest direction in which Gawain would be travelling in order to reach the chapel. The metaphorical use of "grun" as the trap of Satan; the diabolical connotations of north and green; the existence of the form "gren" or "grene"—all would have favored the belief by any except absolute far-northerners that "grun" was both an odd northern form of "green" and a customary metaphor for temptation. Hence the journey of "good Gawain" to the Green Chapel would in all probability have suggested not only the chivalric journey to the Chapel Perilous, but the spiritual journey into the realm of temptation.

NOTES

1. See the interesting and thoroughly documented study by R. E. Kaske, "Gawain's Green Chapel and the Cave at Wetton Mill," in *Medieval Literature and Folklore Studies* (New Brunswick, N.J., 1970), pp. 111–121. The following brief citations to lines descriptive of Gawain's journey are from *Sir Gawain and the Green Knight,* ed. J. R. R. Tolkien and E. V. Gordon, 2nd ed. rev. Norman Davis (Oxford, 1968).
2. *Syr Gawayne,* ed. Sir Frederic Madden (London, 1839), p. 320.
3. *Ibid.,* p. 321.
4. A selection of Mr. McIntire's articles has been published by the *Cumberland News.* The title given by the editor, Thomas Gray, is *Lakeland and the Borders of Long Ago* (Carlisle, 1948).
5. I, lxxxvi.
6. III [D], 1382–1383; 1413–1414; 1448 (*Works,* p. 90).

7. See "Satan, Langland, and the North," pp. 29, 31 below.
8. See Joseph Wright, *English Dialect Dictionary*, under "groyne."
9. See *MED*, under "grin(e n. (b)."
10. II, 294.
11. The history of Holm Cultram Abbey is given in considerable detail in *The Victoria History of the County of Cumberland* (London, 1905), II, 162–173.
12. McIntire, "Wolsty Castle," *Cumberland News* (Oct. 21, 1933); Dante, *Inferno* XX, 115–117; Boccaccio, *Decameron* VIII, IX.

3

Malory and Color Symbolism: Two Notes on His Translation of the "Queste del Saint Graal"

I

THE OLD FRENCH *Queste del Saint Graal*,[1] provides a kind of key to medieval literary taste. Despite a sophisticated but certainly emphatic piety, the work possessed an appeal such as to make it an indispensable part of the most complete and finished version of the Arthurian romance—the so-called Vulgate Arthurian, which was composed in the early thirteenth century.[2] Generally considered to have been written by a Cistercian monk[3] and hence presumably out of accord with romance tradition, the *Queste del Saint Graal* nevertheless does have a very distinct function in the Vulgate version. It serves as a kind of bridge between the immense and brightly colored *Lancelot* and the compact, somber *Mort Artu*.[4] It represents the transition from youth to age—from natural to supernatural values—which the Middle Ages felt to be in accord with the rhythm of existence.[5] Needless to say, not everyone found himself willing to accept piously and graciously this great transition. Amongst those who did not was Sir Thomas Malory. With the youthful feats of Lancelot he felt in sympathy; with the great battle on Salisbury Plain he had enough in common to present its action movingly. However, the *Queste del Saint Graal*, which under the decorous fiction of the eschewing of earthly knighthood for heavenly knighthood really

cried out "Repent! Repent!,"[6] gave Malory difficulty. One difficulty was temperamental. In the *Queste*, earthly chivalry is heavily downgraded. Celestial knighthood, on the other hand, which
evidently held for Malory very limited appeal, is presented as the
supreme ideal. In its presence every earthly ideal withers. The
second difficulty was that, despite his feelings, Malory simply
could not avoid coming to terms with the *Queste*. It was solidly
built into the structure of the Vulgate version, and the Vulgate
was not only Malory's principal source, but constituted the only
major unified pattern of the Arthurian story.[7]

The two following notes concern two incidents in the *Queste*
—both visions—one experienced by an earthly knight, Sir Gawain;
the other by a celestial knight, Sir Bors. The incidents, it is hoped,
may be of interest as providing specific examples of Malory's
spiritual travail in translating the *Queste* and as indicating the
existence, in the *Queste*, of an element proper to the *Queste* alone
—an extensive and consistent pattern of theologically oriented
color symbolism.[8]

As has been intimated, the *Queste del Saint Graal* is the quest
after supernatural values.[9] However, as its author insists, its characters are not abstractions but real people.[10] This is of some
importance, because, as has also been intimated, the *Queste* is
hortatory in nature.[11] It is addressed to those who are in need of
initiating the spiritual search and those who are in need of the
strength to persevere in it. Of the first classification, Gawain is the
outstanding exemplar. The nature of the quest—the search for
salvation—Gawain has consistently refused to understand.
Although he is the first to vow to pursue the Quest, certain fleshly
interests make his chances of success exceedingly remote.[12]
Gawain is an earthly knight, and as such seeks earthly adventures. In these, when they occur, he finds only "meschaance";
when they do not—which is the usual course of affairs—he experiences only boredom.[13] One day, falling in company with Hestor
des Mares, who has had a similar experience in the Quest, the two
companions come upon a deserted chapel. After dutifully saying
his orisons, Gawain has a vision. In Malory's translation:

Sir Gawayne hym semed he cam into a medow full of herbis and
floures, and there he saw a rake of bullis, an hundrith and fyffty,

that were proude and black, save three of hem was all whyght, and one had a blacke spotte.[14]

After further adventures, they arrive at the chapel of Nasciens, the hermit, who explains to Gawain the meaning of the meadow he has seen in vision.

"Sir," seyde [the ermyte unto] sir Gawayne, "the fayre medow and the rak therein ought to be undirstonde the Rounde Table, and by the medow ought to be undirstonde humilité and paciens; tho be the thynges which bene allwey grene and quyk. For that men mowe no tyme overcom humilité and pacience, therefore was the Rounde Table founden, and the shevalry hath ben at all tymes so hyghe by the fraternité which was there that she myght nat be overcom: for men seyde she was founded in paciens and in humilité. At the rack ete an hondred and fyffty bullys, but they ete nat in the medowe, for if they had, their hartes sholde have bene sette in humilité and paciens; and the bullis were proude and blacke sauff only three.

"And by the bullys ys undirstonde the felyshyp of the Rounde Table whych for their synne and their wyckednesse bene blacke; blackenes ys as much to sey withoute good vertues or workes. And the three bulles whych were whyght sauff only one had bene spotted? The two whyght betokenythe sir Galahad and sir Percivale, for they be maydyns and clene withoute spotte, and the thirde, that had a spotte, signifieth sir Bors de Gaynes, which trespassed but onys in his virginité."[15]

Malory's translation of Gawain's vision and its interpretation offers a few insights, relevant principally to Malory's views on spirituality. In the first place, Malory is evidently inclined to give what he considers theological subtleties a brusque treatment. However, the *Queste* author is of an exactly opposite persuasion. His aim is to demonstrate the worthlessness of worldly values, and the necessity of abandoning them in favor of otherworldly values. This he accomplishes by a judicious mixture of romantic knight-errant story and what must have been to him popularized, or popularizable, theology. In Gawain's vision of the bulls and the meadow, what he is presenting is an abbreviated allegory of sin. Since, generally speaking, no one is all good or all bad, the bulls are described as spotted ("vairié") with sin[16]—a familiar image used extensively by Langland in his depiction of Haukyn, the active man's coat:

"Bi Criste," quod Conscience tho · "thi best cote, Haukyn,
Hath many moles and spottes · it moste ben ywasshe."
"ȝe who so toke hede," quod Haukyn · "byhynde and bifore."[17]

However, while almost all of the bulls are as thoroughly spotted as Haukyn's coat, Bors's markings are much more difficult to define. As a result of his evening with King Brangoire's daughter, Bors has acquired a spot.[18] However, as a result of his repentance he is now neither quite spotted nor quite unspotted; he has only the mark of a spot—a "signe de tache."[19] What the author of the *Queste* seems to be doing is presenting a theological commonplace in as mystifying a fashion as he is capable of. Bors has sinned once, but he has since so effectively amended his damaged chastity that his one offense has been entirely forgiven him. His sin has therefore been removed, but the proclivity remains.[20] Hence, Bors has a spot and he doesn't have a spot. This is too much for Malory. To waste time on the gradations of symbolic bulls is the last of his intentions. Like Chaucer's Nun's Priest, after reviewing the arguments for and against free will, he "wol nat han to do of swich mateere."[21] The bulls are black and Bors *had* a spot,[22] the present state of which is no concern of Sir Thomas Malory, Knight.

Malory's translation of the remainder of the passage is equally indicative of his feelings. He has rendered the green field and its symbolism with literal exactness, although he has placed his translation of the term "vert" in the interpretation of the vision rather than in the vision proper.[23] However, what is most interesting is his translation of "la chevalerie a puis esté si fort par la douçor et par la fraternité qui est entr'ax" as "shelvalry hath ben at all tymes so hyghe by the fraternité which was there."[24] Although the translation appears, at first glance, quite adequate, Malory has left out the key term "sweetness" ("douçor") from the phrase "par la douçor et par la fraternité," and hence attributed the strength of the Round Table to the fellowship alone. It is of some interest to observe that, in the course of his translation of the *Queste*, Malory has earlier come across the same two terms, "douçor" and "fraternité," in the same context and has followed exactly the same procedure: he has translated "fraternité" and ignored "douçor." The passage referred to is perhaps worth examining, because, although Malory's nontranslation is in both cases identical, the earlier provides a fuller insight into the extent of the spirituality with which the author of the *Queste* surrounds the Round Table. The passage in question is to be found in a preceding section of the *Queste* which concerns itself with the adventures of Perceval. There Perceval's aunt, from queen become recluse, expounds to Perceval the mysteries of the Round Table and describes to him the process by which a knight becomes a companion of the Round Table:

> And when God gives them such grace that they become companions, they hold themselves happier than if they had gained the whole world: and it is apparent to everyone that for this they have left fathers and mothers and wives and children. You [Perceval] have seen this happen to yourself. For since you left your mother and were made a companion of the Round Table, you have had no desire to return; rather were you suddenly captured by the sweetness and the brotherhood which must exist amongst those who are its companions.[25]

It is evident from the French text that the author of the *Queste* keeps the ideas of "sweetness" and "fellowship" quite separate. It is not the sweetness of the fellowship which takes possession of the Knights of the Round Table. Further, it is to be observed that the reference to God's bestowing grace as antecedent to companionship rather clearly distinguishes the fellowship of the Round Table from any secular fellowship, while the leaving of wives and children indicates with equal clarity that the fellowship is to be a celibate and doubtless monastic one. In this context, "douçor" would seem to be a way of expressing the monastic ideal—the enjoyment of God, the supreme good, which is the common undertaking of an order whose essential activity is meditation. The term "fraternité" would then denote the brotherhood which binds together the contemplatives in their common undertaking. Humility and Patience,[26] represented by the green meadow upon which the Round Table is said to be founded, are the basic virtues upon which such a life, or indeed any life, must be founded—Humility being the attractant of grace and Patience the power to persevere undeterred, which power is the gift of grace. As the recluse has pointed out, it is by the gift of grace that one becomes a companion of the Round Table. To this the recluse adds the "senefiance" of the Round Table. It is the third table from that of the Last Supper—the second being the Grail table of Joseph of Arimathaea. Further, in its circular shape, the Round Table figures the world in its position at the center of the universe, surrounded by the elements, the planets, and the stars.[27] Given these ideals, the knighthood to which the companions are to adhere can be viewed only as purely spiritual.

As has been previously observed, spirituality had, for Malory, little appeal. It is also possible that in Malory's view "sweetness" and "knighthood" were such different conceptions that bringing them together was nothing short of appalling. By simply omitting the highly unmilitant "douçor," the Round Table could be made to return to its proper state. As might be expected, Malory translates the speech of Perceval's recluse aunt:

Hit ys well seyne be you [Perceval], for synes ye departed from your modir ye wolde never se her, ye founde such felyship at the Table Rounde.[28]

II

In the vision of Sir Gawain it would appear that Malory understood perfectly well what was being said, but declined spiritual ascent. In a second vision, however, that of Sir Bors, one has the feeling that while plodding through the desert of religion, Malory has lost his landmarks. In the original *Queste*, the pattern of vision and interpretation of vision is a constant. In the Bors episode, however, the pattern is complicated by the multiplicity of the visions which occur and by the entrance into the narrative of the false or diabolic interpretation. The present study is concerned only with Bors's first vision, that of the swan and the raven, but since in the *Queste* subsequent events are nothing more than the coming into being of what the totality of visions has prefigured, the events directly connected with a given vision are difficult to disentangle from the whole of the narrative.

The events relevant to the vision of the swan and the raven

are more or less as follows. Sir Bors, like all of Arthur's knights, is engaged in the Quest of the Holy Grail. As one absolutely committed to the attainment of the Grail, Bors is mindful of his earlier fleshly failing; he therefore advisedly sleeps upon the floor and avoids soft beds.[29] In the course of his wanderings, he encounters a lady who is about to be unjustly dispossessed of her lands by her elder sister, and he undertakes to do judicial combat on her behalf. On the eve of combat, sleeping in his accustomed fashion, Bors has a vision. In Malory's translation:

> And anone as he was aslepe hym befelle a vision: that there cam two birdis, that one whyght as a swanne and that other was mervey-lous blacke; but he was nat so grete as was that other, but in the lyknes of a raven. Than the whyght birde cam to hym and seyde,
>
> "And thou woldist gyff me mete and serve me, I sholde gyff the all the ryches of the worlde, and I shall make the as fayre and as whyght as I am."
>
> So the whyght birde departed. And than cam the blacke birde to hym and seyde,
>
> "And thou serve me to-morow and have me in no dispite, thoughe I be blacke. For wyte thou well that more avaylith myne blacknesse than the odirs whyghtnesse."[30]

The following morning, Sir Bors encounters with the elder sister's champion, Sir Prydam le Noyre, and despite the fact that Sir Prydam is "the most douted man of thys londe," Bors defeats Sir Prydam and returns the lands to the younger sister, their rightful owner. Bors then proceeds on his journey and shortly afterwards has two adventures: the first is the necessity forced upon him of choosing whether to save the virginity of a maiden or the life of his brother, Lyonell;[31] the second is meeting a man in "religious wede . . . on a stronge blacke horse, blacker than a byry." At Bors's request, he interprets the vision of the swan and the raven in a rather startling fashion. The white bird is a beauti-ful lady who has long loved Bors, and the dark bird is Bors's future sin in refusing her—a sin which will be her death. Under the conduct of the dark man of religion, Bors is taken to the lady's castle. There the lady, who is so beautiful that she seems to possess all the beauty in the world, tells him of her love and her imminent self-destruction should he refuse her. However, Bors does refuse her, and she thereupon mounts to the parapets of the castle with twelve of her ladies. Despite the entreaties of one of the ladies that he be not responsible for their deaths, Bors remains adamant.[32] They then leap—at which terrible sight Bors crosses himself—and with a horrendous noise the castle and all its occupants vanish. Thoroughly confused, Bors arrives at an abbey of white monks where he requests a true interpretation of the dream which has prefigured his adventures with the dark man and the dazzling lady.[33] In Malory's translation, the abbot's explanation is as follows:

[. . . by the blak birde myght ye understande Holy Chirche] whych seyth, "I am blacke," but he ys fayre. And by the whyght birde may men undirstonde the fynde, and I shall telle you how the swan ys whyght withoutefurth and blacke within: hit ys ipocresye, which ys with[oute] yalew or pale, and semyth withouteforth the servauntis of Jesu Cryste, but they be withinfurthe so horrible of fylth and synne, and begyle the worlde so evyll.

Also whan the fynde apperith to you in lyknesse of a man o[f] religion . . . all was for thou sholdist nat fynde the aventure of the Sankgreall. And the thirde fowle betokenyth the stronge batayle ayenste the fayre ladyes whych were all devyls.[34]

Here again, Malory's translation appears generally adequate, but partly out of haste and partly out of what appears to be sheer ignorance, he has in fact scraped the surface off a quite delicate artifact and replaced it with a veneer of his own manufacture. The Bors temptation, of which the vision of the birds comprises the central part, is by all odds the most subtle and complex of all the adventures in the *Queste*, and it is doubtless this special quality which occasioned Malory's difficulties. Curiously enough, the inevitable vision and interpretation, which one expects to be growing weary of, are actually what lend this incident its peculiar interest. For one thing, the vision-interpretation sequence is much more dramatic, in that a diabolic interpretation, which Bors believes comes from a priest and hence thoroughly befuddles him, is interposed between the vision itself and the true interpretation by the abbot.[35] The false interpretation is remarkable for the devil's ingenious use of courtly-love argumentation; the second and true interpretation is perhaps more remarkable for the extended use of a kind of color symbolism rarely to be encountered.

The color symbolism employed by the author of the *Queste* in Bors's temptation is distinctive in that its meaning, when finally and authoritatively interpreted, is the reverse of what the reader expects. It is a symbolism entirely dependent upon scriptural allusions involving color, but allusions in which the standard interpretation of the meaning of color goes exactly counter to the standard interpretation of the meaning of the text. Thus the white swan owes his being to Matthew XXIII, 27:

> Woe to you scribes and Pharisees, hypocrites, because you are like to whited sepulchres, which outwardly appear to men beautiful but within are full of dead men's bones and of all filthiness.

The bird, black but beautiful, is made up directly from the Song of Songs (1, 4): "I am black but beautiful." Since the Song of Songs had long been treated as an allegory of the love of Christ for his Church, it follows that the speaker of the text should be identified with Holy Church.[36] However, the texts are, in the vision proper, alluded to only very vaguely, each bird asserting the superiority of its claim in terms of a color whose normal symbolism has been reversed and then again reversed by the dark tempter, who perverts the true meaning of the vision by recourse to normal color symbolism. In the tempter's interpretation, the white swan is the maiden who will die for love; the black raven is the sin which Bors will commit in refusing her love. Like Bors, the reader is left to disentangle the meanings of the colors as the story proceeds.

For Sir Thomas Malory, the abbot's clarification did not entirely remove the puzzlement. With understanding the white bird as a Satanic figure Malory had no difficulty, whether or not he recognized the allusion. With the Song of Songs allusion, however, he had great difficulty. This he translates, "I am blacke, but *he* ys fayre."[37] This is the more curious because the French renders the text with what one would expect to be perfect clarity. Holy Church is in mourning over the state of the faithful and is hence clothed in black. Accordingly, she expresses the contrast between her outward appearance and her essential being by the statement, "Je suis noire mes je suis bele."[38] However, the text as it stood evidently made no sense to Malory and was hence in need of emendation. This need is possibly related to the unaccountable appearance, in the last line of the abbot's interpretation of Bors's dream, of a "thirde fowle" which "betokenyth the stronge batayle ayenste the fayre ladyes."³⁹ For this the French text offers no parallel. It simply reads: "Now have I told you who was the white bird, and who was the dark, and who was the lady for whom you undertook the battle, and against whom [Satan] you did so [i.e., undertook the battle]."⁴⁰ The third bird as related to the battle against the fair ladies is entirely Malory's creation.

As was previously pointed out, the "I am black, but I am beautiful" occurs not in the vision proper, but in the abbot's explication of the vision. The abbot's use of this quotation from the Song of Songs⁴¹ has been prepared for in the vision by the presence of a strong element of beauty in the description of the black bird: "molt ert bele de la nerté qu'ele avoit."⁴² This Malory seems to have missed, since he fails entirely to translate it. On the other hand, in the *Queste* description of the swan, Malory found the ideas of beauty and whiteness twice combined: "ausi biaus et ausi blans"; "si blans et si biax."⁴³ That the Church should be in mourning and in black is to Malory perfectly comprehensible—he has possibly himself contributed something toward her state. But assuming that no connection between beauty and the Church existed in the mind of Malory, who then is denoted by the term "beautiful"? As Malory sees it, beauty has consistently been combined with whiteness—a combination completely in accord with medieval ideas concerning female beauty. This combination has appeared only in the swan, who, the abbot has explained, is a figure of Satan. Therefore, it is Satan who is beautiful and white, whereas, in Malory's understanding, Holy Church is neither. It is consequently apparent that what Holy Church is really saying is, "I am blacke, but *he* ys fayre"—the concluding word "fayre" being highly appropriate as meaning both beautiful and white.⁴⁴ Such a reading would conform to Satan's two most dazzling and deceptive appearances—as the swan of the vision and as the temptress of the highly volatile castle. Hence the reading, "I am blacke, but he ys fayre."

It would appear that it is to Malory's miscomprehension of the Song of Songs allusion that the genesis of the curious third bird is to be attributed. In the *Queste*, the abbot has said: "Now have I told you who was the white bird, and who was the dark, and who was the lady from whom you undertook the battle, and against whom [Satan] you did so [i.e., undertook the battle]." As Malory sees it, two birds have been explained. Now he has a third allegorical avian, a lady concerning whom Bors did battle and with whom Satan is somehow involved. Who is she? Malory fears that somewhere something has been inadequately defined; he also feels that returning to the material he has already put behind him is not a solution eagerly to be desired.

Malory has apparently put out of mind entirely the uninteresting lady who was being dispossessed by her elder sister and for whom Bors undertook combat.[45] He has also apparently neglected to remember that the abbot has pointed out the symbolic significance of the elder and younger sisters. The younger, whom Bors has defended, represents Holy Church; the older, the Old Law, which is equated with the enemy Satan.[46] However, he remembers very vividly the devilishly attractive temptress of the castle, who with her ladies leaped from the castle walls. They are all certainly beautiful ladies and they are all certainly of demonic origin, as their explosive castle proves. Hence Malory resolves the matter of the third lady most expeditiously. The first step is not to look back to identify her. With the exclusion of the lady actually alluded to—who is also Holy Church—the problem becomes less difficult. Malory simply proceeds to lump together Bors's spiritual antagonists—the "fayre" Satan he has created out of the Song of Songs allusion in the *Queste* with the "fayryst lady that ever [Bors] saw" and her fair attendant ladies whom he has found in the narrative proper.

To this admirably simple solution a difficulty nevertheless does present itself. The difficulty is that neither the number nor the gender of the "fayre ladyes" matches with the reading "he is fayre" which Malory has adopted. However, this turns out to be no real difficulty. The ladies are but ladies in seeming and are in actuality devils. As such they are but minor replicas of Satan himself. The temptation of the "fayre ladyes," though admittedly a "strong batalyle," is but another encounter in the spiritual warfare in which Satan is perpetually engaged. In her mourning, Holy Church is "blacke"; in his temptations, Satan is "fayre."

Only one small detail remains—the necessity of inventing a variety of bird—something to parallel the swan and the raven. A neutral term like "thirde fowle"[47] Malory seems to have judged most expedient. With this insignificant matter taken care of, the true reading, which would have horrified the author of the *Queste*, but which for Malory nevertheless solves all difficulties, emerges: "the thirde fowle betokynth the stronge batayle ayenste the fayre ladyes whych were all devyls."

Not only would the author of the *Queste* have been horrified, but, to a greater degree, Holy Church. Malory's failure to perceive behind the "Je suis noire mes je suis bele" the classic text of the Song of Songs, which describes Holy Church herself, must have caused her to cry out, as she did on an earlier occasion:

"Thow doted daffe," quod she · "dulle arne thi wittes;
To litel latyn thow lernedest · lede, in thi зouthe."[48]

Though for Malory the *Queste del Saint Graal* evidently held little appeal, the *Queste* is nevertheless a remarkable work, and not the least remarkable of its attributes is its use of color symbolism. As noted above, the color symbolism is a theologically oriented symbolism and, as a result, color appears in the narrative rarely if ever, except when a theological matter is involved. However, a theologically trained poet with an eye for color might have found much of interest in it. In *Sir Gawain and the Green Knight*, for example, may not the chalk-white veils of the "auncian" lady of the castle and the green girdle which is adopted as the cognizance of the Round Table owe something to such a poet's rather attentive reading of the *Queste del Saint Graal*?

NOTES

1. All references are to the edition of Albert Pauphilet (Paris, 1923).
2. See Jean Frappier, "The Vulgate Cycle," in *ALMA*, pp. 295–318.
3. A. Pauphilet, *Études sur la queste del St. Graal* (Paris, 1921), pp. 53–83; Étienne Gilson, "La Mystique de la grace dans la *Queste del Saint*

Graal," Romania, LI (1925), 321–337. Frappier gives a very useful summary in *ALMA,* pp. 306–307.

4. Frappier, *ALMA,* p. 296.

5. For the conception of medieval man's living in accord or disaccord with fixed standards, each governing a period of his age, rather than in terms of an individual self, I am indebted to Professor Alfred L. Foulet of Princeton University. He has summarized his views as follows: "Usually medieval man . . . analyzed his thoughts and feelings . . . in relation to fixed external norms. He did not live inside a private, subjective world" ("Lucien Foulet Memorial—Alfred Foulet Testimonial," *Romance Philology,* XXII (1969), 395 [No. 70 of Alfred Foulet Bibliography]). It is to be hoped that a full exposition of this important concept will soon be forthcoming.

6. Reference is made specifically to the vision of Lancelot in which he sees his holy ancestors and his holy descendant, the "Bons Chevaliers." A man in the company of angels descends from heaven and speaks kindly to all except one, whose position is the successor of the holy forebears and the begetter of the holy successor. To this one he says; "Se tu velz, je t'amerai, se tu velz je te harrai." A handy hermit expounds the vision to Lancelot and speaks of the words "don tu te remembres bien"—as well he might. It is difficult to find much mysticism or even Christianity in this (*Queste,* pp. 130–131, 137).

7. The Vulgate version represents the first coming together of the three main elements of the Arthurian romance—the *Lancelot,* the *Queste,* and the *Mort Artu.* To these were added the *Merlin* and the *Estoire del Saint Graal.* No other Arthurian work has the scope and curiously unattributable unity of the Vulgate. See Frappier, "The Vulgate Cycle," in *ALMA,* especially p. 296, note 2.

8. This comment is intended to apply only to the Arthurian tradition. There are Arthurian works, particularly *Sir Gawain and the Green Knight,* which contain infinitely more color than the *Queste,* but the color is by no means exclusively theologically oriented, or even exclusively symbolic.

9. As has been noted, not all of the Questers are seeking for the spiritual values which are the Quest's proper goal. Some of them, like Lancelot (note 6 above) and particularly Gawain, are in need of spiritual prodding. As Pauphilet puts it, the characters are "échelonnés depuis l'impiété jusqu'à la sainteté" (*Queste,* p. x).

10. The best example of this is the tournament between Elyezer, son of King Pellés, and Argustes, son of King Herlen, in which Lancelot takes part. He chooses as usual the weaker party, that clothed in black, so that his prowess in arms may be the more remarked. Despite his best efforts, however, the party in white triumphs. The symbolism of the tournament is set forth in terms of conventional color symbolism, the significance of which is expounded to Lancelot by a recluse (*Queste,* pp. 143–145). What is of interest here is not the interpretation of the recluse, whose admonitions to Lancelot are more or less identical with the admonitions Lancelot receives from all his spiritual advisers, but the insistence upon the reality of the tournament—even though the

tournament possessed more significance than the participants themselves understood: "greignor senefiance qu'il meismes n'i entendoient"
(*ibid.*, p. 143).

11. Pauphilet observes that many factors enter into the *Queste*: "Mais les
morceaux les plus achevés de son livre sont certainement les modèles
de sermons qu'il [l'auteur] y a enchâssés en plusieurs endroits, notam-
ment dans le rôle de Lancelot" (*Queste*, p. xiii). See note 6, above.

12. The grand repository for information concerning Gawain is B. J. Whiting, "Gawain: His Reputation, His Courtesy and His Appearance in
Chaucer's *Squire's Tale*," *Mediaeval Studies*, IX (1947), 189–234.

13. In the *Queste*, Gawain's unwitting killing of Yvains li Avoltres is interpreted as part of the self-destruction of the Round Table as a result
of earthly knights' entering into a holy undertaking (*Queste*, pp. 153,
157). However, in the *Mort Artu*, Gawain is singled out as the greatest
killer of the Quest—eighteen of the thirty-two knights of the Round
Table who fail to return have died by his hand. As Gawain himself
puts it, not because he was the best knight, but by ill-fortune: "la
mescheance se torna plus vers moi que vers nul de mes compaignons"
(*La Mort le roi Artu*, ed. Jean Frappier [Paris, 1954] p. 2). The author
of the *Mort* would appear to be turning the sin of the *Queste* into the
tragic misfortune which pursues Gawain throughout the *Mort*.

14. "Ce que messires Gauvains vit en son dormant, si li fu avis qu'il ert en
un pré plein d'erbe vert, et de flors i avoit plenté. En cel pré avoit un
rastelier ou il menjoient cent et cinquante toriaus. Li torel estoient
orgueillex et tuit vairié ne mes troi. De ces trois n'estoit li uns ne bien
tachiez ne bien sanz tache; ainz i avoit signe de tache; et li autre erent
si blanc et si bel qu'il ne pooient plus estre" (*Queste*, p. 149). Malory's
translation is that found in *The Works of Sir Thomas Malory*, ed.
Eugene Vinaver (Oxford, 1954), p. 680. Cited hereafter as *Malory*.

15. "Or, biau sire, ou pré que vos veistes avoit un rastelier. Par le rastelier
devons nos entendre la Table Reonde: car ausi come ou rastelier a
verges qui devisent les espaces, ausi a il a la Table Reonde colombes
qui devisent les uns des sieges des autres. Par le pré devons nos entendre
humilité et patience, qui toz jorz sont vives et en lor force. Et por ce
que humilité ne puet estre vaincue ne pacience, i fu la Table Reonde
fondee, ou la chevalerie a puis esté si fort par la douçor et par la fraternité qui est entr'ax, que ele ne pot estre vaincue. Et por ce dit on
qu'ele fu fondee en humilité et en pacience. Au rastelier menjoient
cent et cinquante torel. Il i menjoient et si n'estoient pas ou pré; car
s'il i fussent, lor cuers mainsissent en humilité et en pacience. Li torel
estoient orgueilleux et tuit vairié ne mes troi. Par les toriaux doiz tu
entendre les compaignons de la Table Reonde, qui par lor luxure et
par lor orgueil sont chaoiz en pechié mortel . . . si qu'il en sont vairié
et tachié. . . . Des toriax i avoit trois qui n'estoient mie tachié, ce est
a dire qui estoient sanz pechié. Li dui estoient blanc et bel et li tierz
avoit eu signe de tache. Li dui qui estoient blanc et bel senefient
Galaad et Perceval. . . . Li tierz ou il avoit eu signe de tache, ce est
Boorz, qui jadis meffist en sa virginité (*Queste*, pp. 155–156; *Malory*,
pp. 683–684).

16. For this rather universal conception, see "St. Augustine and the 'Parson's Tale.'" For the use of "vairié," see notes 14 and 15 above.
17. *Piers Plowman*, ed. W. W. Skeat (Oxford, 1886), B XIII, 314–316 (I, 404). In the *Tristan* of Gottfried von Strassburg, a skillful use of a similar metaphor saves Brangane (trans. A. T. Hatto [Baltimore, 1960], p. 210).
18. Bors's fall is not a part of the *Queste* proper, but is frequently alluded to. In the *Lancelot*, Bors enters a tournament where his success is so brilliant as to attract the love of the daughter of King Brangoire, who, like Bors, is a virgin. Through the wiles of her governess, who is in possession of a willy-nilly ("ou il voelle ou non") ring, he is induced to enter her bed. From this reciprocal loss of virginity, God feels that something must be retrieved—the devil is only too happy about the whole thing—and Helain le Blanc, future Emperor of Constantinople is born. It is clear in the account that Bors is "de froide nature et virgenes et enfes," and that it is the magic ring which has aroused passion in him (*The Vulgate Version of the Arthurian Romances*, ed. H. Oskar Sommer [Washington, 1909–1913], IV, 262–270).
19. See notes 14 and 15 above.
20. The distinction is between the "culpa," which may be sacramentally removed, and the "poena." Chaucer seems to have been quite conversant with the doctrine. See below, p. 347.
21. VII [B²], 3251 (*Works*, p. 203).
22. "the bullis were proude and blacke sauff only three" (*Malory*, p. 683). The bulls are of course not black, but a heavily spotted white. In order to effect his oversimplification, Malory resorts to his own explanation, which operates in terms of conventional color symbolism: "blackenes ys as much as to sey withoute good vertues or workes." See above, p. 13. There is no parallel in the French.
23. For the *Queste*, see note 14 above; for *Malory*, see pp. 12–13 above.
24. See note 15 above.
25. "Et quant Diex lor en done tel grace qu'il en sont compaignon, il s'en tienent a plus boneuré que s'il avoient tout le monde gaangnié, et bien voit len que il en lessent lor peres et lor meres et lor fames et lor enfanz. De vos meismes avez vos ce veu avenir. Car puis que vos partistes de vostre mere et len vos ot fet compaignon de la Table Reonde, n'eustes vos talent de revenir ça, ainz fustes maintenant sorpris de la douçor et de la fraternité qui doit estre entre cels qui en sont compaignon" (*Queste*, pp. 76–77).
26. See above, p. 13. One of the present authors is preparing an essay on the "green" virtues in connection with *Sir Gawain and the Green Knight*. [A.L.K.]
27. *Queste*, pp. 74–76.
28. *Malory*, p. 659.
29. For the episode of King Brangoire's daughter, see note 18 above.
30. "Et si tost come il fu endormiz, si li fu avis que devant lui venoient dui oisel dont li uns estoit si blans come cisne et ausi granz et cisne resambloit bien. Et li autres ert noirs a merveilles, si n'ert mie de grant corsaige. Et il le resgardoit, si li sembloit une cornille; mes molt ert

bele de la nerté qu'ele avoit. Li blans oisiaux venoit a lui et li disoit: "Se tu me voloies servir, je te donroie totes les richesces dou monde, et te feroie ausi biaus et ausi blans come je sui." Et il li demandoit qui il ert. "Dont ne voiz tu, fet il, qui je sui? Je sui si blans et si biax et puis assez plus que tu ne cuides." Et il ne li respondoit mot a ce. Et cil s'en aloit; et maintenant revenoit li noirs oisiax, et li disoit: "Il covient que tu me serves demain, et ne m'aies mie en despit por ce se je sui noire. Saches que mielz vaut ma nerté qu'autrui blanchor ne fait." Lors s'em partoit d'ilec, qu'il ne veoit ne l'un ne l'autre oisel" (*Queste*, pp. 170–171; *Malory*, pp. 688–689). Malory's basic orientation toward the secular is illustrated by a small touch. When the white swan promises Bors reward for his services, Malory thinks of the services in terms comparable to Chaucer's Squire in the Prologue to the *Canterbury Tales*, who "carf biforn his fader at the table" (I [A], 100 [*Works*, p. 18]). Malory translates the generality "se tu me voloies servir" as "And thou woldist gyff me mete and serve me," for which the French offers no parallel. Malory seems here to be more engaged in reliving the events of his youth than in perceiving allegorical servitude to sin.

31. Bors of course preserves the damsel, and it would appear on correct religious and even practical grounds. Virginity is worth more than corrupt knighthood, and besides Lyonell is still very much alive (*Malory*, pp. 691–692, 697, 698–702). The incident of the damsel is useful chiefly in defining what the author of the *Queste* considered ideal knighthood, and what Malory considered it. The assaulted maiden calls upon Bors for assistance in the name of the lord he serves: in the *Queste* it is clearly God; in Malory, although the influence of the source story has not been completely dispelled, it is Arthur (*Queste*, p. 175; *Malory*, p. 691). See Vinaver's comment in *The Works of Sir Thomas Malory*, ed. Eugène Vinaver, 2nd ed. (Oxford, 1967) III, 1565.

32. The Bors of the *Queste* is an ascetic and not entirely sympathetic seeker after salvation. The appeal of the ladies, whom he believes to be real, falls on ears conscientiously deafened to human appeal. He would rather "that they all lost their souls, than that he alone should lose his" (*Queste*, p. 181). However, it is characteristic of the constant humanizing impulse one feels in Malory's work that he should cause the abbot, who later makes the final interpretation of all Bors's adventures, to attribute the particular form of the earlier temptation— that in which Bors must choose between preserving the virginity of an unknown damsel and preserving the life of his brother Lyonell—to Satan's knowledge that Bors was "tendir-herted" (*Malory*, pp. 691– 697). Bors is not strikingly tender-hearted in the incident of King Brangoire's daughter (see note 18 above), nor in that of the leaping ladies. Malory may find Bors too chilly as he appears in the *Queste* to form a continuity with the quite sympathetic figure he is in the *Mort Artu* and consequently here attempts a certain humanization.

33. The narration immediately preceding occupies pp. 177–182 of the *Queste*.

34. "Par le noir oisel qui vos vint veoir doit len entendre Sainte Eglyse, qui dist: 'Je suis noire mes je suis bele: sachiez que mielz valt ma

nerté que autrui blancheur ne fet.' Par le blanc oisel qui avoit sem-
blance de cisne doit len entendre l'anemi, et si vos dirai coment. Li
cisnes est blans par defors et noirs par dedenz, ce est li ypocrites, qui
est jaunes et pales, et semble bien, a ce qui defors en apert, que ce
soit des serjanz Jhesucrist; mes il est par dedenz si noirs et si horribles
d'ordures et de pechiez qu'il engigne trop malement le monde. . . . Et
einsi t'eust il mis en pechié mortel, par quoi tu eusses failli as aventures
dou Saint Graal. Einsi t'ai ore devisé qui fu li blans oisiax et qui li
noirs, et qui fu la dame por qui tu empreis la bataille et contre qui
ce fu" (*Queste*, pp. 185–186; *Malory*, 697) .

35. *Queste*, pp. 177–180; *Malory*, pp. 693–694.

36. If the author of the *Queste* were a Cistercian, the text could have been
quite immediate to him through the writings of St. Bernard (Henri de
Lubac, *Exégèse médievale* [Paris, 1959], Part I, II, 586 ff. However, the
Song of Songs was in any case a very well-known text. In Chaucer's
Merchant's Tale it is much alluded to (see pp. 330 ff. below).

37. See p. 18, note 34, above.

38. As has been observed (note 36, above) , the Song of Songs was a very
well-known work, yet the French translation in the *Queste* of the
passage in question, "Nigra sum sed pulchra" (I, 4) as "Je suis noire
mes je suis bele," although perfectly accurate, is beset by a peculiar
confusion—one group of manuscripts curiously enough attributes the
verse to Christ and another in the customary fashion to Holy Church
(see Pauphilet's note to the passage [*Queste*, p. 286]). Vinaver believes
that no extant MS of the *Queste* provides a reliable source for Malory's
translation, but he accepts MS BN, fr. 120, as being "nearest to the
'French Book' " (*Malory*, III, 1534–1535) . This reads: "par le noir
oisel qui vous vint veoir doit on entendre Sainte Eglise . . ." (*ibid.*, II,
967) . If this was the French text as Malory had it, it would seem that
there could have been no confusion in Malory's mind, but, as has been
noted, there does exist a confusion regarding the sex of the speaker
in the manuscripts as a whole. Such a confusion could have affected
Malory to some extent, but Pauphilet records no variants in the text
itself (*Queste*, p. 286) , and Vinaver indicates no confusion at all in
Caxton (*Malory*, II, 967) . It would appear that Malory's extraordinary
translation is essentially dependent upon Malory.

39. See p. 18 above.

40. See note 34 above.

41. The Vulgate reading is unequivocal: "Nigra sum sed pulchra." However, the abbot's French translation, "Je suis noire mes je suis bele," is
composed of two distinct clauses, which could be interpreted, if one
were not familiar with the text, as two separate assertions by two
separate personages. This may have combined with other possible
sources of confusion. See note 38, above.

42. See note 30, above.

43. See note 30, above.

44. See *MED*, under "fair."

45. See note 34, above.

46. *Queste*, pp. 168–174; *Malory*, pp. 688–690. Bors's acceptance of the en-

counter with Sir Prydam le Noire and the encounter itself surround the vision discussed as well as a second and immediately subsequent vision which prefigures Bors's preservation of the virginal damsel at the expense of what he takes to be the death of his brother, Lyonell.

47. There is in actuality a "thirde fowle" in the French text. As Bors sets out upon his adventures, he sees a "grant oisel" flying above a rotten tree wherein she has a nest containing numerous dead "oiselez." By striking her own breast and making the blood burst forth, she revives the small birds—at which Bors wonders much (*Queste*, pp. 167–168). Despite the fact that the "great bird" is an obvious figure of Christ (*ibid.*, p. 184), and that in the subsequent diabolic interpretation of Bors's dream concerning the swan and the raven, Malory confuses the "grant oisiax" with the "noirs oisiax"—the "great bird" with the "black bird" (see Vinaver's comment [*Malory*, III, 1566]), the mere numerical presence of a triplicity of birds in the Bors temptation sequence may have suggested the "thirde fowle." Malory was very possibly much more interested in an immediate solution to an uninteresting problem than he was in an exact bird count.

48. *Piers Plowman*, B Passus I, 138–139 (Skeat, I, 32). Actually, the abbot's summary is not very illuminating. Within the visions there are purportedly four elements involved: (1) the white bird, (2) the black bird, (3) the lady for whom Bors undertook battle, and (4) a somebody against whom Bors undertook battle, described in the opaque idiom "contre qui ce fu." There are in fact only two: both the black bird and the lady whom Bors defended are figures of Holy Church; the white bird and the opponent of the lady he is defending are figures of Satan—the last being the Old Law, elsewhere equated with Satan (*Queste*, pp. 185–186). The usual pattern in the *Queste* is a one-to-one allegorical relationship, and the reality of the event from which the allegorical "senefiance" is drawn is insisted upon (see note 10, above). Malory was thus faced with a very difficult passage in a form of literature in which he had little interest and less learning. He may hence have felt an acute need for improvisation.

4

Satan, Langland, and the North

IN DESCRIBING THE FALL OF SATAN Langland comments on Satan's curious action in preferring the north to the south and intimates that an explanation would be forthcoming were it not for his fear of offending the feelings of northern men.

> He and other with hym · that hulde nouʒt with treuthe,
> Lopen out in lothliche forme · for hus false wille;
> He hadde lust to be lyke · hus lord god almyghty.
> *Ponam pedem meum in aquilone, et ero similis altissimo.*
> Lord! why wolde he tho · thulke wrechede Lucifer,
> Lepen a-lofte · in the north syde
> Than sitten in the sonne side · ther the day roweth?
> Ne were it for northerne men · a-non ich wolde telle.[1]

The Latin quotation which Langland inserts in the midst of this passage has generally been considered to be an inaccurate quotation of Isaiah XIV, 13–14:

In caelum conscendam, super astra Dei exaltabo solium meum, sedebo in monte testamenti, in lateribus aquilonis. Ascendam super altitudinem nubium; similis ero Altissimo.[2]

Actually, however, the direct source of Langland's quotation would appear to be St. Augustine's paraphrase of Isaiah rather than the Isaiah text itself. As stated by St. Augustine, it reads:

Reprinted from *Speculum,* XXIV (1949), 413–414.

"Ponam sedem meam ad aquilonem, et ero similis Altissimo."[3]
It may further be pointed out that the conception of the north
and south as symbolic of spiritual states, which lies behind Langland's passage, is likewise indebted to St. Augustine.

In the *Enarratio in Psalmum* XLVII, St. Augustine establishes
the antithesis of north and south and identifies Satan as the north.

Contrarius solet esse aquilo Sion: Sion quippe in meridie, aquilo
contra meridiem. Quis est iste aquilo, nisi qui dixit, *Ponam sedem
meam ad aquilonem, et ero similis Altissimo.* (Isaiah XIV, 13–14)?[4]

In the *De gratia Novi Testamenti liber*, St. Augustine proceeds
to explain by copious allusions to Scripture this antithesis of north
and south and the association of Satan with the north. A short
extract will suffice to show his meaning.

Diabolus igitur et angeli ejus a luce atque fervore charitatis
aversi, et nimis in superbiam invidiamque progressi, velut glaciali
duritia torpuerunt. Et ideo per figuram tanquam in aquilone ponun-
tur: unde cum generi humano diabolus incubaret, ventura gratia
Salvatoris dicitur in Cantico canticorum, *Exsurge, aquilo, et veni,
auster, perfla hortum meum, et fluent aromata* (Song of Songs, IV, 16.)[5]

In these two passages St. Augustine seems to be stating the
familiar concept of the two cities, the one founded on love of
God, the other on love of self,[6] of which latter city Satan is, of
course, the founder and first citizen. The deprivation of grace
which occurs when anyone by an act of his will turns from God is
symbolized by the north wind; the grace of God which removes
the effects of sin and brings man back to God is symbolized by
the south wind.

That all three passages—Isaiah and the two passages from St.
Augustine—came into conjunction and were known as a whole
appears likely. In the *Liber regulae S. Spiritus* one finds these
three passages fused:

Tales [Superbi] dicunt cum dyabolo: ascendam in celum per
altitudinem dignitatis; ponam sedem meam in aquilone, non in austro
per gratiam, set in aquilone per culpam et ero similis Altissimo, ut
sim quasi Deus terrenus, altissimus et fortis, dives et sapiens.[7]

Langland's mystery, then, turns out to be not particularly
mysterious and in fact almost self-explanatory. The answer to

Satan's act is of course "hus false wille."[8] The explanation of Satan's connection with the north which Langland considerately withholds out of deference to the sensibilities of northern men is simply that Satan is traditionally associated with the north as a symbol of the deprivation of the grace of God and that according to St. Augustine the north is never used in a good sense in Scripture.

Austrum, quamvis mortalibus carnibus gravis sentiatur, non tamen uspiam memini in sanctis Libris mali aliquid significare, sicut aquilonem numquam in bono.[9]

It is perhaps indicative of Langland's sense of irony that this idea which he restrains himself from revealing seems hardly more objectionable than the explanation, authoritatively offered by Holy Church, which is supposed to offend nobody:

"Ac ich wolle lacke no lyf" · quath that lady sothly;
"Hit is sykerer by southe · ther the sonne regneth
Than in the north by meny notes · no man leve other.
For thider as the fend flegh · hus fote for to sette,
Ther he failede and ful · and hus felawes alle;
And helle is ther he ys · and he ther ybounde.
Euene contrarie sitteth Criste · clerkus knowen the sothe."[10]

NOTES

1. C Passus II, 109–115 (*Piers Plowman,* ed. W. W. Skeat [Oxford, 1886], I, 31).
2. See Skeat's note on the above passage (*Piers Plowman,* II, 25).
3. *Enarratio in Psalmum* XLVII (*PL,* XXXVI, 534).
4. *Ibid.*
5. *De gratia Novi Testamenti liber, seu epistola* CXL (*PL,* XXXIII, 561).
6. *De civitate Dei,* XIV, XXVIII (*PL,* XLI, 436).
7. "De comminationibus et indulgentijs: capitulum LXXXVII," in *Liber regulae S. Spiritus,* ed. A. Francesco la Cava (Milan, 1947), p. 204.
8. St. Augustine finds the origin of evil in the aversion of the will from God. The will is false in that it deserts God, the perfect and unchangeable good, for a lesser good. The first creature to desert God was, of course, Satan.
9. *Annotationum in Job, liber unus* (*PL,* XXXIV, 876).
10. C Passus II, 116–122 (*Piers Plowman,* I, 31). I have throughout used "Satan" as a generic term for "the fend" rather than Langland's "Lucifer." (See Skeat's notes to C Passus XXI, 297, 315, in *Piers Plowman,* II, 258–259.)

5

Langland and Two Scriptural Texts

T HAT WILLIAM LANGLAND, perhaps best known for his observation of contemporary English life, existed also in a world of biblical allusion is apparent to anyone who turns the pages of *Piers Plowman*. Furthermore, it is equally apparent that the biblical text reached Langland not directly, but surrounded by an accretion of commentary. Yet in relatively few cases is our knowledge sufficiently detailed to indicate with any degree of certainty the form or forms in which a given text reached Langland and the artistic purposes he made it serve. The present essay is devoted to the study in some detail of two such texts.

I. PES SUPERBIAE

In Passus II, 108–111 of the C text, Holy Church says of Lucifer:

> He was an archangel of heuene · on of godes kny3tes;
> He and other with hym · that hulde nou3t with treuthe,
> Lopen out in lothliche forme · for hus false wille;
> He hadde lust to be lyke · hus lord god almyghty.
> *Ponam pedem meum in aquilone, et ero similis altissimo.*[1]

Reprinted from *Traditio*, XIV (1958), 385–398.

The Latin quotation with which the above passage ends, although occasionally attributed to Origen, is manifestly indebted to St. Augustine's compressed paraphrase of Isaiah XIV, 13–14: "Ponam sedem meam ad aquilonem, et ero similis Altissimo."[2] However, what is not equally clear is why Langland chose to alter "sedem" to "pedem."[3] Although this is surely a diminutive, not to say microscopic, problem, its limitations are not without advantage. It is here possible, I think, to see more or less exactly what Langland's sources were and how he shaped them to his own purposes.

In his *Enarrationes in Psalmos,* St. Augustine interprets the word "pes" as a figure of love, of the movement of the soul toward its desired object. Hence one finds expressed, in terms of this image, the central Augustinian doctrine of the two loves: charity, which moves upward toward God, and cupidity, which falls away from God toward the created:

The foot of the soul is rightly understood to be love. When depraved, this love is called cupidity or lust; when righteous, right love or charity. . . . Charity moves toward walking, and perfecting, and ascending; pride moves toward a fall.[4]

Since Satan was the first to fall from pride, it is not surprising to find him singled out as a particularly dark example of wrongly directed love. In commenting on the text, "They shall be made drunk by the plenty of thy house," (Psalm XXXV, 9), St. Augustine points out the perilous position of the creature especially favored by God. When such a one has received abundantly of the gifts of God, he is in danger of regarding them as his own private property and hence as fit subjects for self-congratulation. Pride— or in pedal imagery the foot of pride—is then most to be feared.

Non veniat mihi pes superbiae . . . [Psalm XXXV, 12]. "Beneath the shelter of thy wings the sons of men shall find their hope, and they shall be made drunk by the plenty of thy house." When anyone shall have begun to drink in exceeding plenty from that fountain, let him take care lest he become proud. . . . Why did the Psalmist call that [self-regarding love] "foot"? Because by becoming proud it deserted God and went from Him. The Psalmist declared that one's foot was one's love. Let not the foot of pride come unto me.[5]

Satan, foremost among the angels and the most richly endowed of God's creatures, failed to heed this warning. He became instead a victim of his own charms. Pride moved his love from God to self, and he fell.

Ne des ad movendum pedem meum . . . [Psalm cxx, 3]. Hear first by what means his [foot] was moved who was among the angels, and from an angel became the devil; for, his foot being moved, he fell. What was the cause of his fall? The cause was pride. Pride, and pride alone, moves toward ruin the foot [of the soul].[6]

A second term which Augustine interprets as a figure of love is "pondus." Weight, like foot, is a metaphor which expresses this same movement of the soul toward its goal. In a famous passage of the Confessions, St. Augustine says:

Peace for us lies in good will. The body inclines by its weight toward its own place. . . . Fire inclines upward; a stone, downward. They are moved by their weights; they seek their places. . . . When not well ordered, they are restless; when they are in order, then they are at rest. My weight is my love; by it I am carried wherever I am carried.[7]

It is interesting to observe that these two Augustinian conceptions of "pes" and "pondus" seem to have become so closely associated as to be virtually interchangeable. Thus in the De causa Dei, Thomas Bradwardine, while purporting to give Augustine's interpretation of "pes," actually gives his interpretation of "pondus."

"O bless our God, ye peoples, and make the voice of his praise to be heard, who hath set my soul to live, and hath not suffered my feet to be moved" [Psalm lxv, 8–9]: my feet, that is to say, my desires and loves. But that is common in Augustine. My foot is my love; by it I am carried wherever I am carried.[8]

Hence, when the medieval writer approached the problem of Satan's boasted equality with God, he had available two metaphors by which that self-regarding love, or indeed any love, could be described—"pondus" and "pes." Guido de Columnis adopted the former. In his Historia destructionis Troiae, he wrote of Satan: "Hic elatus superbie pondere . . . dixit, 'Ponam sedem meam ab

Aquilone et ero similis altissimo.' "[9] Langland followed the second alternative and wrote: "Ponam *pedem meum* in aquilone, et ero similis altissimo."

One wonders whether, in choosing this particular version, Langland was observing already established terminology or whether he was himself making a new combination of passages to produce a desired effect. The problem is a difficult one. Although there is some positive evidence to indicate how the line took the form it has in Langland's poem, there is only negative evidence to show who gave it that form. Thus one may suppose that "pedem" replaced "sedem" in the line in question because in two passages of the *Enarrationes* where Satan makes his customary boast, "Ponam sedem meam," St. Augustine applies to him the text "Non veniat mihi pes superbiae."[10] However, this information is not particularly helpful in determining whether or not it was Langland himself who effected this combination. The only real evidence is the existence or nonexistence of such a combination in other medieval allusions to St. Augustine's paraphrase. So far as I am aware, no such example is to be found. Amongst a body of Latin allusion which extends all the way from a bestiary to the excommunication of an emperor,[11] there is no occurrence except in Langland of the reading "pedem" for "sedem." Furthermore, in English translations of the Augustinian compression of Isaiah xiv, 13–14, the alliteration is entirely dependent upon the idea of "seat," and there seems to be no awareness at all of the Satanic foot. Thus the *Cursor mundi* reads: "sett," he said, "mi sete I sall . . . / In þe north side"; and William of Shoreham: "He wolde sette hys sete ryche / Of north half."[12] On the basis, therefore, of what evidence is available, it would seem probable that the combination of the two Augustinian passages was made by Langland himself for his own artistic purposes. And these, I think, become apparent even at a rapid glance. By the substitution of "pedem" Langland has given the line a kinetic quality which accords considerably better with Satan's warlike pretensions than the static "sedem." Furthermore, the use of "pes" vastly increases the connotations of the line. The allusion to Satan now operates in terms of his evil love and thus touches upon the basic problem of love with which *Piers Plowman* is so deeply concerned.

II. GOING TO WESTMINSTER

Satan's vaunted equality with God could not, of course, escape divine retribution. In the mind of the commentator the vengeance visited upon Satan's boast might be seen allegorically set forth in the fate of Pharaoh and his army: "Horse and rider He has cast into the sea. . . . The chariots of Pharaoh and his army He has cast into the sea" (Exodus xv, 1–4).[13] Here also the work of the scriptural commentator seems to have afforded Langland the raw materials of his art and perhaps even a certain measure of inspiration.

After Theology has challenged the legality of the wedding of Mede and Fals, and it has been agreed that the issue is to be settled at Westminster, Fals and Favel gather together a host of questionable witnesses and look about for transportation:

> Ac thanne cared thei for caplus · to kairen hem thider,
> And Fauel fette forth thanne · folus ynowe;
> And sette Mede upon a schyreue · shodde al newe,
> And Fals sat on a sisoure · that softlich trotted,
> And Fauel on a flaterere · fetislich atired.[14]

Simony and Civil are accommodated in a like fashion, and the procession is completed by harnessing the Commissary to Civil's cart, and transforming Liar into a "long cart." Says Civil:

> And cartesadel the comissarie · owre carte shal he lede,
> And fecchen vs vytailles · at *fornicatores*
> And maketh of Lyer a longe carte · to lede alle these othere,
> As freres and faitours · that on here fete rennen.[15]

In its incongruity and satiric violence, the scene is one of Langland's best and apparently most original. Yet it cannot be said to lack antecedents.

In his *Homilies on Exodus*, Origen considers the allegorical meaning of the overthrow of Satan and his army (Exodus xv, 1–4). Since he has already identified Pharaoh with Satan, the problem is the meaning of Pharaoh's horses, riders, and chariots.

Horse and rider He has cast into the sea. All who are born to flesh are, figuratively speaking, horses and have their riders. There are horses whom God mounts, and these go about admonishing the world. Of these it is said [Habakkuk III, 8]: "And salvation is in thy horsemen." There are, however, horses whose riders are the devil and his angels. Judas was a horse, and so long as his rider was the Lord, he was of the company of salvation. . . . But when he surrendered himself to Satan . . . Satan became his rider, and led by his reins he began to attack our Lord and Saviour. . . . *The chariots of Pharaoh and his army He has cast into the sea; his chosen riders, his princes He has plunged into the Red Sea.* Pharaoh, since he is more potent in malice and rules the kingdom of evil, drives four-horse chariots. . . . There are other "picked riders" . . . of whom we have already spoken; now let us see who are the "princes." . . . These princes are evil angels of the army of Pharaoh.[16]

Although the above interpretation of Origen becomes in a sense standard, since, in Rufinus' Latin, it passes by way of Bede and Rabanus Maurus into the *Glossa ordinaria*,[17] there is abundant evidence of a second tradition, hardly less well known, which opposes to Origen's anthropomorphic figure a quite different conception. According to this second interpretation, the human element tends to disappear and the presentation takes the form of an elaborate allegory of warrior vices and vehicles. As is well recognized, the beginnings of the conception of vices struggling for the possession of the soul are to be found in the *Psychomachia* of Prudentius, where the vices encounter and are defeated by the personified virtuous qualities of the soul. Of the numerous scenes of individual conflict which make up Prudentius' poem, one seems to have been of extraordinary popularity. This scene is the dramatic entrance into battle of the gentle vice Luxuria, imperturbably strewing flowers from her bejewelled chariot, and very nearly overcoming the resistance of the ravished virtues.[18] Throughout the following centuries, the influence of the *Psychomachia* was immense, as has been ably demonstrated by Katzenellenbogen and Bloomfield.[19] To this influence was added, almost two centuries later, that of an equally famous literary battle—the assault of the seven deadly sins upon the "miles Dei" in the *Moralia* of Gregory the Great.[20] From the eighth through the twelfth centuries, the influences of Prudentius and Gregory combined to produce a whole series of *Psychomachiae*. In the works of Ald-

LUXURY'S JEWELLED CART WITH RIDERS

From the *Hortus deliciarum* of Herrad von Landsperg, ed. A. Straub and G. Keller, Strasbourg, 1879–1899. Plate 47

helm, Alcuin, Theodulf of Orléans, in the *Liber de conflictu vitiorum et virtutum* and the *De fructibus carnis et spiritus*, both of uncertain authorship, the now traditional theme of moral battle is stated and restated.[21] But for its final form the allegorical struggle of vice and virtue was not indebted to any of the above, but to St. Bernard of Clairvaux.

In the course of his *Sermones in Cantica*, St. Bernard has occasion to comment upon the text, "My love, I have likened thee unto my company in the chariots of Pharaoh" (Song of Songs 1, 8).[22] This passage St. Bernard interprets as a struggle between the forces of the "Amica," the soul and bride of Christ, and the chariots of the vices under the leadership of Satan.[23] The soul, supported as it is by virtues and angelic hosts, is like an army, and, by analogy to the divinely assisted victory of the chosen people over the physical Pharaoh, may be expected to triumph over the spiritual Pharaoh, Satan. The forces arrayed against the soul are, however, imposing. Satan's army is led by powerful princes of vice, among whom St. Bernard singles out three for especial consideration. These are the three "principalia vitia"— Malice, Luxury, and Avarice. They are equipped with three splendid chariots—or, it would appear, four-wheeled carts—which St. Bernard allegorizes in minute detail. For example:

> The cart of Luxury . . . turns upon four wheels: Gluttony, Lust, Softness of Garments, and Laxness of Slumbrous Ease. It is drawn by two horses: Prosperity of Life, and Abundance of Things; their two postilions are Torpor of Sloth and False Security.[24]

Although the preceding account is of necessity extremely brief, it is, I think, sufficient to indicate the nature of St. Bernard's contribution. What he has accomplished is nothing less than an extraordinarily successful fusion of all the elements so far discussed. Most influential and most clearly apparent is the work of the commentators on Exodus. Origen had long before made the same association between the "currus Pharaonis" of Exodus xv, 1–4 and Song of Songs 1, 8,[25] and the idea of Satan's chariots as vices seems first to have been stated by St. Bruno in his *Expositio in Exodum*.[26] Other elements may also be noted. The term "principalia vitia" echoes the classical phraseology of Gregory the

Great,[27] while the "currus Luxuriae" of Prudentius now appears in the ranks of Pharaoh's mobile army. Perhaps most interesting, the "quadriga," the four-horse chariot of the original Origen comment, has been transformed, in accordance with contemporary military practice, into a four-wheeled cart[28]—the vehicle known as the "longa caretta."[29]

It would be most pleasant if, after so prolonged and exhausting a journey through allegorical battlefields and matériel, one could pause gratefully and contemplate St. Bernard's final and authoritative interpretation. However, St. Bernard's admirable synthesis was final only in terms of a single tradition, the *Psychomachia* or vice-virtue tradition. Although Herrad von Landsperg, for example, in her famous *Hortus deliciarum* clearly followed the later *Psychomachia* tradition—note the "gemmatus currus Luxuriae" where the whole tradition from Prudentius to St. Bernard may be traced (Fig. 1)[30]—the opposing conception of Origen remained firmly entrenched in the *Glossa ordinaria*. Whether the army of Satan consisted of vices or of demonic powers remained a difficult question. How many resolutions of this problem were attempted the present writer is not prepared to say. However, in England the most influential seems to have been that of Stephen Langton, later Archbishop of Canterbury. In his *Commentary on the Pentateuch (ca.* 1185),[31] Langton addresses himself to the text basic to both traditions—Exodus xv, 1–4. He begins by summarizing from Origen the horse and rider relationship indicated at the beginning of the present discussion. But when he arrives at the section of Origen which deals with Pharaoh's chariots, he makes a rather surprising reading. Origen had said that whomever one might see excelling others in vice, him he would know "de quadrigis esse Pharaonis," that is, one of the four horses drawing Pharaoh's chariots.[32] Langton, however, quotes Origen as saying "esse quadrigas diaboli,"[33] which makes the sinner not the motive power of the chariot—now extended into a cart—but the cart itself. When Langton turns to St. Bernard for his second major interpretation, he makes another unusual reading. Langton finds that St. Bernard has described the great vices not so much as drivers of carts, but as the carts themselves: "tres eius [Satanae] principes sive currus."[34] The net result of these two readings is that both sinners and sins become identified with carts. One can only conjecture what lies behind this equivalence, but it seems clear that if both sins and sinners are viewed as carts, the opposition between the views of St. Bernard and Origen tends to disappear. By the identification of sin and cart, the devil is borne about in sin-carts in a manner similar to St. Bernard's conception and exactly comparable to that of St. Bruno; by the identification of sinner and cart, the devil may be viewed as proceeding very much as in Origen. Thus Langton maintains both the Satanic rider of Origen and the sin-cart of St. Bernard, and in this fashion he harmonizes the two traditions.[35]

But Langton has a further and highly significant change to make. He quietly suppresses St. Bernard's "Malicia" and transfers her allegorical cart to "Superbia."[36] With this change, the carts now read: Luxuria, Avaricia, Superbia—the customary equivalents for concupiscence of the flesh, concupiscence of the eyes, and pride of life (I John II, 16). As Langton indicates a little further on in his commentary, it is to these three vices that he wishes to make his carts conform.[37] The influence of Langton's interpretation—and in particular of his equation of the sins of I John II, 16 with modes of equine transportation—can be seen in a second English theologian almost contemporary with Langton. In the *Summa de officio sacerdotis* of Richard de Wetheringsett (*ca.* 1230) one finds Satan described as a driver in a fashion highly reminiscent of St. Bernard but in fact identical to Langton:[38] "Pride may be called the devil's cart, whose four wheels are contempt of God, of one's neighbor, of one's own subjection, of ecclesiastical institution." More important for present purposes, Satan is likewise described as a horseman in terms of I John II, 16: "Concupiscence of the Flesh may be likened to the devil's palfrey, Avarice to his rouncy, Pride to his war horse."[39]

If we turn now from the commentators to the poet Langland, two problems seem to require consideration: (1) What evidence is there that Langland was actually familiar with the commentary in question? (2) If he was, in what ways has he reshaped his materials?

In answer to the first question, it may be stated with some confidence that evidences of both traditions are discoverable.

From the sins tradition—that is, the interpretation of St. Bernard further developed in terms of I John II, 16, by the English commentators—Langland drew the three types of horse (palfrey, rouncy, war horse) on which Fals and his friends ride to Westminster. If one compares Satan's horses in the *Summa de officio sacerdotis* (quoted above) with those Favel produces (A text), the parallels are reasonably consistent. The war horse "dextrarius" appears in Langland as "alle denes and sodenes · as destreres dihten"; the "runcinus" or "runcinus trottans" as "Fals on a sysoures backe · that softly trotted"; and the "palefridus" as "lette apparayle prouisours · on palfreis wyse."[40] Also from the sins tradition, in this case from the allegorical four-wheeled carts, comes the "longe carte" into which Liar is so suddenly transformed. It seems likely that Langland, familiar with the "longa caretta" as a traditional conveyance for militant sins, used this term to describe Liar as he bears his burden toward Westminster. It is perhaps worth suggesting that Liar's peculiar shape may be directly indebted to Stephen Langton's commentary, for in Langton, it will be remembered, the vice is not the driver of the cart, but the cart itself. Finally, as will be pointed out below, Civil and Simony would appear to be Langland's adaptation of the three "principalia vitia" of the St. Bernard–Langton commentaries. To Origen, on the other hand, Langland's indebtedness is of a somewhat different nature; it is to be discovered less in particular resemblances than in basic conception. The central and consistent figure of the human horse ridden or driven by demon or vice—Fals seated upon a juror, the Commissary pulling Civil's cart—has its roots in the commentary of Origen.

In answer to the second question, that of Langland's use of his materials, I think two observations may fairly be made. First, Langland seems to have taken the two traditions and synthesized them in a singularly effective fashion. The most difficult problem for the commentator, it has been pointed out, was the make-up of Pharaoh-Satan's army. Was it composed of sins, or was it composed of demons? Later commentators had been faced with the difficult choice of attempting to bridge the two traditions or of following one to the exclusion of the other.[41] Langland, perhaps again influenced by the commentary of Stephen Langton,[42] keeps both traditions and solves the demon-sin problem by placing the two on separate and distinct levels. Satan and his angels he simplifies into the unholy Trinity, Fals-Favel-Liar, three timeless protean figures, suggestive of the father of deceit himself, to whom he gives control over both wedding and journey. The "principalia vitia"—Pride (Malice), Luxury, and Avarice—he converts into those sins of his own age which he considers controlling—Simony and Civil. These become Satan's temporal agents carrying out his commands. Thus, in the company of the timeless manifold figure of deceit, the vices of the age drive on their human victims. A second observation is perhaps also worth making, and that concerns the balance of materials within Langland's synthesis. Aside from the sins Simony and Civil, which, as stated above, appear to be derived from the major vices of the St. Bernard–Langton commentaries, virtually all that the B text retains of formal sin allegory is the representation of Liar as a cart, and this by virtue of its wonderfully incongruous transformation loses all contact with the spirit and tone of St. Bernard's treatment. The whole balance of Langland's presentation is in the direction of Origen's basic metaphor. On the road to Westminster it is the human rather than the abstract view which predominates; it is the human which is saddled or cart-saddled. One is inclined to feel that Langland the satirist found in Origen's image the kind of grotesque, human, and violent metaphor he wanted for his indictment of contemporary society. With a kind of Swiftian sense, he perceived in Origen's powerful inverted image of man degraded to the level of beast a stinging fiction by which to convey the incongruity of human prostitution to evil— of the "up-so-doun" relationship which sin, the perversion of reason, produces.[43]

I I I

Langland was very much a part and an observer of the world of his time, but he existed simultaneously and perhaps even more fully in a world of biblical interpretation and allusion. What the present essay has sought to do is to show in a very fragmentary fashion how elements of this world entered into the fabric of

Piers Plowman. It has tried to illustrate Langland the artist at work—in one case combining passages to gain force and allusiveness, in another giving magnificent satirical point to a metaphor whose grotesqueness and vigor he felt to be at one with his own satirical style and purpose.

NOTES

1. All references to *Piers Plowman* in this essay are to the edition by W. W. Skeat (Oxford, 1886).
2. See above, "Satan, Langland, and the North"; D. W. Robertson and B. F. Huppé, *Piers Plowman and the Scriptural Tradition* (Princeton, 1951), p. 44, note 52. The attribution to Origen is to be found in two Oxford manuscripts, the *Septuplum* (University Collection 71, fol. 29ª) and a *Tractatus de septem viciis principalibus* (Bodleian Laud Misc. 549, fol. 9ª). The former reads: "Origenes enim ait quoniam omnis elatus filius elati qui dixit 'Ponam sedem meam ad aquilonem, et ero similis altissimo.'" If this attribution were accepted, the ultimate source would obviously be Origen, for the unknown writer on whom the two manuscripts depend seems to state quite clearly that it was Origen (or rather his Latin translator, Rufinus) who put the words "Ponam . . . altissimo" in the mouth of the "elatus," Satan. However, the attribution seems to be without foundation. The passage in Origen alluded to actually reads (in the Latin of Rufinus): "Et iterum dicit elatus hic et superbus: 'Ascendam in coelum, supra sidera coeli ponam thronum meum, sedebo in monte excelso supra montes altos, qui sunt ad aquilonem, adscendam supra nubes, et ero similis Altissimo.' . . . Omnis, ergo, qui elatus est et superbus, vel filius est elati huius vel discipulus et imitator" (*In numeros homilia* xii, in *Origines Werke*, ed. W. A. Baehrens [Leipzig, 1921], vii, 105). From the above, it is apparent that Origen has quoted the two verses of Isaiah xiv, 13–14, nearly entire, while the text in question merges one part of each into a single whole; morever, in verse 13 Origen reads "ponam thronum meum" instead of "ponam sedem meam." In the *Vetus Italica,* ed. Pierre Sabatier (Rheims, 1743; Paris, 1751), ii, 543, one may find listed numerous early readings of Isaiah xiv, 13–14, several of them showing a tendency to compress the two verses. It appears, however, that the earliest occurrence of the form "Ponam sedem meam ad aquilonem, et ero similis Altissimo" is in Augustine. There seems, therefore, to be every reason for taking Augustine as the source of the compressed form Langland used. I am indebted to Professor Bernard Peebles of Catholic University for valued assistance with this passage.
3. Robertson and Huppé (*Piers Plowman,* p. 44, note 52) tentatively attribute the reading "pedem" to a scribal confusion of *p* and *s.* Langland's rephrasing of "Ponam pedem" in the lines immediately following, "hus fote for to sette" (C ii, 119), shows that "pedem" was not an error but the reading intended. The possibility of such a confusion

having occurred before Langland is also remote. As the subsequent discussion will indicate, there is no evidence of such a reading before Langland.

4. "Pes animae recte intelligitur amor: qui cum pravus est, vocatur cupiditas aut libido; cum autem rectus, dilectio vel charitas" (*Enarratio in Psalmum* IX, 15 [*PL*, XXXVI, 124]. "Ad ambulandum et proficiendum et ascendendum charitas movet; ad cadendum superbia movet" (*Enarratio in Psalmum* CXX, 5 [*PL*, XXXVII, 1608]).

5. "*Non veniat mihi pes superbiae.* . . . Sub umbraculo alarum tuarum sperabunt filii hominum, et inebriabuntur ab ubertate domus tuae. Cum coeperit quisque isto fonte uberius irrigari, caveat ne superbiat. . . . Quare illum [amorem sui] pedem dixit? Quia superbiendo Deum deseruit, et discessit: pedem ipsius, affectum ipsius dixit. Non veniat mihi pes superbiae" (*Enarratio in Psalmum* XXXV, 17 [*PL*, XXXVI, 353–354]).

6. "*Ne des ad movendum pedem meum.* . . . Sed prius attende unde motus est [pes] illi qui erat inter angelos, et moto pede cecidit, et de angelo factus est diabolus: moto enim pede cecidit. Quaere unde cecidit: superbia cecidit. . . . Ad ruinam non movet pedem [animae] nisi superbia" (*Enarratio in Psalmum* CXX, 5 [*PL*, XXXVII, 1608]).

7. *Confessions* XIII, ix, 10. The translation followed is that by Vernon J. Bourke (*The Fathers of the Church: A New Translation* [New York, 1953] XXI). For a brief discussion of the conception of "pondus," see Étienne Gilson, *Introduction à l'étude de saint Augustin* (Paris, 1943), pp. 173–174. See also H. R. Patch, "*Consolatio philosophiae*, IV, m. vi, 23–24," *Speculum*, VIII (1933) 41–51.

8. "Benedicite gentes Deum nostrum, et auditam facite vocem laudis eius, qui posuit animam meam ad vitam, et non dedit in commotionem pedes meos, id est, affectus et amores meos; sed illud commune Augustini, Pes meus, amor meus, illo feror quocumque feror" (*De causa Dei*, ed. Henry Saville [London, 1618], p. 481). There is of course the possibility that St. Augustine himself applied the same language to "pes" as to "pondus," but I have been unable to find any example of it. It is perhaps more probable that "foot" had become as well known a symbol for love as "weight," and that this circumstance effected an interchange between the two images. See Wetheringsett: "pede amoris" (*Summa*, fol. 49ᵃ; full citation below, note 39); Ludolf of Saxony: "pedem, id est . . . affectum mentis" (*Vita Christi*, C XXII); Anselm of Laon: "pedem, id est affectum mentis" (*Enarratio in Matthaeum* IV [*PL*, CLXII, 1274]); Radulphus Ardens: "in pedibus, id est, in affectibus" (*Homilia* XLIV [*PL*, CLV, 2101]): St. Bruno: "pedes, id est, affectiones" (*Expositio Pauli in epistolas Pauli ad Ephesianos*, VI [*PL*, CLIII, 349]).

9. Guido de Columnis, *Historia destructionis Troiae*, ed. N. E. Griffin (Cambridge, Mass., 1936), p. 96.

10. *Enarratio in Psalmum* I, 4; XXXV, 17 (*PL*, XXXVI, 68–69, 353).

11. The bestiary is MS Oxford, Bodleian Ashmole 1511, fol. 41ᵇ. The excommunication is that of Henry IV by Gregory VII in 1080. Gregory says of Henry that in his pride he imitates his spiritual father, "qui dixit, 'Ponam sedem meam ab aquilone et ero similis Altissimo.'" The

record here cited is actually that of the publication of the excommunication "Delectis fratribus et coepiscopis per Principatus et Apuliam et Calabriam constitutis," rather than the excommunication itself (*Das Register Gregors VII*, ed. Erich Caspar [Berlin, 1920], p. 522). Examples of the same Satanic speech are to be found in scriptural commentaries (Cassiodorus: *PL*, x, 279); in treatises on the sins (Peraldus, *Summa de vitiis* [Lyons, 1500], fol. 102ª; *Septuplum*, MS Oxford, University College 71, fol. 29ª; *Tractatus de viciis*, MS Oxford, Bodleian Laud Misc., fol. 9ª); in chronicles (Guido de Columnis, *Historia*, p. 96). For the citation from Gregory VII, I am indebted to Miss Beryl Smalley, St. Hilda's College, Oxford.

12. *Cursor mundi*, ed. Richard Morris, *EETS O.S.* No. 57 (lines 457–459); "On the Trinity," lines 394–395, in *William of Shoreham's Poems*, ed. M. Konrath, *EETS E.S.* No. 86, p. 143.

13. Rupert of Deutz says: "Olim ascensorem istum 'In coelum ascendam,' dicentem, 'et supra astra Dei exaltabo solium meum' [Isaiah xiv]. [Dominus] detraxit et projecit in istum aerem caliginosum" (*In Exodum commentariorum* ii, 37 [*PL*, clxvii, 645]).

14. B ii, 161–165.

15. B ii, 179–182. It is not entirely easy to make out what is happening in these lines. It would appear, however, that there are two carts here described. The first is that pulled by the Commissary, the business of which is to bring back easy money (see Skeat's note to C iii, 191). The second, into which Liar is dramatically stretched, is directed by Civil to "lede alle these othere." Whether this means "to draw in a cart all these others," or simply "to precede" is not clear. However, since the same word "lede," as used two lines above in conjunction with the Commissary, clearly means "draw," and since pictorial representations of what the present writer takes to be comparable carts of sin show the forces of evil being transported in long carts (see note 29 below), the first reading seems preferable.

16. "*Equum et adscensorem proiecit in mare* . . . omnes, qui in carne nati sunt, figuraliter equi sunt, sed hi habent adscensores suos. Sunt equi, quos Dominus ascendit, et circumeunt omnem terram, de quibus dicitur: 'et equitatus tuus salus' [Habakkuk iii, 8]. Sunt autem equi, qui adscensores habent diabolum et angelos eius. Iudas equus erat, sed donec adscensorem habuit Dominum, de equitatu salutis fuit . . . sed ubi se diabolo substravit . . . adscensor ipsius effectus est Sathanas, et illius habenis ductus, adversus Dominum et Salvatorem nostrum coepit equitare. . . . *Quadrigas Pharaonis, et exercitum eius proiecit in mare, electos adscensores, ternos statores demersit in rubrum mare,* Pharao velut potentior in malitia et regnum nequitiae tenens 'quadrigas' agit. . . . Sunt alii 'electi adscensores' . . . sed iam de adscensoribus supra diximus; nunc etiam qui sint 'terni statores' videamus. . . . Isti ergo 'terni statores' sunt angeli nequam de exercitu Pharaonis" (*In Exodum homilia,* vi, 2–3 [*Werke* (Leipzig, 1920), vi, 193–195]). The biblical text used by Rufinus in his translation is a form of the Old Latin close to the version printed by Sabatier (i, 164) from a Rheims Psalter manuscript. On the term "terni statores," cf. IV Kings vii, 2, and see A. Souter, *Glossary of Later Latin* (Oxford, 1949), p. 387. J. H. Baxter

and C. Johnson (*Medieval Latin Word List* [Oxford, 1934], p. 427) define the word (in the form "ternistator") as "title of wicked angel." It would appear likely that it was Origen's exposition of Exodus xv, 1–4, or something similar, that gave to "ternistatores" the meaning adduced by Baxter and Johnson. In arriving at his conclusion that the "ternistatores" are "angeli nequam," Origen plays insistently upon the three element in the biblical term.

17. Bede, *Explicatio in Exodum* xv (*PL*, xci, 311–312); Rabanus Maurus, *Commentarium in Exodum* iv (*PL*, cviii, 67–75).

18. *Psychomachia*, lines 310–343 (in *Prudentius*, trans. H. J. Thomson [Cambridge, Mass., 1949), i, 300–302).

19. Adolf Katzenellenbogen, *Allegories of the Virtues and Vices in Medieval Art* (London, 1939); Morton W. Bloomfield, *The Seven Deadly Sins* (Lansing, Mich., 1952).

20. *Moralia in Job*, xxxi, 45 (*PL*, lxxvi, 620).

21. See Bloomfield's excellent and extremely useful index under "Psychomachiae" (cited in note 19 above).

22. *Sermones in Cantica* xxxix (*PL*, clxxxiii, 977–981). I have not translated "equitatus" in the customary fashion as "company of horsemen" because I am unable to find that St. Bernard interpreted his text in that fashion. Actually, the usage of "equitatus" about the time of St. Bernard identified it more or less with "exercitus" (see Du Cange, *Glossarium*), and Bernard seems to observe this equivalence (*Sermones in Cantica* iv): "Sed vide iam similitudinem de Pharaone et exercitu eius, ut de Domini equitatu. Non inter ipsos *exercitus* similitudo data est" (*PL, clxxxiii, 978*).

23. One notices that such an interpretation offers certain grammatical difficulties, since "in curribus Pharaonis" does not accord particularly well with the idea of battle *against* Pharaoh's chariots. Stephen Langton (discussed below) seems to have felt this difficulty, and in his own *Glossa in Cantica* is at pains to show that God is fighting with the "equitatus" against the "currus," and modifies the grammatical form to fit: "ego [Deus] militabam veluti in curribus, id est, in currus Pharaonis" (MS Oxford, Bodley 87, fol. 153ᵃ).

24. "Luxuriae vero currus quadriga nihilominus volvitur vitiorum, Ingluvie videlicet ventris, Libidine coitus, Mollitie vestium, otii soporisque Resolutione. Trahitur equis aeque duobus, Prosperitate vitae, et rerum Abundantia; et qui his praesident duo, ignaviae Torpor, et infida Securitas" (*PL*, clxxxiii, 980). I have translated "auriga" as "postilion" rather than as "charioteer" because the arrangement here alluded to would seem to be that of a principal driver, in this case the "vitium principale," and the postilions governing the individual horses. Illustrations of this method are to be found in the *Bible moralisée* (cited in note 29 below) and in the *Hortus deliciarum*, plate 5 (ed. Canon Joseph Walter [Strasbourg, 1952]), where the postilion of the chariot of the sun is labelled "auriga."

25. *In Cantica canticorum* ii (*Werke* [Leipzig, 1925], viii, 151).

26. "Quot enim sunt vitia, tot sunt et currus, quibus diabolus fertur" (*PL*, clxiv, 265).

27. The phrase "principalia vitia" occurs repeatedly in Gregory's description

of the seven deadly sins in *Moralia*, xxxi, 45: "septem principalibus vitiis," "septem nimirum principalia vitia," etc.

28. It is to be observed that Origen uses the reading "quadriga" in referring to Pharaoh's chariots and shows that he is using the term in its classical sense by having the "quadriga" drawn by four horses (*In Exodum homilia*, vi, 3 [*Werke*, vi, 194]). St. Bernard, however, evidently understood "quadriga" and "currus" as both referring to a four-wheeled vehicle. Thus he says: "Habet namque Malitia currum suum rotis quattuor consistentem. . . . Trahitur autem duobus admodum pernicibus equis. . . . Tunc namque *quadriga* ista Malitiae" (*PL*, clxxxiii, 980). The same terminology is used in describing the four-wheeled cart of Luxuria (see note 24 above). St. Bernard is here doubtless following established usage. In antiquity "currus" had meant a four-wheeled wagon as well as a chariot, and in England in 1238 one finds "currum cum quattuor rotis" (*Calendar of the Liberate Rolls*, Henry III: 1226–1240, p. 333). "Quadriga" was apparently also used in this sense in St. Bernard's time. Baxter and Johnson print "quadriga" as meaning a four-wheeled wagon in about the year 1160 (*Medieval Latin Word List*, p. 342).

29. The "longa caretta" seems to have been a well-recognized form of military transportation. From its great length, it must, like the "currus," have had four wheels. Henry III maintained ten of these carts in each of the principal castles of Winchester, Bristol, and Gloucester. In 1227 he gave orders for their construction, and in 1229 for their repair (*Calendar of Liberate Rolls*, pp. 19, 140). The carts were clearly intended for military use. Thus in the *Bible moralisée*, ed. A. Laborde (Paris, 1911), I, plate 48, one may see Pharaoh advancing into the Red Sea in his long cart filled with soldiers and drawn by postilion-mounted horses. The *Hortus deliciarum* of Herrad von Landsperg, discussed below, offers a similar illustration. For information relative to "currus" and "longa caretta" I am indebted to Dr. E. M. Jope.

30. The bejewelled cart, Luxury herself, and five of the cart's armed passengers, Iocus, Petulantia, Amor, Pompa, Voluptas, all go back to the original *Psychomachia* of Prudentius (lines 310–444). The label "principale vicium," seen near Luxuria's head, is due ultimately to Gregory the Great (see note 27 above), while three of the passengers, Immundicia, Turpiloquium (scurrilitas), and Mentis Excecatio (caecitas mentis), are also due to him (*PL*, lxxvi, 621). From the later *Psychomachiae* further armored passengers are drawn. Alcuin furnishes Lascivia (*Liber de virtutibus et viciis* [*PL*, ci, 634] and the *De conflictu vitiorum et virtutum* provides Ignavia (*PL*, xl, 1092). The four-wheeled cart, with the "principale vicium" as driver of the cart, shows immediate and doubtless controlling indebtedness to St. Bernard (see note 28 above). The illustration is reproduced from the edition of the *Hortus deliciarum* by Canons A. Straub and G. Keller ([Strasbourg, 1879–1899], plate 47).

31. MS Oxford, Trinity College 65, fols. 110ᵇ–111ᵇ. The hand is English and dates from about the second quarter of the thirteenth century. For this information I am indebted to N. R. Ker, Esq., Reader in

Paleography, Oxford University. For the date of composition of the commentary and for checking my transcriptions, I am indebted to Miss Beryl Smalley, Oxford. All future references to Langton are to this manuscript.

32. *In Exodum homilia*, VI, 4 (*Werke*, VI, 194).

33. "*Currus Pharaonis*, etc. . . . super hoc dicit Glosa: 'Quos videris in luxuria turpiores, in crudelitate seviores, in avaritia deteriores, scito esse quadrigas diaboli' " (fol. 111ᵃ).

34. St. Bernard has said only that Satan equipped his three princes with carts: "his suis principibus Pharao praeparavit currus" (*Sermones in Cantica* XXXIX, vi (*PL*, CLXXXIII, 980). Langton, however, goes considerably further and quotes Bernard as identifying princes and carts: "Nota quod Pharao habet currus, habet et principes duces exercituum. Super hunc locum vero in *Canticis canticorum,* 'Equitatui meo assimilavi te in curribus Pharaonis,' assignat Sanctus Bernardus qui sint currus Pharaonis et appendicia eorum. Sic Pharao est diabolus, qui est, ut dicit Dominus ad Job, rex super omnes filios superbie (Job XLI, 25). Tres eius principes sive currus sunt hec tria vicia: Superbia, sive Malicia, Avaricia, Luxuria" (fol. 111ᵃ).

35. Having identified both sinners and sins as carts, Langton is now ready to show that demons are the riders. Thus he says: "*Electi principes,* etc. Principes, ut habemus, sunt vicia principalia vel demones eis presidentes" (fol. 111ᵇ). This makes clear that the demon is the rider or driver and sin the conveyance. I do not find, however, that Langton has specifically shown the comparable relationship between demon and sinner. He would seem to be interested in harmonizing the two main elements of each tradition: the sin-cart of St. Bernard and the demonic rider of Origen. In this solution he is very close to the earlier interpretation of St. Bruno, to aspects of which St. Bernard is himself perhaps indebted (see note 26 above).

36. Langton begins by mentioning Malicia as an equivalent for Superbia, but after making this initial equivalence, he makes no further mention of Malicia at all. Thus: "Superbia sive Malicia . . . Primus ergo est currus Superbie," etc. (fol. 111ᵃ). The lines quoted are a continuation of the passage reproduced in note 34 above.

37. "Tria principalia vitia, scilicet, concupiscentia carnis, concupiscentia oculorum, et superbia vite" (fol. 111ᵇ).

38. It will be observed that the devil is here the driver and the vice the cart. In St. Bernard, the vice is the driver and the cart is made up of subdivisions of the vice. Satan is nowhere treated as the driver of the vice, nor in St. Bernard is there a "currus Superbie" (see note 34 above).

39. "Currus diaboli protest dici superbia, cuius quattuor sunt rote: contemptus Dei, et proximi, et proprie subjectionis, et ecclesiastice institutionis"; "Item carnis concupiscentia est quasi palefridus diaboli, et avaricia quasi runcinus, superbia quasi dextrarius" (MS Oxford, New College 94, fol. 49ᵃ, 47ᵇ). For a brief discussion of Richard de Wetheringsett and the *Summa de officio sacerdotis,* or "Qui bene presunt," see below, "St. Augustine and the 'Parson's Tale,' " note 8.

40. A II, 150, 135, 148. For examples of the "runcinus trotans" as a common type of rouncy, see Du Cange, *Glossarium*, "runcinus."

41. In addition to the examples already discussed, see Rupert of Deutz: "exercitum eius [Sathanae] tam vitiorum quam daemonum" (*PL*, CLXVII, 647). In this he is followed by Gerhoh of Reichersperg, *Expositio in canticum Moysis* I (*PL*, CXCIV, 1021).

42. I have not been able to find any hint of Langland's solution except in Langton's *Commentary on the Pentateuch*. Here the demons are manifestly of higher position in Satan's army than the sins, as the phrase "demones eis [viciis] presidentes" indicates (see note 35 above). However, if the "electi principes" are both the "principalia vicia" and the demons driving them, the relationship of demon and vice remains indefinite. This indefiniteness is continued in Langton's identification of "adversarios" (Exodus xv, 7) as "demones et vitia" (fol. 112ᵃ). One suspects that Langton was more interested in the homiletic advantages of viewing Satan's army from different points of view than he was in establishing a precise Satanic chain of command.

43. For the significance of the phrase "up-so-doun," see Chaucer's *Parson's Tale*, lines 260–266 (*Works*, ed. F. N. Robinson, 2nd. ed. [Boston, 1957], p. 234).

6

Langland's "Canes Muti": The Paradox of Reform

In the tenth passus of *Piers Plowman* (B 256 ff.), Clergy defines Dobest as "to be bolde · to blame the gylty," but adds the qualification that the priest, to carry out his duty of just reproof, must himself be blameless: *"Si culpare velis · culpabilis esse cauebis. . . ."* However, Clergy continues, few are they who obey this injunction, and little are the people benefited by their blind guides:

> Ac it semeth now sothly   ·   to the worldes syght,
> That goddes worde worcheth nauȝte   ·   on lered ne on lewede,
> But in suche a manere as Marke   ·   meneth in the gospel,
> *Dum cecus ducit cecum, ambo in foveam cadunt.*
> Lewed men may likne ȝow thus   ·   that the beem lithe in ȝowre eyghen,
> And the festu is fallen   ·   for ȝowre defaute,
> In alle manere men   ·   thourgh mansed prestes.
> The bible bereth witnesse   ·   that alle the folke of Israel
> Byttere abouȝte the gultes   ·   of two badde prestes,
> Offyn and Fynes;   ·   for her coueytise,
> *Archa dei* myshapped   ·   and Ely brake his nekke.
>   For-thi, ȝe corectoures, claweth her-on   ·   and corecteth fyrst ȝow-seluen,

Reprinted from *Essays in Literary History* (in honor of J. Milton French), ed. Rudolf Kirk and C. F. Main (New Brunswick, N.J., 1960).

And thanne mowe ʒe saufly seye · as Dauid made the sauter:
Existimasti inique quod ero tui similis: arguam te, et statuam
contra faciem tuam.
And thanne shal borel clerkes ben abasched · to blame
ʒow or to greue,
And carpen nouʒte as thei carpen now · and calle ʒow
doumbe houndes,
Canes non valentes latrare (B x, 274–287).[1]

The significance of the "doumbe houndes" epithet with which
Clergy closes his remarks remains largely unexplored.[2] It has,
of course, long been recognized that the words "canes muti non
valentes latrare" make up a portion of the indictment of the priest-
hood of Israel found in Isaiah LVI, 10: "Speculatores ejus caeci
omnes . . . canes muti non valentes latrare." Beyond this, however,
very little of Langland's allusion has been explained. Why, for
instance, are the secular clergy called "doumbe houndes," and
who are the "borel clerkes" who so accuse them? Finally, how
are we to interpret the passage as a whole? Are we to interpret
it as Langland's delight at the deserved rebuke of the corruption
practiced by the secular clergy or as his concern over criticism
which, if unchecked, might well endanger the existence of the
Church itself?

The relevance of Isaiah LVI, 10, to the secular clergy, English
or otherwise, is easily made out. In all the commentaries the
"speculator," watchman, and the "canis," watchdog, are interpreted as figures of the priest. Of the two, the "canis" metaphor
seems to have been much the more popular. Thus the *Glossa*
ordinaria says: "Just as it is the duty of dogs to protect a flock, so
is it the duty of prelates to protect the people."[3] The failure of
the watchdog to bark is the failure of the priest to correct evil
when he sees it appear among his flock. Thus in the *Cura*
pastoralis (II, iv), Gregory says:

Let the spiritual leader [rector] be discreet in silence, useful in
word, lest he utter those things which ought to be kept silent, or keep
silent those things which ought to be spoken out. For just as incau-
tious speech drags into error, so does indiscreet silence abandon in
error those who were capable of being taught. For often improvident
leaders [rectores] fearing to lose human favor, tremble to speak out
freely those things which are right, and according to the voice of

Truth (John x, 12), keep their flocks not with the zeal of shepherds, but in the manner of mercenaries, for when they hide themselves beneath silence, they flee at the approach of the wolf. And thus the Lord reproves them through the mouth of the prophet, saying: "Dumb dogs, not able to bark."[4]

In the British Isles, the Isaiah passage seems to have been as well known as on the Continent. It appears first, so far as the present writer is aware, in the famous *De excidio et conquestu Britanniae* (sixth century), where Gildas speaks of the duty of priests to reprove the sinful, "lest we be 'dumb dogs, not able to bark.' "[5] In Anglo-Saxon England, the text is found in the first pastoral letter of Aelfric, and in Wulfstan's brief treatise concerning lazy, timid, and negligent pastors.[6] In the fourteenth century, it appears, amongst other places, in the *Speculum Christiani*: "If he [the curate] es not salt or sau*er*y in wysdom, he es an hounde a-boute the floc of god, but he dryue₃ not a-wey the wolfe with berkynge of p*r*echynge."[7]

From the above references, it is clear that the priest was expected to be a faithful watchdog, barking vociferously to warn of evil. This warning might be made directly in the form of personal rebuke—as for instance Chaucer's good priest, who would "snybben sharply for the nonys"[8]—or less directly in the form of preaching.[9] It will be noted, however, that in the *Piers-Plowman* passage reproduced above, Langland seems to have in mind less an abstract treatment of the duties of the good priest than a specific group or groups—"borel clerkes"—who are calling the secular clergy "doumbe houndes." Who might these be?

No group of Langland's time was more consistent in pointing out the failings of the secular clergy than the friars. Though themselves open to many criticisms, there was one criticism they were not open to, and that was failure to preach. In a curious monitory poem, *De concordia inter fratres et rectores ecclesiae* (early fifteenth century), the monk John Audelay contrasts the activity of the preaching friars and the indolence of the parish priests:

Trule, I trow, þis rewme where chamyd *and* chent
  Nere þe foreþeryng of þe frerys *and* here p*r*echyng,
For þe seculars p*r*estis take no*n* entent
  Bot to here leudnes *and* her lust *and* here lykyng.[10]

What the friars had to say in their sermons about the non-preaching and materially inclined secular clergy is fortunately readily available in the *Summa predicantium*, the great compilation of preaching material for friars put together not long before 1348 by the Dominican John Bromyarde.[11] Under the head of "Avarice" one finds much relevant material. Here Bromyarde, in his characteristic narrative form, declares that against the avaricious man, in this case evidently the avaricious priest, the three great masters of deceit, the world, the flesh, and the devil, join forces. At the beginning of his career, the new priest attacks the triple temptations facing him with great energy; but the world, the flesh, and the devil, though duly put to flight by his eager assault, take care to drop tempting bits in their precipitous retreat.

Thus many seek to pursue vigorously, and in this labor begin [to attack] the world—that is, sinners living unto the world and evilly—by correction; their own flesh by maceration; the devil by humiliation. But the world scatters rewards, and while they are busy about these, the evil escape. . . . And thus they mock the receivers of rewards. . . . These [receivers of rewards], made sport of through entreaty and bribe, put off their corrections, and about these [corrections] being both negligent and timid, permit many to go off to hell, with whom they themselves go for the sake of company. Therefore it is said to Moses, Exodus xviii [21]: "Provide out of all the people wise men, able and fearing God, in whom there is truth, and who hate avarice," for they who hate avarice and are not busy about rewards, will not permit sinners to go off into damnable perdition. . . . Those who give up their pursuit because of the aforementioned impediments [the temptations of the world, the flesh, and the devil] are like dogs which cease to bark when bread is thrown them by a thief, and permit the thief to carry out his intention. Thus they are *dumb dogs, not able to bark*.[12]

Another group equally critical of the failings of the secular clergy and equally devoted to the practice of preaching were the Lollards. Wyclif's own views on the avariciousness of the secular clergy and their disinclination to preach are well enough known to require no further discussion. What is perhaps more relevant is to examine the kind of popularization of Wyclif's views which might have come to the ears of Langland. An example of such a popularization is the vast and discursive tractate *On the Seven Deadly Sins*, thought to have been written about 1385 by Nicholas Hereford, one of the best known of Wyclif's followers.[13] Although a few years too late for the usually accepted date of the B text (*ca.* 1377), the *Seven Deadly Sins* provides a useful compilation of typical Lollard opinions, which by the year 1377 were being actively circulated by Wyclif's "poor priests."[14] Particularly instructive are Hereford's views on preaching. "Þo moste hye servise þat men have in erthe," says Hereford, "is to preche Gods worde,"[15] and "herfore Jesus Crist occupyed hym mooste in þo werke of prechyng, and laft oþer werkes; and þus diden his apostils, and herfore God loved hom."[16] But now, continues Hereford,

no more covetouse men schal men fynde in erthe, ne ferrer fro hevenly lif, ne more wrappid wiþ worldly causes. And it semes to mony men þat þei gon hedlyngis to helle, and drawen men aftir hom þat þei schulden bere to heven. . . . Ffor prest is a spyere in his castel [Isaiah LVI, 10], to loke ofer perels of schepe; and if he be blynde in his soule for pouder of temporal goodis . . . and þus perel come to schepe, þo Lord þat owis þo schepe by skil schulde dampne hym for negligense.[17]

The reference to the priest's being a "spyere in his castel" is of course a reference to the beginning of the text under discussion, "Speculatores ejus caeci omnes . . . canes muti non valentes latrare" (Isaiah LVI, 10). Given the presence of this allusion, it is no great surprise to discover elsewhere in Hereford's text this same image of spiritual blindness merging into an image of spiritual muteness occasioned by the devil's casting a highly material bone to the watchdogs:

And as eyne in þo hed reulen al þo body for to go right weyes and profitable to mon, so prelatis of þo Chirche schulden lede hit in Gods wey. Bot Crist seis in his Gospel, þat if a blynde lede a blynde mon in þo wey, þei fallen bothe in þo dike [Matthew xv, 14]. And þus þo wey of charite, þat schulde be brood to alle men, is streyned by envye, and lettis men to sue Crist. And so þo fend haves cast a boon, and made þese honndes to feght; and by a bal of talow lettis hom to berke.[18]

It is apparent, I think, that the Dominican Bromyarde and the Wyclifite Hereford are making essentially the same accusation. Worldly goods have blinded the Church to the needs of its sheep and made mute the mouths which should warn the flock of approaching disaster. As a result, the blind pastor accompanies the blind sheep down the road to hell. In place of spiritual leaders, there are only blind—and mute—mouths. All this is to be found in Langland: the covetousness, the blindness, the failure of reproof. However, between Langland and the two groups whom the present writer takes to be the "borel clerkes"[19] in question there is a long and large difference. Whereas the Wyclifite and the friar either relished destructive criticism or lacked effective concern about its consequences, Langland feared what might happen to the unity of the Church should unbridled criticism be permitted to gain currency. What Langland hoped to see was a reform movement within the secular clergy strong enough to refute, through its own example, the slurs cast upon it. One of the numerous paradoxes of Langland the man[20] is that Langland the reformer had a very exact sense of the dangers of reform:

> For-thi I conseil alle creatures · no clergie to dispise,
> Ne sette schort be here science · what so thei don hemselue.
> Take we her wordes at worthe · for here witnesse be trewe,
> And medle we nau3t muche with hem · to meuen any wrathe,
> Lest cheste chafen vs · to choppe vche man other;
> *Nolite tangere christos meos, etc.*[21]

NOTES

1. All references to *Piers Plowman* are to the edition by W. W. Skeat (Oxford, 1886).
2. Brief comments are to be found in Cardinal F. A. Gasquet, *Old English Bible,* 2nd ed. (London, 1908), p. 67, and H. B. Workman, *John Wyclif* (Oxford, 1926), II, 208.
3. "Sicut canes gregem, sic prelati debent custodire plebem" (*PL,* CXIII, 1208).
4. "Sit rector descretus in silentio, utilis in verbo, ne aut tacenda proferat, aut proferenda reticescat. Nam sicut incauta locutio in errorem pertrahit, ita indiscretum silentium hos qui erudiri poterant, in errore derelinquit. Saepe namque rectores improvidi humanam amittere gratiam formidantes, loqui libere recta pertimescunt; et juxta Veritatis vocem (John x, 12), nequaquam jam gregis custodiae Pastorum studio, sed

mercenariorum vice deserviunt, quia veniente lupo fugiunt, dum se sub silentio abscondunt. Hinc namque eos per prophetam Dominus increpat, dicens: *Canes muti non valentes latrare*" (*PL*, LXXVII, 30). For this citation I am indebted to the kindness of Professor Morton W. Bloomfield of Harvard University.

5. "Ne simus 'canes muti non valentes latrare'" ("Gildae Sapientis *De excidio et conquestu Britanniae*," in *Monumenta Germaniae Historica* [Berlin, 1898], XIII, 48).

6. *The Homilies of Wulfstan,* ed. Dorothy Bethurum (Oxford, 1957), pp. 240, 350. These passages were kindly pointed out to me by Professor Rudolph Willard of the University of Texas.

7. *Speculum Christiani,* ed. Gustaf Holmstedt, *EETS O.S.* No. 182 (London, 1933 [for 1929]), p. 172.

8. "General Prologue" to the *Canterbury Tales,* line 523.

9. Preaching seems to have been a very popular interpretation of the hound's bark. In addition to the *Speculum Christiani* passage cited above, see Haymo of Halberstadt, "latratus predicationis" (*PL*, CXVI, 1010); Hervey of Bourg-Dieu, "canes enim dicuntur praedicatores" (*PL*, CLXXXI, 514); and Nicholas of Lyra, "sine voce predicationis" *Biblia sacra cum glossa ordinaria* (Lyons, 1589), IV, 562. The gloss last noted is the interlinear gloss.

10. Lines 599–602 (*The Poems of John Audelay,* ed. E. K. Whiting, *EETS O.S.* No. 184, p. 31). It is interesting to observe that the poem seems to be a deliberate imitation of *Piers Plowman,* both in its imitation of Langland's alliteration and in its concern with the peril to the unity of the Church posed by the strife between the secular and regular clergy.

11. The *DNB* ("John Bromyarde") puts Bromyarde's period of activity at around 1390. However, recent researches (see H. C. Beeching, "The Library of the Cathedral Church of Norwich," *Norfolk Archaeology,* XIX [1915], 72–73, indicate that the *Summa predicantium* was written certainly before 1352 and that its author probably died in the plague of 1348. For information relative to the dating of the *Summa* I am indebted to the Rev. James A. Weisheipl, O.P., and to the Rev. Leonard E. Boyle, O.P.

12. "Sic multi conantur fortiter persequi, et hoc opere incipiunt mundum, i.e., peccatores mundialiter et male viuentes correctione; carnem propria[m] maceratione; dyabolum humiliatione. Sed mundus spargit munera, circa que dum intendunt, mali fugiunt. . . . Et sic illudunt receptoribus munerum. . . . Sic illusi prece et precio, correctiones differunt, et circa eas negligentes et timidi, multos ad infernum abire permittu[n]t, cum quibus et ipsimet vadunt ratione societatis. Ideo dicitur ad Moysen (Exodus XVIII [21]): *Prouide de omni plebe viros sapientes, potentes, et timentes Deum, in quibus sit veritas, et qui oderint auariciam . . .* quia qui odio habent auariciam, circa munera non intenti, peccatores abire non permittunt in perditionem damnabilem. . . . Propter predicta impedimenta cessantes, canes sunt qui pane sibi a latrone proiecto, latrare cessant, et furem propositum suum persequi permittunt. Sic *canes muti non valentes latrare*" (*Summa predicantium* [Basel, *ca.* 1484], Art. A, XXVII, 58). Punctuation has been

normalized throughout and biblical quotations have been italicized. For checking my translation I am indebted to the Rev. James A. Weisheipl, O.P.

13. The tract is published by Thomas Arnold in *Select English Works of John Wyclif* (Oxford, 1869–1871), III, 119–167. Arnold believed the work to be by Wyclif himself, but in 1907, Edmund D. Jones attributed it, on the basis of dialect study, to Nicholas Hereford (see *Anglia*, XXX, 267–268). He is followed in this by H. B. Workman (*John Wyclif* [Oxford, 1926], I, 330; II, 135); and H. E. Winn (*Wyclif: Select English Writings* [Oxford, 1929], pp. 146–147). Workman assigns the *Seven Deadly Sins* to about the year of Hereford's return from Rome (1385). See *John Wyclif*, II, 135, and Winn, *Wyclif*, p. 147.

14. Workman finds Wyclif's first reference to the persecution of the "poor priests" in the year 1377 (*John Wyclif*, II, 205).

15. Arnold, *Select English Works*, III, 143.

16. *Ibid.*, III, 144.

17. *Ibid.*, III, 150.

18. *Ibid.*, III, 133. Unlike Bromyarde's hound story, Hereford's occurs under "Envy," and hence the more complicated image of dogs fighting over a bone.

19. "Borel (burel)" is a word of frequent occurrence in Middle English. Numerous examples are to be found in Chaucer, but none in conjunction with "clerk" (see article on "burel" in J. S. P. Tatlock and A. G. Kennedy, *A Concordance to the Complete Works of Geoffrey Chaucer* [Washington, 1927]). Gower, however, in the Prologue to the *Confessio amantis* (line 52), uses the exact phrase: "Thus I, which am a burel clerk." The *MED* which cites the Gower passage, interprets the phrase as meaning: "clerk with little learning;? also, an educated layman" (see article "burel"). The word "burel" may of course tend to suggest the garb of Wyclif's "poor priests" (see Workman, *John Wyclif*, II, 203), but it is highly doubtful that Langland could have known much of their activities by the time of the B text (see p. 55 and note 14 above). It seems more likely that "borel clerkes" was used as a simple term of abuse, of which Langland had a considerable store.

20. For the paradoxical nature of Langland's character, see the excellent discussion by E. T. Donaldson, *Piers Plowman: The C Text and Its Poet* (New Haven, 1949), chap. VII.

21. B XII, 123–127 "Touch not my anointed" (Psalm CIV, 15 [Vulgate]). The speaker here is Ymagynatyf, who in Passus XII answers the doubts set forth by the dreamer in Passus X. He may therefore, I think, be taken as a reliable spokesman for Langland's considered opinions.

7

Amatory Psychology and Amatory Frustration in the Interpretation of the "Book of the Duchess"

T he *Book of the Duchess* is not only a superb poem, but that Chaucerian rarity—an occasional poem of which the occasion is known. From numerous topical references, as well as from Chaucer's own testimony,[1] it is clear that the *Book of the Duchess* is an elegy upon the death of Blanche, Duchess of Lancaster, who perished in September, 1369, during one of the periodic recurrences of the Black Death. Thus the poem was presumably one of consolation directed toward the bereaved husband, John of Gaunt, Duke of Lancaster. In terms of the conventions of the "consolatio," the poem could be expected to take the form of the dream vision, in which a supernatural being appears to the dreamer and by gentle but adamant argumentation brings him to perceive the meaninglessness of the mortal and the transcendency of the divine. The outstanding example of this sort of poem is of course the *Pearl*.[2]

To a court poet, such a poem would seem to present no insurmountable difficulties. What is obviously called for is a conventional set of theological arguments accompanied by, or climaxed by, a conventional vision of the Lady Blanche amidst the joys of Paradise, the net effect being the illumination of the bereaved's earthly mind, and his consequent movement from despair to consolation. However, the elegy Chaucer produced can hardly be termed conventional. First, there is the virtually unexampled introduction of humor into an elegy, and humor of an uneven and curious sort. Second, the humor comes into being largely through the agency of a most extraordinary literary personage. This personage is the complex Narrator-Dreamer, the fictive creation through whom the totality of the poem is communicated, and whose position in the poem is therefore central. However, though firmly embedded in the poem, the Narrator-Dreamer does not afford a particularly secure base for literary exploration. What one learns from the Narrator, who recounts what he, as Dreamer, has experienced, is the stupidity of the latter—a stupidity so incredible as to have forced criticism of the poem into two apparently opposite opinions. The most modern and most generally held is that the Dreamer within the poem is not really stupid at all, but is using his feigned stupidity as a psychiatric tool to purge the bereaved husband of his grief; the second possesses at least qualified faith in the reality of the Dreamer's stupidity, but finds its nature difficult to define.[3]

The present essay will deal with (1) the occasion of the poem, and the possible relation of the strange element of elegiac humor to the quite unfictional Geoffrey Chaucer, husband as well as poet; (2) Chaucer's use of an amatory psychology which would have made the non-comprehension of the Dreamer quite comprehensible to a contemporary audience; and (3) an analysis of the poem in terms of the humor and psychology mentioned.

I

To those familiar with the essential humanity of Chaucer, it seems very natural and fitting that his earliest extant work should be a work in which sorrow and laughter find a balance, and from which sentimentalism is firmly excluded. However, one needs to remind himself that this is not merely a poem, but a particular kind of poem, and that it is addressed to John of Gaunt, Duke of Lancaster, a man of known and positive sensibilities, who was in the process of becoming the most powerful man in England.[4] A poem delicately attuned to John of Gaunt's sensibilities—probably abject flattery—could do much for the advancement of a very minor civil servant, who was also a poet; failure or, worse, offense could have disastrous consequences. A system of literary patronage is after all simply the obverse of a system of literary censorship.

It is therefore odd that Chaucer the future diplomat, having adopted the graceful device of placing the praise of the lost Duchess in the mouth of the noble lover who has experienced the loss, should have caused the bereaved lover, in the person of the Black Knight, to make statements capable of quite unpietistic interpretation. Thus, the Black Knight, in accordance with the accepted rhetorical tradition of describing female beauty from top to bottom,[5] makes an enraptured descending catalogue of the Lady's person, but a catalogue curiously annotated with negatively informative data. The Black Knight begins appropriately enough with the exquisite gold of the Lady's hair; but, in making his next major stop, her eyes, he describes not only their singular qualities, but the unwarranted conclusions drawn by presumptuous gazers beneath their half-closed lids[6]—unwarranted because the objects of her love were exclusively "goode folk," and her manner of loving unexceptionable:

> She loved as man may do his brother;
> *Of which love she was wonder large,*
> *In skilful places that bere charge.* (892–894)

After this muddily worded and completely uncalled for explanation—which would seem to fit rather exactly Pope's remarks on explaining a thing till all men doubt it—the Black Knight continues his downward progress, arriving at such destinations as "visage" (895), "nekke" (939), "shuldres" (952), and concluding his anatomical journey at:

> Rounde brestes; and of good brede
> Hyre hippes were; a streight flat bak.
> I knew on hir noon other lak
> That al hire lymmes nere pure sewynge
> *In as fer as I had knowynge.* (956–960)

The gratuitousness of this last line—if it is indeed gratuitous—can hardly be exaggerated, since John of Gaunt, by this time almost thirty, had acquired and was continuing to acquire a distinguished reputation for precisely this kind of knowing,[7] and hence could hardly be expected to relish—particularly as emanating from the mouth of his representative in the poem, the Black Knight—a line which could be construed as a nervous disclaimer of any sort of amatory impropriety in his wooing of the Duchess. A further example of the same sort of thing is found near the end of the poem, where the disclaimer occurs in connection with the climactic act of the courtship—the bestowal of the Lady's mercy upon her long-serving and long-suffering lover. She

> . . . yaf me al hooly
> The noble yifte of hir mercy,
> *Savynge hir worship, by al weyes—*
> *Dredles, I mene noon other weyes.* (1269–1272)

Here again celescalation of tone carries the reader aloft, only to be abruptly brought back to earth by the introduction of a doubt the lyricism of the passage had never permitted him to entertain. It is hardly necessary to note that of all the phases of the conventional love process, the "gift of mercy" was perhaps the most vulnerable to cynical interpretation.[8]

Are we to believe that these lines are attributable to the ineptness of a young poet, or are they the expression of the feelings—voluntary or involuntary—of a very real, nonfictional Geoffrey Chaucer, squire of low degree, toward one of the greatest magnates of the land—John of Gaunt, Duke of Lancaster? Since the *Book of the Duchess* is so highly finished a poem, the first alternative may be classed as an improbable possibility. The second may, however, bear examination, since the circumstances surrounding Chaucer's composition of the *Book of the Duchess* appear to involve not only John of Gaunt, ostensible patron of the poem, but John of Gaunt's involvement with Philippa Chaucer, wife of Geoffrey Chaucer, civil servant and occasional poet.

The marriage of Geoffrey Chaucer, esquire to Edward III, and Philippa Roet, damoiselle to Queen Philippa, which occurred *ca.* 1366,[9] could not have created much of a stir at court. The positions of Philippa and Geoffrey were relatively equal, and not particularly exalted. Since the households of Edward III and

Philippa had been constrained to merge because of the latter's extravagance,[10] Geoffrey and Philippa served together, and may previously have served together, in comparable capacities, in the household of the Countess of Ulster.[11] As a reward for their services to the royal couple, they both received modest annuities in successive years (1366–1367).[12] Further parallels between Philippa and Geoffrey are not lacking, the most important being that marriages between squires and damoiselles were very frequent.[13] Here, however, similarity appears to reach an abrupt end. Much stress has been placed on Chaucer's bourgeois London background, and much is known of his career. The relatively little that is known of Philippa has received correspondingly little attention. A highly imaginary biography, on which facts occasionally obtrude, is here inserted, with a view to explaining Philippa's inubiquitousness as regards Geoffrey, and the effect this lack of connubiality may have had on the poet's feelings at the time of the writing of the *Book of the Duchess*.

Philippa came from Hainault, one of the tiniest and most intensely chivalric-minded of areas, and her father was Sir Payne Roet, who served the English crown as Guienne King of Arms, and hence was chivalric-minded on a professional basis. Her sister, Katherine Roet, had early obtained a position in the Lancastrian household as damoiselle to the Duchess Blanche, a position quite comparable to that of Philippa in the Plantagenet household. Katherine had been married to Sir Hugh Swynford, a knight of John of Gaunt's and a man of established family; she was now, however, a widow, her husband having been killed in battle in Aquitaine. Katherine's position was undisturbed by Sir Hugh's death, and she remained on in the Lancastrian household to become the mistress of John of Gaunt—probably before the death of Blanche—and to attain a level of excellence in mistresshood possibly never equalled—more than twenty years of active service, retirement upon marriage to the Duke, and legitimization of her children, the Beauforts.[14] Since the Savoy, the principal Lancastrian residence, was in London, and John of Gaunt was very much a figure at court, Philippa must have had an extensive opportunity to observe, and probably to know him. After her marriage to Geoffrey Chaucer, Esquire, also much at court, Philippa must have found herself frequently engaged in gazing upon two portraits. One was that of the man she had married: a witty, entertaining raconteur and poet, adept with words, but showing little promise of rapid advancement—also now rather inclining to rotundity, and more and more to be found with his head in an unentertaining book. The other, with whom her sister Katherine lived, was a man of dazzling splendor. His lands were a palatinate, a kingdom unto itself, collecting its own revenues and dispensing its own justice. His London palace, the Savoy,[15] rivalled if not excelled that of Edward III at Windsor. Furthermore, the Duke of Lancaster's values were those heraldry recorded and romance proclaimed—chivalry and love. And, incidentally, he was known as one who rewarded liberally and reliably those who served with excellence in these noble professions. Marie de St. Hilaire, the Duke's first known mistress—like Philippa from Hainault and again like Philippa, damoiselle to the Queen—received a royal annuity of twenty pounds, rather higher than Philippa's ten marks, and in addition, as late as 1399, a continuing pension from John of Gaunt.[16] In Marie, Philippa may have found an example appropriate to her own situation. On at least one occasion, Philippa's royal pension was to be collected for her by Lancastrian hands together with Marie's—and on that occasion they were the only ones of the damoiselles of the deceased Queen to be paid.[17] For Philippa, also, the future might hold a Lancastrian as well as a royal pension.[18] That John of Gaunt took excellent care of those descended from those he loved is established fact. The Beauforts, his illegitimate children by Katherine Swynford, were legitimized, and became distinguished members of the nobility; Blanche, the daughter of Marie de St. Hilaire, was married well and splendidly.[19] One Thomas Chaucer, the son of Philippa, was to thrive under Lancastrian patronage.[20]

All this, of course, lay in the future, and how far Philippa's eye could pierce we cannot tell. But if, in the course of her future stay in the household of Lancaster, chivalry and love were to be proposed in place of philosophy and old books—for a Hainaulter, what choice?

The somehow inevitable choice seems to have come with the death of Queen Philippa in August, 1369. Her damoiselle,

Philippa Chaucer, was left without employment. Since Geoffrey Chaucer was in fact a squire of low, or, more properly, lesser degree, with an annuity of twenty marks,[21] and since Philippa could expect, as a reality of court life, that her own annuity of ten marks would, after the death of the Queen, be paid irregularly, a second position had to be sought. The Chaucerian income was obviously inadequate for a private establishment. With the death of Blanche, Duchess of Lancaster, almost exactly one month after the death of the Queen, Philippa's decision—if it had not already been made—was finally made. Katherine, who had long been damoiselle to the Lady Blanche, was now in fact mistress of the ducal household, and was in a position to provide for her sister. From September 1, 1369, when robes of mourning for the death of Queen Philippa were issued to the royal household, among the recipients being Philippa and Geoffrey,[22] until almost three years later, no record of Philippa's whereabouts exists. However, on August 30, 1372, her name reappears—this time, however, in the records of the house of Lancaster. Before taking ship for France on one of the numerous and always dangerous campaigns which marked the period, John of Gaunt bethought himself of those for whom he had failed to make antecedent provision. One Philippa Chaucer seems to have been very present to his mind, and an annuity of ten pounds was made out to her.[23] The reason given for the grant was the "bon et agreable service" she had rendered and would in future render to Queen Constance. The exclusive reference to Constance, though by no means remarkable, does suggest the possibility that Philippa was in the entourage of John of Gaunt when, in 1371, he set forth to claim his Spanish bride and titular Spanish kingship, and that she then remained in the position of damoiselle to the new bride, Queen Constance.[24] After all, Tristan fell in love with Yseult on a sea voyage, and why should not the Duke of Lancaster? He had done it many times.

In any case, Philippa had found the splendid life she wanted, and she clung to it with determination. Though a son, Thomas, was born,[25] and though, possibly in consequence, she was emphatically returned to Chaucer in 1374, she was in 1377 again back in the Lancastrian household. The frequent appearance of

Philippa's name amongst the recipients of New Year's gifts to the Lancastrian household indicates her continued presence there.[26] The last record we possess of Philippa is dated February 19, 1386, and concerns her induction into the Fraternity of Lincoln Cathedral, along with a whole group of the younger Lancastrian family,[27] chief of whom was the Count of Derby, the future King Henry IV. As the only woman in the group, this event must have been for Philippa, the most splendid moment of her life and, John of Gaunt being present, it necessarily occurred in a profoundly religious setting. The next year Philippa was dead.

It is hoped that the foregoing may have cast some light on the emotional state of Geoffrey Chaucer, Esq., at the time of the writing of the *Book of the Duchess*. Queen Philippa had died on August 15, 1369; Blanche, the Duchess, on September 13, 1369. Sometime before November 7 of the same year, it would appear that Philippa departed the court.[28] However, before Philippa left, it is more than probable that Geoffrey had accepted the commission to write the elegy of the Duchess. Had he not, it is very difficult to understand why he wrote no elegy for Philippa, Queen of England, beyond question infinitely more colorful than the Duchess Blanche, and infinitely more widely loved.[29] It was, after all, to the Plantagenet, not to the Lancastrian, household that Chaucer was attached.

Chaucer's feelings on attempting to fulfill the task he had undertaken must have been very mixed. At the time he assumed the writing of the elegy, he must have known that his wife would inevitably depart for the Lancastrian household. Philippa's position was gone, and the Chaucers had no home. Furthermore, he must have known the nature of his wife's aspirations, and, from an infinity of sources, he must have known the reputation of John of Gaunt: "he had manye paramours in his youthe and was not verye contynente in his age."[30] Chaucer thus found himself in the unenviable position of celebrating the perfect love between a much loved lady and a much loving lover, whose next mistress his own wife might become. Should he be successful in pleasing the Duke, he might be incorporated into the vast Lancastrian palatinate in a much advanced position, but perhaps also as a convenience of convention to cover the activities of John of Gaunt and Philippa. The situation could hardly be considered conducive to the elegiac mood.

II

> I dream of a Ledean body, bent
> Above a sinking fire, a tale that she
> Told of a harsh reproof, or trivial event
> That changed some childish day to tragedy—
> Told, and it seemed that our two natures blent
> Into a sphere from youthful sympathy,
> Or else, to alter Plato's parable,
> Into the yolk and white of the one shell.
>
> —*Yeats, "Among School Children"*

Although the preceding account of the state of Chaucer's feelings at the time of the composition of the *Book of the Duchess* may, it is hoped, afford some basis for a fuller understanding of the poem, it obviously does nothing toward solving the principal difficulty, that of the opaque Dreamer, whose climactic discovery at the end of the poem—"She ys ded"—is identical with what he has heard and duly recorded at the beginning of the poem— "my lady . . . is fro me ded and ys agoon" (477–479). However, the parable of Plato so movingly alluded to by Yeats, the blending of two separate natures into a single sphere, may conceivably do so. Since the relationship of Platonic parable to the *Book of the Duchess* may not be immediately apparent, a brief examination of the chronological and geographical movement of the parable in question, that of the divided soul, may prove useful.

The Yeats allusion is of course to the speech of Aristophanes in the *Symposium*, in which he describes man's original state. Man was once spherical in shape, possessed four arms and four legs, and could walk or whirl like a cart wheel. So indestructible did he think himself that in his pride he dared assault the citadel of heaven. Zeus, forced to some sort of action but disinclined to absolute annihilation, since this would inevitably entail a disastrous loss of worshippers, devised a plan by which the number of worshippers should, in fact, be doubled:

He spake, and cut mankind in two . . . as you cut an egg through with a hair. . . . So now, when the single nature was thus cut in two, each half, longing for the other, rejoined it, and they threw their arms about each other, and entwined, in desire that they might grow together.

Since that time, every human being cleaves to what is like to him:

The reason lies herein that this was our original nature, and once we were complete. Now the longing for completeness, the pursuit of it, is known as love.[31]

Despite Plato's apparent intention that it is Socrates who is to be listened to, the imaginative power of Aristophanes' account of the coming into being of love is such as to have exerted for centuries a powerful influence on the poetic imagination, rather to the detriment of the great truth Socrates learned from the sublime, but hard to understand, Diotima. It is of course superfluous to note that in the East classical knowledge was engulfed by Arabian conquest, but it is important to observe that by the ninth century the parable of Aristophanes had become well enough known to find a place in the *Kitab az-Zahra* (Book of the Flower) of Ibn Dawoud, amatory anthologist and son of the founder of the Zahirite (literalist) sect. He says:

Some of the followers of philosophy claim that God, be He praised, created all spirits in a round shape, in the form of a sphere; then He cut them in two, put in each body one half, and whenever a body meets another, in which the other half is placed, cut from the same sphere, there arises between the two bodies a passionate love due to their former relation; and the condition of people will show different effects, according to the subtlety of their natures.[32]

However, it would appear that it was not through the anthology but through the tractate that amatory theory developed, and for present purposes the most important of these is the *Dove's Neck Ring* of Ibn Hazm al-Andalusi, written in 1027, and as the author's name implies, in Moslem Spain.[33] The *Dove's Neck Ring* is an incomparable record of an incomparable period—one in which theology, philosophy, music, poetry, and love all were assimilated into a culture unique but, by its very nature, doomed to a brief existence.[34] Ibn Hazm's book is a tractate on love, but a very unusual one. In theology Ibn was a Zahirite, a kind of Mohammedan Wyclif, who denied any authority other than the Koran. In the interest of literalism, Ibn consequently recorded only what he had himself experienced and witnessed. The personages and occasions which serve as subjects for his "anecdotes" are, in fact, real and historically verifiable. The poetry, or, more exactly, poetic comment, which follows his anecdotes is his own—the poetry of his youth. However, imposed upon youthful experience is the logic of the mature theologian. The *Dove's Neck Ring* is not only logically organized; it possesses a kind of double organization. Within each of the thirty chapters, a generality is stated, together with its subdivisions. After this follow the anecdotes and poetical observations noted, invariably in that order. The more important organization, however, is to be found in the form he gives to the totality of his book. "I have," he says, "in effect, followed the natural development of things, their chronological order."[35] Since things tend to be mortal, as Ibn is constantly reassuring us, the *Dove's Neck Ring* is really the birth, life, and death of love—and lovers. Thus Ibn, having neatly concluded his disquisition on love as an earthly phenomenon, has placed himself in an excellent position to view the same subject in terms of eternal values. At this point, Ibn the human being and onetime lover disappears, and in the last two chapters, "The Ugliness of Sin" and "The Merits of Continence," the harshness of the puritanical theologian unequivocally expresses itself. The gates of hell and heaven are flung open simultaneously, and human love is revealed as a neutral something, in and of itself valueless. If in love, as in any other human activity, the Law of Allah is obeyed, the result is eternal heavenly reward and such happiness as the mutable world affords. Conversely, if the Law is not obeyed, the result is damnation. To make matters somewhat worse, no matter how pure the love which runs counter to the Law of Allah, or how perfect, it is doomed to turn to hate. Such a love is capable of yielding only acrid misery.

It has been thought useful to take an overall view of the *Dove's Neck Ring*, because, precisely at the point Ibn becomes the dogmatic moralist, his terminology alters in a highly important and highly confusing fashion. Ibn has initially defined love as a "fusion of souls," very much in the manner of Ibn Dawoud, but with the difference that he is able to support his own definition with a Koranic text.[36] At the beginning of the first of his two concluding chapters, "The Ugliness of Sin," "soul" takes on a very forbidding meaning, and "heart" a very exalted one:

We know that Allah, the Powerful and Great, has placed in man two opposing natures. One counsels only good, and urges nothing except what is good. . . . This nature is Reason, which has for its guide, Justice. The second, on the contrary, counsels only what the appetites desire, and leads only to perdition. This is the Soul, which has for its guide Desire. Has not Allah, the most Exalted, declared: "The soul is naturally borne toward what is evil?" The "heart" Allah has metaphorically termed "Reason," and he has said, "There is in that a lesson for those who possess a heart. . . ."[37]

To understand what Ibn is saying, it is necessary to go back to Arabic thought in general and in particular to Arabic medical theory. Although one school was labelled that of the "physicians," and the other that of the "philosophers," Arabic medicine was never purely physiological. There was always something more. Thus Galen (130–200?), Greek anatomist and father of the "physician" school, included in his system of physiology the Platonic idea of the triple soul; while Avicenna (980–1037), a contemporary of Ibn Hazm and the foremost exponent of the philosophical school, was in general accord with Galen as to the actual organic composition of the human body. Avicenna's concept of the psychic system and its operation within the body, however, was not only different from that of Galen but vastly more complex. Arabic medicine, therefore, imparted to the West no simple dichotomy of body and soul but rather distinct philosophies as to the relationship between the physical and the psychic.[38]

For the fourteenth century, the best representative of the thought of Galen is the Bolognese anatomist, Mondino dei Luzzi, whose *Anatomia Mundini*, written about 1316, exerted, within the school of the physicians, a dominant influence for some two hundred years.[39] Mondino's work is essentially a handbook of dissection, proceeding on the highly practical assumption that the

more perishable organs are in need of the most immediate consideration. Hence, his order of examination and exposition proceeds from bottom to top. However, in this very practical method
of procedure, he is governed by an ancient tradition inherited
from early Greek medicine. According to this notion, the body is
made up of three major cavities: the abdominal, whose principal
organ is the liver; the thoracic, whose principal organ is the heart;
and the cranial, whose principal organ is the brain. However, as
noted above, Galen's physical system owes its operation to a
psychic system ultimately derived from Plato. Central to this system is the term "pneuma" (in Mondino, and in Latin generally,
translated "spiritus"). Within the body, there exists a triplicity
of "pneumata," corresponding to the previously noted triplicity of
principal organs. Thus the lowest, the liver, is the body's cook;
and the function of the "pneuma" proper to the liver is the super-
vision of nutriment. The medial "pneuma," that of the heart, sees
to the composition and movement of the blood; the highest
"pneuma" presides over the functioning of the rational processes.
On an ideal day, devoid of internal dissension, pneumatic bliss
would be accomplished in the following fashion. The jaws chew;
the stomach receives the conditioned nutriment and converts it
into chyle; the liver performs its culinary duties by changing the
chyle into blood. In its turn, the heart, through the action of its
right ventricle, draws the blood from the liver and passes it by a
process of purification to the left ventricle. In this ventricle, the
"spiritus," a kind of vaporous distillate, is produced, and the now
spiritous blood is conveyed throughout the body, nourishing the
organs in both their physical and psychic faculties.[40] For the
brain, however, there is reserved a distinct and very deliberate
further digestion or purification, which takes place in the "rete
mirabile," the delicate network of arteries, through which the
blood reaches the brain. Through this additional process of
refinement, the brain is supplied with the special nutriment
appropriate to its exalted station.[41] Thus for Galen and for his
followers, as it was for Plato, the supreme organ is the brain.

However, opposed to the view of the physicians was that of
the philosophers. Their ultimate authority was Aristotle and their
champion was Avicenna. As previously observed, Avicenna's con-

ception of anatomy is not entirely divorced from that to which Galen had given rise, but his system and his emphasis are very different. In his *Canon of Medicine*, Avicenna views the human being not as a simple composite of three interconnected "ventres," an interpretation to which Galenic anatomy was particularly vulnerable,[42] but as a single entity pervaded by a single vital principle—the heart. As against the physicians who accorded only a secondary importance to the heart, Avicenna sees the heart as transcendent. Within the body, the heart is, by divine emanation, the first moved of all that is moved. Through its indwelling "pneuma" or "spiritus"—in Avicenna probably best rendered as "breath"—the heart is endowed with a double power. It is both initiative and retentive. In its primary function as breath it visits the other organs (brain, liver, genitalia) with its life-giving powers and thereby enables them to carry out their function; in its second, or retentive, function, it becomes the repository of the essential properties of all the organs it has visited. The heart is thus the vital principle of animate being: it cannot therefore be understood simply as organ, or simply as metaphor. The heart extends to the lowest activities of physical existence; more important, it comprehends the highest faculties of psychic knowing. "The 'heart' is the instrument of spiritual apprehension, either mystical or intellectual";[43] it is the reigning king of the body. In the words of John Gower, all organs

> . . . unto the herte ben
> Servantz, and ech in his office
> Entendeth to don him service. . . .
> For as a king in his Empire
> Above alle othre is lord and Sire,
> So is the herte principal,
> To whom *reson* in special
> Is yove as for the governance.[44]

To return to the *Dove's Neck Ring*, it is to be remembered that although Ibn's ideas are difficult to comprehend without reference to the philosophical background against which he is writing, Ibn is a moralist as well as a philosopher. In the *Dove's Neck Ring*, he is primarily interested not in the heart's relation to the senses, but in its relationship to the desires the senses are capable of arousing. For him, the heart is king of the body in its moral function as Reason, the suppressor of the desires of the body.[45]

However, to consider the activities of the heart as confined within the bounds of the moral, the medical, and the philosophical would hardly be realistic in any literature. The heart seems always to have been endowed with the power to transcend the simply rational. In Arabic poetry there exists a plenitude of examples of the heart's suprarational powers, among which one image appears to be dominant—that of the lover's heart being a dwelling place for the beloved. Perhaps the most imaginative is a poem by Ibn himself:

Would that my heart were split with a knife, that you might be placed therein and, once within my bosom, the opening closed. . . . You should live there as long as I should live, and at my death, you should dwell in my heart in the night of the tomb.[46]

From the preceding it should be apparent that the Western heritage of Arabic ideas concerning the heart consisted essentially of a loose aggregate of ideas contributed by physician-philosopher, philosopher-physician, theologian-poet, and, to a somewhat lesser extent, poet. Since the ideas noted occur in combinations which make discrete analysis virtually impossible, a brief chronological treatment appears to be the only feasible method for studying the movement of the heart myth—later doctrine—from the eleventh-century world of Ibn Hazm to the fourteenth of Geoffrey Chaucer.

To begin with the troubadours, an excellent example of the idea of the heart's ability to unite itself to the beloved is to be found in the "Pro ai del Chan essenhadors" of Jaufré Rudel. In the following passage, Jaufré describes quite simply the heart's movement from lover to lady, a movement which, despite its apparent indebtedness to Arabic tradition, seems, interestingly enough, to represent something of a reversal of a favorite image of Arabic poetry. No longer is it lady who dwells with lover:

There is my heart so entirely, that elsewhere
May be found neither branch nor root;
And while, beneath covers, I sleep—
There, with her, my spirit dwells.[47]

This passage, which has been termed "the myth . . . in all its original purity,"[48] nevertheless, in its allusion to "branch nor root," indicates rather clearly its debt to the treelike nutritional system of the heart, as described by "olde Galen" and his followers.[49] The related idea of the heart's ability to communicate with the beloved, no matter what the distance, appears in its most exalted form in the famous "amour lointain," of the same poet, Jaufré Rudel. A more practical consideration of the problems of the voyaging heart appears in Bernard de Ventadorn's "Tant ai mo cor ple de joya." If tradition is to be trusted, Bernard's devotion to Eleanor of Aquitaine caused Henry II, who took a very practical interest in his wife's activities, amatory or otherwise, to pluck the unhappy Bernard back from France to damp and frosty England, thus separating him—physically at least—from his lady. Despite such brutal and simplistic measures, Bernard's heart, like that of any true lover, is with his lady:

> But the body is here . . .
> Far from her, in France.[50]

As a final indication of the pervasiveness of Arabic amatory ideology, it is of some importance to notice that the dichotomy of heart and body, so strongly emphasized at the end of the *Dove's Neck Ring*, has entered the troubadour vocabulary. In the "Apres mon vers" of Raimbaut d'Orange, for instance, it appears in the formulaic alliterative form which is destined to last through the fourteenth century, and probably beyond. In this poem, Raimbaut does not know how much time is left for him to live, and decides to give over concern for the body in favor of the heart: "mon cors al cor liure."[51]

Bernard de Ventadorn, mentioned above, was, of course, not the only poet or man of letters who sought the patronage of Eleanor of Aquitaine, and of her children.[52] Hence, if one wishes to ascertain the appeal and currency of any given literary motif during the latter part of the twelfth century, he might expect a fairly accurate indication to be forthcoming from the works of those writers traditionally associated with Eleanor and her family. Of these, three would seem especially worthy of consideration— Andreas, Chrétien, and Thomas.

As the foremost codifier and reprover of love, Andreas Capellanus holds a special position in the history of the erotic ethic. By incorporating a series of eight debates into the Ovidian structure of his great work, the *De amore*, he united troubadour "tençon" and scholastic disputation in so effective a fashion as ultimately to win for his work the distinction of formal ecclesiastical condemnation.[53] In those sections in which Andreas speaks "in propria persona"—and "persona" would here appear to be an appropriate term—the heart doctrine is central. Thus, in Andreas's initial definition of love: "Love is a certain inborn suffering proceeding from the sight of, and immoderate meditation upon, the form of the opposite sex"; the immoderate meditation is described as taking place in the heart, and is termed "lust of the heart" ("concupiscentia cordis")—in the courtly love vocabulary a quite improper term, and consequently tidied up by both his French and Italian translators.[54] Perhaps more revealing is Andreas's definition of love as a union of hearts, in itself striking because of its echoes of the *Symposium*, but the more striking when one is forced to notice that it follows immediately after Andreas's not particularly incorporeal derivation of "amor" from "amus," meaning "hook"—to which he makes it clear a line is attached.[55]

In those dialogues of the *De amore* in which Andreas does not speak "in propria persona," the heart doctrine is also frequently made use of. A few examples will suffice. In the Eighth Dialogue, the uniting of hearts serves to define the celebrated concept of "amor purus";[56] in the Fifth Dialogue, there is to be found a most interesting example of the heart's moral role, stated in terms highly reminiscent of Ibn Hazm. In this dialogue, the would-be lover has so completely won over the lady's will ("voluntas") that she professes to be more than willing to grant him her love, but a certain difficulty arises in the fact that her heart ("cor") absolutely refuses. In her pseudo-dilemma, the lady disingenuously inquires: "If my heart forbids me to love, I beg you to inform me which is to be given preference—heart or desire?"[57] Since the lover is obviously not in a position to have completed his reading of the *De amore*, he is unprovided of an answer, and departs disconsolate.

In Chrétien de Troyes, as in the trouvères generally, the heart myth—by this time more properly doctrine—is a constant. Two examples may, however, be cited as indicating the formulaic pattern which the heart doctrine progressively assumes, and the interrelationship of amatory diction and Arabic medical philosophy. In Cligès, Fenice animadverts upon the rather facile accommodation which Yseult has made between the rival claims of lover Tristan and husband Mark:

> . . . her heart ["cuer"] belonged entirely to one, and her body ["cors"] to two renters. In this manner she spent her whole life; nor did she ever refuse herself to either. Such a love was not reasonable. . . . The possessor of the heart is the possessor of the body.[58]

In Chrétien's *Perceval*, the theme of the detachable heart appears in a context which renders a knowledge of Galenic anatomy almost obligatory. Gawain is directed by a noble huntsman to a castle where the huntsman's sister is instructed to entertain him as if he were her brother. The sister is so attentive to her brother's wishes, and to those of her companion Gawain, that both seem to be proceeding from the prescribed familial relationship to a more immediate one. However, at just this moment, they are interrupted by a "vavasors" who knows more about certain past and rather unpleasant familial relationships than does either of the two incipient lovers. Accordingly, he denounces the enthusiastically compliant young lady in a most abusive fashion:

> Unhappy and foolish woman, splendidly are you accomplishing what you ought to accomplish! Rather with your hands should you pluck out his heart from his bosom ["ventre"] than with your mouth. If your kiss touches his heart, you have drawn his heart from his bosom ["ventre"].[59]

If one perceives in this a parodic comment of the "vavasors" as to the location of Gawain's heart, he is in error. The location of Gawain's heart, as that of anyone else's, is in the medial or thoracic "venter"—where Galen put it; Mondino found it; and where it is reputed still to be present.

Of the various forms of the heart doctrine, the rarest would seem to be the full-scale amatory *Psychomachia* of "cuer et cors." In the twelfth century, the outstanding example of this genre is the *Tristran* of Thomas, the more so because Thomas does not present the heart as the more or less physical space traveller, but as the presumed possessor of the power of suprarational, telepathic communication—a power, however, by no means infallible. Tristran, exiled to Brittany, senses that the heart of his beloved Queen Yseult, which has supported him in his exile, has now changed. In actuality, it is his own physical desire for a new and proximate love which convinces him that Yseult is disporting herself in loveless sexual pleasure with her husband, Marc. In Tristran's disoriented mind, it therefore follows that he must make trial of the same "ovre . . . contre amur" by marrying Yseult of Brittany. But on the night of his wedding, in his haste to experience what he presumes his love Yseult to be experiencing, he dislodges the ring given him by Yseult as a token of her love for him. In an involved but extraordinarily symmetrical debate, Love and Reason confront Lust and Nature; love-vow to a distant love confronts marital-vow to an immediate love. Not unexpectedly, the distant love triumphs:

Love and *reason* restrain him, and conquer the lust of his body. The great love he has for Ysolt takes away what *nature* wills, and conquers the loveless *lust* which had possessed his mind.[60]

By the thirteenth century, the heart doctrine has, in secular literature, reached the end of its development, but rather obviously not of its popularity. The first part of the *Roman de la rose*, by Guillaume de Lorris, seems to have been intended as a versified tractate on that particular practice of love proper to a courtly milieu. For purposes of the present study, Guillaume's section of the *Roman* is interesting in that the simple division of "cuer et cors," which had remained a constant in the Vulgate Arthurian,[61] is largely abandoned in favor of an infinitely more complex amatory *Psychomachia*, which takes place within the lady rather than within the lover, and in which the field of combat is expanded to include, in personified form, the whole of the lady's emotions, urging and opposing love. Rather less sophisticated is the remarkable thoracic operation performed by the God of Love, through which the heart of the lover is locked within his bosom by a tiny gold key, as the gage of his submission to the God of Love. Upon the completion of his operation, the God of Love rather curiously proceeds to instruct the lover as to how he, the lover, is to bestow his presumably imprisoned heart (2240), and how, having bestowed it, what torments he will suffer. The most interesting of these is a highly imaginative variation on the venerable detachable-heart theme. When the lover is distant from his lady, he suddenly realizes he cannot see her for the adequately sufficient reason that his eyes are not with her. Struck with horror he cries, "Why did I send my heart alone?" (2303). Since eyeballs seem incapable of the volatility of hearts, he decides to take them himself.[62]

It is obvious that in the mechanical operation of the spirit, there is always something of the grotesque. The vulnerability of the detachable-heart conception is apparent to Guillaume de Lorris, but his is a playful and delicate spirit. The true parody is forthcoming from the anonymous creator of Sir Dinadan, comic hero of the prose *Tristan*. Sir Dinadan, having heard out the lonely lamentations of Sir Palomides, unsuccessful competitor of Tristan for the love of Queen Yseult, delivers a magisterial pronouncement on the importance of maintaining firm control of one's heart:

To tell the truth, I have never been without my heart; on the contrary, I never fail to feel it beating and moving within my breast. . . . But I know very well, of my own knowledge and from what I have heard from many people, that Madame Yseult carries with her the heart of Tristram, the nephew of King Mark of Cornwall, and yours also, as you yourself tell me. Therefore, since the truth of the matter is that she has so many hearts in her bosom— which, by the way, is by no means too capacious—and if by some chance I should desire to place mine there, do you believe that those who have already taken up lodgings in her bosom would suffer me to remain with them? Absolutely not! For they are too rough, and too villainous, and too cruel, and too quick to combat. Rather mine would be chased out to my great shame and dishonor. And for this reason, I shall keep my heart ever with me. I have no desire that lady or maiden gain title to it.[63]

However, if the idea of the detachable heart lent itself admirably to parody, another form of the heart doctrine—amorous oblivion—was perhaps somewhat less vulnerable, even though carried to ridiculous extremes. It will be recalled that in both Chrétien's *Perceval* and *Lancelot,* a reminder of the lady causes unconsciousness to descend upon her lover. In the case of Lancelot, the cause is the finding of a comb, containing tresses "si biax, si clers et si luisanz," that Lancelot demands of his attendant damsel whose they are. The damsel replies in rather earthy terms that they are "from the head of the queen; they never grew in any other field." When Lancelot is informed as to what queen, he appears to faint. And indeed he has, for he is kept from falling off his horse only by the energetic efforts of the attendant damsel.[64] Perceval's experience is somewhat different, since it involves a further element. Three drops of blood upon new-fallen snow remind Perceval of the coloring of the face of his beloved, and as he muses upon them, they become the face of his beloved. Propped up by his lance, he spends the morning in a trance, until observed by Sir Sagremor, who obtains Arthur's permission to bring him in out of the cold. However, it would appear that through passage of time, Perceval is emerging from his trance at the moment Sagremor demands that he come to the king, for Perceval only "gives the appearance of not hearing." When Sagremor, angered at his silence, draws back and rather elaborately charges upon him, Perceval is more than ready for Sir Sagremor and for Sir Kay, who not unexpectedly follows.[65]

Chrétien, the master of narrative suspense and mystery, has little interest in explicating the psychological mechanism of chivalric oblivion. However, the author of the thirteenth-century Provençal *Flamenca* takes considerable pleasure in discursive commentary upon the events he is engaged in narrating. The hero of his story, Guillaume de Nevers, has, at the instigation of Love, come to assuage the sorrows of Flamenca, effectively incarcerated in a tower by her superlatively jealous husband. In a brief respite from what turns out to be a rather laborious seduction, Guillaume listens to the song of the nightingale, and through the magic of the nightingale's song, loses awareness of all about him. The author comments:

The truth is that love blinds a man, deprives him of hearing and speech, and makes him, to all appearances, a fool; while on his part, the lover believes himself most fully possessed of sense. Guillaume hears nothing, sees nothing, apprehends nothing. His eyes, his hands, his mouth are motionless . . . he is blind, deaf, and dumb.[66]

Thus the joy which animates his heart, the poet continues, causes a certain unavailability of the senses, because:

To share this joy, each sense must return to the heart; for the heart is lord and father. If then, good or evil befall the heart, each of the senses comes to him to know his will; and when they are thus met within, the possessor of the heart is left like one in a trance. And since pleasure and pain make the senses thus return to the heart, I am not surprised in the least that the joy of love, since it is of the heart and compounded of pleasure and pain, makes the senses run like spurred horses back to their lord.[67]

When the song of the nightingale ends, Guillaume comes to himself.

From the parodic remarks of Sir Dinadan, and from the central position which the heart doctrine occupies in *Flamenca*, it is clear that toward the middle of the thirteenth century the doctrine was enjoying a well-established popularity. Hence, in accordance with the Christian conviction that whatever possessed popularity was in urgent need of Christianization, the heart doctrine was found readily adaptable to the story of Mary Magdalene and her love for her Lord, Jesus. At some time, possibly in the early thirteenth century, there appeared a highly rhetorical and highly dramatic *Homily on Mary Magdalene*,[68] attributed to Origen, but certainly not his. The time of the drama is the Resurrection; the place is the tomb of Christ; the action is entirely conducted by the Rhetorician-Preacher, who as rhetorician shows an unexcelled mastery of the rhetorical question. He begins by addressing his audience, but then proceeds to lash Mary and Christ—both of whom appear to have taken refuge in the audience —with punishing questions. Thus, concerning Mary, he demands of the audience:

Why has she not accepted Christ's promise of His Resurrection? Why has she not accepted the consolation of the angels, which would have been immediately forthcoming, had she simply answered the question: "Whom do you seek?"[69]

The answer to this harsh question has fortunately not escaped the Preacher. Despite the Preacher's own earnest advice that she accept the consolation forthcoming from the angels, the Preacher understands that his own limited advice is not the solution. Mary does not seek discourse with the angels; she seeks Him who created the angels. Living or dead, she will not be separated from Christ, and through the perseverance of her love, she will find Him. Christ Himself is the only consolation she is willing to accept.

This is, in fact, the particular answer to Mary's obdurate unknowing that the Preacher wishes to bring out, and his concluding address to the audience is set in these terms. However, it is evident throughout that Mary's state of unknowing is not simply willed; it has other sources. Her failure to recognize Christ as the "hortulanus" is in no way willed, but is rather the result of the state to which love and ensuing sorrow have reduced her. Through sorrow,

She had been rendered lifeless: sentient, she sensed nothing: seeing, she saw not: hearing, she heard not. Nor was she, indeed, where she was, because her whole being was where her Master was, though where He was, she knew not.[70]

This difficult to understand state is explained to the audience in terms highly reminiscent of the romantic heart doctrine:

Believe me, if she had recognized Christ, she would not be seeking him in the tomb; and if she had retained His words in her heart, she would not be mourning over the dead, but rejoicing over the living. . . . But, alas! her heart had been filled with an excess of sorrow, and erased the memory of those words; no understanding remained in her, all wisdom had perished.[71]

To Christ, the Preacher explains the situation of Mary in the orthodox terminology of "spirit" and "soul," but with such force and directness that it would seem to suggest a fear on the part of the Preacher that, in the course of his sermon, somnolence might have drifted across the Divine Mind:

When Joseph placed your body in the tomb, Mary likewise there buried her spirit, and thus indissolubly joined, and, in a certain way, united it to your body, so that it would have been easier to separate her living soul from her live body, than her spirit, loving you, from your dead body. . . . Where she lost your body, with it she lost her spirit. What wonder if she who had lost her spirit possessed no sense? What wonder if she did not recognize you, she who had no spirit capable of understanding. . . . And thus her error proceeded not from error but from love and sorrow. . . . Oh, how full of wisdom was her ignorance, and how learned her error![72]

At the height of his eloquence, the Preacher demands of Christ: "Return, therefore, her spirit, and soon she will recover her senses . . ." The Abchurch version reads, "soon she will recover her heart."[73]

From Alceste's spirited defense of one Geoffrey Chaucer in the Prologue to the *Legend of Good Women*, we learn that the said Geoffrey had in fact written—a long time ago—a poetical version, now lost, of the *Homily* attributed to Origen:

> He made also, goon ys a gret while,
> Orygenes upon the Maudeleyne. (F 427–428)[74]

III

The length of the two preceding sections, which must have taxed if not overcome the reader's tolerance, may, it is hoped, prove excusable. If one understands something of Chaucer's emotional state at the time of the composition of the *Book of the Duchess* and is also aware of Chaucer's familiarity with a psychology in which the state of the heart determines the state of the lover, certain barriers to comprehension may possibly be removed. As Mason in his *Musaeus* compassionately observed concerning Chaucer's verse:

> Whanne shallow brooke yrenneth hobling on,
> Ovir rough stones it makith full rough song;
> But, them stones removen, this lite rivere
> Stealith forth by, making plesaunt murmere.[75]

There can be little question that it is the sympathetic but predominantly opaque state of the Dreamer which initiates the dialogue beween Dreamer and Knight, which in turn becomes the central action of the poem. It thus becomes evident that the Dreamer's stupidity is not simply stupidity, nor simply amatory stupidity; in terms of the art of the poem, it might better be considered structural stupidity. If for a moment the reader sets aside the problem of defining the Dreamer's experience, and looks rather to how that experience is organized, he finds himself in the presence of an artifact the intricacy of which the sheer energy of the poem has hardly permitted him–to glimpse.

Like Keats's "Eve of St. Agnes," the *Book of the Duchess* is organized within a framework. One encounters first the Narrator's state and his consequent reading of the story of Ceyx and Alcione (1–290), and finally the dream itself (291–1323). At the end of the poem, the path is retraced—from dream, to book, to the real world as the artist knows it—a world in which literary composition is not a dream but a necessity of existence (1324–1334). This outer structure is, in its way, as formal a one as Chaucer ever attempted. However, the dream contained within the frame is not only formally organized but infinitely more complex. Its first element is the hunt, which, although located within the dream, constitutes a kind of intermediate structure between the outer frame and the inner structure of the encounter of the Black Knight and the Dreamer. Though faintly traced, it begins with the Dreamer's being aroused by the sound of the huntsman's horn and his joining the hunt (291–386); remains only as background after the blowing of the "forloyn" (386)—the signal that the "hert" has stolen away from the hunters; and resumes at the end of the dream with the huntsman's "strake forth," which announces the finality of the "forloyn" and the abandonment of the "hert-huntyng" (1311–1323).[76] Contained within the outer and intermediate structures is the Dreamer's encounter with the Black Knight (387–1313). In its complexity, this inner structure renders distinct the considerably simpler outer and intermediate structures, and hence, in a sense, solidifies them in their function as frame. The inner structure proper consists of a transition from hunt to Black Knight (387–442), and a series of four blunders—or alternatively, absolute failures of comprehension on the part of the Dreamer—(740–741); (1042–1044); (1126–1135); (1298). Of these, all but the second (1042) are followed by the Black

Knight's mournful refrain. At the close of the last of these blunders—"Where is she now?" (1298)—the hunt and dream end, and the return to the awakening Narrator takes place.

To the present writer, the divisions indicated above constitute the main divisions of the poem. What follows is an attempt to analyze the poem as a whole within these divisions, and in terms of the materials, biographical and psychological, adduced in the first two sections of the present essay.

The outer structure of the *Book of the Duchess* (1–290) is essentially an introduction to the state of the Narrator: his sleeplessness, his dazed consciousness, his "sorwful ymaginacioun." All these, it is generally agreed, add up to a conventional, but not necessarily unreal, lovesickness which the Dreamer has suffered "this eight yeer."[77] As a relief from his sleeplessness, he bids an undefined somebody—an "oon"—to hand him a book, a "romaunce." It is here that the reader gets his first insight into the social position of the Narrator. He is certainly not Geoffrey Chaucer, who as "damoiseau" of the King's chamber must have had rather similar duties to perform, but a man of substance with servants attentive to his every wish. A further revelation of his incredibly opulent state is afforded by the Dreamer's reaction to the reading of the "romaunce" of Ceyx and Alcione. As a reward for much needed sleep, the Narrator is prepared to offer Morpheus the finest of beds; send around certain unidentified artisans, obviously available at his immediate command, to paint with gold the walls of Morpheus's cave; and in addition to provide munificently for any contingent claims on the part of Morpheus's "goddesse, dame Juno" (243). This visionary opulence, together with the proven necessity of blowing a horn in Morpheus's ear to inform him that the painters are coming (182), completes the tone of the poem which has been earlier set by the interaction of the speeches of Ceyx and Alcione in what must be considered one of the key passages in the poem. Animated by Mercury, the body of Ceyx stands before the bed of his bereaved wife and says:

> ". . . farewel, swete, my worldes blysse!
> I praye God youre sorwe lysse.
> To lytel while oure blysse lasteth!" (209–211)

Alcione's reaction to the fact of her bereavement, conveyed as it is in a speech which is a kind of distillate of all complaints against worldly mutability, is somewhat astonishing:

> . . . "Allas!" quod she for sorwe,
> And deyde within the thridde morwe. (213–214)

Lingering but eloquent melancholy is undercut by human reaction so abrupt as to verge on the comic. This interaction, taken together with the Mercury-Morpheus incident which immediately precedes, yields, in the present writer's opinion, the tone which is to prevail throughout the poem. It is a mixed tone, difficult to define, but the elements of which may perhaps be distinguishable. It is a complex tonality composed of oppositions—the consistent statement of the romantic love-death theme and its equally consistent undercutting—around which plays a kind of comic spirit dominated by an irresistible and irresponsible comic compulsion. In a philosophical sense, this tonality is representative of a view of life in which the tragic is inseparable from the comic,[78] but this philosophical and objective view finds itself coexistent with powerful subjective feeling—feeling which finds expression in a kind of parodic humor which delights in language itself and has as its objects everything and nothing, and an apparently guileless but edged humor which has as its object John of Gaunt. Both are irrepressible. One would be tempted to apply to Chaucer's elegy Socrates' dictum that "he who is through art a tragic poet is a comic poet also," were it not that the implied rational separation of genres is something not to be looked for in the *Book of the Duchess*. From the time we enter the Dreamer's world, we are made aware that it is a world in which Reason must exercise great care before seating herself upon her throne.

With Morpheus's apparently instant acceptance of the Narrator's offer the central action of the poem is reached, and the frame left behind. Narrator becomes Dreamer, and the reader the inhabitant of a world of dreams (291). In this world it is apparent that one material matter has not changed—the overwhelming wealth and unmistakably exalted position of the Narrator, now become Dreamer. When he is awakened by the "solempne servise" of the birds without, the Dreamer is awakened to a bedchamber no less magnificent than that promised Morpheus. Although the walls are described as simply "ful wel depeinted" (322)—obviously a supremely modest understatement —the true glory of the room is its windows. In them are magnificently depicted the wealthy Dreamer's favored literary subjects: the stories of Troy and the *Roman de la rose*. However, the most striking attribute of the room is not the windows themselves but their superb condition; not a single pane of this magnificent vitreous creation is even cracked ("ycrased")—a rather rare condition for windows, especially in the Middle Ages.[79]

The Dreamer, in accordance with his social position obviously an ardent sportsman, unhesitatingly mounts his horse and rides out of his ornate bedchamber to join the hunt. He is of course gratified to find that the hunt is being conducted under the auspices of the Emperor Octavian, an obviously suitable hunting companion.

At the beginning of the transitional section (387–442), the "hert" has "rused" and stolen away. The "forloyn" has been blown, and the Dreamer has little confidence that the track of the hart will be recovered. As he leaves his hunting station, he is greeted by a marvellously affectionate "whelp" which has strayed from the hunt, and acts "ryght as hyt hadde me yknowe" (392). As the Dreamer seeks to gather up the lovable little creature, it eludes his grasp and "was fro me goon" (396). As he follows down a green and flowery path, the Dreamer finds himself in a glade of a kind of magic forest, in which all manner of beasts, including the hart and his mate, live strangely undisturbed. Within the forest, the huge trees stand apart "wel ten foot or twelve," and rise up "clene withoute bowgh or strikke" to a fantastic height—"fourty or fifty fadme lengthe"—and then interlace their boughs to create a shadowy light beneath (416–426). In this somber yet highly natural setting, the Dreamer first perceives the Black Knight and hears his lament:

> ". . . my lady bryght . . .
> Is fro me ded and is agoon" (477–479)

the phrasing of which seems to echo that of the Dreamer in attempting to capture the lovable whelp—which also was "fro me goon." In the dialogue which follows, the verbal parallel is reinforced—both have experienced loss, and both are suffering from lovesickness. Aside from this unity of suffering, however, the two are carefully differentiated. The Knight has lost his Lady through death, but the form his malady takes is that of the sporadic amatory oblivion experienced by the chivalric lover separated from his lady. It is in relation to the state of the Black Knight that the comments of the unknown author of the *Flamenca* (alluded to on pp. 79–80) become most valuable, for they provide a virtually complete commentary on the Black Knight's state:

> His sorwful hert gan faste faynte,
> And his spirites wexen dede;
> The blood was fled for pure drede
> Doun to hys herte, to make hym warm—
> For wel hyt feled the herte had harm—
> To wite eke why hyt was adrad
> By kynde, and for to make hyt glad;
> For it is membre principal
> Of the body. . . . (488–496)

A further characteristic of the Black Knight's lovesickness is his conviction that the only remedy for his condition is death. The Dreamer's affliction is, however, quite different. He suffers from amatory "melancolye," with its sleeplessness, "sorwful ymaginacioun," and paradoxical "drede I have for to dye" (24). The Knight's malady, therefore, is characterized by the amatory trance, from which it is possible to emerge with rational powers virtually unaffected; the Dreamer's is a kind of deepening twilight in which the physical heart and its sympathies remain with him, but the heart's higher faculties of reason and perception are with his lady.[80] A further distinction between the two sufferers is perhaps discoverable. From Chaucer's exhaustive use of Machaut's *Jugement dou Roy de Behaingne*, it is more than probable that the dialogue between the Black Knight and the Dreamer is constructed upon the love debate in the *Jugement*: the Black Knight corresponding to the lover who has won his lady and lost through death; the Dreamer to the lover who has won his lady and lost through rejection. The final distinction between the two is the evident one of social station. As he recovers from his oblivion, the Black Knight shows himself by his Galvanic "courtesie" to be unmistakably of high degree. By contrast, the multi-estated Dreamer seems to have shrunk in stature, and stands before the Black Knight, hood ın hand, like the ingénu Perceval of the Middle English romance, the "fole of the filde," who emerges from pure woodland nature, and finding himself in the presence of a knight, dutifully removes his hood as his mother has told him to.[81] However, no matter how great the differences, it becomes evident that the common suffering of the two has united them in a kind of natural sympathy. Through love, the Dreamer has become a "foole naturel,"[82] and as such he instinctively seeks to assuage the Black Knight's suffering, an undertaking in which Pan, god of Nature, is already engaged (512).[83] From natural instinct, the Dreamer is capable of diagnosing with extraordinary accuracy the Black Knight's illness, but as to what has occasioned that illness he is curiously blind and deaf—although exceedingly un-dumb. It is thus the Dreamer's simultaneous will to comfort and absolute failure to comprehend what he is trying to be comforting about which constitutes the essential action of the poem.

The dialogue between the Black Knight and the Dreamer (443–1310) is composed, as earlier indicated, of four blunders. The Black Knight, although initially resistant to the idea that any cure for his sorrow is possible—"For y am sorwe, and sorwe ys y" (597) —seems, on his own part, intuitively to sense the kindly earnest of the Dreamer, just as the Dreamer has sensed the suffering of the Black Knight. Thus, although his responses make it more than clear that his emotions are controlled by an iron code of manners, the Black Knight seems to feel no real offense at the direct and quite personal request of the now lowly Dreamer:

> ". . . telleth me of your sorwes smerte;
> Paraunter hyt may ese youre herte,
> That semeth ful sek under your syde." (555–557)

After a brief outcry against the state to which his sufferings have reduced him, the Black Knight replies: "Allas! and I wol tel the why" (598) and proceeds to recount the loss of his lady under the transparent fiction of a chess game in which Fortune took his queen. Against such a loss there can be no remedy except death (690). The Dreamer is, to be sure, affected by the pity of the tale, but the pity he feels is overwhelmed by sheer horror at the implications of what he has just heard:

> "A, goode sir," quod I, "say not soo!
> Have som pitee on your nature . . ." (714–715)

He therefore resolutely places himself between the Black Knight and death by recounting with aquilian erudition a catalogue of famous suicides for love, all of which were really quite ridiculous —"Dido . . . which a fool she was!"—but anything so preposterous as death over the loss of a chess queen no book has ever recorded. There follows the mournful answer of the Black Knight:

> "Thou wost ful lytel what thow menest;
> I have lost more than thow wenest." (743–744)

It is precisely what has escaped his understanding that now further arouses the Dreamer's interest. His previously simple natural urge to alleviate pain has become mingled with an eagerness as yet undefined, but clearly present:

> "Loo, [sey] how that may be?" . . .
> Good sir, telle me al hooly
> In what wyse, how, why, and wherfore
> That ye have thus youre blysse lore." (745–748)

The Black Knight, however, is now somewhat less than eager to comply. He has encountered a creature of such opacity that it is questionable that he can ever make his loss understood. As a gentleman, he replies "blithely," but as one who has learned from experience, he considers it judicious to extract from the Dreamer an oath that he will expend his last ounce of energy in the pursuit of comprehension. The Dreamer's oath is a model of precise definition:

> "I shal right blythely, so God me save,
> Hooly with al the wit I have
> Here yow, as wel as I kan." (755–757)

The Black Knight replies, "A Goddes half!" and addresses himself to answering the astonishingly journalistic "Who, what, where, when, and why" of the Dreamer. What follows is an idyllic story of his dedication to the God of Love (759–774); the bestowing of his love on Nature's masterpiece, "goode faire White" (817–948); a catalogue of her physical charms—interrupted, as earlier noted, by what appear to be some curious embarrassments on the part of the Black Knight[84]—together with a complementary catalogue of her social and moral virtues; the whole concluded by:

> ". . . certes she was, that swete wif,
> My suffisaunce, my lust, my lyf,
> Myn hap, myn hele, and al my blesse,
> My worldes welfare, and my goddesse,
> And I hooly hires and everydel." (1037–1041)

The Dreamer is curiously unmoved. He knows something of what love can do to the eyesight, and the Black Knight has not only presented Blanche in visual terms, but, what is even more revealing, has actually used the phrase "to myn yë" (981). Furthermore, the lover who proclaims his lady to be absolute perfection must expect coldness if not outright incredulity on the part of one who himself loves. Hence the restraint of the Dreamer's reply:

> "I leve yow wel, that trewely
> Yow thoghte that she was the beste,
> And to beholde the alderfayreste,
> Whoso had loked hir with your eyen." (1048–1051)

Understandably, the Black Knight is driven into a paroxysm of hyperbole. *All* who saw her knew her worth; and even if he, her lover, had combined in himself all the virtues of all the greatest men of history, he would not have been worthy of her love. His emotion for the moment exhausted, the Black Knight reverts to his first sight of his lady, and to the constant delight of seeing her:

> "And yet she syt so in myn herte,
> That, by my trouthe, y nolde noght,
> For all thys world, out of my thoght
> Leve my lady; noo, trewely!" (1108–1111)[85]

Well, says the Dreamer, if that's the situation:

> "Me thynketh ye have such a chaunce
> As shryfte wythoute repentaunce." (1113–1114)

The misunderstanding of "repentaunce" brings another outburst from the Black Knight, concluding:

"I nyl foryete hir never moo." (1125)

The Dreamer's reason has proved utterly inadequate to penetrate the fiction of the chess game, but more than adequate to perceive what folly it is to be taken in by the ravings of a fanatic. The Dreamer's third blunder is, however, probably the most important. It is different in kind, since it is purely misunderstanding and does not tread upon the Black Knight's feelings. More important, it tends to define the Dreamer's stupidity and hence prepares for the fourth and climactic blunder, with which the poem concludes. The Dreamer, after his failure to understand the chess metaphor, had asked:

"In what wise, how, why, and wherfore
That ye have thus youre blysse lore." (747–748)

In reply to his question, the Dreamer had been favored with a fascinating and palatably sorrowful love story, the continuity of which has regrettably been interrupted. The Dreamer has heard enough of how the Black Knight first saw his lady and under what circumstances. Now he wants to hear the next episode in the story.

"But wolde ye tel me the manere
To hire which was your firste speche . . .
And how she knewe first your thoght,
Whether ye loved hir or noght. . . ." (1130–1134)

And then as an afterthought:

"And telleth me eke what ye have lore,
I herde yow telle herebefore." (1135–1136)

What has happened is that the Dreamer's multiple question as to how the Black Knight had his "blysse lore" has been answered by an enchanting description of how the Black Knight first saw his lady. The Dreamer is impatient to hear what happened next. For the Black Knight the loss of his "blysse" is, as it has been throughout, the loss of his lady. For the Dreamer, however, this is entirely untrue. Foremost in his mind is the love story he has been listening to, the continuation of which he is eager to hear. However, in the background of his bemused consciousness, there remains a faint recollection of his original question, as to what the Knight has lost, but the question itself has been almost completely overlaid by the Dreamer's urgent desire to hear the story out. For a second time, the Knight's mournful refrain is heard:

> "Yee!" seyde he, "thow nost what thow menest;
> I have lost more than thou wenest." (1137–1138)

Yet meeting the mounting intensity of the Dreamer's questions, "For Goddes Love, telle me al" (1143), there is a mounting willingness on the Black Knight's part to tell all: " 'Before God,' quod he, 'and I shal' " (1144)—and this despite the Dreamer's now fully demonstrated inability to understand what has been told him. Within the Black Knight something is happening.

Aside from increased emotion, however, within the Dreamer nothing is happening. As to what the Black Knight's loss is, he is as opaque as ever:

> "What los ys that?" quod I thoo . . . (1139)

but in the following lines the reason for his inability to understand first becomes defined:

> "Nyl she not love yow? ys it soo?
> Or have ye oght doon amys,
> That she hath left yow? ys hit this?" (1140–1142)

In the course of the eight-year illness occasioned by his rejected love, the Dreamer has become progressively incapable of conceiving of lovesickness as anything other than the product of thwarted love. It is in this sense, not in the grotesquely physical sense parodied by Sir Dinadan, that the Dreamer's heart is with his lady. He can literally think in no other way. Thus he can "ful wel . . . reherse" the lay the Black Knight speaks, but its meaning cannot penetrate his consciousness. Through love, his state has become very like that of Mary Magdalene.

> Byholde here the wonderful worchynge of loue. A litel bifore sche [Mary Magdalene] herde of an aungel that he was risen/ and after of tweyne that he leuede; and ʒit sche hadde it nouʒt in mynde/ but saide: I woot nouʒt. And all that made loue. For as origene seith/

here *herte* and here mynde was not there sche was in body/ but it was there as here loue was. . . .[86]

Mary cannot understand that Christ is risen; the Dreamer cannot understand that the Lady is dead. It is no small part of Chaucer's art that he has given the Dreamer very little occasion to. The reader knows the Lady is dead; in a distant fashion, the Dreamer may know it too, and it may be one of the functions of the refrain to suggest this distant truth trying to break through to the Dreamer. But if one will go back over the interchange between Knight and Dreamer, it becomes apparent that the Black Knight has spoken of events in the past tense, but never of the Lady as anything but present, as, for instance, "she syt so in myn herte" (1108). The Black Knight's inability to express his loss as death adapts perfectly to the Dreamer's inability to conceive of loss as anything other than the loss of a living love. Hence the Dreamer's eagerness to participate with the Black Knight in his love experiences. It is not impossible that in the Dreamer there exists a proto-Pandarus.[87]

The Black Knight is as good as his promise, and he does tell all in a tone of mounting lyricism. In a narrative replete with heart imagery, he recounts the events of his courtship of Blanche, and their life together. Notable among the heart references in his narrative are lines which seem to descend from Chrétien's *Cligès*, through the *Roman de la rose*, to the *Book of the Duchess* —the image of the detachable heart:

> "She was the lady
> Of the body; she had the herte,
> And who hath that, may not asterte." (1152–1154)[88]

and in the concluding rhapsody of the Black Knight, a related image closely approaching Andreas Capellanus, Ibn Hazm, and, with a change in terminology, the *Symposium*:

> "Oure hertes wern so evene a payre,
> That never nas that oon contrayre
> To that other, for no woo.
> For sothe, ylyche they were both glad and wrothe;
> Al was us oon, withoute were,
> And thus we lyved ful many a yere
> So wel, I kan nat telle how." (1289–1297)

The Dreamer is doubtless moved by the beauty of the description, but he is also disappointed at not hearing the end of the story: "Where is she now?" (1298). At this catastrophic failure to understand, the Black Knight "wax as ded as stoon" (1300), and heroically seeks to explain, exhorting the Dreamer to remember how he has said before:

> "Thow wost ful lytel what thow menest;
> I have lost more than thow wenest." (1305–1306)

But the astonished Dreamer, as fixed in his conception as to what constitutes loss as he was at the beginning of the dialogue, replies in almost exactly the same words:

> "Allas, sir, how? what may that be?" (1308)

Out of his own agony, and the uncomprehending intensity he senses in the Dreamer, the Black Knight finally externalizes the truth he has only been able to express under a veil: "She ys ded!"

Within a forest glade which suggests a Gothic cathedral,[89] there appears to the sorrowing lover not a creature of supernatural reason, Boethius's Dame Philosophy, but a virtual parody of supernatural reason—a comforter who cannot understand what he is trying to be comforting about—a "foole naturel." Yet within the natural cathedral, the thrice iterated conviction on the part of the Knight that his is a sorrow unique and hence irremediable —"I have lost more than thou wenest"—yields to the Dreamer's bumbling efforts, and the ultimate and inescapable truth about the Lady is expressed—"She ys ded"—a truth the Dreamer cannot understand because his heart is with his lady, and a truth the Black Knight cannot express because the vision of his lady dwells ever in his heart, and his heart cannot abandon its search for her. Once the expression has been made:

> . . . al was doon,
> For that tyme, the hert-huntyng. (1312–1313)

All this should leave the reader with an ungovernable urge to rush out and observe a natural phenomenon; but somehow it does not. If the *Book of the Duchess* is less about the death of the Duchess herself than about the consolation of the Black Knight, it is also less about the Black Knight than about the Dreamer. It is the Dreamer whom we encounter at the beginning of the poem; it is through the Dreamer's eyes that we read the story of Ceyx and Alcione; it is again the Dreamer whose severely limited comprehension governs the dialogue with the Black Knight. At the "strake forth," hunt and Black Knight disappear, and we return to the Narrator and the book he has read, and the book he will now "fonde to put . . . in ryme" (1332). If there is a truth to be found in the central action which culminates in the consolation of the Black Knight, may there not also be elements of truth of a different sort, but a sort highly relevant to their creator, in what the Narrator narrates and the Dreamer dreams, elements which are sometimes part of the central action and sometimes quite distinct from it? The Black Knight is a single figure—stylized, distanced, who comes to life only to pass from view.[90] The Narrator-Dreamer, as noted above, is the reader's constant companion throughout the poem. He is, in fact, more a presence than a figure, and, as mask for the poet,[91] his presence is the poet's presence—all that in the year 1369, Geoffrey Chaucer, was, suffered, and hoped to be. There is Chaucer the artist, whose artistic conscience forbids him the use of clichéd pietism, but not the introduction of comedy into an elegy. There is Chaucer the incipient philosopher, who perceives the necessity of a balance of the tragic and the comic in any meaningful vision of life, but who quite irresponsibly yields to the curious necessity of presenting his self-creation, the Narrator-Dreamer, in a visionary array of guises which do not seem entirely necessary to a measured vision of existence—as the litterateur whose book for the evening contains only such trivia as the lives of kings and queens (56–57); as the very model of a model monotheist, who has never heard of pagan gods (237); as the man of burgeoning wealth whose "largesse" is unlimited, even to pagan gods he has never heard of; as the patron of art who possesses stained-glass windows portraying his literary interests— all without a crack and all on twenty marks. One can only think of the visionary ascent of the somewhat impecunious Leopold

Bloom to the highest positions of State and Church: "Gaudium magnum annuntio vobis: habemus carnificem."[92]

But underneath it all is Chaucer the human being, the suffering lover of his wife,[93] who, in her turn, sees him as a bad risk. Chaucer, the everyday civil servant, who knows perfectly well how advancement is to be gained, but cannot bring himself to pay the price. Chaucer, who knows the hearts of men, and who knows that a man may have many mistresses and yet only one lady, who understands that the loss of the Duchess Blanche is to John of Gaunt an infinitely real loss. Chaucer, who knows that his wife may be willing to assuage the grief of the Duke of Lancaster.

Perhaps the quite accurate comments of the early editors concerning the immediate relationship of the *Book of the Duchess* to the death of Blanche might be complemented in a fashion in conformance with the wording of Sir Robert Cotton's librarian concerning the single other great elegy of Chaucer's age, the *Pearl*: "Vetus poema Anglicanum de morte Blanchiae Ducissae Lancastriae, in quo sub insomnii figmento, multa ad vitam et artem Galfridi Chaucer pertinencia explicantur."[94]

NOTES

1. *Works*, p. 266.
2. See the excellent study by John Conley, "*Pearl* and a Lost Tradition," *JEGP*, LIV (July, 1955), 332–347.
3. G. L. Kittredge, *Chaucer and His Poetry* (Cambridge, Mass., 1915), pp. 37–72, was the first to bring out this aspect of the poem. Wolfgang Clemen, in *Der junge Chaucer* (1938), recently translated by C. A. M. Sym as *Chaucer's Early Poetry* (New York, 1964), initiated the idea of the conscious use of stupidity as a means to psychic purgation. The idea was further developed by James Kreuzer in his essay "The Dreamer in the *Book of the Duchess*," *PMLA*, LXVI (1951), 543–547. The most complete and finished statement of the position is to be found in Bertrand Bronson, "The Book of the Duchess Re-opened," *PMLA*, LXVII (1952), 863–881. For a tentative opinion to the contrary, see E. T. Donaldson, ed., *Chaucer's Poetry* (New York, 1958), pp. 952–953.
4. The ailment contracted by Edward, the Black Prince, in the Spanish campaign of 1367 steadily reduced him to the point of virtual political insignificance. This, plus the growing senility of Edward III (both King and Prince died in virtually the same year, 1376–1377), left a

political vacuum which Lancaster's vast wealth and personal army made it possible for him to exploit. For a full-scale study of John himself and his administrative system, see Sydney Armitage-Smith, *John of Gaunt* (London, 1904).

5. E. Faral, *Les Arts poétiques du XII et du XIII siècle* (Paris, 1924), pp. 214 ff., and the *Poetria nova of Geoffrey of Vinsauf*, trans. Margaret F. Nims (Toronto, 1967), pp. 36 ff.

6. Lines 871–873. The description of the lady's eyes "opene by mesure,/ and close" provides perhaps the most striking example of Chaucer's verbal dependence on Machaut. The description is an exact translation of Machaut's "s'estoient clungnetant par mesure" (*Jugement dou Roy de Behaingne*, line 321, in *Oeuvres*, ed. E. Hoepfner [Paris, 1908], 1, 69). For a table of parallels to Machaut, see Robinson's note to line 816. For detailed comparisons, see articles cited in Robinson's explanatory note to the *Book of the Duchess* (Works, p. 773, col. 2). However, the larger pattern of the enamorment and subsequent progress of love depend upon Lorris's first section of the *Roman de la rose*. Machaut's ideology is limited.

7. The most acerbic chronicler of the Duke's erotic behavior is the Monk of St. Albans, whose diatribe against Gaunt indicates that the Duke's incontinence was known to have existed during the period of his marriage to the Duchess Blanche as well as that of his later marriage to Constance of Castile. The passage follows (italics mine): ". . . relicto licito matrimoniali thoro, *tam primam uxorem suam, domini et nobilissimi Henrici primi ducis Lancastriae, quam domini Petri regis Hispanorum filiam, moechus infamis decepit et adulter.* Et non solum in abdito talia et occulto praesumpsit, sed in earum lecto meretrices iniquissimas, ipsis dolentibus sed non audentibus contradicere, collocavit" (*Chronicon Angliae* [1328–1388], ed. Edward Maunde Thompson [London, 1874], p. 75). Armitage-Smith is quite aware of the Monk of St. Albans, and he further publishes Percy MS 78, which also states his infidelity "in diebus Domine Blanchie prime uxoris sue" (*John of Gaunt*, pp. 464–465). To compound the difficulty, there is the matter of John's liaison with Marie de St. Hilaire, and the birth of a daughter Blanche, which Armitage-Smith calls "a very early *liaison* (?1358 or 9)," as against John's marriage to Blanche, which occurred on May 19, 1359 (*ibid.*, pp. 461, 14). This, however, seems to present no real difficulty to Armitage-Smith, since he is able to state flatly, "There is no evidence that any *amour* disturbed the married life of John of Gaunt and Blanche of Lancaster." Perhaps it is the "disturbed" that is in need of italics (*ibid.*, p. 461). In any case, Armitage-Smith is far from denying the existence of the Duke's reputation, including that of his having died of venereal disease (*ibid.*, pp. 463–464), which perhaps explains the rather curious statement of the Monk of St. Albans (quoted above) concerning the attitude of professional lovemakers toward the wealthy Duke. Marjorie Anderson ("Blanche, Duchess of Lancaster," *MP*, XLV [1948], 159) is aware of the problem, but explicitly follows Armitage-Smith's opinion. See also note 14 below.

8. See, for instance, *Merchant's Tale*, where the "pitee" of May is subject

to a series of ironical allusions (IV [E], 1979, 1986, 1995), of which the medial (1986) is itself an ironical allusion to the *Knight's Tale* (I [A], 1761). In regard to the earlier passage (892–894), one might compare the *Shipman's Tale* (VII [B²], 1621) and Mercutio's "Queen Mab" speech (Shakespeare, *Romeo and Juliet*, I, iv, 93–94).

9. To be more precise, it must have occurred antecedent to September 12, 1366 (*Chaucer Life Records*, ed. Martin M. Crow and Clair C. Olson [Oxford, 1966], p. 68, cited hereafter as *Life Records*). Anyone interested in the life of Chaucer must feel indebted to this monumental piece of scholarship.

10. *Ibid.*, p. 69.

11. J. M. Manly, *Some New Light on Chaucer* (New York, 1926) contains an extended discussion of the problem (pp. 57–63). See also *Life Records*, p. 69, note 3.

12. *Ibid.*, pp. 67, 123. Though Philippa's was the earlier, it was for the exceedingly modest sum of 10 marks. Geoffrey's was for 20 marks. Joan and Marie de St. Hilaire, the latter (see note 16 below) a personage of considerable interest, both received annuities of £20 (*ibid.*, p. 69).

13. Russell Krauss, "Chaucerian Problems," in *Three Chaucer Studies* (Oxford, 1932), pp. 14–16 (cited hereafter as *Three Chaucer Studies*).

14. For Sir Payne Roet, see *Life Records*, p. 69 and note; for Katherine, see *DNB* and *Life Records*, passim. It may, or may not, be worth noting that the Percy MS (cited in note 7 above) specifies Katherine Swynford as participant in the Duke's extramarital activities during the life of Blanche; "Katerinam de Swynfurth, de qua genuit, in diebus Domine Blanchie prime uxoris sue, Johannem Bowfurth," etc. (*John of Gaunt*, pp. 464–465).

15. It is of some interest to observe that it was at the Savoy that King John of France, after his capture at Poitiers, awaited his ransom, later fixed by the Treaty of Brétigny (1360) at 3,000,000 crowns. Released to raise the funds for his huge ransom, John later returned to England of his own free will when the hostage for the collection of the ransom, his son, the Count of Anjou, took flight. It was again at the Savoy that he lodged. This is an abridged account.

16. For the career of Marie, see *Three Chaucer Studies*, pp. 150–151.

17. May 21, 1379, by John de Yerneburgh, who held numerous positions in the Lancastrian household (*Life Records*, pp. 80, 83).

18. It is to be remembered that Philippa would not surrender her royal annuity by receiving a Lancastrian. Rather her ability to collect an annuity for which there was no consideration, Queen Philippa being for a considerable time dead, was very much improved. The court influence of John of Gaunt was by no means inconsiderable.

19. *Three Chaucer Studies*, pp. 150–151.

20. *Ibid.*, pp. 31–56, passim; *Life Records*, passim.

21. June 20, 1367 (*Life Records*, pp. 123–125). It is interesting that the grant to Chaucer was made at Queenborough on the Isle of Sheppey, which Edward III characteristically used for privacy with his immediate family. We know from the *Retraction* that Chaucer had written "many a song and many a leccherous lay"—less harshly stated, amusing

poetry. If he were in fact with the royal family at Sheppey, the nature of his position at court might be a little further clarified. The annuity of 20 marks was, however, not an overwhelming one (*ibid.*, p. 123).

22. *Ibid.*, p. 98.

23. *Ibid.*, pp. 85–87. It is worth noting that the grant is a separate document, and not part of a series of grants.

24. The political situation being what it was, John obviously could not expect to find his bride in Spain. As heiress to her vanquished father, Constance was an émigrée at Bordeaux. The marriage was apparently performed at Rocquefort, (Armitage-Smith, p. 93), but John did manage to return with something of a Spanish entourage. Krauss seems to favor the idea that Philippa was in attendance (*Three Chaucer Studies*, p. 151, note 41). The language "ad fait et ferra en temps avenir a nostre . . . campaigne la roine" could fit only Constance (*Life Records*, p. 86).

25. The paternity of Thomas is a subject unto itself, and has been dealt with by Professor Krauss in *Three Chaucer Studies*. The record (*Life Records*, p. 271) is actually the grant by John of Gaunt of an annuity to Chaucer himself, since he is the designated payee. However, no services of Chaucer are specified, while those of Philippa to both Queens, Philippa and Constance, are. Furthermore, the customary language (note 24 above) "ad fait et ferra," which implies future continued service, are replaced by the double use of "ad fait," which more than implies that the services of the person named—Philippa Chaucer—are terminated. The timing of the series of bounties which befell Chaucer shortly after John of Gaunt's return in 1374—including his position in the Customs—gives the appearance of the work of a good angel, but could just as well be the work of one of a different sort. On the whole subject, see *Three Chaucer Studies*, especially pp. 155 ff.

26. *Ibid.*, 154.

27. *Life Records*, p. 91.

28. Her pension was collected for her by one John of Hermesthorpe, an official of the royal household. Previously she had collected in person. (*Three Chaucer Studies*, p. 24; *Life Records*, Table 1, p. 71.)

29. Philippa had an eye for the dramatic, and invariably for the dramatic in terms of the medieval ideal of womanhood. Her intercession for the burghers of Calais is well known; less well known is her intercession for the lives of certain unfortunate builders of viewing stands for a tournament, which collapsed to the great detriment of a considerable part of the female English nobility. See *DNB*.

30. Thynne, *Animadversions* (quoted in *Three Chaucer Studies*, p. 149).

31. *Plato*, trans. Lane Cooper (Oxford, 1938), pp. 236–239.

32. A. R. Nykl, *Hispano-Arabic Poetry* (Baltimore, 1946), p. 123. The name of the work, *The Book of the Flower*, seems to have been a matter of controversy, and the name of its author a source of confusion for the non-Arabist—in particular, the present writer. In Nykl's translation of Ibn Hazm's *Dove's Neck Ring* (Paris, 1931), the author is given as "Abū Bakr Muhammad Ibn Dāwūd al-Isfahānī" (p. lxi), which I present in its full form, since Ibn Hazm (discussed below)

refers to him as "Muhammad b. Dāwūd"; Nykl elsewhere calls him "Ibn Dāwūd al-Isfahānī" (*Hispano-Arabic Poetry*, pp. 122–123); and the same Dāwūd is elsewhere discoverable as "Abū Bakr Muhammad." Curiously enough, Nykl gives no indication of recognizing the source of Dāwūd's quotation as the *Symposium* (*ibid.*, p. 123).

33. I have preferred to follow the edition and translation of Léon Bercher, *Le Collier du pigeon* (Algiers, 1949).

34. A very readable account of this civilization is to be found in Edwyn Hole, *Andalus: Spain under the Muslims* (London, 1958). However, his grouping of Ibn Hazm with the "amor purus" school finds little support in the *Dove's Neck Ring*. In the sexual attitudes to which Ibn gives personal support, he is very much the literalist follower of the Koran.

35. "J'ai, en effet, suivi le développement naturel des choses, leur ordre chronologique" (Bercher, p. 11; Nykl, p. 5). Although, earlier in this same passage, Ibn professes to have followed chronology only as a departure from a more elaborate order, a glance at the total organization will indicate that the order is in fact chronological.

36. This would appear to be an oversimplification, since, as earlier noted, Ibn refuses the Platonic definition of Dāwūd, and takes the position that love is a conjunction of diverse parts of souls, distributed amongst expectant beings in their supernal abode, and which, on earth, act as affinities—but still in the spiritual manner derived from their original state. These parts Allah created from a single soul (Koran 7.189). Love is thus a union of spiritual affinities produced by supernatural agency in an antecedent state of the soul. The earthly attraction produced by physical beauty is not love, although the soul, being itself beautiful, is necessarily attracted to what is beautiful (Bercher, p. 25; Nykl, p. 11). However, if beyond the beautiful image presented to sense perception, the lover does not perceive a corresponding spiritual trait (affinity), the union which follows is not love. A complicating element which is not properly a part of Ibn's definition is the term "heart." All "hearts are in the hand of Allah" (Bercher, p. 13; Nykl, p. 6), and the great loves listed by Ibn as entirely praiseworthy would seem to belong to this class, because within the law of Allah. Further, there is a suggestion that the "heart" is the governing agent in a love which cannot be explained by physical attraction (Bercher, p. 17; Nykl, p. 8). However, although in his first chapter, "The Nature of Love," Ibn discusses the ramifications of his definition, these more subtle elements tend to occur in rather noncontiguous locations, while the simple phrase "fusion of souls" (Bercher, p. 21; Nykl, p. 9) or "union of souls" (Bercher, p. 19; Nykl, p. 9) occurs without qualification. It is hence this definition, very close indeed to that of Ibn Dāwūd, which tends to leave its impression upon the reader.

37. Bercher, p. 317; Nykl, p. 176. According to Bercher, the references are to Koran 12.53; 50.37; 49.7; 39.22.

38. For Galen, I have relied on M. T. May, *Galen on the Usefulness of the Parts of the Body* (Ithaca, 1968); and for Avicenna, on O. C. Gruner, *A Treatise on the Canon of Medicine of Avicenna* (London, 1930).

39. The edition of the *Anatomia Mundini* which has been available to me is the Marburg edition of 1541. All references are to this edition. The position of Mondino in the history of medicine and his relationship to Galen are discussed by George Sarton, *Introduction to the History of Science* (Washington, 1947), III, 1, pp. 842–845.

40. "et tunc ocurret tibi statim ventriculus dexter, et videbis in eo duo orificia . . . quorum unum est versus epar, et est orificium per quod, vel a quo, ingreditur vel egreditur vena chilis; et est orificium maximum, quia per hoc orificium cor trahit sanguinem ab epate, et ipsum expellit ad omnia alia membra. . . . Hoc viso, scinde ventriculum sinistrum . . . hic ventriculus debet generare spiritum ex sanguine" ("De anatomia cordis," p. 37b). The obvious difficulty in quoting Mondino is that he is interested primarily in actual dissection, and presupposes a knowledge of the essentially Galenic theory on which he is proceeding. May, cited in note 38 above, gives a thorough exposition of the theory (*Galen*, pp. 52–56).

41. "invenies rete mirabile . . . In illo rete sive in venis istius retis, continetur spiritus vitalis, ascendens a corde ad cerebrum, ad hoc ut fiat animalis. Et quia spiritus hic melius alteratur, divisus ad minima, et tunc maxime ad minima, quando est contentus in arteriis parvissimis et subtilissimis, ideo istud rete fuit contextum ex venulis sive arteriis minimis subtilissimis, ut spiritus contentus in eis faciliter alteretur et temperetur, et ad formam animalis spiritus convertatur" ("De anatomia cerebri," p. 55b). A full discussion of the concept and operation of the "pneuma" or "spiritus" is to be found in May, *Galen*, pp. 46–47.

42. See, for instance, *The Early South-English Legendary*, ed. C. Horstmann, *EETS O.S.*, 87, in which certain physiological data are attached to the life of St. Michael, beginning (1.736): "In eche manne þreo soulene beoth: ake nouȝt alle I-liche guode" (p. 320).

43. J. W. Sweetman, *Islam and Christian Theology* (London, 1967), II, 38, note 2. What precedes is an attempted summary of the "breath" and its relation to the heart, as found in Gruner, *Avicenna*, in particular pp. 107 ff. An excellent brief treatment of Avicenna is to be found in Armand A. Maurer, *Medieval Philosophy* (New York, 1962), pp. 94–100.

44. "Confessio amantis," VII, 466–468, 485–489, in *The Complete Works of John Gower*, ed. G. C. Macaulay (Oxford, 1901), III, 246; italics mine.

45. As has been noticed (note 36 above), Ibn introduces the term "heart" into his first chapter, but its relation to "soul," though implied, is by no means explicit. However, if the reader, accustomed to thinking of "heart" and "head" as opposite, and "heart" and "soul" as companionate, goes back over what Ibn has said in the intervening chapters, he will find that Ibn is unobtrusively consistent in making the satisfaction of "soul" a physical experience in which little regard for the feelings of the object of desire is evident (Bercher, pp. 117, 119; Nykl, pp. 65–66). "Heart," however, is detached from physical desire, and incapable of being satisfied by fulfillment of desire (Bercher, pp. 155, 157, 161; Nykl, 87–89, 90–91). The actual opposition of "heart" and "soul" is, however, made explicit only in the last two chapters. For example,

concerning one who has conquered sexual temptation in obedience to the law of Allah, Ibn remarks: "What is to be said of him who has secured his *heart* against a fire hotter than that of the tamarinth . . . who has compelled his *soul* to avoid the object of its desire, an object sure of attainment, which it was already preparing to enjoy . . .?" (Bercher, p. 375; Nykl, p. 205).

46. Bercher, p. 161; Nykl, p. 90. For other examples, see Nykl, *Arabic Poetry*, pp. 106, 111, 157, 170, 188, etc.

47. Lai es mos cors si totz c'alhors
    Non a ni sima ni raïtz
    Et en dormen sotz cobertors
    Es lai ab lieis mos esperitz

(*Anthology of the Provençal Troubadours*, ed. R. T. Hill and T. G. Bergin [New Haven, 1941], p. 26.)

48. "Chez Jaufré Rudel le mythe figure dans toute sa pureté originelle: 'Mon coeur,' dit-il, 'est là tout entier. . . . Mon esprit est là-bas auprès d'elle.' . . . Ailleurs, le thème peut se trouver altéré par l'abus de la préciosité" (René Nelli, *L'Érotique des troubadours* [Toulouse, 1963], pp. 210–211). I am throughout much indebted to the work cited.

49. The reference is to the structure of the coronary artery, which has the appearance of an inverted tree. Mondino says: "Figura etiam apparebit . . . figurae pinealis . . . et est maxima juxta cor, sicut stirps arboris" ("De anatomia cordis," p. 37b). The noted anatomical observer, Alicia de Badone, described the "herte roote" as being affected by thoughts of youth (III [D], 469–471).

50. "mas lo cors es sai, alhor,/lonh de leis, en Fransa" (Bergin, *Anthology*, p. 47). For the tradition, see Amy Kelly, *Eleanor of Aquitaine* (Cambridge, Mass., 1950), p. 86.

51. W. T. Pattison, *The Life and Works of the Troubadour Raimbaut d'Orange* (Minneapolis, 1952), p. 78. The rather stronger idea of the heart's forbidding is also present ("Mos cors m'o veda" [p. 79]). The formulaic "cuer et cors," which seems to provide a romantic counterpart for the Christian "body and soul" is to be found in Balade xxxiv of Chaucer's contemporary, John Gower. In the ballad, he uses the refrain "U li coers est, le corps falt obeir" (*Complete Works*, I, 365).

52. See the two comprehensive articles of Rita Lejeune, "Rôle littéraire d'Aliénor d'Aquitaine et da sa famille," *Cultura neolatina*, xiv (1954), 5–57; "Rôle littéraire de la famille d'Aliénor d'Aquitaine," *Cahiers de civilisation médiévale*, I (1958), 319–337.

53. See the introduction to J. J. Parry's translation of *The Art of Courtly Love* (New York, 1941), and that of Salvatore Battaglia to his edition *Trattato d'amore* (Rome, 1947). Aside from the very thoughtful introduction, the latter edition is notable for facing texts of the Latin (Trojel ed.) and Battaglia's own edition of two fourteenth-century Italian translations.

54. "Amor est passio quaedam innata procedens ex visione et immoderata cogitatione formae alterius sexus . . . statim eam incipit concupiscere corde" (Battaglia, *Trattato d'amore*, pp. 4, 8). The Italian translates:

"Desiderarla nel cuore" (Battaglia, p. 9), and the French: "Dedenz son cuer la loe et prise/Et a couvoitier la commence." It is to be noted in the French translation that although "couvoitier" does appear, whatever force its appearance might have is rather effectively diluted by the antecedent ideas of praising and honoring (*Li Livres d'amours de Drouart la Vache,* ed. Robert Bossuat [Paris, 1926], p. 7). The date of the translation, as given by Drouart himself, is 1290.

55. Capitulum III: "Unde dicatur Amor." "Dicitur autem 'amor' ab 'amo' verbo, quod significat 'capere' vel 'capi.' Nam qui amat, captus est cupidinis vinculis, aliumque desiderat suo capere hamo . . . [et] incorporali vinculo corda unire" (Battaglia, *Trattato d'amore,* p. 12). The extraordinary verbal agility of Andreas will be perceived in his not only depriving "hamus" (fish hook) of its initial "h," but in first introducing it in the ablative case "amor ab [h]amo," so as to make the two visually parallel. I have somewhat altered the punctuation for the purpose indicated.

56. "Et purus quidem amor est, qui omnimoda dilectionis affectione duorum amantium corda coniungit" (Battaglia, p. 212; Parry, p. 122).

57. "Mea namque voluntas esset, quae proponitis, adimplere, sed cor contradicit omnimodo. . . . Ergo, si cor contradicit amare, quaeso, ut mihi asseratis, cui potius sit favendum: cordi scilicet an voluntati?" (Battaglia, pp. 140, 142; Parry, p. 89). At this point Parry appears to give preference to present-day idiom, and translates "my heart or my head?" The text is, however, quite explicit. (Battaglia, pp. 141, 143.)

58.   ". . . ses cueurs fu a un entiers,
Et ses cors fu a deus rentiers.
Ensi tote sa vie usa
N'onques les deus ne refusa.
Ceste amors ne fu pas resnable. . . .
Qui a le cuer, cil a le cors. . . ." (3113–3123)

(*Cligès,* ed. A. Micha [Paris, 1957], p. 95.) I am aware that "renters" is not an exact equivalent of "rentiers," but I believe it approximates the sense. Cf. "rentier" in glossary of edition cited.

59.   "Feme maleurose et fole
Tu fais bien ce que tu dois faire,
Qu'a tes mains li deusses traire
Le cuer del ventre ainz qu'a la boche.
Se tes baisiers al cuer li toche,
Le cueur del ventre li as trait."

(*Le Roman de Perceval,* ed. William Roach [Geneva, 1956], p. 172.) The significance of the term "ventre" and its relationship to the anatomists is pointed out by Zara P. Zaddy, "Chrétien de Troyes and the Localization of the Heart," *Romance Philology,* XII (1959), 257–258. A more general study of the heart doctrine of the trouvères is that of Roger Dragonetti, *La Technique poétique des trouvères dans la chanson courtoise* (Bruges, 1960), pp. 232–241. In the passages adduced by Dragonetti, the formulaic pattern of "cuer et cors," noticed above, is

observable. He terms the heart "siège de toute pensée et de tout amour"
(p. 232). I am indebted to Professor Alfred L. Foulet of Princeton
University for pointing out to me the above studies, and for relieving
me of my misconception concerning the meaning of the term "ventre."

60.   Amur e raisun le destraint,
        E le voleir de sun cors vaint.
        Le grant amor qu'ad vers Ysolt
        Tolt ço que la nature volt,
        E vaint icele volenté
        Que senz desir out en pensé. (601–606)

Les Fragments du Tristan de Thomas, ed. Bartina H. Wind (Leiden, 1950), p. 87. For the sense of "desir" (606), see glossary.

61. Rational: "Merlin" sot quanques cuers pooit savoir de toute perverse science (21; also 35, 163, 226). Detachable: the Lady of Malehot would willingly have known "en quel lieu il [Lancelot] avoit mis son cuer" (226; also 161, passim); "cuer et cors," 27, 225, 260. (*The Vulgate Version of the Arthurian Romances*, ed. H. Oskar Sommer [Washington, 1910], Vol. III.)

62. *Le Roman de la rose,* ed. Ernest Langlois (Paris, 1920), II, 1955 ff.; 2299 ff.

63. "Ne onques voir sanz mon cuer je ne fui, ançois le sent touz jourz dedenz mon piz debatre et remuer. . . . Mes itant sai je bien tout de voir, et par ce que a pluseurs genz l'ai oï dire, que madame Yseult porte avecques lui le cuer de Trystram, le neveu au roy Marc de Cornoaille, et le tien cuer autresint, si comme tu meesmes le contes. Doncques, puisque il est ainsi que ele a tant de cuers dedenz son ventre, qui ne par est mie trop grant, et se je le mien i vouloie metre par aucune aventure, cuides tu que ceuls qui dedenz son ventre sont hebergiez me vousissent avecques euls souffrir? Certes, nenil; car ils sont trop durs pautonniers et trop felons et trop cruieus et trop orgueilleus durement: si chaceroient le mien hors a grande honte et a grant deshonnour. Et pour ce garderai je mon cuer avecques moi, que je ne vueill pas que dame ne damoiselle en ait ja saisine" (Eugène Vinaver, *Études sur le Tristan en prose* [Paris, 1925], p. 97). Gratitude is due to Professor Vinaver for having extracted Sir Dinadan from the mass of the prose *Tristan*.

64. Chrétien de Troyes, *Le Chevalier de la Charrete,* ed. Mario Roques (Paris, 1958), lines 1414 ff.

65. *Perceval,* ed. Roach, lines 4164 ff.

66.   Vers [es] qu'Amors homen encega
        E l'auzir e-l parlar li tol,
        E-l fai tener adonc per fol
        Cant aver cuja plus de sen!
        Guillems non au ni ve ni sen,
        Ni-ls oils non mòu, ni ma ni boca (2345–2350)

(*Les Troubadours*, ed. and trans. René Lavaud and René Nelli [Bruges, 1960], p. 764).

67.
Ans coven que, per joi menar,
Cascus dels sens al cor repaire;
Car le cors es seners e paire,
E per so, cant ha mal ni be,
Cascus dels sens a lui s'en ve
Per saber tost sa volontat;
E quan son laïns ajostat
Om es defors totz escurzitz
E estai quais esbalauzitz;
E pos mals o bes dins los fai
Tornar, meravilla non ai
Si jois d'amors, cant es corals
E mescladamens bes e mals,
Los fai tornar ad espero
A lur senor. . . . (2357–2371)

(*Ibid.*, 766.) It is to be noted that either love or sorrow makes the senses rush to the heart. An example of Nature despairing of the cure of a heart afflicted with love is to be found in lines 3015 ff. (p. 801).

68. *Opera originis* (Paris, 1604), II, 291–294. "This identification was suggested by Tyrwhitt, Glossary, s.v. 'Origenes'" (Robinson's note to *Legend of Good Women*, line 417). It is the above text I have followed, although I have noted variants of some interest in a separate copy of the *Homily* in the British Museum (col. 122. 19b) attributed to W. Faques, and conjecturally dated 1504. It is stated to have been printed in Abchurch Lane, London.

69. Summary of *Opera originis*, II, 292, col. b.

70. Facta erat exanimis, facta insensibilis. Sentiens non sentiebat, videns non videbat, audiens non audiebat; sed neque erat ubi erat, quia tota ibi erat ubi magister erat, de quo tamen ubi esset nesciebat (*ibid.*, p. 292, col. 1).

71. Credite mihi, si ipsum cognosceret, in monumento eum non quaereret, et si verba illius corde retineret, non de mortuo doleret, sed de vivente guaderet . . . sed, pro dolor, nimius dolor cor illius repleverat, et memoriam horum verborum deleverat; sensus nullus in ea remanserat, omne consilium in ea perierat (*ibid.*, p. 292, col. a). See also 293, col. b; 294, col. a.

72. Denique Ioseph posuit in monumento corpus tuum, Maria sepelevit ibi pariter spiritum suum, et ita indissolubiliter iunxit, et quodammmodo univit eum cum corpore tuo, ut facilius posset separare animam se vivificantem a vivificato corpore suo, quam spiritum suum te diligentem a defuncto corpore tuo. Ubi perdidit corpus tuum, perdidit cum eo spiritum suum. Quid igitur mirum si sensum non habebat quae spiritum amiserat? Quid mirum si te nesciebat, quae non habebat spiritum quo scire debebat? . . . et sic error non procedebat ab errore, sed ab amore et dolore. . . . O quam scienter nescit, et quam docte errat (*ibid.*, 293, col. b).

73. Redde ei itaque spiritum suum . . . et mox recuperabit sensum suum.

(Idem) Abchurch: "Redde itaque ei spiritum suum . . . Moxque re-cuperabit cor suum (no pagination; I should read it as page 13).

74. *Works*, p. 493. Although no manuscript exists, Chaucer's translation must have been well known, because a "Complaynte of Mary Magdalene" is found in all the early editions.

75. "Musaeus: A Monody to the Memory of Mr. Pope," in *Poems* (London 1764), p. 7.

76. A full discussion of hunting terms in Chaucer is to be found in O. F. Emerson, and those which appear in the *Book of the Duchess* are thoroughly discussed ("Chaucer and Medieval Hunting," *Romanic Review*, XIII [1922], 115–150; rpt. *Chaucer Essays and Studies* [Cleveland, 1929], pp. 320–377).

77. R. S. Loomis, "Chaucer's Eight Year Sickness," *MLN*, LIX (1944), 178–180.

78. *Plato*, ed. Cooper, p. 276.

79. It is not impossible that this scene is something of an inverted version of the later Chaucer's *Complaint to His Purse*, (*Works*, 539–540).

80. Cf. *Flamenca*, p. 80; *Homelia*, pp. 80–82; note 73, above.

81. "Sir Perceval of Galles," lines 505, 401–403, in *Middle English Metrical Romances*, ed. W. H. French and C. B. Hale (New York, 1930), II, 548, 544–545.

82. The term is borrowed from Thomas Usk's *Testament of Love*: "yet thinke on thy servaunt that for thy love spilleth . . . the hete of my brenning tene hath me al defased. . . . My conninge is thinne, my wit is exiled; lyke to a foole naturel am I comparisoned (Skeat, VII, 6).

83. The "foole naturel" here appears to function as agent.

84. See pp. 61–62 above.

85. The passage is more than reminiscent of the Arabic. See p. 73 above.

86. Nicholas Love, *Mirrour of the Life of Christ*, ed. L. F. Powell (Oxford, 1908), p. 267.

87. There is also a curious parallel in language. The Dreamer: "I stalked even unto hys bak (458); Pandarus: "Tho gan I stalke hym softely byhynde" (II, 519). In both cases, the action is undertaken to hear what gives promise of being a confession of love; in both cases the hearer is able to rehearse more or less word for word what he has heard (*Works*, pp. 271, 407). As a small contribution to the history of science, it should be observed, on the most reliable authority, that Guilhem Adhemar had much earlier contrived a "jeu à l'oreille" which permitted him to hear amorous discourses, and hence rendered obsolete the crude method noted above (Jehan de Nostredame, *Les Vies des . . . poètes provençaux*, ed. Chabaneau and Anglade [Paris, 1913], p. 30).

88. "Qui a le cuer, cil a le cors" (*Cligès*, ed. Micha, line 3123); "Il est assez sires dou cors/ Qui a le cuer en sa comande" (*Roman*, ed. Langlois, lines 1996–1997).

89. According to lines 419–425, the trees rise up, without branches, to a height of 240–300 feet ("of fourty or fifty fadme lengthe") and then interlock overhead, not an inch apart.

90. For the technique of distancing, see Bronson, *PMLA*, LXVII, 878.

91. On Chaucer's use of the "persona," see E. T. Donaldson, "Chaucer the Pilgrim," *PMLA*, LXIX (1954), 936. Though the article deals with the *Canterbury Tales*, it has great applicability throughout Chaucer. I have not so much followed Donaldson's approach as found myself arriving at much the same conclusions from a rather different approach. The same may be said of my agreement with Donaldson as to the role of the natural in the consolation. See *Chaucer's Poetry*, ed. Donaldson (New York, 1957).

92. James Joyce, *Ulysses* (New York, 1934), p. 473.

93. This is pure conjecture.

94. The present article is not intended as a total interpretation of the *Book of the Duchess*, but simply as a discussion of the interaction of two major elements within the poem. It says nothing, for instance, except by implication, of the artistic success of the elegy *qua* elegy. This is beyond the scope of an article which it is difficult to believe anyone would wish longer. A selective listing of works dealing with this and other aspects of the poem may be found in Albert C. Baugh's recent bibliography: *Chaucer* (New York: Appleton-Century-Crofts, 1968). Goldentree Bibliographies.

8

Chaucer's St. Valentine: A Conjecture

THE PRESENT ESSAY is an attempt to trace the development of the legend of a remote saint, whose day of decapitation was rather curiously judged in the fourteenth century and later to be an appropriate occasion for the writing of love poems and comparable amatory observances—connected, it would appear, only very invisibly with reverence for Christian martyrdom. The particular objectives of the essay are to define the state of the legend at the time of the composition of the *Parlement of Foules*, and the attitude toward St. Valentine Chaucer takes in the *Parlement*.

I

The first step in the evolution of St. Valentine as a fertility figure—as was suggested a great while ago by Francis Douce (1757–1834), antiquary and onetime keeper of manuscripts in the British Museum[1]—seems to have been the Roman Lupercalia, celebrated on February 15. The rites of the Lupercalia are mentioned by numerous ancient writers. For instance, Varro (116–27 B.C.) in the *De lingua latina* interprets the significance of the rites in the course of his discussion of the various months which make up the Roman year:

Of those which were added to these [numerically named months], the prior was called *Ianuarius* "January" from the god who is first in order [Janus]; the latter, as the same writers say, was called *Februarius* "February" from the *di inferi* "gods of the Lower World," because at that time expiatory sacrifices are made to them; but I think that it was called February rather from the *dies februatus* "Purification Day," because then the people *februatur* "is purified," that is, the old Palatine town girt with flocks of people is [purified ("lustratur")] by the naked Luperci.[2]

Plutarch more exactly defines the idea of purification in the Lupercalian rites:

As for the Lupercalia, judging by the time of its celebration, it would seem to be a feast of purification, for it is observed on the inauspicious days ["Dies nefasti"] of the month of February, which name can be interpreted to mean *purification*, and the very day of the feast was anciently called Febrata.

He continues, after interpreting the Lupercalia as meaning "feast of wolves":

. . . the actual ceremonies of the festival are such that the reason for the name is hard to guess. For the priests slaughter goats, and then, after two youths of noble birth have been brought to them, some of them touch their foreheads with a bloody knife, and others wipe the stain off at once with wool dipped in milk. The youths must laugh after their foreheads are wiped. After this they cut the goats' skins into strips and run about, with nothing on but a girdle, striking all who meet them with thongs, and young married women do not try to avoid their blows, fancying that they promote conception and easy childbirth. A peculiarity of the festival is that the Luperci sacrifice a dog also.[3]

Although the Romans seem to have been somewhat vague about the origins of the rites described by Plutarch, they nevertheless entertained very positive notions concerning the function of those rites. As Dr. Franklin puts it in her extensive study, *The Lupercalia*:

Very frequently the blows dealt by the Luperci are mentioned as assuring to women productivity. In later times this idea of propagation was extended also to the crops. In the minds of the ancients fertility was closely related to purification, for it was by purification from evil powers that the forces of life became active. Consequently, by the time of Varro the Lupercalia was regarded as one of the most important lustrations of the state.[4]

That the celebration of the Lupercalia had as its purpose human fertility cannot be doubted, but that this should have been its sole purpose is highly questionable. It seems very strange that the oldest of Rome's religious festivals should not from the beginning have included both crops and herds. The earliest known Roman gods were gods of agriculture—Jupiter was originally a sky god, and a bringer of rain; Saturn was not only an agricultural god, but one of the earliest identifiable professors of agriculture; Ceres was a goddess of crops; and Mars was both a vegetation deity and a protector of the fields.[5] All that is known concerning the relationship of the Luperci to the crops is that they exercised their rites in behalf of the increase of the crops, and that no implication of late development exists.[6]

Earlier than the earliest Roman gods were the cult divinities of the Ligurians, the first known inhabitants of Italy, as the related Pelasgians were the first known inhabitants of Greece. These earth divinities were constructs in animal form of the perils which threatened a primitive agricultural society and required propitiation for the nonexercise of their malevolent powers.[7] An extremely ancient divinity of this sort was the serpent of Lanuvium, whose cult perhaps goes further back into antiquity than that of the Lupercalia. This remarkable serpent, who later became a symbolic attendant of Juno Sospita[8] of Lanuvium, had in his charge the safety of the city. As such, he required tribute in the form of sacrificial cakes presented to him by a certified virgin. If there had been an unfortunate error in the process of selection, he spurned the cakes and consumed the maiden. If, however, the maiden possessed the necessary qualifications, he graciously accepted the cakes, and a bountiful harvest was expected to follow.[9] A more imminent danger than the failure of a good harvest was the threat posed by the wolf, whose depredations threatened not only herds and flocks but man himself. From this wolf terror emerged a wolf deity whose propitiation involved not only an offering but an act of expiation or purification.[10] In its primitive Greek form, as Franklin would have us believe, a child was offered, its entrails tasted by the celebrant, who then fled to escape the penalty of his sacrificial impiety, and often underwent an expiation—such as becoming, for a period of time, a werewolf.[11] The Lupercalia, however, was not simply a cult, but in Dr. Franklin's terminology a "cult-complex."[12] In its earliest form:

The Luperci endeavored to avert from the people the deity's malignant power by offering it sacrifice. They sought to share the mysterious potency of the sacrificial animal by eating of its entrails. Yet they felt that the act of slaying an animal consecrated to the god was a sacrilege; therefore they fled, as from a crime, and expiated their guilt by being stoned. Having been thus purified, they returned to the Lupercal, and ate in sacramental fashion the flesh of the sacrifice.[13]

In this conjectural earliest form, the Lupercalia would seem generally comparable to the conjectural form of the wolf cults of Greece and Italy. However, as a cult-complex, the original apotropaic form of the Lupercalia was so completely lost under successive overlayings that even the learned Greek student of Roman antiquities found himself puzzled by the apparent non-relation of the events which made up its celebration.[14] The partial assimilation of the ancient cult by the maternally motivated wolf who nursed Romulus and Remus seems a readily understood development. However, it is of some relevance to observe the direction further changes took. The addition of the sacrifice of the dog was possibly initiated by the Sabines. Its purpose seems to have been purification.[15] From Ovid's account, the goat sacrifice appears to be a borrowing from the cult of Juno Lucina, at whose command, "Let the sacred goat enter into the Italian matrons," the sterility of the Sabine women was—"Gratia Lucinae!" —effectually ended. The means employed was the application of the goat thongs later so evident in the Lupercalia.[16] What is important here is that although the Romans associated with the Lupercalia Lupercus, Faunus, Inuus, and Pan Lycaeus—all earth gods and fertility gods—by the time of Ovid the center of the stage was held by Juno, the guardian deity of women. It is exclusively as the imparter of human fertility—the goat-thong whip was called the "amiculum Junonis"[17]—and as the bringer-into-light (Juno Lucina) of the fertility she had herself made possible that Juno was invoked. The advent of Juno meant, of course, her coexistence with the ancient earth gods, not her displacement of them. The addition of her rites simply gave a further meaning and a further complexity to the Lupercalia.

That the rites of the Lupercalia are complex and hence highly controversial would seem to go without question. The present writers, as a result, find themselves in much the same relation as Study to Theology in Langland's *Piers Plowman*:

> The more I muse there-inne   ·   the mistier it semeth,
> And the depper I deuyne   ·   the derker me it thinketh.
>   (B x, 181–182)

However, there does seem to be a perceptible movement from concern for the fertility of cattle and fields to a concern for human fertility—an historical evolution which probably explains the emergence and importance of Juno. However, this emphasis upon the human in no way changed the underlying conception of purification as the necessary antecedent of fertility. If Ovid is to be believed, the Luperci beat the fields as well as the females.[18] In his edition of Ovid's *Fasti*, Sir James Frazer says of the Lupercalia:

> . . . the festival was one of purification, which, by ridding the community of the evil powers of barrenness and disease that had infested it in the past year, set free the kindly powers of nature to perform their genial task of promoting the fertility alike of women, of cattle, and of the fields.[19]

II

The Lupercalia was probably the oldest of Rome's festivals—founded even before the Romans settled on the Palatine Hill—and it was possibly the last to succumb to Christianity. When, in 495, Pope Gelasius finally abolished the Lupercalia, his procedure followed the accepted pattern. He set in its place a Christian festival of comparable meaning and almost exact date—the Purification of the Virgin, or Candlemas, celebrated on February 14.

The choice of Candlemas possessed a further advantage. Among the most ancient and prominent festivals of the Church was the Presentation of Christ in the Temple, to which the festival of the Purification of the Virgin was obviously readily assimilable, since the Presentation could take place only after the traditional forty days of purification had been observed. However, the date of the Presentation depended directly upon the date assigned the birth of Christ, which was in the Eastern Church January 6, and in the Western, December 25.[20] This disparity was ultimately to prepare for the advent of St. Valentine.

The first notice of the institution of Candlemas occurs in Jerusalem in the second half of the fourth century. The *Peregrinatio* of Etheria describes it under the name of "Quadragesimae de Epiphania," but no specific mention of the Virgin is there made. Since, as noted above, the feast of the Nativity was originally kept in the East on January 6, the Presentation was celebrated on February 14.[21] The observances attached to February 14 then coalesced into a feast of Our Lord, a feast of the Purification of the Virgin Mary, and, as indicated below, a feast of lights.[22]

As described in the eighth-century Saint-Amand manuscript, there was at early dawn a gathering at the Church of Santo Adriano in the Roman Forum. All the regions and parishes were represented, and with lighted candles the populace awaited the Pope at the church. It was a meeting of the "plebs," on the side of the Comitium, near the Curia, where in bygone years the *Comitia tributa* had assembled. The choice of Santo Adriano for this gathering was therefore not without importance in the history of the festival, since this had been the traditional location of the Lupercalian rites. The Pope and deacons, vested in black, appeared, and the procession was formed with two lighted candles carried before the Pontiff. The procession then left the Forum for the Church of Santa Maria Maggiore. The black vestments and the hushed chanting of the Gloria lent a special note of solemnity to the service.[23]

Further evidence that the Church, since it could not well abolish the antique pagan fertility rites at one stroke, effectively Christianized the Lupercalia is very directly attested to by Bede in the *De temporum ratione*, XII.

The Christian religion has changed these customs; for in the same month on Saint Mary's day [Candlemas Day], all the people, with priests and ministers, go forth with hymns through the churches and the chosen places of the city; and all carry in their hands the lighted tapers they have received from the bishop. . . . And this is no longer done, as in pagan times, for the purification of an earthly kingdom, but for the commemoration of that heavenly one, in which, according to the parable of the prudent virgins, all the elect, with the lamps of good works burning, will go to meet the Spouse their King, and enter with Him into the nuptials of the heavenly city.[24]

Thus the related ideas of purification and fertility embodied in the Lupercalia became the inheritance of the Virgin Mother and found their observance in the Feast of Candlemas on February 14. The month of February thereby retained its ancient associations, and the substituted feast of Candlemas gained wide dissemination throughout the Christian world. In the north of England, for instance, Candlemas was known as the "Wives' Feast Day."[25] Since the present study is most immediately concerned with England, it is perhaps worth noting that plays of the Purification of Mary are prominent in the repertories of companies performing in Coventry, Digby, York, and Chester—a rather clear indication of how important an observance it was considered.[26]

Although the popularity of Candlemas remained constant, the date of its observance did not. As has been noted, Candlemas was transferred from February 14 to February 2, a transferal made necessary by the final establishment throughout the Church of December 25 as the date of Christmas.[27] Such a change was of no small consequence, since it left a liturgically highly important day without an incumbent. February 14 was the day of St. Valentine, but it was also the day of numerous other saints. Why was Valentine regarded as so appropriate a saint for this day that other candidates were thrust into oblivion?

The great repository of saints' lives is the Bollandist-edited *Acta sanctorum*.[28] Under date of February 14, one finds several St. Valentines, but only two of the lives are recorded in any detail. These are the lives of Valentine, priest of Rome, and Valentine, Bishop of Terni. Following these is the *Veneration of the Head of St. Valentine*, by Baudri de Bourgueil, Bishop of

Dol during the early twelfth century. Since the first of these lives, that of Valentine, priest of Rome, is, on the one hand, involved with a second martyrology and, on the other, provides a singularly bare narrative, discussion will be limited to the life of Valentine, Bishop of Terni, and to the *Veneration* of Baudri de Bourgueil.

The account of Valentine, Bishop of Terni, is complex in style, but direct in narrative and restrained in its description of the acts of the saint. The story begins in Rome at the house of one Crato, who is a rhetorician and teacher, apparently one of considerable note. With him are lodged three noble Athenians: Proclus, Ephebus, and Apollonius, who, one is led to believe, have exhausted all of Greek learning and have come to Rome to learn whatever Greece has failed to provide. At a point in their instruction by Crato, his son Chaeremon falls prey to an ailment which no physician in Rome can cure. One Fonteius, an undefined acquaintance or friend of Crato's, happens to mention that a young relative of his had suffered from an even worse attack of the same disease and had been cured by a certain St. Valentine, Bishop of Terni. Crato immediately sends to Valentine several distinguished friends to discover whether the bishop will deign to come. He accepts.

Upon St. Valentine's arrival, Crato beseeches him to cure his son, as he had cured the boy relative of Fonteius. The saint replies, "Tu si vis, curabitur" ("If it is your wish, he will be cured"). The delighted father then promises Valentine a tenth of his estate—which appears to be an ample one—if he can bring about the cure. St. Valentine's reply to this munificent offer is somewhat startling. "I marvel that you, a skilled master of rhetoric, did not observe that I said, 'Tu si vis, curabitur.'" The saint thereupon proceeds to attack Crato's belief in false gods and brazen images, and declares that only by faith in Christ can his child be cured. St. Valentine's logic is not easy to follow, but what he apparently means is that he is using "vis" in the sense of "will" rather than "wish," and that the will which does not draw its power from Christ possesses no power. It is in this vein that he concludes:

Believe therefore the son of God to be the true God, Jesus Christ, and renounce all images, and you will see your son saved.[29]

But Crato, who bears the title "orator," is practiced in argumentation, and he finds the concept of the transferability of faith not without its difficulties. "I don't know much about your religion," he says, but

> . . . I have heard it said that everyone is to be saved by his own faith: nor may the faith of one avail another, nor the lack of faith of one be a hindrance to another.[30]

St. Valentine is not impressed by Crato's argument. He concedes only that the nature of a father's faith cannot prove an obstacle to a child who is a believer in the true faith, and he then proceeds to produce example after example of the faith of others saving the sick or even the dead (Lazarus); and, by contrast, the lack of faith of a single individual (Pharaoh) being the ruination of a whole people.

Buried beneath the avalanche of exempla, Crato makes an immediate and abject profession of faith. However, it is rather obvious that there are many dark spots in his mind, and as the saint painstakingly endeavors to illuminate them, Crato makes a rather practical observation: "As our disputation grows longer, the life of my son Chaeremon grows shorter." St. Valentine proceeds undeterred in his doctrinal exposition, but he in turn makes a practical observation. He realizes that he cannot then and there bring the worldly-wise Crato to a state of belief adequate to the salvation of his son. He therefore substitutes his own. He says:

> Since the wisdom of the world, in which you appear to be thoroughly versed, is in the presence of God, stupidity, and you cannot so perfectly believe as the faith itself demands, pledge me your faith in the form of this promise: if your son is saved through my faith, you, through the salvation of your son, shall, with all your household, be converted to Christ.[31]

The promise is of course made, St. Valentine retires with the boy to a locked cubicle, the cure is worked, and the ecstatically happy parents soon hear their son singing the praises of God. Understandably they plead with St. Valentine to unlock the door. "Not until I have completed the canonical number of prayers and hymns," the saint replies. Only at dawn does he unlock the door.

A final incident concludes the miracle. Proclus, Ephebus, and

Apollonius, who have been present throughout and have themselves received baptism:

> . . . casting aside the studies of human wisdom, betook themselves so completely to God that from that time forth they would read absolutely nothing of human letters, but gave themselves over to spiritual studies under the guidance of a master [St. Valentine] whose deeds as well as his words proved miraculous.[32]

The rest of the account, which one would expect to constitute the major and most dramatic part of the narrative, is treated briefly, if not abruptly. As a result of the miracle, conversions without number take place; St. Valentine is imprisoned and tortured; his joyful endurance of his torture comforts the souls of those who "through him believed in Christ." Ultimately he is taken from prison at night and beheaded. His body is removed, again by night, to his church at Trevi, and buried decently in a "purchased spot of earth outside the city." Proclus, Ephebus, and Apollonius persist in daily prayers and vigils by his grave, suffer the same torture and execution, and are buried near him.

There is much in the account of the "ancient writer" which gives his work character. First, there is but one miracle described, and that tinged with a realism not often encountered in a saint's legend: the father's pointed remark that as their argument lengthens, his son's life shortens; St. Valentine's perception that a mind trained in argumentation is not in a moment to be changed by argumentation. There is also perhaps concern for the faith, in that the author seems to see "human letters" as in need of castigation, and concern for the Church in his insistence, rather like that of Chaucer in his portrait of the Parson, that it is by action that belief is to be gained and held.

It should be added that the arguments are themselves relatively skillful, and apparently imitative of the tradition initiated by the *De consolatione philosophiae* of Boethius. The work is more like the sermon of an earnest churchman on what the heroic self-dedication of a single man can do, and, perhaps by implication, what the lack of it can undo. One is reminded of Langland's puzzled meditation on the critical shortage of miracles in his own day. Most remarkable, however, is the lack of mention of relics or of continuing miracles. The account of St. Valentine by the "auctor anonymus antiquus" is not a work intended to establish a prestige shrine for the discriminating pilgrim.

The account of St. Valentine written about 1120 by Baudri de Bourgueil, Bishop of Dol in Brittany, is very different. In the first place, Baudri's version depends not on the saint himself, but on the nature of his death—decapitation. Baudri's narrative is thus not primarily concerned with the "acta" of the saint, but with the adventures of his head: its removal from a hiding place in Rome; its translation to the monastery of Jumièges in Normandy; and the miracles ensuing upon its arrival there. The title, *On the Veneration of the Head of St. Valentine*, quite precisely defines the subject of the work. Another rather curious matter is Baudri's sources. In an age which venerated authority, Baudri's sole authority is oral—what he has heard from the monks themselves concerning these miracles.[33] In fact, one of Valentine's most notable miracles was related to Baudri by the sufferer saved—Brother Hugo, Precentor of Jumièges, who was near death from loss of appetite.[34] Finally, there is the question of Baudri's motives. From scattered remarks which grow more emphatic as the account proceeds, it is clear that Baudri, being often at Jumièges as a refugee from the "uncivilizable Bretons" of whom he was bishop, finds himself a kind of repository of the miracles of St. Valentine related to him at Jumièges, and hence under a moral and religious obligation to elevate the bushel which has obscured the miraculous deeds of the saint, and to let the light shine forth. As he puts it:

To remain silent about Valentine is impious; to speak out concerning him is an act of piety to which one is compelled. They who fail to make themselves heard are to be rebuked for their impious silence and ingratitude, and especially those who are his very own, who see these and others of his acts and are silent—they who conceal the glory of Valentine when it is only right that he be openly praised. Let these silent ones correct their error and speak out; let them add testimony to testimony, for the supreme Creator ceases not to add miracles to miracles.[35]

In the same hortatory tone, one finds statements to the effect that the aid of Valentine is inexhaustible, and is at hand for all who, with devotion, will but seek him. To remain silent about Valentine is in fact to utter sacrilege. The pen of Baudri will therefore not be idle.

Baudri is at least as good as his word. As recorded by him, the history of the head begins in a rather more than slightly mysterious fashion. A certain priest has come to Rome for the sake of prayer, but also with the desire of obtaining relics of the saints, presumably for the benefit of those who had no access to the relics, in which Rome was so rich. In the hospice where he was lodged, he revealed to his fellow lodgers his desire, in the hope that he might find satisfaction for it. In the course of discussion, someone who was present spoke of Valentine, priest of Terni. He declared that he would give the priest the head of St. Valentine, not for the sake of gain, but that the relic might gladden and make resplendent the land beyond the mountains. The undefined someone, as mysterious as the priest himself, did in fact know the hiding place of Valentine's head, and duly presented it to the priest, who, with God's aid, virtually flew across the rough and unfriendly mountains and arrived in Normandy. By divine will, he came to Jumièges, became a monk, and conferred the "patrocinium" of the head upon the monks of Jumièges. However, the monks at that time had not heard the works of St. Valentine, and when they did, they feared lest the head be taken from them or, alternatively, that it might be the head of another. In the meantime, they deferred any decision, and the head continued to repose in an ivory case behind the altar of the Virgin Mary.[36]

At last the time came when God willed to chasten the inhabitants of the town of Jumièges, and in so doing to see to it that his servant Valentine should no longer remain unknown. He therefore sent a plague of mouselike creatures to devastate the newly sown fields. This they did by eating day and night, until almost nothing of the new crops remained. At this point, St. Valentine appeared to one of the monks and addressed him in an imperious tone:

"Go," he said, "and tell the brothers to carry our head—concerning [the identity of] which some are in doubt—I am indeed Valentine!—through the fields and countryside; [tell them] to go about through the crossroads and through the streets of towns—for God will indeed be propitious unto them, if henceforth they are quicker to remember us."[37]

The monk thought it but a dream, and did nothing. However, on Valentine's second appearance his voice, as he reprimanded the otiose monk, was overheard. His third appearance proved more than convincing, and the head of Valentine was carried about in ceremonial procession. The previously avid rodents plunged into the Seine and were drowned:

> The Omnipotent, indeed, to display the power of his dear [Valentine], exterminated the exterminating horde, and by that means propagated the name of His own Valentine.[38]

After Valentine's intervention on behalf of the "tendre croppes," Baudri recounts one fire and two plagues suffered by neighboring inhabitants, in which the aid of St. Valentine was sought not without avail. A further intervention, perhaps less dramatic than that of the rodents but of similar significance, fol-. lowed. On one occasion, presumably at harvest time, the heat was so great that

> The grass had withered, the grain grown white, for the unseasonable drought had parched the earth. Every field was becoming powdered dust, and threatened sterility; and every God-fearing man was in lamentation.[39]

A procession was made to the church of St. Philbert, not far from Jumièges, and apparently in the midst of the area of devastation. (At this point, Baudri is seized by such a fit of religious exaltation that he feels himself virtually unable to continue his narrative. However, he does.) As the monks began the service, the sky, previously devoid of clouds, became dark, thunder was heard, and rain suddenly poured down. The monks were for the moment fearful that they might not be able to return to their monastery, but their fears were groundless. A clearing of the skies took place, and what rain descended was parted to the right and to the left of the monks as they bore their own Valentine back to Jumièges.[40]

From a comparison of the life of St. Valentine discussed above with the *Veneration of the Head of St. Valentine*, several conclusions may be drawn. First, for the world beyond the Alps—France and England—there was but one St. Valentine. In the Jumièges version of the head reported by Baudri—the only account of these miracles to be found in the *Acta sanctorum*—the differences between Valentine, priest of Rome, and Valentine, bishop of Terni, are erased. In Baudri's account, Valentine is everywhere called "priest"; conversely, Valentine is nowhere called "priest of Rome," but "priest of Terni."[41] When Valentine makes his first dramatic appearance, the only one in which his apparel is described, it is as a priest that he is clothed.[42] Second, it is clear that the monastery of Jumièges had something to gain by seeing to it that a definitive, composite Valentine was their very own personal possession—"noster Valentinus"[43] being the term by which the monks were accustomed to refer to their saint. Jumièges was a powerful Benedictine monastery with a commercial port on the Seine, one of a very considerable concentration of monasteries in the vicinity of Rouen. Of ancient foundation, it had been ravaged by Viking incursions, but was in the tenth century restored by William Longsword. In the following century, Jumièges benefited by the interest in monastic establishment and endowment which characterized the earlier Dukes of Normandy and which, between 1035 and 1066, became a passion with the lesser nobility.[44] At some point in approximately this same period of monastic fervor, Robert I granted a foundation charter to Holy Trinity, Rouen, to which the "venerated relics" of St. Catherine had been conveyed.[45] In June, 1067, in the course of the triumphant progress through Normandy which marked his conquest of England, William I

. . . reached Jumièges, where he was met by Maurilius, the aged metropolitan of Rouen, who arrived in time to perform the last public act of his own distinguished career. On 1 July, in the presence of a large company, including the bishops of Lisieux, Avranches, and Evreux, Maurilius solemnly hallowed the abbey-church which had been begun more than twenty years before by Abbot Robert, later archbishop of Canterbury.[46]

The King also participated in the ceremony.

Could a distinguished monastery on such an occasion, or indeed on any occasion, afford to be devoid of relics? Whether or not on this particularly splendid occasion the head of St. Valentine was a part of the abbey's treasure the present writers are unable to say. However, Baudri de Bourgueil, writing about 1120, makes it eminently clear that at the time his work was composed, the head was a cherished possession of the abbey of Jumièges. Furthermore, he intimates that the abbey had been its repository for a very long time, but how very long a time he judiciously neglects to make clear. However, the reader is informed that the mysterious priest who carried the head across the Alps did so at a period much anteceding the eleventh century, for the head is said to have arrived at Jumièges before the deeds of St. Valentine were known and to have remained in its receptacle at Jumièges long after they were known. It is therefore not without interest that the Abbot Robert, who was present with William the Conqueror at the dedication of the abbey church, was Robert of Jumièges, who had been successively Abbot of Jumièges, Bishop of London, and Archbishop of Canterbury.[47] England and Normandy were now firmly linked, and the appearance in England of the legend of a Jumièges saint was as likely a development as the appearance of the same legend in France. Nothing seemed to bar the adoption of so useful a saint on either side of the Channel.

A comparison of the life of St. Valentine with the *Veneration of the Head of St. Valentine* may also cast some light on the capabilities of the Jumièges *legenda* for general consumption. The life is dry, argumentative, and makes no promises. Its author is unknown. Baudri, on the contrary, as bishop of Dol and pretender to an archbishopric, was not only a man of position, but a man of letters whose poetry, written in Latin, embraced a large range of pious subjects, especially the epitaph for the noble dead.[48] However, he was by no means exclusively the pious moralist. He also conducted a kind of epistolary correspondence which he directed to a wide range of personages, including the nobility. "Adèle, countess of Blois, daughter of William the Conqueror, and Cécile, her sister, abbess of Caën, both well versed in literature, honored him with their friendship."[49] Thus any work by him was capable of circulating at the highest levels particularly, perhaps something like a saint's legend, since Baudri possessed a considerable reputation for piety and yet never recognized an opposition between poetry and religion.

However, the most important aspect of Baudri's *Veneration* is not the unifying of St. Valentine or the rendering of him exportable. The real value of his work is the clear indication that by the beginning of the twelfth century St. Valentine had taken on a new dimension. He was by this time thought of as a saint efficacious in countering that which would destroy the growth and maturing of the natural. This new attribute may perhaps be described by the term "fertility saint" or "nature saint." The ancient fertility deity has been defined as a "giver of fertility and a protector from evil."[50] However, as has been indicated, the process by which fertility is achieved is not direct but dependent upon the antecedent neutralizing of the forces of evil. The whip of the Luperci, the "amiculum Junonis," did not of itself impart fertility. Juno appears in the Lupercalia as Juno Februata—Juno the Purifier—and it is only after purification that fecundity may take place. As Frazer puts it, the purificatory powers of the Lupercalia "set free the kindly powers of nature to perform their genial task of promoting the fertility alike of women, of cattle, and of the fields."[51]

St. Valentine fits the pattern of the fertility god with considerable exactness. Flowers do not spring up beneath the feet of the devoted brethren who bear about his head. What Valentine does is to inhibit that which destroys the natural—the rodents, the drought, the plague[52]—and thereby frees nature to exert her powers. That Baudri's account should be devoid of references to St. Valentine's promotion of maternity is not entirely astonishing. In general, the fraternal orders were not in search of a saint with a thoroughly validated incubic reputation.

III

When St. Valentine next appears, the time is some two centuries later. As far as the present writers' admittedly limited knowledge extends, there exists no literary record of St. Valentine between Baudri de Bourgueil in the twelfth century and Oton de Grandson in the fourteenth.[53] What happened or did not happen to St. Valentine is simply unknown. However, some sort of continuum must be posited, because when he emerges in the fourteenth century it is as a fully developed and obviously recognizable personage—no poet found it necessary to explain who St. Valentine was. Fortunately, however, although knowledge concerning St. Valentine is absent during this very extensive gap in time, the genial resource of conjecture remains available. Hence it is possible to suppose that the evolution of the cult of St. Valentine followed in general the same course as the cult of the Lupercalia. Both moved with the evolution from a simple agricultural society to a highly sophisticated society with quite different values. The twelfth-century St. Valentine is a deity of the fields; the fourteenth-century St. Valentine is the patron saint of mannered love, which may exist in and for itself, or have as a natural adjunct fertility. How the transition was actually made is not apparent, but it may be further conjectured that it was through an existing association of long standing—love, the season of May, and the song of the birds. In the poetry of the troubadours, these three elements are constants. Thus in the famous "Lanquan li jorn" of Jaufré Rudel, all are found in the first four lines:

> When the days are long in May,
> I delight in the sweet song of distant birds,
> And when I am departed thence,
> There comes to me remembrance of a distant love.[54]

and in the immensely influential *Roman de la rose*, the opening scene of the dream contains the same three elements of May, the song of the birds, and love.[55] Hearing the birds, the Dreamer comes to the conclusion:

> Hard is the hert that loveth nought
> In May, whan al this mirth is wrought. . . . (85–86)[56]

Further, the song of the birds is said to constitute a "servise" to the God of Love.[57] To maintain his dignity, the God of Love required saints—as Chaucer learned to his cost[58]—and the saint was not infrequently sought out by the inhabitants of the natural world. St. Jerome had his lion, and St. Cuthbert his birds. As St.

Valentine was the patron saint of the natural world, so was the spring song of the birds symbolic of the resurgent forces of nature. Given the hierarchical and parallelistic pattern of medieval thought, Valentine, the natural saint, could hardly avoid becoming associated with the God of Love and the surroundings in which he lived—the verdure of May and the song of the birds. In his *L'Érotique des troubadours*, René Nelli comments on the rather unsaintly cult of Valentinage, and in so doing indicates the association of St. Valentine with the triplicity—love, May, song of birds:

In Valentinage, it is the birds who symbolize the renewal of the forces of love and of nature, for it was believed in the Middle Ages that the birds paired on the 14th of February.[14] And this belief has likewise played a major role in the elaboration of the love of May. . . . An attentive reading of the troubadours is sufficient to establish the fact that at the beginning of their poems, the song of birds breaks upon the scene more frequently than floral or plant settings or the murmur of flowing water. . . . The song of the birds is almost never absent, which is in no way astonishing, since it [the song of the birds] is charged with an almost objective erotic significance, and because it constitutes a sort of natural hymn to love.[59]

It must be observed, however, that Nelli nowhere states that the troubadours gave a place in their poetry to St. Valentine. The earliest text mentioned by him is Chaucer's *Parlement of Foules*.

From what has been adduced, the following conjectures may be made. The popularity of St. Valentine began at a time antecedent to 1120, with his taking on the characteristics of protector of the crops—a counter-sterility figure and, conversely, a fertility figure.[60] He was thus, head in hand, able to occupy the position of presiding saint of February 14, with its Christian heritage of the Purification and the Presentation, and its pagan heritage of the Lupercalia.[61] One may further conjecture that, as saint, Valentine was readily assimilable into the religion of love, and as natural saint, was assimilable into the traditional love poetry of the troubadours, where love had its celebrants—the songbirds—and its proper season—May.

Something further may perhaps be said of May, the month famed for its verdure and its flowers, because, through the agency of St. Valentine, it appears linked to February, a month not similarly famed.[62] In the *Parlement of Foules*, the garden in which the birds are to make their choice on St. Valentine's Day is comparable to the May-garden of the *Roman de la rose*. The walls of the garden are constructed of green stone (122); verdure and flowers are everywhere. The garden itself is situated on a "grene mede" (184); the trees are covered with leaves eternally as green as emerald (173–175); and the goddess Nature is enthroned "upon an hil of floures" (302). From the rondel in honor of Nature and St. Valentine which the birds sing at their departing —"Now welcome, somer, with thy sonne softe" (680)—the time of year would appear to be that immediately preceding summer, presumably May, and it is within this "place/ . . . that was so sote and grene" (295–296) that the birds choose their mates on St. Valentine's Day. In view of this disparity in weather, it is quite possible that it is not because the birds mate on February 14 that human beings follow their example, but rather because the association between St. Valentine and the birds had become so strong in observances of the vernal season that on the day liturgically designated as being given over to the veneration of St. Valentine, the birds were placed under the cruel presumption of overwhelming erotic emotions under the most inclement of conditions. In the Celtic calendar, the middle of February marks the beginning of spring[63] and is hence perhaps an appropriate time for symbolic mating, but as an actuality February 14 would differ little if at all from winter. Although amatory epistles on the occasion of St. Valentine's Day were certainly written, any mention of verdant fields, "jolie saison," or the like is difficult to find, simply because such phenomena were not in existence at that time of year. Because February 14 was the day of St. Valentine in legend, the birds were considered under the rigorous necessity of choosing their mates, but of actual amorous avian activity we hear nothing. As a patron saint of the natural world, St. Valentine obviously considered further demands, given the state of the weather, unsaintly.

Charles d'Orléans, a prisoner in England, looking out his window on St. Valentine's Day, wrote:

On this day of St. Valentine
When one must choose his mate,
I have chosen something little to my taste:
Rain, wind, and wretched roads.[64]

The state of the Valentine legend as Chaucer knew it is best represented by two French poets,[65] for differing reasons very closely connected with England. The first of these is Oton de Grandson (1340?–1397), a Savoyard nobleman, almost exactly Chaucer's contemporary, who served Edward III and Richard II in much the same capacities as did Chaucer.[66] The second is Charles, duc d'Orléans (1394–1465), quoted immediately above, whose poetic activity coincided, rather curiously, almost exactly with his capture at Agincourt and his subsequent imprisonment in England. The major part of his poetry was composed between 1415, the date of his capture, and 1441, the date of his release.[67] Hence it is possible to know through Grandson, the first of these poets, in what way Valentine figured in the poetry familiar to the English court in the time of Chaucer, and through Grandson's successor, Charles d'Orléans, what trends in Valentine poems were to become dominant. The amount of documentation afforded by Grandson and Charles d'Orléans is the more valuable, since the troubadour poets have much to say about May, love, and the song of birds, but nothing, so far as the present writers are aware, concerning St. Valentine.[68] Guillaume de Lorris, whose *Roman de la rose* was to become the model for virtually all subsequent amatory poetry of the Middle Ages, never mentions him. Gower,[69] knew of St. Valentine and associates him with May, but gives him little prominence. It would appear that Baudri de Bourgueil's seminal work fell on fertile ground but was extremely slow in germinating. In Oton de Grandson, Baudri found an effective if distant continuator.

Oton de Grandson was for his age an idyllic figure. He was of noble birth, and a knight of very considerable reputation. As lover of the "non pareille de France," though eternally unsuccessful, he was nevertheless eternally faithful. As a poet, he wrote only of love, and, in terms of his time, very successfully. His verse was particularly influential in Spain, but also much esteemed in

France and England. As is well known, Chaucer calls him in the *Complaint of Venus* the "floure of hem that make in Fraunce."

The reading of Grandson's poetry is a rather puzzling experience. From the oblivion into which his reputation fell, one is prepared for poetry which had a very powerful appeal to a taste which was and is no more. Yet the anticipated dullness never quite makes itself felt. If, on the other hand, one looks for an especially striking or moving poem, he does not find his search a rewarding one. Rarely is the mildly melancholic surface of Grandson's poetry disturbed by emotions the reader can accept as real; more rarely yet by humor. To sharpen what ought to be the dullness of his poems, Grandson writes almost entirely within a single genre, the "complainte," and within a single convention, the unloved yet ever faithful lover. As might be expected, Grandson's language is the established language of the genre and convention he is following. All in all, his poetry contains virtually nothing the twelfth-century troubadour had not already written. Thus his "complainte" is to his unattainable lady Isabel; his love is an agony which, unless his lady's mercy intervenes, can only end in death; his heart is punctured, may on occasion leap out through his eyes, and is constantly with his lady. So stated, Grandson's poetry would seem more likely to produce oblivion than emotion. However, within his constant form and convention, Grandson manages to bring together varying combinations of language with varying aspects of the convention he is dealing with, and to state them in a style whose sentiment, smoothness, and decorum seem to reflect the ideal of ordered manners the courtly world of his day so eagerly strove to attain.

Grandson's Valentine poems in general fit this pattern, but they seem as a group rather more interesting, because less formulaic, more inventive, and closer to the feelings of the human being, Grandson. The first of these is the *Complainte de St. Valentin*,[70] very possibly the first poem of Grandson's now extant. He here represents himself as inconsolably bewailing the death of his lady, a lady who must, in the natural order of things, have anteceded the Isabel of his subsequent poetry. As he utters his complaint to his dead lady, he sees St. Valentine hastening toward him to assuage his sorrow:

And the better to accomplish his design,
He [St. Valentine] brought with him the God of Love,
Who came up and took me by the hand,
And gently spoke to me.[71]

What the God of Love has to say is that, as his vassal, Oton cannot cease to love. Since his lady is dead, Oton is released from his obligations to her. Furthermore, the God of Love will reveal to him the lady most worthy to be loved—the "merveille de ce monde." Despite Oton's earlier protestations of inconsolability, he does gaze upon the lady, and at once accedes to the demands of his feudal obligations:

Thus did Love command it to be,
Whom it is my will and my duty to obey.
With the most perfect willingness,
I will to carry out all his will.
Therefore, without a moment of repentance,
I shall serve her to the end.
Thus, without deceit, did I promise him,
On the day of St. Valentine.[72]

Here Oton presents himself to us in a somewhat more human form than his customary guise of ideal perfection. The story of Tristan and Yseult, which he on occasion echoes, had long before set the pattern for the actions of the perfect lover in the situation in which Oton finds himself. At the beginning of the poem, he has, as is usual in his later poetry, declared death to be his only remedy. However, the God of Love has by direct pronouncement made clear what his ruling in Oton's case is. As a faithful servant to the God of Love, he has no choice but to obey.

Aside from revealing Oton's inclination toward love and delicately rationalized disinclination toward untimely death, the poem gives us one of the rare glimpses of how the fourteenth century conceived of St. Valentine. On his day, when love is the rule, St. Valentine quite properly intercedes in behalf of the bereaved and grief-stricken lover. However, his intercession brings in the God of Love himself, who thereupon assumes complete control over the action of the poem—to the exclusion of the saint. Although in the saint's legend, the power exerted by the saint is always understood to be of divine origin, it is the saint himself who holds the forefront of the drama and who himself performs the miracles. Valentine is here not much more than the God of Love's helper, who, when his errand is completed, may be dispensed with.

The somewhat depressed dignity of Valentine is indicated in another poem of Grandson's, the *Balade de Saint Valentin double*.[73] Here the poet, after complaining to the "non pareille" of his seven and a half years of service and the proximity of his death, suddenly turns to St. Valentine and requests an undefined miracle, possibly the extinction of the lover's customery allegorical antagonists—Dangier, Reffus, Paour, and Durte[74]—adding, beguilingly, the benefits which might accrue to the saint should this miracle become known:

> For by many you will make yourself adored
> And sought after by many a loyal lover,
> If in this case you stand true helper to me.[75]

The prayer does not radiate hope, nor is St. Valentine again mentioned. There would seem further to be an implication that the saint's miracles are not considered very reliable, and that the number of his worshippers may even stand in need of augmentation. One would like to believe he is here in the presence of that rarest of literary commodities—Grandsonian humor. In any case, the "noster Valentinus," the treasured miracle worker of Jumièges, is not the Valentine of Grandson.

One other aspect of St. Valentine which Grandson is useful in illuminating is the extent and constancy of the association between the saint and the birds. In Chaucer's three uses of St. Valentine— the *Complaynt d'Amours*, the *Complaint of Mars*, and the *Parlement of Foules*, most notably the last—St. Valentine is always associated with birds. This is not, however, true of Grandson. Of some eight Valentine poems, six are one form or another of the usual complaint, for which St. Valentine affords a convenient occasion. However, two are of a distinctly different type. In these the birds are not simply decorative, as in the troubadours, the trouvères, and the *Roman de la rose*; it is they who are the designated actors in the poem, and the poet is the bystander. The less interesting poem of the two is *À l'entrée de ma jeunesse*.[76] The situation presented is the familiar one of the poet's overhearing the lament of the forsaken lover, and asking him to tell all. The overheard lover explains that as a very young man he was deeply attracted by a falcon ("esprevier"), whom he had first seen the day following St. Valentine's Day. He persisted in his attempts to lure her, and eventually she swooped down upon his wrist. For a long time their bliss was complete—but alas! During that time his "enfance" terminated, and shortly thereafter he was seized by a mad passion to capture a "pelerin" falcon, who, unfortunately for him, was attracted to a splendid and obviously noble falcon ("tier-cellet"), and "c'estoit la paire." After some quite polite and absolutely non-Chaunteclerian lovemaking, they flew off. When he returned to look for the falcon who was his first and true love, the perch was empty. The lover then bitterly bewails the loss of his falcon through his own treachery. The whole of this story is of course the most unsophisticated of allegories, but what lends it interest is the curious fact that the poet-auditor is entirely unable to see through it. In fact he, Grandson, seems to intimate rather sternly that unrestrained bird-loving is, at its very best, irrational:

> It seems to me folly for anyone
> To get himself into such a state over a bird
> That he loses his strength and vigor,
> And goes about sighing night and day,[77]

and he continues in the same vein. It might be observed that a poet who cannot understand lovesickness over the loss of a falcon sounds very much like a poet who cannot understand lovesickness over the loss of a chess queen.[78]

If *À l'entrée de ma jeunesse* tells us something of the state of the Valentine legend in the fourteenth century, the second of Grandson's bird poems, the *Songe St. Valentin*,[79] tells us virtually nothing about St. Valentine, but presents us with a poem which Chaucer either thought well enough of—or found it expedient—to draw upon rather extensively in his early poetry, particularly in the *Parlement of Foules*.[80] This brings up the nature of the appeal of a poet who has manifestly not stood the test of time, and the influence—or lack of influence—of Grandson's poetry upon Chaucer, when the popularity of that poetry was at its peak. At the beginning of the present section, something was said of Grandson's style and of his popularity. The *Songe St. Valentin* makes it possible to be more specific concerning his style, his popularity, and the extent to which his poetry had meaning for the poet and apprentice philosopher, Geoffrey Chaucer.

The poem begins with a first-person narrative in which the poet, wearied by a night during which love has reft him of his rest, falls asleep in utter exhaustion on the morning of St. Valentine's Day. He dreams that he has left a diamond and a ruby in a grove, and, upon awakening, hastens to retrieve them. Instead of his jewels, however, he finds in the grove a gathering of the whole of birddom, presided over by an eagle, all engaged in choosing their mates on this the appointed day. Oton is challenged by the eagle to show cause why he should not be evicted *vi et armis,* since he gives no satisfactory indications of intention to mate. The same challenge is addressed by the presiding eagle to a peregrine falcon, who is perched alone upon a nearby tree, and is equally unbusy about making himself appear an acceptable mate. The answer of both to the eagle's challenge is the same—each has already made his choice, but his beloved has chosen to make herself—to him—inaccessible. To seek another mate would be betrayal. Not only are both answers the same, but both poet and falcon would seem to be means of presenting, under a very thin allegory, the amatory agonies of one Oton de Grandson.

The more one looks at these two poems, apparently rather different in kind, the more they come to resemble the rest of Grandson's poetry. Grandson as objective observer is Grandson the eternal complainant. What is on the surface a rather novel conception—birds as actors rather than as decorative devices— turns out to be part and parcel of the same tradition. The eagle is feminine,[81] and it is she who has rather clearly made the choice of her meek mate who sits passively beside her. What she is ruling over is an assemblage of birds, but what is decided is essentially a "demande d'amours," and the assemblage is thereby turned into a court of love.[82] Grandson is virtually without exception of a total sameness. Other poets, contemporary with him—one thinks of Machaut and Froissart—wrote at least as well and within the same tradition, but were quite overshadowed by him. What gave him his remarkable fame? Arthur Piaget, editor and virtual discoverer of Grandson's poetry, explains this phenomenon as follows:

One must not forget that the poetry of Grandson was intended for readers, and especially feminine readers, of the fourteenth century. In that era one entertained a different idea of poetry than that of the present day, just as one spoke of love in a different fashion. Lovers of "poetry" and lovers read and reread Grandson's verses in despite of their monotony, their poor rimes, their impoverished vocabulary. This poetry revealed a man, timid [in amatory affairs], excessive in sensibility, faithful to the death, having in his heart one single passion—to serve his lady. But this submissive lover, whose single value was love, was not a comfortable canon like Guillaume de Machaut, but a great lord who spent his life in battle, who had many times risked his life and was known in both the English and French armies as a redoubtable champion. To be a great lover and a great knight—these were in the Middle Ages two "professions" tightly bound together. The author of the *Livre des faicts du Mareschal Boucicaut* shows how: "Love takes away fear and replaces it with bravery, brings forgetfulness of labor, and grateful acceptance of what one must bear for the sake of the beloved . . . as one reads of Lancelot and Tristan, and of many others whom Love ennobled and caused to attain renown—and likewise in our own days . . . as one speaks of Messire Othe de Gransson."[83]

The true continuator of the poetry of Grandson was Charles d'Orléans. His father, Louis d'Orléans, was a great patron of the arts and a protector of the best-known poets of his period. By the age of ten, Charles was already composing poetry, but he had hardly made a beginning when the assassination of his father, procured by the Burgundians, required him to devote all his energies to a war of vengeance. In 1414, his partisans were successful, and he would then have had the opportunity, had Fortune been willing, for the pursuit of his poetic interests. That this was in fact his intention would appear from his having had sewn upon the sleeve of one of his robes the beginning of a poem now lost: "Madame, je suis plus joyeulx."[84] However, his long awaited joy was of exceedingly short duration. In 1415, he was captured at the battle of Agincourt, and for a quarter of a century England was to be the scene in which he was constrained to practice his poetic and amatory arts. Interestingly enough, Alice Chaucer, Duchess of Suffolk and daughter of Thomas Chaucer, was very possibly one of the ladies to whom he addressed his poems.[85]

Charles d'Orléans was the last great poet in the French courtly tradition, and unquestionably one of the most sophisticated. Unfortunately, he seems to have been limited by the circumstances of his life or by aristocratic poetic tradition, or by both, to essentially occasional poetry. Hence Valentine's Day received from him annual tributes, as did May 1. Unlike the May poems, however, the Valentine poems are bare of verdure and, with one exception, of birds.[86] They are sometimes vaguely bawdy, as when Charles is awakened on Valentine morning, not by the song of the birds but by the knock of his "butin" upon the door[87]—a situation rather comparable to that described in Ophelia's interesting ditty:

> To-morrow is Saint Valentine's day,
>   All in the morning betime,
> And I a maid at your window,
>   To be your Valentine.
> Then up he rose, and donned his clo'es,
>   And dupped the chamber door;
> Let in the maid, that out a maid
>   Never departed more.[88]

The rest of the poems deal with such matters as the collision of St. Valentine's Day and Lent; his "nonchaloir," or renunciation of the pursuit of love; his increasing cynicism at the conflict between the not-so-young poet and a day devoted to amorous observance. However, after his return to France in 1441, he did not abandon his long-established practice of writing poems in observance of St. Valentine's Day until virtually the end of his life. In one of his last poems, the vitriolic mood produced by his conflicting emotions gives birth to a line of an intensity rarely to be discovered in his poems:

> Vielle relique en viel satin . . .[89]

a line in which one finds it difficult to distinguish St. Valentine and Charles d'Orléans.

IV

Chaucer's Valentine was, then, a saint, executed at Rome in the third century and claimed by both Rome and Terni. In the two early lives, his principal attribute seems to have been that of miraculous healing. However, as successful claimant to the position successively held by the Lupercalia and the Purification of the Blessed Virgin, there must have been something more of the natural in the traditions surrounding him than is recorded in the early lives, or, alternatively, in the passage of time some sort of unrecorded natural tradition, later than the lives, must have accreted. In any case, by the early twelfth century the story of the translation of his head to Jumièges and the miracles attendant upon it had become established. While at Jumièges, Baudri de Bourgueil took down the story and the miracles, and gave the whole a credibility and literary acceptability which his position as bishop and fashionable man of letters almost uniquely qualified him to do. Baudri's account, however, did not gain the popularity one might have expected. From the early twelfth century to almost the late fourteenth St. Valentine seems to have been denied literary effulgence. It is perhaps during this gap in our knowledge of the Valentine tradition that through a combination of troubadour poetry and Jumièges monastic fervor, Valentine's association with bird-life and romantic love took place at a fashionable poetic level, and his position as friend of life and folk saint of holy matrimony—at least in England—took form at a lower social level. In any case, Valentine became the fashionable saint of lovers, and this was accomplished through the poetry of Oton de Grandson, whose verbal facility and personal embodiment of the ideals his poetry described made the name of St. Valentine as valid a piece of amatory verbal coinage as "noble yforged newe." However, Valentine is for Grandson something of a game, as Manly remarks, similar to the *Flower and the Leaf*.[90] Like Grandson, Charles d'Orléans made Valentine a kind of play saint, an occasion for poetic composition, and his connection with birds, or with any form of natural life, became severely attenuated.

For Chaucer, St. Valentine must have been essentially the creation of Grandson. He could obviously not have known Charles d'Orléans, but parallels in the *Book of the Duchess,* and the *Parlement of Foules,* as well as his explicit indebtedness in the *Complaint of Mars,* show that he had read Grandson thoroughly. He may very well have been indebted to the *Songe St. Valentin* for the idea of overcoming the inclement weather of St. Valentine's Day by incorporating it into a dream vision in which the state of the weather is the prerogative of the Dreamer.[91]

However, Chaucer's indebtedness to Grandson is limited to what one might call the mechanical arts—situations and poetic devices such as that suggested above. Chaucer did not follow the fashionable trend of toy saint and occasion for annual poetic effusion. The presiding deity of the *Parlement of Foules* is Nature, and Chaucer treats Valentine accordingly. It is upon his day that the great concourse of birds assembles, and must assemble—"So priketh hem Nature in hir corages."[92] Chaucer restores Valentine to nature and makes him again the natural saint he must have been.

NOTES

1. Douce's is the earliest such opinion the authors are aware of. The authority is a note of Skeat's, the source of which he does not reveal (I, 516). Douce is probably best known for his donation to the Bodleian Library of the important collection of manuscripts which bears his name. See *DNB.*

2. "Ad hos qui additi, prior a principe deo Ianuarius appellatus; posterior, ut idem dicunt scriptores, ab diis inferis Februarius appellatus, quod tum his paren[te]tur; ego magis arbitror Februarium a die februato, quod tum februatur populus, id est Lupercis nudis lustratur antiquum oppidum Palatinum gregibus humanis cinctum" (*De lingua latina,* trans. Roland G. Kent [Loeb Classics, Cambridge, Mass., 1938]. Chap. VI, 204–206). We have ventured to change the translation of "lustratur" in the above passage from "is passed around" to "is purified," as being more consonant with sense of the passage. However, the idea of purification has earlier been plainly stated, and Kent's translation has the advantage of bringing out the running of the Luperci about the old Palatine city. The most eminent Lupercus to run the course was Marc Antony, and the occasion one of singular importance—the offering of the crown to Caesar. For an account of the event, see Ovid's *Fasti,* ed. Sir James G. Frazer (Loeb Classics, Cambridge, Mass., 1931), pp. 391–392.

3. "Romulus," xxi, in *Lives,* trans. Bernadotte Perrin (Loeb Classics, London and New York, 1928), I, 157–159. Plutarch sees the feast as derived from an ancient Greek (Pelasgian) wolf cult, and connects it

with the "lupa," who nursed Romulus and Remus. The Luperci, however, seem not to have been simply "noble youths," but members of the two colleges of priests (later three) who conducted the Lupercalia. Ovid's account in *Fasti*, Bk. II, 267–452, is important. He organizes his narrative around the Romulus and Remus story, but interrelates both Faunus and Juno. For modern commentary on this very vexed subject, see Alberta M. Franklin, *The Lupercalia* (New York, 1921), the most extensive study; the articles "Lupa," "Lupercalia," "Luperci," and "Lupercus" in Pauly-Wissowa, *Real-Encyclopädie der klassischen Altertumswissenschaft* (Stuttgart, 1927), XIII, 1814–1842; and the brief but very useful summary of Frazer in his edition of the *Fasti*, pp. 389–394.

4. P. 19. Italics added.

5. For immediate reference, we have found the *New Century Classical Handbook* (ed. Catherine B. Avery and Jotham Johnson [New York, 1962]) very useful. See entries under gods named.

6. The most frequently quoted authority for the idea that the Lupercalia had as its purpose the fertility of the crops is one Joannes Laurentius Lydus (490–565?), a Byzantine antiquary, whose particular distinction lies in his knowledge of works on Roman institutions and customs now lost. Hence in his *De mensibus*, a work on Roman calendar customs, he quotes one Anysius, whose treatise had the same title as his own. The quotation (a translation from the Greek in which Lydus wrote) reads as follows: "Anysius autem in libro De mensibus Februum inferum esse Thuscorum lingua ait, et coli a Lupercis pro fructuum incremento" (*Joannes Lydus*, ex recognitione Immanuelis Bekkeri [Bonn, 1837], pp. 61–62, in *Corpus scriptorum historiae Byzantinae*). This would seem to describe some expiatory rite to the gods of the lower world; Ovid declares (II, 31–32) that the Luperci purify the land with their accustomed instruments of lustration: "pelle Luperci/ omne solum lustrant idque piamen habent" (*Fasti*, ed. Frazer, p. 58).

7. This idea, which runs throughout Franklin's work, is perhaps most succinctly stated in her concluding "Résumé": "From their remote ancestors they [the Ligurians] had inherited a religion that was mainly of fear, and that sought to propitiate the invisible forces that seemed lurking to do harm" (*Lupercalia*, p. 96).

8. Franklin takes the reduction of the serpent, which was the original deity of Lanuvium, to a symbolic appendage of Juno Sospita (see note 9 below) as the grafting upon an ancient cult of a newer and more powerful one; i.e., the goat-goddess, and proceeds to make an analogy with Juno and the Lupercalia (*ibid.*, pp. 58–59). However, it is doubtful that the wolf was ever so obscured; cf. "lupa," the nurse of Romulus and Remus; "Lupercal," shrine and cave where they were nursed; "Lupercus," a remote fertility god who seems at least to have given his name to the feast of the Lupercalia; "Luperci," the celebrants of the Lupercalia. However, the question is simply one of degree, and the overlaying process in each case seems evident.

9. The shrine of Juno Sospita at Lanuvium was a famous and prized one, and a condition of the peace following the Latin War (340–338

B.C.) was that her worship at Lanuvium was to be shared by the Romans. Juno Sospita (Protectrice) was a war goddess, but her costume, involving goat horns and skin, associated her with the fertility of the goat. A temple to her was built at Rome in 194 B.C., the same year temples to two other goat-deities—Faunus and Veiovis—were dedicated (*ibid.*, pp. 58–59). Juno Sospita was incorporated into the state religion of Rome, just as Lanuvium was incorporated into the Roman state (Pauly-Wissowa, XIII, 1120). The story of the ancient serpent is told by Propertius, among others, (*Elegies*, IV, 8, ed. and trans. H. E. Butler [London and New York, 1924], p. 315).

10. Franklin argues from the Greek "Lycaeus" and the Latin "Lupercus" that, after propitiation ceremonies had lost meaning, the divinities, by a rather devious process, became beneficent and were understood as protectors of the flocks (*Lupercalia*, pp. 21–48).

11. *Ibid.*, pp. 22–23.

12. *Ibid.*, pp. 19, 39.

13. *Ibid.*, pp. 41–42. For the stoning, see pp. 40–41.

14. The reference is of course to Plutarch. See above, p. 109.

15. See Franklin, *Lupercalia*, chaps. VII and VIII. Her conclusions may be found summarized on p. 80. Also, *Fasti*, ed. Frazer, p. 390.

16. "et dea per lucos mira locuta suos: /Italidas matres," inquit, "sacer hircus inito" (*Fasti*, II, 440–441; ed. Frazer, p. 88). For the whole account, see Frazer, pp. 88–89.

17. Pauly-Wissowa, "Lupercalia," col. 1824; Franklin, *Lupercalia*, pp. 62–63; *Fasti*, ed. Frazer, p. 390. The temple of Juno Sospita at Lanuvium had a statue of the goddess in which she was clothed in a goatskin.

18. *Fasti*, II, 31–32; ed. Frazer, p. 58. See note 6 above.

19. P. 394.

20. The Eastern Church had long considered January 6 as the date of the birth of Christ. When December 25 became the established date, the date of the Purification of the Virgin had to be moved ahead to February 2, because of the traditional "churching" of women that occurred forty days after childbirth. However, although this would seem quite relevant to the Eastern Church calendar, the question arises as to why it should affect the Western, which had always observed Christmas on December 25. The reason would seem to be that Candlemas was a feast of the Eastern Church imported to Rome and celebrated there prior to its official acceptance into the liturgy. It was probably observed in the Western Church, as in the Eastern, on February 14, until it was incorporated into the official liturgical calendar of Rome as February 2 (*New Catholic Encyclopedia* [New York, 1967], III, 23; 656). In England, references to "old Candlemas day" are not infrequent.

21. See note 20 above, and L. Duchesne, *Christian Worship: Its Origin and Evolution*, trans. M. L. McClure, 5th ed. (London, 1923), pp. 271–273.

22. *Encyclopedia of Religion and Ethics*, ed. James Hastings (New York, 1911), III, 190.

23. *Ibid.*, III, 190–191; Archdale A. King, *Liturgies of the Primatial Sees* (Milwaukee, 1957), pp. 375–376.

24. J. Vriend, *The Blessed Virgin in the Medieval Drama of England* (Purmerend, Holland, 1928), p. 115.

25. Hastings, *Encyclopedia*, III, 193.

26. Vriend, *Blessed Virgin in Medieval Drama*, pp. 114–123.

27. See note 20 above.

28. Paris, 1863–1883.

29. "Crede ergo filium Dei, verum Deum esse, Jesum Christum, et omnibus renuncia simulacris, et videbis salvum filium tuum" (*Acta sanctorum*, I, 757, col. 2, sec. 3).

30. "audivi tamen, quod unusquisque per fidem suam salvetur, nec prosit alteri alterius fides, nec obesse poterit alteri alterius infidelitas" (*ibid.*).

31. "Quoniam sapientia mundi, in qua tu magister esse videris, stultitia est apud Deum, et non potes tam perfecte credere, quam fides ipsa deposcit . . . da mihi fidem tuam sub hac pollicitatione, ut si filius tuus per meam fidem salvetur; tu per salutem filii tui cum omni domo tua convertaris ad Christum" (*ibid.*, I, 758, col. 1, sec. 7). It is worth noting the incorporation into the Valentine legend of II Cor. iii, 19: "Sapientia enim huius mundi stultitia est apud Deum."

32. "abjicientes studia humanae sapientiae, ita se contulerunt ad Dominum, ut ultra penitus nihil humanarum legerent litterarum: sed conversi ad Dominum, spiritalibus se studiis tradiderunt magistro, cujus non tantum verba, sed etiam facta probarentur mirabilia" (*ibid.*, I, 758, col. 2, sec. 9).

33. "monachorum Gemmeticensium puram relationem *pro auctoritate* recompensans, litteris perstringere procuravi, quod de capitis translatione *audivi*: nec non et pauca quae de multis miraculis, quae per eum [Valentinum] Dominus operari dignatus est, ipsorum testimonio credulus *cognovi*" (*ibid.*, I, 759, col. 2, sec. 1).

34. "Hoc ex ipsius [Hugonis] ore hausimus, Fratribus aliis, qui cum eo illud attestati sunt, audientibus" (*ibid.*, I, 762, col. 1, sec. 17). The same miracle is again recorded toward the end; in this case, however, the beneficiary was the Prior (*ibid.*, I, 762, col. 2, sec. 19).

35. "Impium est silere de Valentino, pium est autem, sicut coactus fuerit, de Valentino loqui. Taciturnitatis impiae et ingratitudinis redarguendi sunt, et praecipue sui, qui vident haec et alia, et silent, qui contegunt Valentini gloriam, quem decet publice commendare. Corrigant igitur culpam suam et loquantur, adjiciant scriptis scripta, quia summus Opifex non cessat adjicere miraculis miracula" (*ibid.*, I, 761, col. 2, sec. 13). The term "sui" would seem to refer to brothers of the abbey of Jumièges, who suffer from indolence in proclaiming the merits of the saint.

36. This is a summary of a rather extensive narrative which occupies something like the equivalent of a full column (I, 759, col. 2). The marginal commentary reads: "Obtinetur a Sacerdote Romam profecto caput Sancti Valentini Martyris; defertur Gemmeticum; deponitur absque veneration in theca eburnea, quibusdam dubitantibus."

37. "Vade, inquit, et dic Fratribus, ut caput nostrum, de quo quidam ambigunt (Valentinus siquidem ego sum) per agros et regionem istam deferant, compita vel plateas circumeant: quia revera Deus eis propi-

tiabitur, si nostri ex hoc nunc festinius reminiscentur" *(ibid.,* I, 760, col. 1, sec. 5).

38. "Omnipotens etenim, ad ostendendam cari sui virtutem, illum exterminatorem cuneum exterminabat, et Valentini sui nomen per hoc propagabat" *(ibid.,* I, 760, col. 1, sec. 6).

39. "Herbae marcuerant, segetes exalbuerant, quoniam terram intempesta siccitas siccaverat: omnis ager pulverulentus sterilitatem minabatur, et omnis homo timoratus conquerebatur" *(ibid.,* I, 761, col. 1, sec. 12). For the rather specialized meaning of "timoratus," see *Harper's Latin Dictionary.*

40. "Ea re nudus aer modicum quid exalbuit, et nubium densitas latices suos sustinuit, et tempus illis Fratribus redeundi opportunitatem permisit. Revertebantur, et pluvias imminentes reverebantur: nec tamen a pluviarum elapsu fatigabantur: videlicet quae magis stupeas, pluviae a dextra et a laeva ipsis videntibus cadebant, nec tamen processionem offendebant" *(ibid.,* I, 761, col. 1–2, sec. 12).

41. "Valentino Presbytero Interamnensi" *(ibid.,* I, 759, col. 2, sec. 2). By choosing one term from the title "priest of Rome," and a second from "bishop of Terni," a composite Valentine is made to emerge.

42. "sacerdotali decoratus indumento" *(ibid.,* I, 760, col. 1, sec. 5). However, the term "sacerdotalis" may here have a more inclusive meaning than "priestly" in a technical sense.

43. "nostrum Valentinum" *(ibid.,* I, 761, col. 1, sec. 11).

44. See article "Jumièges" in *New Catholic Encyclopedia*; also the chapter "The Ecclesiastical Revival," in David C. Douglas, *William the Conqueror* (Berkeley, 1966), pp. 105–132; especially pp. 105–118.

45. Douglas, *William the Conqueror,* p. 111, and authorities there cited (note 2).

46. *Ibid.,* p. 209.

47. Robert of Jumièges played a very lively part in the struggle between Edward the Confessor and Earl Godwine. Against Godwine he was alternately successful and unsuccessful. He arrived in England in 1043, and was forced to flee in 1052. He has been termed head of the Norman faction which opposed Godwine. See *DNB.*

48. See *Les Oeuvres poétiques de Baudri de Bourgueil,* ed. Phyllis Abrahams (Paris, 1926).

49. "Adèle, comtesse de Blois, fille de Guillaume le Conquérant, et Cécile sa soeur, abbesse de Caën, très-versées l'une et l'autre dans les lettres, l'honorèrent de leur amitié" *(Histoire littéraire de la France,* XI, 97).

50. Franklin, *Lupercalia,* p. 49.

51. *Fasti,* ed. Frazer, p. 394. See also p. 392.

52. In the *Life* discussed earlier (pp. 114–118), the central event of the narrative is St. Valentine's healing of Chaeremon. In the *Veneration,* this aspect of St. Valentine receives only irregular notice and little emphasis (see pp. 118–121 above). Baudri's real emphasis is upon St. Valentine's relation to the natural—his preservation of the crops from the rodents, and his bringing down rain upon the drought-stricken earth—this again a preservation of the crops. The association of rain-bringing with the earth divinity is obviously a very early one.

53. Since St. Valentine remained in the liturgy until the second half of the present century, liturgical notices no doubt exist. However, since the present writers' concern is primarily literary, no study of other possible appearances of St. Valentine has been made.

54.
> Lanquan li jorn son lonc en may
> M'es belhs dous chans d'auzelhs de lonh,
> E quan mi suy partitz de lay
> Remembra · m d'un' amor de lonh . . . (1–4)

(*Les Chansons de Jaufré Rudel*, ed. Alfred Jeanroy, 2nd. ed. [Paris, 1965], pp. 12–13).

55. Lines 45–81, ed. Ernest Langlois (Paris, 1920), II, 3–5.

56. Chaucer's supposed translation (*Works*, p. 566).

57. Lines 661–664 (*Roman*, ed. Langlois, II, 34–35). To say that the birds sing to the God of Love may be going too far, but given the presence of the God of Love, his controlling power (lines 865–872), and the general earthly-paradise tone, the assumption may be permissible.

58. The reference is to the penance imposed upon Geoffrey for his heresies against the God of Love, the chief of them being the writing of *Troilus and Criseyde*. He is to compose a kind of *Legenda aurea* of those women who have died faithful to love, and hence have attained sainthood in the religion of love. The "glorious legende" is, of course, the *Legend of Good Women*. The reality behind the fiction and Chaucer's feelings on the burden of the *Legend* imposed upon him are well treated by E. T. Donaldson (*Chaucer's Poetry* [New York, 1958], pp. 956–959).

59. "Dans le Valentinage ce sont les oiseaux qui symbolisent le renouvellement des forces d'amour de la nature, car on croyait, au Moyen-âge, que les oiseaux s'appariaient à la Saint-Valentin, le 14 février. Et cette croyance . . . a joué également un grand rôle dans l'élaboration de l'amour de mai. . . . Il suffit de relire attentivement les troubadours pour constater qu'ils font intervenir beaucoup plus souvent, au début de leurs poèmes, le chant des oiseaux que le décor floral et vegetal ou le murmure des eaux vives. . . . Le chant des oiseaux n'en est presque jamais absent, ce qui n'a rien d'étonnant, puisqu'il est chargé d'une signification érotique presque objective et qu'il constitue une sorte d'hymne naturel à l'amour" ([Toulouse, 1963], pp. 37–38).

60. Nelli, *L'Érotique des troubadours*, p. 37.

61. See Karl Löffler, *Schwäbische Büchmalerei* (Augsburg, 1928), plate 24. "Valentinus halt in der Linken die Martyrerpalme, in der Rechten sein abgeschlagenes Haupt" (p. 49). The drawing is in the form of a wheel, in the center of which is the Presentation in the Temple, with the caption "Purificatio Mariae."

62. In England, the evidence that there was a direct association between St. Valentine and the month of May is slight, yet existent. Gower's *Cinkante Balades*, for instance, does seem to indicate such an association. In Balade xxxiv, he first states Valentine's control over the erotic instincts of the birds:

> Saint Valentin l'amour et la nature
> De toutz oiseals ad en governement . . . (1–2)

At the beginning of Balade xxxv, he speaks of St. Valentine's day as a day of choosing, and he speaks of the birds, likening his lady to "la fenix souleine." He then ends Balade xxxv in lines highly reminiscent of the *Parlement of Foules,* and continues on into Balade xxxvi and hence into May, carrying with him all the principal characters of the *Parlement*:

> XXXV. Chascun Tarcel gentil ad sa falcoun,
> Mais j'ai faili de ceo q'avoir voldroie:
> Ma dame, c'est le fin de mon chancoun,
> Qui soul remaint ne poet avoir grant joie. (21–24)

> XXXVI. Pour comparer ce jolif temps de Maii,
> Jeo le dirrai semblable a Paradis;
> Car lors chantont et Merle et Papegai,
> Les champs sont vert, les herbes sont floris,
> Lors est Nature dame du paiis;
> Dont Venus poignt l'amant au tiel assai,
> Q'encontre amour n'est qui poet dire Nai. (1–7)

(John Gower, *Complete Works,* ed. G. C. Macaulay [Oxford, 1899–1902], I, 365–366.) The capitalization of "Nature" (xxxvi, 5) is not to be attributed to the editor. The obvious solution to the February-May problem would seem to be pledging on St. Valentine's Day and amorous disport in May. Such an arrangement seems to be present in the *Cuckoo and the Nightingale.* The birds trip out of their nests, and sing their "service" to May. Then, in accordance with their earlier February choice:

> They proyned hem, and made[n] hem right gay,
> And daunseden, and lepten on the spray,
> And evermore two and two in-fere;
> Right so as they had chosen hem to-yere
> In Feverere, on seint Valentynes day. (76–80)

(*Chaucerian and Other Pieces,* ed. W. W. Skeat (Oxford, 1897), p. 350). Vol. VII (Supplement) to *Complete Works of Geoffrey Chaucer,* ed. W. W. Skeat (Oxford, 1894). In France, *Valentinage* appears to have carried over from February to May, and from century to century. *Valentinage* appears to have been more or less frankly adulterous, and as late as the seventeenth century, Jean-Pierre Camus, Bishop of Belley (Savoy) attacked it in his *Diotrephe, histoire valentine* (Lyons, 1626), stressing the fact that the husband was forbidden to deny the Valentine, chosen in February, access to his wife over so long a period of time that the survival of virtue seemed unlikely. If we are to accept Nelli's analysis, *Valentinage* was very much a part of the love of May (*L'Érotique des troubadours,* pp. 37–39).

63. "[February] was sometimes divided into two halves, named, the first, the winter *Faoilleach,* the second, the spring *Faoilleach*" (*British Calendar Customs,* ed. M. Macleod Banks [London, 1939], II, 142).

64.
> A ce jour de saint Valentin,
> Que l'en prent per par destinee,
> J'ay choisy, qui tresmal m'agree,
> Pluye, vent et mauvais chemin . . . (1–4)

("Rondeau cx," in Charles d'Orléans *Poésies*, ed. Pierre Champion [Paris, 1956], II, 353). Lydgate describes the "blisful night" of St. Valentine: "In Fevrier, whan the frosty mone/Was horned . . ." ("The Flour of Curtesye," lines 1–2, in Skeat, *Chaucerian and Other Pieces*, p. 266).

65. What is forthcoming from the English poets Gower and Lydgate has already been indicated (see notes 62 and 64 above). Until after Chaucer, there is little in English concerning Valentine. This contrasts with the very considerable amount available from the fifteenth century onwards.

66. For the life of Grandson and the definitive edition of his poetry, see Arthur Piaget, *Oton de Grandson* (Lausanne, 1941); for his relationship to the English court and his influence on Chaucer, see Haldeen Braddy, *Chaucer and the French Poet Graunson* (Baton Rouge, 1947), and articles cited there.

67. The excellent edition of Champion (cited in note 64 above) gives an informative life, and a careful chronology of the poems. A brief but more critically oriented study by Daniel Poirion is to be found in the *Dictionnaire des lettres francaises: Moyen Age* (Paris, 1964).

68. See p. 125 above.

69. See note 62 above.

70. Piaget, *Grandson*, pp. 183–193.

71.
> Et, pour mieulx son fait acomplir,
> Le dieu amoureux admena,
> Qui par la main me vint saisir
> Et doulcement m'araisonna . . . (93–96)

(*Ibid.*, p. 186.)

72.
> Amours l'a ainsi commandé,
> A qui vueil et doy obeir.
> De tresparfaicte voulenté,
> Veuil tout son vouloir acomplir.
> Pour ce, san jamaiz repentir,
> La serviray jusqu'a la fin.
> Ainsi lui promectz sans mentir,
> Le jour de la Saint Valentin. (265–272)

(*Ibid.*, p. 193.) The "her" of line 6 is presumably the "merveille" he has just seen; the "him" of the following line, the God of Love. The puns on "will" are such that the reader needs the reassurance that this is in fact an early poem.

73. *Ibid.*, pp. 256–258.

74. See "Le Souhait de Saint Valentin" (*ibid.*, p. 204, line 53). The terminology indicates the continuing pervasive influence of Guillaume de Lorris's first part of the *Roman de la rose*, written almost a century and a half earlier.

75.   Car de plusieurs vous ferez aourer
           Et requerir de maint loyal amant,
           Se en ce cas vous m'estes bien aidant. (42–44)

(*Ibid.*, p. 257.)

76. Piaget, *Grandson*, pp. 428–434. This is not in actuality a separate poem, but part of the *Le Livre messire Ode*, a kind of autobiographical sentimental novel in verse, interspersed with various incidents. Since the birds are rather transparent allegories for human beings, we have altered the genders accordingly.

77.   Il me semble que c'est folour
           Pour ung oysel mener tel fin
           Que d'en perdre force et vigour
           En souspirant soir et matin. (1364–1367)

(*Ibid.*, p. 435.)

78. The allusion of course is to the failure of the Dreamer in the *Book of the Duchess* to comprehend the Black Knight's allegory of having lost his queen in a chess game. This parallel does not seem to have been remarked. Braddy (*Graunson*, p. 59) makes a list of parallels of which this is not one.

79. Piaget, *Grandson*, pp. 309–323.

80. Braddy has an extensive discussion of Chaucer's use of the *Songe* (*Graunson*, pp. 64–66, 72, 86).

81. Lines 120–121: "L'aigle qui bien l'apparcevoit,/Comme celle qui cler y voit . . ." (Piaget, *Grandson*, p. 313). See also lines 73, 306. Genders are less clearly defined in the falcon love story (*ibid.*, pp. 313–319).

82. For courts of love, see W. A. Neilson, *The Origins and Sources of the Court of Love* (London, 1899). He discusses Grandson (p. 75), but does not seem to make this point.

83. "Comment expliquer le succès de Grandson, en France, en Angleterre, en Espagne? Il serait difficile, malgré toute la sympathie qu'inspire l'auteur du *Livre messire ode*, de ratifier le jugement de Chaucer qui le tenait pour un grand poète ou du moins pour le plus grand poète de son temps. Mais il ne faut pas oublier que les poésies de Grandson étaient destinées à des lecteurs et surtout à des lectrices du XIVe siècle. A cette époque, on se faisait de la poésie une autre idée qu'aujourd'hui, comme on dissertait de l'amour d'une autre manière. Les amateurs de poetrie et les amoureux lisaient et relisaient les vers de Grandson, en dépit de leur monotonie, de leurs pauvres rimes, de leur pauvre syntaxe et de leur pauvre vocabulaire. Ces poésies révélaient un homme timide, sensible à l'excès, fidèle jusqu'à la mort, n'ayant dans le coeur qu'une seule passion, servir sa dame. Or cet amoureux soumis et total n'était pas un confortable chanoine comme Guillaume de Machaut, mais un grand seigneur qui passait son temps à se battre, qui avait maintes fois risqué sa vie et qui était connu comme un champion redoutable dans les armées anglaise et française. Grand amoureux, grand capitaine, s'étaient, au moyen âge, deux 'mestiers' étroitement unis. L'auteur du *Livre des faicts du Mareschal Boucicaut* montre comment: 'Amours oste paour et donne hardement, fait oublier toute peine et

prendre en gré le travail que on porte pour la chose aimée. . . . Si comme on lit de Lancelot, de Tristan et de plusieurs autres que Amours fist bons et a renommée attaindre, et mesmement en noz vivans . . . si comme on dit de messire Othe de Gransson' " (Piaget, *Grandson*, pp. 176–177, note 2).

84. Champion, *Poésies*, I, xxiii.

85. *Ibid.*, I, v.

86. By this is meant the actual presence of birds, as in Grandson's *Songe St. Valentin*, or of the poet's hearing their song.

87. "Rondeau CCXLIX" (*ibid.*, II, 433).

88. Shakespeare, *Hamlet*, IV, v, 46–53 (ed. John Dover Wilson, 2nd ed. [Cambridge, 1936], p. 99).

89. "Rondeau CCLXXVI" (Champion, *Poesies,* II, 449).

90. J. M. Manly, "What is the *Parlement of Foules?*," in *Festschrift für Lorenz Morsbach* (Halle, 1913); No. 50 in *Studien zur englischen Philologie*.

91.   Th' air of that place so attempre was
      That nevere was ther grevaunce of hot ne cold . . .

(*Parlement,* lines 204–205.) The air was imported via Boccaccio's *Teseida*. See Robinson's note to lines 183 ff. (*Works*, p. 794).

92. I [A], 11 (*Works*, p. 17). Compare Nature's address to the birds in *Parlement,* line 319: "as I prike yow with pleasaunce" (*Works*, p. 315).

9

How Dares Collaborated with Dictys

GUIDO DELLE COLONNE'S *Historia destructionis Troiae* is a "very curious, very strange" work, as C. S. Lewis says in reference to Martianus Capella's *De nuptiis*. Like Martianus, Guido wrote when he was old; like Martianus he was a scholar and a pedant; and like Martianus he produced a work that became for later ages both a textbook and a quarry. Boccaccio mined it for his *Filostrato*, Chaucer both the *Historia* and the *Filostrato* for his *Troilus and Criseyde*. Though at a considerable remove, Shakespeare, in *Troilus and Cressida*, is not without his debt to Guido.

Like Geoffrey of Monmouth's celebrated and rather comparable *Historia regum Britanniae*, Guido's *Historia* is not devoid of difficulties. One of the more curious problems to be encountered in the *Historia* occurs in the Prologue, where Guido firmly rejects Homer and Virgil as reliable sources for any account of the Trojan war, and states that it is his intention to depend exclusively on two eye-witnesses: Dictys, who was present throughout on the Greek side, and Dares, who witnessed all from the Trojan side.[1] Moreover, he intends to translate these immediate sources directly, rather than use an earlier Latin version by one Cornelius, who, out of an undue concern for brevity, "improperly omitted those particulars of this history which are best able to attract the minds of its auditors."[2] In its general outlines, what Guido purports to be doing is thus pretentiously clear. However, when the reader comes to a detailed consideration of Guido's Prologue, it is not easy to determine with any exactitude what he meant the reader to understand as his distinctive accomplishment. What he did in fact do is a matter of scholarly record, and one not particularly creditable to Guido or his profession: he rendered back into authoritative Latin Benoit de St. Maure's *Roman de Troie*, a translation into Old French of a concordance of Dares, *De excidio Troiae historia*, and Dictys, *Ephemeris belli Trojani*—the same two sources which Guido claims as his very own but,—of course, with omitted acknowledgment.[3] Precisely what Guido wished his reader to understand as his personal historiographical triumph is the problem to be dealt with here.

The problem lies first of all in the obscurity of Guido's language, particularly in the Prologue to the *Historia*. It is in the Prologue that Guido discusses his great undertaking, and it is here that the difficulty begins:

Sed ut fidelium ipsius ystorie vera scribentium scripta apud occidentales omni tempore futuro vigeant successive, in utilitatem eorum precipue qui gramaticam legunt, ut separare sciant verum a falso de hiis que de dicta ystoria in libris gramaticalibus sunt descripta, ea que per Dytem Grecum et Frigium Daretem, qui tempore Troyani belli continue in eorum exercitibus fuere presentes et horum que viderunt fuerunt fidelissimi relatores, in presentem libellum per me iudicem Guidonem de Columpna de Messana transsumpta legentur, *prout in duobus libris eorum inscriptum quasi una vocis consonantia inventum est in Athenis.*[4]

Mary E. David's revised translation of this passage is perhaps as close to a literal one as the convolutions of Guido's Latin allow:

However, so that the true accounts of the reliable writers of this story may endure for all future time hereafter among western peoples, especially for the use of those who read Latin, so that they may know how to separate the true from the false among the things which are written of the said story in Latin books, those things which were taken over by me, Justice Guido delle Colonne of Messina, from Dictys the Greek and Dares the Phrygian, who were at the time of the Trojan War continually present in their armies and were the most faithful reporters of those things which they saw, are collected in the present little book, *just as it was found written with, so to speak, one agreement of voice, in their two books in Athens.* [Italics ours.][5]

Now let us consider another translation of the italicized passage, this from Anne G. Johnson's recent translation of the *Historia*: ". . . just as the record of them was found in Athens in two books, written as it were in complete agreement."[6] Mrs. David's first translation of this concluding passage was as follows: ". . . just as it was written in their two books which were found in Athens and in which there is an agreement as with one voice."[7] It may be noted that all three translations manifest a curious blend of singular and plural: "it was" or "record . . . was" occurring in juxtaposition to a reference to what appear to be two separate and distinct books. In her revised translation, Mrs. David no longer reads "two books [found] at Athens," but rather "it" is found "in their two books."

Moreover, the later "one agreement of voice" is closer to what Guido wrote than "an agreement as with one voice" and certainly closer than "in complete agreement." Furthermore, "one agreement of voice" is possibly suggestive of co-operation rather than of circumstantial similarity. Guido's phrase, "una vocis consonantia," is in fact a crux, and a difficult one. Dr. Johnson, whose translation has previously been noted, has also recognized the problems posed by the passage:

The Latin here is difficult to translate. Guido seems to be saying that both Dares and Dictys said the same thing. This, of course, is not true; but Guido has many of his facts in this preface wrong and probably had not at this point seen either of the two books he refers to.[8]

In an earlier study, an attempt was made to examine in some detail the problem of precisely what it was that Guido meant by this statement concerning Dares and Dictys. The hypothesis there arrived at was stated as follows:

This passage has been taken to mean that Guido thought, mistakenly, that in their accounts of the Trojan War, Dares and Dictys agree "as with one voice" [Mrs. David's first translation of the phrase]. Aside from the fact that this would flatly contradict Guido's own epilogue in which he relates in detail the significant points on which Dares and Dictys differ in their description of the actual fall of Troy (beginning with the treason of Antenor and Aeneas), it appears to me that Guido is referring to his *source* as a harmony, a combination, of the histories of Dares and Dictys: notice that the facts to be found in Dares and Dictys ("vera . . . scripta," "ea") are taken over ("transsumpta") by Guido in his book ("presentem libellum"), *just as* in *their* two books—but their two books written just like Guido's own, as *one* ("prout in duobus libris eorum *inscriptum quasi una vocis consonantia* inventum est in Athenis"—italics ours). . . . According to Guido, as I read him, not their *two* books, but the combination of them ("inscriptum quasi una vocis consonantia") was found in Athens. Now, Benoit's *Roman*, Joseph of Exeter's *De Bello Troiano*, and Albert of Stade's *Troilus* are of precisely this nature, a consonance of Dares and Dictys. . . . In other words, Guido pretends to be the translator of the original concordance of Dares and Dictys, a concordance that he assumed to be behind both Benoit's *Roman*, which he never mentions, and Joseph's Latin poem, which he mentions only to belittle. . . . As regards the problem raised by Guido's notion of the origins of the Troy Story as to who made this concordance, a sixteenth-century reader of the *Laud Troy Book* seems to have solved it to his own satisfaction. An inscription from that century on the first page of the *Laud Troy Book* reads as follows: "Dares a troian haralte and dictus a grecian haralte writt this book in Greek and lost it in Athens and there it was found by Guido de Columpnia a notary of Rome and digested into lattyn." According to this, the original concordance was no less than the original work, written as a joint effort by Dares and Dictys! One has a pleasant picture of the two erstwhile enemies getting together after the war to produce a work of superlative historical accuracy, combining as it would the points of view of both sides.[9]

In the course of subsequent research, the third volume of Alfonso el Sabio's *General estoria*, particularly that section containing the history of the Trojan war, attracted the authors' attention.[10] Since the *Estoria* is somewhat earlier than Guido's *Historia* (*ca.* 1270 as against 1287) and offers a detailed version of the composition of the Dares-Dictys concordance in complete agreement with the brief notation scribbled in the sixteenth-century *Laud Troy Book*, the *Estoria* may be taken as a complete and reliable rendering of a very extensive tradition. A translation of the relevant passages contained in the chapter "Of those who composed this history" follows:

> With that Antenor of Troy, who was a man of power and of the grand manner, there was also a good Trojan clerk named Dares. And when he saw the deeds of the Greeks and knew those of the Trojans, he understood that it was a great matter and one long to endure. And so he concentrated all his attention on keeping his eyes on the facts of Troy, how they came about, and wrote them all down. And in the Greek host there was also another good master clerk. And they called this one Dictys, and he was an astute man and well informed.
>
> And after the destruction of Troy, these two, Dares and Dictys, found themselves thrown together. And since they were good and learned men, when they began to speak they understood each other and became companions. And in their companionship they went on speaking together, and came to the matter of Troy, and they marvelled at such an event as that was, and at such destruction and so great a massacre of men. And they came to the conclusion that it would be a very good thing if someone should write it all down. And then Dares said: "All that was done in Troy from the beginning to the end I saw very well and know it." And when Dictys saw that, he said: "All that the Greeks did I also saw, and was in the midst of it all, and know it very well." And then they both agreed as one that they would write this history; and they did it, and they wrote it in Greek.
>
> And because these two wise gentlemen, Dares of Troy and Dictys of Greece, made themselves perfect in knowledge of the whole matter of Troy—the one [being] with the Trojans and the other with the Greeks, and there made this writing—good and wise men conclude that this history, as we have told it here, is the truest that there is.[11]

In the light of this description of the dual composition of the authoritative history of Troy, the obscurity of Guido's account is cleared up, and the conjecture, mentioned earlier, verified. We now know that before Guido wrote, a tradition concerning the composition of an authoritative history of the Trojan war was in existence. This history was composed by Dares and Dictys working in concert, and drawing upon the *ephemerides*, or daybooks, which they were presumed to have used to establish an unassailably factual record of the war. Nor was either version contaminated by the other. The account in Alfonso's *General estoria* specifies that Dares, on the losing side, had recorded his observations before he ever met Dictys. Finally, the close correspondence in language between Guido's "inscriptum quasi una vocis consonantia" and Alfonso's "acordaron amos en uno" is worth observing. Neither Guido nor Alfonso el Sabio is maintaining that the two short Latin histories of the Trojan war, as originally written, were in agreement with each other: what they are maintaining is that, subsequent to the production of these separate works, Dictys and Dares joined forces; hammered out their differences; and, agreeing together as one as to what the final version should be, produced their definitive history.

As regards these separate works by Dictys and Dares, they are clearly referred to in Guido's Epilogue, in which he lists some of the specific differences between the two works. We have already seen an example of the hitherto almost universal view that the Epilogue is in flat contradiction to Guido's statement in the Prologue; that the assumed contradiction is to be explained in terms of Guido's belated discovery that the position he took in the Prologue was wrong; and finally that he was forced to write the Epilogue to conceal the fact that he had not been following Dares and Dictys at all—meanwhile neglecting to correct the Prologue. But since it is now certain that Guido presented himself as translating the original concordance produced by the collaboration of Dictys and Dares, the Epilogue in no way contradicts the Prologue. Adhering rigidly to the same lofty standards of scholarship that prompted Alfonso to append to his history of the Trojan War a series of divergent and additional accounts culled from less authoritative histories, Guido is not to be outdone in indicating how the journals kept by Dares and Dictys during the course of the war differ from each other. These journals he appears to identify with the two Latin works which have come down to us under the names of Dictys and Dares. To Guido, however, these works are nothing more than the day-to-day records, the notes, that the two erstwhile enemies compared and harmonized as they worked together on their final history. These journals would accordingly be of infinitely less authority than the later work, where the two authors could correct each other's mistakes and fill in each other's blank spots. A due comparison of them would, moreover, persuade the learned reader[12] that here indeed was the definitive, authoritative history of the Trojan War translated from the Greek concordance of Dares and Dictys, and itself in turn collated with the original documents.

With his translation of this magnificent resolution of opposites concerning a war whose consequence was the founding of the whole western world by Trojan refugees, Guido must have felt very content:

> Fortassis autem gliscit contrariorum natura,
> Et ex his facere consonum, non ex similibus.
>
> —*De mundo*, x, 3

NOTES

1. Guido de Columnis, *Historia destructionis Troiae*, ed. N. E. Griffin (Cambridge, Mass., 1936), p. 4.
2. "particularia ystorie ipsius que magic possunt allicere animos auditorum" (*ibid.*). Cornelius is said to be "quidam Romanus . . . Salusti magni nepos" (*ibid.*). The translation, as yet unpublished, was kindly provided by Mary E. David (née Meek). The new translation represents Dr. David's continuing struggle against the innumerable problems presented by Guido's text, the largest concentration of which is to be found in the Prologue. Her initial translation is contained in her doctoral dissertation: Mary E. Meek, "A Translation of Guido delle Colonne's *Historia destructionis Troiae*" (unpublished, 2 vols., Radcliffe College, 1956).
3. It was not until 1869 that H. Dunger first conclusively demonstrated the relation between Guido's *Historia* and Benoit's *Roman* (*Die Sage vom troyanischen Kriege in die Bearbeitungen des Mittelalters und ihre Antiken* [Leipzig], p. 61–64). For an account of the Latin Dictys and Dares, as well as an English translation of these works, see *The Trojan War: The Chronicles of Dictys of Crete and Dares the Phrygian*, ed. R. M. Frazer, Jr. (Bloomington, Ind., 1966). For a study of Guido's sources other than Benoit's *Roman de Troie*, see W. B. Wigginton, "The Nature and Significance of the Late Medieval Troy Story: A Study of Guido delle Colonne's *Historia destructionis Troiae*" (unpublished dissertation, Rutgers University, 1964).
4. *Historia*, ed. Griffin, p. 4.
5. For the source of the translation, see note 2 above. The phrase "gramaticam legunt" may indicate not only an ability to read Latin, but a stage in education. Thus in the *Prioress's Tale*, the older boy whom the "litel clergeoun" beseeches to translate the "Alma redemptoris" is unable to do so, because "I lerne song, I kan but smal grammeere"

(VII [B²], 536 [*Works*, p. 162]). If this is true, Guido would appear to be offering his correct version of the Trojan War to the "gramaticus," or teacher, who would be instructing in the "libris gramaticalibus," so that his students might be freed from the horrendous errors of previous versions.

6. Anne G. Johnson, "Guido de Columnis' *Historia destructionis Troiae: A Literal Translation*" (unpublished Ph.D. dissertation, Tulane University, 1964), p. 2.

7. Meek, "Guido delle Colonne's *Historia*," I, 2.

8. Johnson, *Historia*, p. 2, note 1.

9. Wigginton, "Late Medieval Troy Story," pp. 87–90. The passage concerning the *Laud Troy Book* is to be found in E. B. Atwood, "English Versions of the *Historia troiana*" (unpublished dissertation, 2 vols., University of Virginia, 1932).

10. Alfonso el Sabio, *General estoria*, ed. A. G. Solalinde (Madrid, 1961), III, Part 2.

11. "Con aquel Antenor de Troya, que era omne poderso e de grand guisa, andaua vn buen clerigo troyano otrosi e auie nonbre Dayres. E quando vio la fazienda de los griegos e sabie el lo de los troyanos, entendio que grand cosa era e que mucho durarie. E por ende puso toda su entençion en tener ojo en los fechos de Troya commo se fazien, e escriuiolos todos. E en la hueste de los griegos auie otrosi otro maestro buen clerigo. E a este dezian Ditis, e era omne ardit e sabidor.

"E aquestos dos, Dayres e Ditis, fallaronse en vno despues de la destruyçion de Troya. E commo eran omnes buenos letrados, quando se començaron a fablar, entendieronse e aconpannaronse. E fueron fablando en vno en conpanna, e vinieron a la razon de Troya, e marauillaronse de tal fecho commo aquel, e de tal destruymiento e tamanna mortandat de omnes. E retrayen que serie muy bien quien lo ouiese todo escrito. E dixo estonçes Dayres: "Todo quanto fue fecho en Troya del comienço fasta la fin yo lo vi muy bien e lo se." E quando Ditis aquello vio, dixo: "Quanto los griegos fizieron yo lo vi otrosi, e delante estude a todo, e se lo muy bien." E estonçes acordaron amos en vno que escriuiesen esta estoria. E fizieronla e escriuieronla en griego. . . .

"E por que aquellos dos caualleros sabios, Dayres de Troya e Ditis de Greçia, se açertaron en todo el fecho de Troya—el vno con los troyanos e el otro con los griegos, e fizieron ellos ende este escrito—departen los omnes buenos e sabios que esta estoria, segunt que la aqui auemos contada, es la mas verdadera que y ha" (*ibid.*, pp. 159–160).

For assistance with the translation of the above passages, the authors are indebted to Professor Charles Africa and to Mrs. Sonia Helfer, both of Idaho State University.

The association of Dares with Antenor is an adroit touch. In the tradition followed by Benoit de St. Maure and Guido, Antenor was the prime traitor of Troy. As the text indicates, he was indeed a noble of high rank, and a man of great power. As such, he was received into the Greek camp both as purported negotiator for peace between

Greece and Troy, and ultimately as traitor, with great honor. It is therefore natural to suppose that, after the fall of Troy, Dares, his personal learned clerk, would fall in company with a like "master clerk" on the Greek side. It is perhaps worth while observing that the connection of Dares with Antenor is not matched by a comparable association of Dictys with any of the known Greek magnates. The career of Antenor may be traced through the indices of *Le Roman de Troie,* ed. Leopold Constans (Paris, 1908), and *Historia destructionis Troiae,* ed. Griffin. Antenor was not a particularly savory character, and it is doubtful anyone would have wished to associate Dares with him to any further extent.

12. See note 5 above.

10

Chaucer's May 3 and Its Contexts

THE MONTH OF MAY seems from the earliest times to have been regarded in a highly ambivalent manner—it was at once a month of celebration and a month of fear. In Rome, the Floralia, a celebration of the goddess Flora and of spring, extended from the end of April to the first days of May,[1] yet in Roman society May was one of the periods during which marriage was not to take place.[2] In medieval France, "l'amour de Mai" was celebrated; yet here again, as regards marriage, May was a time to be avoided.[3] In the Celtic world, May Day (May 1) was observed in the form of the festival of Beltane, a goddess associated with the sun and with fertility. However, in the ceremony of the Beltane fires, a characteristic form of the observance, there was present an element of death. He who received a particularly blackened portion of the Beltane cake was spoken of as dead.[4] In the realm of literature, Malory seems to provide a good example of a writer sensitive to the ambivalent meanings of May. In the *Knight of the Cart*, he says of the coming of May: "hit gyvyth unto all lovers corrayge, that lusty moneth of May. . . . But nowadayes men cannat love sevennyght but they muste have all their desyres. That love may nat endure by reson . . ." As Malory sees it, the lack of human "stabilité" simply will not permit such love long continuance: "so faryth hit by unstable love in man and woman . . ."[5] For Chaucer, as for Malory, it seems entirely probable that the month of May possessed an ambivalence not undescriptive of the nature of man and of the world he lives in.

What is curious, therefore, is not Chaucer's use of the month of May, but his triple use of a specific date in May. In three major works—*Troilus and Criseyde,* the *Knight's Tale,* and the *Nun's Priest's Tale*—an allusion to May 3 occurs, and it occurs in a fashion which suggests its presence as a counterbalance to the conventional romantic "lusty" aspect of May. Whether used seriously or parodically, Chaucer seems to have expected this date to convey the idea of ill fortune of a tragic sort.

To what may we attribute Chaucer's insistence upon May 3? First of all, it has long been established that May 3 was considered a day of ill fortune.[6] However, so also was May 6, the date of Dorigen's rash promise to Aurelius in the *Franklin's Tale*[7]—yet to this date Chaucer never returns. An even better date for conveying a sense of the tragic is May 1. For the author of the Middle English *Morte Arthure,* May 1 is a tragic date, but a tragic date for the Romans who oppose Arthur's continental campaign.[8] Malory, however, makes May 1 a tragic date for Arthur himself— indeed, a day so tragic that from it will proceed the destruction both of Arthur and of the Round Table itself. Arthur has unknowingly begotten upon his half sister, Morgawse, a son, Mordred, and has thereby incurred God's anger. In a futile attempt to outwit fate, Arthur:

. . . lette sende for all the children that were borne in May-day, begotyn of lordis and borne of ladyes; for Merlyon tolde kynge Arthure that he that sholde destroy him and all the londe sholde be borne on May-day. . . . And all were putte in a shyppe to the se. . . . And so by fortune the shyppe drove unto a castelle, and was all to-ryven and destroyed the moste party, save that Mordred was cast up, and a good man founde hym, and fostird hym tylle he was fourtene yere of age, and than brought hym to the courte, as hit rehersith aftirward and towarde the ende of the MORTE ARTHURE.[9]

Since Malory's source for this passage is the so-called *Suite de Merlin,*[10] the connotations of May 1 would seem to have been as communicable to a French-speaking audience as the same reference in the *Morte Arthure* to an English-speaking audience. Such a date would thus seem to conform exactly to Chaucer's linguistic needs. Why then did he choose to ignore so convenient a date, and emphasize instead May 3?

As might be anticipated, the solutions offered have not been few. In addition to those summarized in Robinson's edition,[11] the further suggestion has been made that May 3 is the traditional date for the Invention of the Holy Cross by St. Helena, and her casting down of the idol of Venus. It is thus an evil day for lovers, at least of a certain kind.[12] Another suggestion is that, according to Ovid, the concluding act or acts of the Floralia took place on May 3, and, given Chaucer's knowledge of Ovid, would have been understood by him as an entirely proper day for feeling the influence of love. The three allusions, then, would have less to do with ill fortune than with love.[13] There has, however, been a general consensus that Chaucer uses May 3 as an evil day, but no solution so far adduced has shown it to have had a reputation adequate to explain Chaucer's repeated use of it. As has been indicated, it does not appear to rank with May 1.

A solution which possibly meets the requirements of adequate horrendousness involves the protagonist of the first of the Monk's "tragedies"—Lucifer. In *Witchcraft and Second Sight in the Highlands and Islands of Scotland*, J. G. Campbell says he has searched far and wide, but can discover for the evil reputation of May 3, the "Avoiding Day of the Year," no explanation except one:

It was on this day that the fallen angels were expelled from Paradise, and on it people should avoid doing any kind of evil. If caught in the act, they will be similarly expelled from the regions of forgiveness, and be visited with "judgement without mercy."[14]

Campbell's solution would appear to have gained rather wide acceptance, since it is the only one recorded in *British Calendar Customs*,[15] an interesting collection from which one may learn something more of the significance to the Celtic mind of May 3. As the "Avoiding Day of the Year," it was a day on which never to begin anything of importance, particularly if May 3 falls on a Friday. Beginning a journey is much discouraged. However, although the Celtic observances noted all indicate the day as possessing a notably bad eminence, it seems also to have been notable in a quite different fashion. The other names for May 3 are all derived from St. Helena's Invention of the Cross. They are, as listed by Banks, "Rood Day. Invention of the Holy Cross. St. Helen's Day in Spring."[16] Nevertheless, though undoubtedly associated with St. Helena and the Cross, there is curiously enough no indication that May 3 had any reputation as a lucky day, but rather the reverse.

An entry in Bede's *Ecclesiastical History* indicates that the Anglo-Saxon mind also was aware of the sinister suggestions of May 3.

In the same year of our Lord 664, there occurred an eclipse of the sun on May 3 about four o'clock in the afternoon; in which year a sudden pestilence first depopulated the southern part of Britain and afterwards attacked the kingdom of Northumbria, raging far and wide with cruel devastation and laying low a vast number of people. . . . The plague did equal destruction in Ireland.[17]

Though Bede makes no comment, evidence does exist that the Anglo-Saxon would have considered May 3 a proper day for such events.[18]

After some glimpses of what May 3 may have been doing in Celtic and Anglo-Saxon minds, there is to be considered what significance May 3 held for the mind of Geoffrey Chaucer, Esq., diplomat and poet, who was nevertheless once Geoffrey Chaucer, Esquire—in the full meaning of the term. Following the stunning victories of Crécy (1346) and Poitiers (1356), Edward III could hardly refrain from pondering whether he might not himself be able to effect at Rheims his own coronation as King of France—a dignity he claimed in right of his mother, and a dignity obtainable, as he then saw it, by simple force of arms. In 1359, the internal difficulties facing the Dauphin were such that the time seemed to Edward opportune for the assertion of his right.[19] At the end of October, 1359, he set sail for France. After a pause of four days at Calais, Edward

. . . departed at dawn in the full array of his great power, and took the field with the entirety of the vastest and best equipped supply train which anyone had ever seen come out of England. It was said that he had more than six thousand well-equipped vehicles, all of which had made the voyage from England. Then he ordered his battles, all so nobly and so richly apparelled that it was a solace and a delight to gaze upon them. . . .[20]

According to Froissart, whose account of Edward's army has been followed above, so great was the enthusiasm that no Englishman between the ages of twenty and sixty who gave intimations of viability failed to embark.[21] If we are to judge from later portraits, amongst the serried ranks which set forth from Calais, not the least imposing figure was an amply proportioned fighting man— one Geoffrey Chaucer, Esquire.[22]

However, the great army which Edward had prepared and which shared Edward's magnificent aspirations was not destined for great deeds. Between the battle of Poitiers in 1356 and Edward's arrival in 1359, French military thinking had changed radically. The French had temporarily lost their passion for the grand charge; though highly dramatic, it had proved no match for the English long-bow. John, the blind king of Bohemia, who was said to have taken part in the charge at Crécy chained to a knight on each side was long dead. John, King of France, who had been captured at Poitiers, was awaiting payment of his ransom, ultimately set at the immense sum of 3,000,000 crowns.[23] The total strategy of the French consisted in refusal to give battle. As a result, the French starved in besieged city and ravaged countryside; the English starved and rotted in the field. In one of the minor engagements which characterized the war, very possibly in the vicinity of Rheims, Geoffrey Chaucer was captured and ultimately ransomed.[24] With the coming of spring, it became clear to the English that they could win no military victory, and to the French that, with the English in the field, they could expect no crops. Agreement was very considerably hastened by the "Black Monday" following Easter Day, 1360. On this well-remembered day, there appeared over the English host a "dim cloud," which produced hailstones so large that they killed men and horses. So violent was the storm that it was believed that the world was coming to an end.[25] The whole miserable campaign was concluded initially by the Treaty of Brétigny, which was later ratified at Calais.[26]

Peace talks began at the hamlet of Brétigny, near Chartres, on 1 May 1360. A week later a truce was concluded to last until Michaelmas, 1361, and the Black Prince and the Dauphin accepted a draft treaty to be confirmed later by the sovereigns of both nations.[27]

There is, however, reason to distrust the traditional dating, as represented above. Before the conclusive hail-storm, both sides had been in constant session, and the negotiable and nonnegotiable points were known. Hence no great length of time was needed to arrive at agreement, and a probable date for that agreement was May 3. As R. Delachenal, author of the authoritative *Histoire de Charles V*, puts it:

"I am inclined to believe that agreement was reached on *May 3*, and that the following days were devoted to drawing up the text of the treaty and resolving questions of detail, thorny perhaps, but not of a nature to compromise the result obtained. From receipts given by Charles de Montmorency, Ainard de la Tour, Jean de Grolée, and Artaut de Beausemblant on *May 3*, it is to be concluded that peace had been arrived at by that date. It even seems that these four knights [all members of the Dauphin's council and sent by him from Paris as negotiators] left Chartres that very day, considering their mission as negotiators concluded . . ."

The receipts ("quittances") in question were acknowledgements of payment of expenses incurred at Chartres during the course of negotiations. The formula for each is "despenz *faiz* en la dite ville de Chartres durant le traictié de la pais et acors *faiz* devant la dite ville de Chartres." If one compares the language of these quittances with the language of an earlier quittance (April 26, 1360) given at Paris by Montmorency [Boucicaut] for expenses incurred and to be incurred—"*faiz et a faire*"—it is evident that the May 3 quittances are not for continuing services, but represent a final accounting.[28]

If the treaty were concluded on May 3, the date could not have failed to impress itself on Chaucer's mind. The campaign had been for the youthful Chaucer a bitter and black experience, unalleviated by the brilliance of English arms which had marked the previous campaigns. In retrospect, the mature Chaucer must have seen the Treaty of Brétigny for what it was: the downturn of English arms, which marked the beginnings of ever increasing chaos within England itself—a current never to be reversed in his lifetime. It may be the totality of Chaucer's moral and physical sufferings in the campaign of 1359–1360, which began so brilliantly at Dover and ended so miserably at Brétigny, which answers Robinson's question as to whether "Chaucer had some personal reason" for his repeated references to May 3. After all, if one accepts the evidence adduced by Delachenal to the effect that the Treaty of Brétigny was effectually concluded on May 3, and that Chaucer, at Calais, subsequently had a part in drawing up its ratification,[29] the date of May 3 could hardly have failed to remain, for Chaucer, a highly meaningful one.

It is hoped that the above study of the origins of the ill reputation of May 3 and its meaning to Chaucer may serve to supplement existing scholarship on the subject. In embarking on such a study, one hopes at best to solve only a puzzling factual problem. However, the May 3 allusions turn out not simply to be allusions, but—whether "by aventure, or sort, or cas"—form a quite perceptible pattern. In the contexts in which they occur, they may perhaps be said to form a kind of limited intellectual autobiography.

I

The first reference to May 3 occurs in *Troilus and Criseyde*, and in a rather striking position. Immediately following the imposing rubrics "Explicit prohemium secundi libri" and "Incipit liber secundus" follow the lines:

> In May, that moder is of monthes glade,
> That fresshe floures, blew and white and rede,
> Ben quike agayn, that wynter dede made,
> And ful of bawme is fletyng every mede;
> Whan Phebus doth his bryghte bemes sprede,
> Right in the white Bole, it so bitidde,
> As I shal synge, on Mayes day the thrydde. . . . (II, 50–56)[30]

What actually "bitidde" is that Pandarus, having gone to bed of "a teene/In love," is awakened by the sorrowful song of the swallow Progne, and bethinks himself of his mission to Criseyde. Before departing, however, he takes the precaution of consulting the phase of the moon. Finding that

> . . . in good plit was the moone
> To doon viage . . . (II, 74–75)

he goes about his business.

Arrived at his destination, he finds a maiden reading to Criseyde and two accompanying ladies the story of the "siege of Thebes." Although he knows perfectly well what is being read, he addresses to Criseyde and her ladies a supremely disingenuous question:

> "Is it of love? O, som good ye me leere!" (II, 97)

and receives in reply exactly the answer he wants:

> "Uncle," quod she, "youre maistresse is nat here." (II, 98)

The result is laughter. Pandarus's self-humor concerning his established amatory insuccess has removed any suspicion as to the deep earnestness of his visit. He has also, by this same opening question, simultaneously introduced the subject he has come to introduce—the love of Troilus for Criseyde, a love which he is commissioned to bring to consummation.

It is as a part of the complex fabric Chaucer has here woven that the May 3 allusion is to be viewed. The story Chaucer is telling is—to all appearances—a love story, and moreover that great medieval rarity, a love story with humor. The Prologue to Book II tells us that Troilus's love for Criseyde is emerging from the blackness of despair to the light of hope, and the docile reader is thereby led to assume a happy ending. This impression is reinforced by the remainder of the Prologue's being devoted to a kind of theoretical disquisition on amatory language and amatory procedures (II, 22–49). When the story proper resumes, the setting is a joyous one:

> In May, that moder is of monthes glade,
> That fresshe floures, blew and white and rede,
> Ben quike agayn, that wynter dede made. . . . (II, 50–52)

The month is May, the literary month,[31] and the natural month in which nature is everywhere reawakening. At the home of Criseyde, love is the subject introduced, and that amidst laughter. The

Narrator, who throughout controls the tone of the poem, is himself the announced servant of the servants of love—"I that God of Loves servantz serve" (1, 15). He is hence understandably ecstatic over the beginnings of Pandarus's "grete emprise":

> Now Janus, god of entree, thow hym gyde! (11, 77)

But beneath the love story runs a current of allusion which suggests that the joyful surface of the poem may not remain forever unruffled. May is indeed a "glade" month, but May 3 is not a glad day. In its direct linkage with the ill fortune of Pandarus's own love affair, and in its association with the beginnings of Pandarus's maneuverings in the love affair of Troilus and Criseyde, there is a suggestion that Pandarus may prove something less than the supreme manipulator he appears to be—that in the heavens there is stored up more than Pandarus can perceive in his "lunarium."[32] Further, in the same allusion to May 3, there is counterposed to the love which Pandarus is so enthusiastically purveying another kind of love which will find its full expression only in the Epilogue.[33] Finally, the domestic tableau of Criseyde and her ladies listening complacently to the "siege of Thebes" is harshly ironical when presented in the context of the siege of Troy—a city which every listener and reader knew must likewise perish.[34]

This same ambivalence is present in the enamorment scene. Troilus falls in love with Criseyde in the springtime joy of "Palladiones feste":

> . . . whan clothed is the mede
> With newe grene, of lusty Veer the pryme,
> And swote smellen floures white and rede . . . (1, 156–158)

All this sounds properly festive, except that the Palladium is the guarantee of the safety of Troy, and, again as every listener and reader knew, its theft by Antenor and Aeneas is the means by which Troy is to fall.[35] The Palladium allusion and the May 3 allusion are exactly parallel. They both present the two levels of the poem: the springtime gaiety of romance and the underlying chill of tragedy.

II. THE "KNIGHT'S TALE"

At the end of *Troilus and Criseyde*, the Narrator, at this point bearing a striking resemblance to Geoffrey Chaucer, announces a distinct change in what shall henceforth be his subject matter:

> Go, litel bok, go, litel myn tragedye,
> Ther God thi makere yet, er that he dye,
> So sende myght to make in som comedye! (v, 1786–1788)

However the term "comedye" be interpreted, its basic sense is invariably that of upward movement. It is not difficult to suppose that in the process of completing *Troilus and Criseyde*, Chaucer had lost his appetite for the tragic, and that in the *Canterbury Tales* he was seeking a kindlier and more expansive view of man and of the world in which he lives.

The emergence of this new attitude is apparent in the *Knight's Tale*, the first of the tales narrated on the road to Canterbury. As in *Troilus and Criseyde*, there is here also an allusion to May 3. It is perhaps worth considering whether the kind of use Chaucer makes of May 3 in the *Knight's Tale* may not serve as a measure of the extent to which his attitudes changed in the course of his composition of *Troilus and Criseyde*.[36]

The *Knight's Tale* is large and amply proportioned. As the Knight himself remarks, "I have, God woot, a large feeld to ere" (I [A] 886). A summary of its action is therefore not a particularly attractive undertaking. However, a commentary on events left undefined is perhaps an even less attractive alternative. Hence, for those to whom it may be of use, a summary follows. "Whoso list it nat yheere" is requested to turn over several leaves.

On Theseus's triumphal return from his conquest of the "regne of Femenye," bringing with him his bride Ypolita and her younger sister Emelye, he is met by a group of widowed noblewomen whose husbands were killed in the expedition of the Seven against Thebes, their bodies refused burial by Creon. At the appeal of the noblewomen, Theseus sets aside all personal concerns and executes justice upon Creon—an act perhaps reminiscent of the great model of justice, Trajan.[37] After Theseus's successful assault on Thebes, in the course of which he meets Creon in the field and kills him "manly as a knyght," there are found lying side by side in the same arms two cousins of the royal blood of Thebes, Palemon and Arcite. They are carried wounded from the field and condemned to perpetual imprisonment.[38] On a May morning, Emelye, in observance of the season, walks in the garden beneath the great tower in which Palemon and Arcite are imprisoned. Both fall in love with her violently and in succession—Palemon sees her first and believes her a goddess; Arcite sees her second, but quite correctly views her as a mortal woman. Rather unrealistically, given the circumstances, each claims her for his own. A heated argument ensues which is temporarily brought to an end by the intervention of Perotheus, a mutual friend of Arcite and Theseus. As a result, Arcite is freed from prison, but banished from Athens on pain of his head. After he has returned to Thebes and dwelt there a "yeer or two," a prey to the pains of love, Mercury appears to him in a vision and informs him that he is to return to Athens, for there his sorrows are to have an end. Arcite perceives that the horrid sufferings love has visited upon him have so changed his face that in Athens no man can recognize him. Hence, disguised as a laborer and with a squire similarly disguised, he proceeds to Athens to the court of Theseus to see and serve the lady he loves. He labors to such good effect that Emelye's chamberlain takes notice of him and appoints him page of the chamber of the beauteous Emelye. There he assumes the name of Philostrate. However, after a "yeer or two" in this position, Arcite's combination of industry, tact, and imported Theban gold brings him such renown that he is elevated by Theseus not only to the estate of esquire, but esquire to the bedchamber of Theseus himself. In peace and in war, Arcite bears himself so well that to Theseus is no man dearer.

Seven years—a minimal but certifiable period for amatory agony—have passed when Palemon escapes from prison and, fleeing until dawn, takes refuge in a grove. The season, astonishingly enough, is May, and the following morning is so merry that Arcite is constrained to ride out from Athens to do his "observaunce" to the season. As a part of his observance of May, he wishes to make himself an appropriate garland, and happens to choose the grove in which Palemon has concealed himself. In the great tradition of the overheard lover, Palemon recognizes Arcite, and their earlier struggle is resumed in the form of a duel, for which Arcite provides absolutely equal arms. As they fight "Breme as it were bores two,"³⁹ Theseus, Ypolita, and Emelye enter the grove in pursuit of a hart reputed to be there. When the identity of the combatants is revealed to him, Theseus wishes to proceed immediately to their execution. However, the cause of the duel being love, the ladies intercede in behalf of the two knights, and Theseus conceives the idea of a magnificent tournament to decide which is to be the fortunate lover and which the unfortunate. Before the tournament, each of the three principals prays to his particular divinity: Palemon to Venus; Emelye to Diana; and Arcite to Mars. As a result, the heavens are shaken by an altercation between Venus and Mars as to which of their favorites is to have the victory. Saturn stills the strife by assuring Venus that, although Mars may be of some assistance to his knight, it is Venus's wishes that shall prevail. The tournament is fought, and Arcite, the favorite of Mars, emerges victorious. However, as he rides in triumph, an infernal specter, sent by Saturn,⁴⁰ causes his horse to rear and fall upon him. Fatally injured, he magnanimously commends to the grief-stricken Emelye his rival Palemon. After a period of mourning which extends for many years, Emelye finally is granted to Palemon.

The above summary has been given in some detail, because virtually no event in the narrative is presented without an accompanying reference—direct or indirect—to the presence of destinal forces. The Theban ladies who implore Theseus's aid attribute to the agency of Fortune both his happy state and their wretched one (I [A], 915–925). When by "aventure or cas" (1074)—Chaucer's favorite method of making clear that an event did *not* happen by chance—Palemon is struck to the heart by the sight of Emelye beneath his prison window, Arcite, hearing his cry, attributes it to the injuries Fortune has inflicted upon them both (1086). The subsequent freeing of Arcite also occasions a kind of antiphonal crying out against destinal forces which both feel are mocking them (1219–1333). In prison, Arcite has desired nothing so much as freedom, but once freed he finds exile from Emelye worse than prison itself: Palemon suffers from a double sorrow—

prison and the pains of love. Of the two complaints, Arcite's, which concerns itself especially with the vanity of human wishes, contains the richer language:

> "We witen nat what thing we preyen heere:
> We faren as he that dronke is as a mous.
> A dronke man woot wel he hath an hous,
> But he noot which the righte wey is thider,
> And to a dronke man the wey is slider." (1260–1264) [14]

Up to this point, "destinee"—also called with varying shades of meaning "Fortune," "purveiaunce," "prescience"[42]—has been treated less as an active force than as a felt presence. However, in the Mercury-Arcite incident, the supernatural, although primarily continuing to be felt as a presence, makes one of its few appearances in perceptible form. When, in a dream, Mercury comes before the suffering love-sick Arcite and bids him be merry, he says:

> ". . . To Atthenes shaltou wende,
> Ther is thee shapen of thy wo an ende." (1391–1392)

Since, amongst his many duties, Mercury has that of "psychopomp," or guide of the dead to their final abode, Arcite might have suspected an "amphibologie,"[43] but he does not, and immediately proceeds to Athens and to the court of Theseus. This intervention of the supernatural is not in Chaucer's source, the *Teseida*. It is entirely of Chaucer's invention.[44]

The escape of Palemon, the next link in the chain of causality, takes the more usual form of allusion. The allusion is to May 3, and it is underlined by some of Chaucer's customary destinal verbiage:

> It fel that in the seventhe yer, of May
> The thridde nyght . . .
> Were it by aventure or destynee—
> As, whan a thyng is shapen, it shal be—
> That soone after the mydnyght Palamoun,
> By helpyng of a freend, brak his prisoun. . . . (1462–1468)

and at dawn Palemon takes refuge in a nearby grove. Palemon's choice of the grove as a place of refuge prepares, of course, for the all-important scene which gathers together the various threads of the preceding narrative, and then leads directly to the dénouement.

Arcite, the next to arrive in the grove, comes there "By aventure" (1506), and in the leafy shadows of the grove utters his "complaynte" against love—a complaint, it is to be noted, not uncolored by a sense of destiny:

> "Love hath his firy dart so brennyngly
> Ystiked thurgh my trewe, careful herte,
> That shapen was my deeth erst than my sherte.
> Ye sleen me with youre eyen, Emelye!" (1564–1567)

Curiously enough, he utters his complaint while walking up and down a path next to which is a bush, where "by aventure" (1516) Palemon is hiding. From the overheard complaint follows the duel in the grove. In his gathering of garlands, what Arcite has failed to see is that the same supernatural forces which brought him from Thebes to Athens have now transported him from Athens to the grove:

> [Arcite] litel wiste how ny that was his care,
> Til that Fortune had broght him in the snare. (1489–1490)

Theseus, accompanied by Ypolita and Emelye, is the third to arrive in the grove. His arrival is explicitly connected to the most powerful statement of the agency of destiny the poem contains:

> The destinee, ministre general,
> That executeth in the world over al
> The purveiaunce that God hath seyn biforn,
> So strong it is that, though the world had sworn
> The contrarie of a thyng by ye or nay,
> Yet somtyme it shal fallen on a day
> That falleth nat eft withinne a thousand yeer.
> For certeinly, oure appetites heer,
> Be it of werre, or pees, or hate, or love,
> All is this reuled by the sighte above. (1663–1672)[45]

Yet the occasion of the arrival of Theseus is a rather trivial one, quite comparable to that of Arcite's. It is simply that Theseus loves to hunt, and especially in May to hunt the "grete hert." He has been told that a hart to his taste is to be found in the grove and, the weather being fine, he brings along Ypolita and Emelye. In the grove he finds Palemon and Arcite engaged in the genial chivalric pastime of dealing each other blows which would fell an oak, and in consequence fighting up to their ankles in blood (1699–1702; 1660). Once their identity is revealed, Theseus, being a direct man, sees no reason not to execute them without delay. It is here that the presence of the two ladies, whose participation in the hunt seems strictly of negative importance, becomes suddenly of the greatest importance. It is by their intercession that Palemon and Arcite are preserved from immediate execution; it is therefore also by their intercession that Theseus is forced into a more reflective state of mind without being relieved of the dual obligation of treating his prisoners as prisoners and at the same time treating them as knights of noble birth, in every way worthy of marriage to Emelye. Theseus, who is capable of thinking only in terms of the utmost magnificence, decides on a tournament, but hardly an ordinary tournament. Both Arcite and Palemon are to have a year in which each is to collect a hundred knights to be of his party—knights, it is understood, of no small station and renown. For this splendid occasion Theseus will himself make ready an appropriately splendid setting.

The scene in the grove is of prima facie importance because it leads directly to the great and supposedly conclusive tournament. However, the encounter in the grove is actually of considerably more than superficial import. When Palemon enters the grove, he is fleeing for his life; Arcite comes there to do honor to May; Theseus, Ypolita, and Emelye are out hunting—yet all arrive at the grove. The ubiquitous power of destiny is nowhere so fully sensed, nor its power so clearly demonstrated.

The tournament, which is to resolve in the most chivalric fashion the problem of what to do with Emelye, is itself heavily loaded with a sense of predestination. Theseus does not announce the tournament as a means of discovering which of the two knights possesses the greater bravery or the greater skill in the use of edged weapons; his intention is to make of the tournament a means of discovering the will of the gods. Each of the two knights is to "have his destynee/As hym is shape" (1842–1843). When destiny has manifested itself, Theseus declares:

"Thanne shal I yeve Emelya to wyve
To whom that Fortune yeveth so fair a grace." (1860–1861)

Before the tournament, each of the three whose destinies are to be determined by the tournament prays to the divinity whose aid he seeks—not in a random fashion, but in the astrological hour over which the particular divinity presides.[46] Palemon arises some two hours before dawn, and in "hire houre" proceeds to the temple of Venus. There he promises Venus to become her servant, and makes a heroic vow to "holden werre alwey with chastitee" (2236).[47] He declares further:

"I kepe noght of armes for to yelpe,
Ne I ne axe nat tomorwe to have victorie,
Ne renoun in this cas, ne veyne glorie
Of pris of armes blowen up and doun;
But I wolde have fully possessioun
Of Emelye, and dye in thy servyse." (2238–2243)

A sign from Venus indicates the granting of his prayer, and with glad heart he leaves the temple. Considerably later, again in the proper astrological hour, Arcite proceeds to the temple of Mars. There he pledges himself to the service of Mars, and prays, by the sorrow that Mars felt when Vulcan found him "liggynge by his wyf, allas!" (2390)[48] that Mars will, out of sheer compassion, grant him victory and thus save him from the comparable sufferings he endures for love of Emelye. At the conclusion of his prayer, the hauberk of Mars rings, and from the statue Arcite hears the word "Victorie!"

Aside from certain bits of humor on the part of the Knight, there is little to make these two scenes memorable. But Emelye's experience in the temple of Diana is rather more complex and portentous. Emelye prays to "Dyane the chaste," and like her suitors observes the ritual of the astrological hour. Her prayer is that Diana will act in some undetermined supernatural fashion to preserve her chastity and keep her from the "hoote love" of her two suitors; however, she seems to sense that her prayer will not be granted, and she therefore also prays that if her "destynee be shapen so" that of necessity she must take one of them, she may have him who desires her most. Diana's answer, which, as Diana herself makes clear, is but a reflection of "eterne word," is conveyed through the sacrificial fires on her altar:

> For right anon oon of the fyres queynte,
> And quyked agayn, and after that anon
> That oother fyr was queynt and al agon:
> And as it queynte it made a whistelynge,
> As doon thise wete brondes in hir brennynge,
> And at the brondes ende out ran anon
> As it were blody dropes many oon . . . (2334–2340)[49]

Terrified and confused, Emelye retires from the temple of Diana.

The brilliance of Chaucer's reporting of the myriad rumors and activities which precede a great tournament, and his astonishingly effective use of alliteration in the description of the great charge at the beginning of the tournament—

> Ther shyveren shaftes upon sheeldes thikke . . .
> Up spryngen speres twenty foot on highte;
> Out goon the swerdes as the silver brighte;
> The helmes they tohewen and toshrede . . . (2605–2609)[50]

distract the reader from the augury Emelye has seen. But as events unfold, the augury of the fires proves its credibility. Palemon is "by the force of twenty" taken unyielded but nonetheless vanquished; the brilliance of Arcite's triumph is swallowed up in his death; Palemon is presumably returned to Thebes and then ultimately recalled from the darkness to which he has been relegated, to win—or rather be granted—Emelye.[51]

With the death of Arcite, the action proper ceases. The rest of the poem consists essentially in a looking back and meditation upon the great mystery of the events which have brought simultaneous triumph and death to Arcite. It is in fact only as a result of Theseus's extended period of reflection that Palemon is brought back from Thebes and the marriage of Emelye to Palemon takes place. Since the resolution of the poem, therefore, depends so heavily upon this process of looking back, it may be useful to examine what it is that Theseus has seen in these events at the time of their occurrence, and what as a result of meditation he has come to see. As against this, it may be equally useful to examine what it is the reader, for whom no period of meditation has been provided, has all along been seeing.

As concerning Theseus, it must first and foremost be realized that he is not, like Calkas in *Troilus and Criseyde,* a "forknowynge wise." No divinity has descended or ascended to whisper in his ear, and he is not presented to us as one, by virtue of his "calkulynge," able to peer into "Goddes privitee." What we do know about him is that he is the exemplar of knighthood; with military valor he combines that deference to womanhood and commitment to the defense of womanhood which was judged to make knighthood complete. These are of course chivalric and romantic values. At the other extreme, Theseus represents justice in its fullest sense. As was pointed out earlier, like Trajan, the medieval personification of justice, he abandons all personal concern to execute justice on Creon.[52] What is more important, the justice he represents is not only prompt justice, but pure justice. In the war against Thebes he has undertaken at the behest of the widowed ladies, he has been looking for no personal profit of any kind, particularly pecuniary profit. It is twice specified in connection with the capture of Palemon and Arcite—both of the royal blood of Thebes—that "he nolde no raunsoun" (1024, 1205).

But Theseus is not merely a composite of ideals the Middle Ages held dear, he is also a human being. Although we certainly see him in the exalted roles of defender of womanhood and executor of justice, throughout most of the poem what is most evident about him is his passion for conferring a kind of golden magnificence upon all he does, notably in the ornate vastness of the stadium in which the tournament takes place, and in the magnitude and splendor of Arcite's funeral rites. If this be pride of life, neither Theseus nor his kingdom seems to show any ill effects. Only in a certain overzealousness in the exercise of justice —as in the case of Palemon and Arcite in the grove—is any weakness of character implied.

It is precisely this much stressed concern for justice which, after the death of Arcite, becomes central to the poem. Theseus has been concerned not only with the exercise of temporal justice, but also in a very real sense with divine justice—he has employed the device of the tournament as a means of arriving at the will of the gods as expressed in the outcome of the tournament. In this tournament, which despite its vastness is conceived as a kind of pagan judicial combat, Arcite triumphs, and Theseus, in accord with his devout plan, promptly awards Emelye to the victor whom Fortune has chosen:

"Arcite of Thebes shal have Emelie,
That by his fortune hath hire faire ywonne." (2658–2659)[53]

A moment later, Arcite, who had earlier become Theseus's cherished friend, and now, at the conclusion of the tournament, has, like Theseus, become a conqueror, receives his death wound.

One gathers that for Theseus, the man of arms, the causes of death in battle have previously presented no particular obscurities. Before the tournament begins, he proscribes, through his herald, the use of weapons and battle tactics he himself knows to be lethal, so that the combatants "shal nat dye" (2541). But despite all Theseus's preparations on the human and divine levels, Arcite the victor alone dies (2707–2708), and in a most incomprehensible fashion.[54] Theseus is thus suddenly thrust face to face with problems which have for all time troubled the minds of men, but apparently not his own. Theseus has piously set up the tournament as a kind of arena in which divine justice is to be demonstrated by the victory of one knight over the other. But the knight who conquers in this judicial combat is instantly destroyed by a force beyond human control, and specifically beyond the control of the mighty Theseus. Is man then merely the plaything of random irrational forces, and the gods merely man's fictional creation? If gods do exist, what kind of gods must they be whose justice is the greatest imaginable injustice?

The injustice of the death of Arcite, which to Theseus seems so overwhelmingly clear, is rather less so to the reader. Theseus, being endowed with no special insight, cannot—at least at this point—penetrate beneath the surface of things. The reader, however, occupies a privileged position. He sees what Theseus sees and understands his bewilderment. However, from his privileged position, the reader can see what Theseus cannot—the actual operation of destinal forces proceeding from the Supreme Intelligence, of which Theseus can perceive only the results. By virtue of his special position, the reader has witnessed the forging of a chain of causality which takes its beginning in Theseus's chivalric war against Thebes, and finds its ending only in the marriage of Emelye to the Theban, Palemon. It is thus not possible for the reader to see the world as devoid of providential government, nor is it much easier for the reader to view that government as captious and cruel, as Gloucester in *King Lear* so eloquently puts it:

> As flies to wanton boys are we to the gods.
> They kill us for their sport.[55]

On the contrary, the reader has seen the characters of Arcite, Palemon, and Emelye slowly unfold in a progressive development which seems somehow geared to the movement of the poem as a whole. In terms of the personalities so developed, destiny does not seem quite so harsh as Theseus has found it.

The character of Arcite, the unsuccessful suitor, is accorded the fullest treatment, and rightly so. This seems at first rather strange, until one sees that Arcite is the only character in the poem who is made up of operative contradictions, which are curiously enough also conventional contradictions, or more exactly contradictions imposed by convention. Arcite is in fact a Shavian Ferrovius or Anthony Anderson manqué.[56] What they are, he is —but the self-knowledge they attain never comes to him. For Arcite, courtly convention completely obviates the possibility of self-knowledge. Arcite has this peculiarity—he is quite capable of self-revelation, but not to himself.

Perhaps the scene which is most useful in getting at Arcite's state of mind throughout the poem is his dying lament:

> "What is this world? what asketh men to have?
> Now with his love, now in his colde grave
> Allone, withouten any compaignye." (2777–2779)

This is addressed to Emelye, his love, at the point of death, but despite the gravity of the moment, and the prevalence of the belief that at such a moment truth prevails, is it Emelye who is Arcite's love, or is his real love the field of battle? In his prayer to Mars, he first prays for victory only as a means of winning Emelye, but in his final words:

> "Yif me victorie, I aske thee namoore" (2420)

victory seems to emerge as an entity in itself, somehow assuming primacy over the possession of the lady for whom he purposes doing battle. This is a self-revelation of the first order, but there is reason to doubt that the revelation which reaches the reader reaches the mind of Arcite. Is he conscious, as is Palemon, that victory and Emelye can be conceived of as separate entities?

The fact would seem to be that the mind of Arcite is convention-bound. In terms of the actual combat to which he is committed, victory would necessarily entail the acquisition of Emelye. In more general practical terms, great knights were not infrequently rewarded with ladies of high estate, as in the case of the famous William Marshall.[57] In terms of another convention, perhaps less practical but no less pervasive, surpassing knighthood depends on superlative love. As the Green Knight's lady presents the argument to Sir Gawain, all great knights are great lovers;[58] ergo, Arcite, being a great knight, must necessarily be a great lover. If he had not had Emelye for his lady, in order to be socially acceptable he would have had to invent one.

Jacques de Lalaing, a fifteenth-century knight-errant from Hainault, the chivalric-minded land of Philippa Chaucer's birth and childhood, was perhaps the most perfected practitioner of arms in the whole Middle Ages. Though he adroitly avoided women—among them Marie de Clèves—he felt it necessary to state, in the "articles" under which he did combat, that it was for the advancement of the honor of his unnamed and nonexistent lady that he fought.[59] The difference between Jacques de Lalaing and Arcite is, however, quite distinct. Jacques seems never to have been under the illusion that he was fighting for love. Arcite, however, believes he is. After Palemon falls in love with Emelye, Arcite falls in love with Emelye. When separated from his lady, he suffers amorous torments of a nature not to be exceeded by any knightly lover. After his failure to comprehend Mercury's double-tongued pronouncement, the love-ravished Arcite proceeds to Athens to see and serve his lady. Quite astonishingly, as the course of true love is said to go, his desires to see and serve her are not only not denied him but, on the contrary, are fulfilled to the fullest degree—he becomes "Page of the chambre of Emelye the brighte" (1427). In the troubadour tradition, this should have been sheer ecstasy, and it is in this tradition that the original of the *Knight's Tale*, Boccaccio's *Teseida*, proceeds. In Boccaccio's version, Arcite, become Penteo, enters the service of Theseus, but only as a means of attaining to the presence of Emilia. His sole purpose is to serve her, and his sole delight to gaze upon her radiant beauty. So intense is his passion that on warm days he is in need of the solace of a cool grove in which to utter his doleful laments—the volume of which proves to be the cause of his discovery in the grove by Panfilo, squire of Palemon.[60]

Chaucer's Arcite is a rather different person than his original. Although he has assumed the highly romantic, and ultimately ironic, name of "Philostrate" ("prostrated by love"), he seems unable to comprehend the sublimity of the bliss into which he has been snatched up. According to the romantic ethic, one of the great rewards of love was the bestowal by the lady upon her unworthy servant of the vision of her unveiled beauty.[61] This both Boccaccio's Penteo and Emilia understand perfectly, although, since Penteo never attains to the position of page to his lady's chamber, his opportunities are limited.[62] As presumed aspirant for possession of Emelye, Philostrate's position despite its lowliness confers upon him overwhelming privileges. He could not be more proximate to the "luoc del marit," unless he were the "marit" himself[63]—who of course does not exist. It is perhaps this absolute lack of connubial competition which is the cause of Arcite's distressing lack of interest.[64]

In any case, Arcite's amorous activities sink to an indescribably low level. There is simply nothing to describe. We hear no further of amorous illnesses which could have brought his lady to comfort him; no lays of love secretly delivered and secretly disposed of; no insufferable agony at his being promoted away from her to become squire of the chamber of Theseus (1440), and ultimately "chief squier" (1730). Arcite, the man of war, after a "yeer or two" (1426) with Emelye gravitates toward the conqueror Theseus. Only in the company of Theseus is he described as being in "blisse" (1449), and to Theseus is no man dearer (1448).

Palemon and Emelye are considerably less complex. Emelye is highly decorative, and in appearance indistinguishable from any of the female abstractions who people the Garden of Love in the *Roman de la rose*. Her Amazonian heritage, however, makes her disinclined toward love as a way of life, and she has a professed dislike for being with child (2310). Despite all this, however, the "freendlich ye" she directs toward Arcite immediately after his victory in the tournament—

> For wommen, as to speken in comune,
> Thei folwen alle the favour of Fortune . . . (2681–2682)

gives some intimation that the regrettable effects of her childhood training may yet be overcome. Palemon, the third of the triad, is the knight-lover. In him there are no discrepancies between profession and action. For seven years in prison his love has continued unabated, and his escape is planned not simply as escape but as the initial move in gathering together in Thebes an army capable of carrying off Emelye by force of arms (1482–1484). One notices readily that Palemon's prayer is purely and simply for the possession of Emelye, and expressly repudiates name-in-arms as a goal. It is equally important to observe that Emelye's prayer is directed less toward her continuance in a virginal way of life—which she clearly feels is not to be her destiny—than it is toward her being granted possession of the suitor for whom she constitutes the primary and all-inclusive motivation.[65]

From his privileged position, the reader is able to perceive that the granting or nongranting of the prayers of the three principals operates in terms of a very definite plan. The universe the reader is given to contemplate is not one in which the gods kill for their sport.

Theseus, however, is denied the vantage point of the reader. He dwells in the flux of things. As has previously been observed, he is no astrologer, nor has he been the host of supernatural visitants. The strangely mute Emelye has not even communicated to him the one augury—that of the two fires in the temple of Diana—which could have conveyed to him the sense that in the supernal regions there did exist a kind of order beyond his comprehension. Theseus is natural man endowed with natural reason. He is "payen" man presented in his most presentable form—very possibly, as has been suggested, in the form of the great pagan emperor Trajan. Like Trajan, Theseus is a just and noble pagan, but unlike Trajan, he is the just man in search of a justice he finds incomprehensible. In Aegeus, his "olde fader," he can find consolation of a sort (2843–2849), but it is not a consolation he ultimately finds meaningful.

It is only after the passage of several years that Theseus brings forth from his "wise" breast (2983) the address which climaxes the poem. It is a curious piece of declamation with a structure somewhat like an hourglass. It moves upward inspirationally from a solid basis of doctrine:

> "The Firste Moevere of the cause above,
> Whan he first made the faire cheyne of love,
> Greet was th'effect, and heigh was his entente." (2987–2989)

However, in terms of human attitude, the great effect and high intent are something less than inspirational, since the same "Prince and Moevere"

> "Hath stablissed in this wrecched world adoun
> Certeyne dayes and duracioun
> To al that is engendred in this place,
> Over the whiche day they may nat pace . . ." (2995–2998)

In other words, man must die. This is hardly more comforting than Aegeus's "Deeth is an ende of every worldly soore" (2849), which Theseus has himself not found entirely satisfying. Furthermore, Theseus has used the highly connotative term "wrecched world," which occurs in innumerable works devoted to contempt of the world—among them *Troilus and Criseyde*;[66] finally he has expressed the universality and inevitability of death in phraseology which goes as far back as the Old English *Wanderer*, and at least as far forward as Richard II's "For God's sake let us sit upon the ground/And tell sad stories of the death of kings."[67] As Theseus states it:

> "He moot be deed, the kyng as shal a page;
> *Som* in his bed, *som* in the depe see,
> *Som* in the large feeld, as men may see . . ." (3030–3032)

Consolation is nipped thin at the waist. But with the lines

> "What maketh this but Juppiter, the kyng,
> That is prince and cause of alle thing . . .?" (3035–3036)

the tone of the speech changes abruptly, and its vision begins to move upward and outward. There is no denial of the reality of mutability and death, but they are viewed from a different perspective. Are not these precisely the sort of thing, as Joyce somewhere says, that makes life's work leaving? Arcite has escaped all of this, and with it the agony of seeing his fame, his name in arms, dulled by age:

> "And certeinly a man hath moost honour
> To dyen in his excellence and flour,
> Whan he is siker of his goode name . . .
> And gladder oghte his freend been of his deeth,
> Whan with honour up yolden is his breeth,
> Than whan his name apalled is for age . . .
> Thanne is it best, as for a worthy fame,
> To dyen whan that he is best of name." (3047–3056)

This is not a medieval Christian sentiment; it in fact resembles in idea and even vocabulary Housman's "To an Athlete Dying Young," one stanza of which reads:

> Now you will not swell the rout
> Of lads that wore their honors out,
> Runners whom renown outran
> And the name died before the man.[68]

But Housman's poetry is negative and purportedly pessimistic, as the *Knight's Tale* is not. Theseus's final statement is no praise of death; it is an affirmation of something very different:

> "What may I conclude of this longe serye,
> But after wo I rede us to be merye,
> And thanken Juppiter of al his grace?
> And er that we departen from this place
> I rede that we make of sorwes two
> O parfit joye, lastynge everemo." (3067–3072)

It is in this passage that one experiences the greatness of the poem. The first half of Theseus's speech has been devoted to the rigorous demonstration of human mortality—no class is exempt. The second, however, begins by demonstrating that death can be a triumph over life, and then, as if transformed by some kind of revelation, concludes with an affirmation of the values of life which can only be conceived of as ultimate—the apparently ridiculous assertion that out of two sorrows can be made a perfect joy, lasting forever. No argument Theseus has presented has denied the sorrows of life; none the imperfection; none the mutability.

As has been said, of insight into the operations of the forces which control the world, Theseus has previously shown no knowledge. Nor in the course of a very extensive narrative has there been any indication that the supernatural world has taken the pains to communicate with him. What now comes from his "wise brest" may be taken as an expression of intuitive reason, but it is more likely that it is the product of experience and prolonged meditation. What Theseus the human being, snatched by the death of his friend Arcite from godlike felicity[69] and plunged into the welter of life, has come to see is the emotional poverty and intellectual bankruptcy of the view set forth by his father, Aegeus. What he now perceives is the absolute human need to assert human values in a world where nothing seems more evident than the total disregard of them. The final heroic vision of Theseus is exactly complemented by what has step by step been revealed to the reader. He has seen that the world is not governed by chance, and that destiny, despite its apparent harshness, has awarded to Arcite, to Palemon, and not the least to Emelye, the self-fulfillment most desired by them—"Wel bettre than they kan hemself devyse" (1254).

May 3 is again a destinal date, but the destiny is of a nature very different from that of *Troilus and Criseyde*. Though still not relieved of her more unpleasant duties, Fortune seems to revolve her great wheel more with a view to depositing worldlings in their proper places than to crushing them out.

III. THE "NUN'S PRIEST'S TALE"

Chaucer's third allusion to May 3 is a most complex one.

> Whan that the month in which the world bigan,
> That highte March, whan God first maked man,
> Was compleet, and passed were also,
> Syn March bigan, thritty dayes and two . . . (VII [B²], 3187–3190)

The lines, when worked out, yield the date of May 3,[70] and the reader is made acutely aware that the day cannot conceivably pass without its usual tragic consequences. It would appear that under cover of the darkness of the preceding night, a "col-fox, ful of sly iniquitee" (3215)—one Daun Russell by name—has slunk into Chauntecleer's domain, and lies hidden there, with murder at his heart. Both Chauntecleer's father and mother, we later discover, have been in Daun Russell's house—to his own great personal satisfaction—and he plans to give himself the same pleasure with Chauntecleer.

As is his usual custom, Chauntecleer sleeps tranquilly upon his perch in the midst of his seven wives—who are also "his sustres and his paramours" (2867). But May 3 is never a day for the customary or the usual. Just before dawn—"in a dawenynge" (2882)—Chauntecleer is assailed by a most terrifying dream. As he later explains:

"Me mette how that I romed up and doun
Withinne our yeerd, wheer as I saugh a beest
Was lyk an hound, and wolde han maad areest
Upon my body, and wolde han had me deed.
His colour was bitwixe yelow and reed,
And tipped was his tayl and bothe his eeris
With blak, unlyk the remenant of his heeris;
His snowte smal, with glowynge eyen tweye." (2898–2905)

Pertelote, Chauntecleer's favorite and immediate companion upon his perch, is suddenly awakened by the terrified "roaring" occasioned by Chauntecleer's horrid dream. When Chauntecleer informs her of the cause of his terror, her womanly bosom is torn by the most violent conflicting emotions. In her dual role of courtly lady, loved *par amours*, and devoted comforting wife, she is at first outraged at the unchivalric terror of her lord:

"Avoy," quod she, "fy on yow, hertelees!
Allas!" quod she, "for, by that God above,
Now han ye lost myn herte and al my love. . . .
Have ye no mannes herte, and han a berd?" (2908–2920)

However, mindful of her second role, she is also deeply concerned at the state of a digestive tract capable of producing so dreadful

a dream. She assures Chauntecleer on the authority of the great
Cato[71] that dreams are meaningless, and after precisely diagnosing the red and black coloration of the fearsome dream-beast as
indicating in her beloved husband a dominance of the choleric
and melancholic humors, she prescribes a mild laxative treatment
which will purge him both upward and downward—the necessary
ingredients of which are, by the greatest good fortune, available
in their very own yard:

> "Pekke hem up right as they growe and ete hem yn.
> Be myrie, housbonde . . ." (2967–2968)

Chauntecleer, however, finds nothing to be particularly merry
about in the proposed course of treatment, and chooses rather to
face death by supernatural causes than to suffer the ghastly demise
he quite advisedly suspects will be the result of Pertelote's treatment.[72] He therefore stoutly maintains the prophetic role of
dreams, and recites an imposing list of men who have come to
frightful ends as a result of hearkening to advisers who scoffed
at the significance of dreams. At the conclusion of his address, he
is seen to take on the stature of the true tragic hero. He proclaims:
"I shal han of this avisioun/Adversite . . ." (3152–3153) and
heroically descends, accompanied by his wives, to the courtyard—
there to meet his destiny.

How is the ignorant, non-medicinally oriented reader to
understand the state of Chauntecleer? Is he, as Pertelote per-
suasively argues, simply a sick rooster whose dream is attributable
entirely to natural causes; or is he, as he prefers to view himself,
a tragic hero forewarned of his coming doom by an "avisioun"
of divine origin?[73] A rather direct hint lies in the timing of
Chauntecleer's dream. In antiquity it was believed that

. . . the soul could reach its greatest power when it was independent of the digestive activity of the body and, therefore, most free
from bodily influence. Then it was nearest to the divine, could enter
into communion with the other world, and receive messages there-
from.[74]

Of the prevalence of this belief, Dante provides considerable
evidence. In *Inferno* XXVI, 7, he speaks, in passing, of true dreams

occurring close to morning: "presso al mattin del ver si sogna"; and in *Purgatorio* IX, 13–18, he again speaks of the mind at dawn existing—like a pilgrim—detached from the flesh and to a lesser degree from thought. In this state, the mind is in its vision almost divine:

> Nell'ora che comincia i tristi lai
>   la rondinella presso alla mattina,
>   forse a memoria de'suo'primi guai,
> e che la mente nostra, peregrina
>   più dalla carne e men da' pensier presa,
>   alle sue visïon quasi è divina.[75]

By the timing of the dream, a pervasive sense of the tragic has been introduced. Chauntecleer's dream has occurred at a time when dreams come true and is hence an "avisioun," as Chauntecleer has pronounced it to be. The reader is therefore constrained to view Pertelote's apparently realistic interpretation as in fact tragic. The reality is that Chauntecleer, the tragic hero, has, by supernatural agency, become the recipient of divine truth—but his wife has refused to believe him. As the Nun's Priest ominously remarks:

> Wommennes conseils been ful ofte colde;
> Wommannes conseil broghte us first to wo,
> And made Adam fro Paradys to go . . . (3256–3258)

Day has now dawned—the day of May 3—and the reader is informed that the entrance into Chauntecleer's domain by the iniquitous col-fox has from all eternity been foreseen by divine prescience—"By heigh ymaginacioun forncast" (3217). Furthermore, the absolute factual accuracy of the account which sets forth the imminent tragic downfall of the great Chauntecleer is beyond question:

> This storie is also trewe, I undertake,
> As is the book of Launcelot de Lake,
> That wommen holde in ful greet reverence. (3211–3213)[76]

However, with Chauntecleer poised upon the very brink of disaster, the Nun's Priest's narrative is suddenly brought to a halt by a theological difficulty: Is prescience in fact predestination? Because Divine Intelligence has foreseen from all time that the fox will burst into Chauntecleer's yard, is the noblest of roosters necessarily doomed? Or is the truth not the reverse: that the coming of the future event is the cause of the divine fore-knowledge, and therefore no necessity exists, and therefore free choice prevails? Or may it not be that the divine knowledge is simultaneous for all periods of time, and necessity simply a con-dition of that knowledge? Here is a problem not without diffi-culty, and the Nun's Priest is uncertain of his own ability to solve it:

> . . . I ne kan nat bulte it to the bren
> As kan the hooly doctour Augustyn,
> Or Boëce, or the Bisshop Bradwardyn,
> Wheither that Goddes worthy forwityng
> Streyneth me nedely for to doon a thing,—
> "Nedely" clepe I symple necessitee;
> Or elles, if free choys be graunted me
> To do that same thyng, or do it noght,
> Though God forwoot it er that was wroght;
> Or if his wityng streyneth never a deel
> But by necessitee condicioneel. (3240–3250)[77]

The Nun's Priest will have nothing further to do with this supremely confusing topic, and abruptly returns to the story of the doomed Chauntecleer. He proceeds to narrate how the sly, iniquitous fox has cynically played upon Chauntecleer's pride in his magnificent singing voice, and has thereby induced him to assume a position ideal for the projection of sound, but equally ideal for rapid transportation:

> This Chauntecleer stood hye upon his toos,
> Strecchynge his nekke, and heeld his eyen cloos . . . (3331–3332)

Whereupon the fox seizes him, and carries him off toward the wood.

Now that the disaster has actually happened, the narrator is overcome:

> O destinee, that mayst nat been eschewed!
> Allas, that Chauntecleer fleigh fro the bemes!
> Allas, his wyf ne roghte nat of dremes!
> And on a Friday fil al this meschaunce. (3338–3341)

The reference to Friday deepens the tragic tone of the poem. Friday, a day unlucky in itself, is unimaginably unlucky when it falls on May 3.[78] Furthermore, it is a day associated with Venus, and we learn to our increasing horror that Chauntecleer is actually a dedicated subject of the pagan goddess and in her service:

> . . . dide al his poweer,
> Moore for delit than world to multiplye . . . (3344–3345)

When one adds to this rebellious pagan delight in pleasure the whole irregularity of Chauntecleer's sexual life—his wives being also his sisters and paramours—and to this that he has unquestionably unreasonably used his wife Pertelote in the very first hour of a day on which sin is unforgivable—

> He fethered Pertelote twenty tyme,
> And trad hire eke as ofte, er it was pryme (3177–3178)

—the state of Chauntecleer's moral life is at best highly questionable, and the certainty of his downfall entirely unquestionable.

Yet another chasm yawns when the narrator points out that Friday is directly connected with the death of another great man, Richard I. The obvious resemblance between the two heroic characters causes the Nun's Priest to bewail his lack of the "sentence and lore" of the great rhetorician Geoffrey of Vinsauf, who, in his handbook on poetic composition, the *Poetria nova*, so eloquently bewailed the death of King Richard.[79] Did he, the humble Nun's Priest, but possess such knowledge, his own hero, Chauntecleer, should be with equal eloquence lamented. Lamentations are now heard from the hens, who have discovered the loss of their lord, Chauntecleer—lamentations such as were never heard at the fall of Troy or the burning of Carthage. The doom of Chauntecleer is evidently complete.

Fortune, however, could not be herself were she not changeable, and as Daun Russell proceeds triumphantly toward the wood with the cock upon his back, a ruse—apparently attributable to Fortune—enters Chauntecleer's quite uncluttered mind, and as a result, he escapes. Unaccountably, the fox has become Fortune's enemy:

> Lo, how Fortune turneth sodeynly
> The hope and pryde of hir enemy! (3403–3404)

But what of Chauntecleer's prophetic dream which the reader has all along been led to believe was true? Contrary to all omens, Chauntecleer has escaped from his prefigured doom, and is apparently to be returned to the very top of Fortune's wheel, there to dwell in bliss amongst his "wyves alle." Is this not the grossest form of literary deceit? Deceit there is, but only of the reader's making. Chauntecleer's dream presented to him a fearsome beast which "*wolde* han maad areest" upon his body, and "*wolde* han had [him] deed (2900–2901). All this is perfectly true. The fox had the same intentions concerning Chauntecleer as he had earlier had toward Chauntecleer's previously pleasurably assimilated parents. Whatever signs and portents his ancestors may have received, Chauntecleer's told him only of the fox's intent, and left his will free to the unaccountably unfatal persuasion of the fair Pertelote.

Although a seemingly self-sufficient story, the *Nun's Priest's Tale* has a very definite setting within the *Canterbury Tales*. Immediately preceding the *Nun's Priest's Tale* comes the Monk's interminable series of "tragedies," a monotonous repetition of a single idea, that earthly joy must end in sorrow, more specifically in "wrecchednesse," and all through the agency of Fortune. The Knight, who has in his own tale specifically repudiated this gloomy view of existence, feels that he can survive no more of the Monk's tragic exempla, and interrupts:

> "Hoo!" quod the Knyght, "good sire, namoore of this!
> That ye han seyd is right ynough, ywis,
> And muchel moore; for litel hevynesse
> Is right ynough to muche folk, I gesse.
> I seye for me, it is a greet disese,
> Whereas men han been in greet welthe and ese,
> To heeren of hire sodeyn fal, allas!
> And the contrarie is joye and greet solas . . ." (2767–2774)[80]

The "contrarie" is precisely what the Nun's Priest—"This sweete preest, this goodly man sir John"—has provided. There is "joye and greet solas" in the story of Chauntecleer, over whose noble brow—"battailled as it were a castel wal"—all the tragic portents the medieval mind could conceive were gathered, but who, nevertheless, inexplicably found Fortune his friend, and

> ". . . clymbeth up and wexeth fortunat,
> And there abideth in prosperitee." (2776–2777)

IV

It would be foolish to fail to observe that each work in which the date of May 3 figures has a different narrator, and that each narrative is permeated by the personality of the individual narrator. However, there would seem to be a steady movement from *Troilus and Criseyde* with its expressed deference to the "moral Gower" and the "philosophical Strode" to the humanism of the *Knight's Tale* and finally to the pure and almost disembodied humor of the *Nun's Priest's Tale*. When a poet can find delight in burlesquing his own work as well as the whole of the world of medieval letters, he would seem to have reached the fullest extent of objectivity, and hence of pure humor. Amidst the parodies of dream lore, medieval medicine, rhetoric, and the rest, one finds another on the predestination–free will controversy. Is not this debate concerning the undoomed Chauntecleer an exquisite parody of the debate on the same subject concerning the doomed Troilus (*TC*, IV, 953–1082)?

However this may be, Chaucer's poetry is never unidimensional. The Nun's Priest's concluding reference: "al that writen is,/To oure doctrine it is ywrite" finds its echo in Chaucer's *Retraction*.[81]

NOTES

1. For the Floralia in general, see Hastings, *Encyclopaedia of Religion and Ethics*, IV, 903, 905. John P. McCall, in "Chaucer's May 3" (*MLN*, LXXVI [1961], 201–205), provides excellent examples of the Christian view of the Floralia.
2. Otto Kiefer, *Sexual Life in Ancient Rome*, trans. Gilbert and Helen Highet (New York, 1935), p. 18. For the pervasiveness of the view see *Ovid's Fasti*, v, 487–490 (ed. and trans. Sir James G. Frazer [London, 1931], p. 296).
3. René Nelli, *L'Érotique des troubadours* (Toulouse, 1963), p. 32.

4. J. A. MacCulloch, *The Religion of the Ancient Celts* (Edinburgh, 1911), p. 266.
5. *The Works of Sir Thomas Malory*, ed. Eugène Vinaver (Oxford, 1954), pp. 790–791. Because of its greater availability, all textual citations are to this one-volume edition, rather than to the three-volume edition cited in note 10, below.
6. J. M. Manly in his edition of the *Canterbury Tales* (New York, 1928) indicates two arrangements of evil days, in both of which May 3 figures (pp. 550, 551). Robinson gives an extensive summary on scholarship concerning May 3 (*Works*, pp. 673–674). However, there are also in Manly's second calendar (p. 551) very unlucky days, for which May 3 does not seem to qualify—as Robinson points out (p. 674).
7. v. [F] 906. (*Works*, p. 137; Robinson's comment, p. 674).
8. *Morte Arthure*, lines 2371–2374 (ed. Edmund Brock, *EETS O.S.* No. 8), p. 70. For the meaning of "kalendez of Maye," see *MED*, "calende(s" 1 (a).
9. Vinaver, p. 44. For the occasion of the begetting, see p. 32.
10. *The Works of Sir Thomas Malory*, ed. Eugène Vinaver, 2nd ed., (Oxford, 1967) III, 1281 ff.
11. See note 6 above.
12. D. W. Robertson, "Chaucerian Tragedy," *ELH*, XIX (1952), 19.
13. McCall, *MLN*, LXXVI, 201–205.
14. (Glasgow, 1902), p. 273. The theological implications of "If caught in the act"—assuming the statement is to be taken literally—are certainly not devoid of interest.
15. *British Calendar Customs*, ed. M. Macleod Banks (London, 1939), II, 246–247. It is interesting, if not particularly relevant, that the same feeling concerning the incompatibility of May and marriage as has earlier been noted is very much in evidence: "None get married on that day of the week upon which this day fell" (*ibid.*, p. 247).
16. There are some indications of various sorts of assimilation. The Invention of the Holy Cross obviously has been drawn from the Roman calendar; a less obvious assimilation is Beltane. Both May 1 and May 3 were associated with her (*ibid.*, p. 246; see also MacCullough, *Religion of the Ancient Celts*, p. 266).
17. *Bede's Ecclesiastical History of the English People*, Book III, Chapter 27, ed. and trans. Bertram Colgrave and R. A. B. Mynors (Oxford, 1969), pp. 311–313. The translation has been altered slightly, and the punctuation made to conform to the punctuation of the Latin text as there printed. The passage was brought to our attention by Dr. Frederick S. Frank of Boston University.
18. Roland M. Smith, "Two Chaucer Notes," *MLN*, LI (1936), 314–317.
19. May McKisack, *The Fourteenth Century* (Oxford, 1959), p. 140.
20. "Si se parti li dis rois, l'endemain au matin, de le ville de Calais à tout son grant arroy, et se mist sus les camps à tout le plus grant charoy et le mieulz atelé que nulz veist onques issir d'Engleterre. On disoit qu'il avoit plus de six mil chars bien atelés, qui tout estoient apasset d'Engleterre. Puis ordonna ses batailles, si noblement et si ricement parés uns et aultres, que c'estoit solas et deduis au regarder" (*Les Chroniques de Jean Froissart*, ed. Simeon Luce [Paris, 1874], v, 199).

21. "Et ne demora nulz chevaliers et escuiers, ne homs d'onneur, qui fust hettiés, de l'eage de entre vingt ans et soixante, que tout ne partesissent: si ques priès tout li conte, li baron, li chevalier et li escuier dou royaume d'Engleterre vinrent à Douvres" (*ibid.*, v, 198).

22. Although his works as a whole give little indication of it, Chaucer did see action at first hand. See following discussion. Upon Chaucer's configuration, the most eloquent testimony is that of the Eagle in the *House of Fame*: "Seynte Marye!/Thou art noyous for to carye . . ." (lines 573–574 [*Works*, p. 287]).

23. McKisack, *Fourteenth Century*, p. 140.

24. From Chaucer's testimony at the Scrope-Grosvenor trial, it is clear that Chaucer took part in an engagement at Rhetel near Rheims, and it is equally clear that at some time between late 1359 and early 1360, he was captured and ransomed (*Life Records*, pp. 23–28). Nothing else remains which might be called indisputable; however, it may be presumed that Chaucer, with the rest of the English host, experienced the "Black Monday" discussed in the note following.

25. The conditions under which the English attempted to wage warfare are amply described by Lady Mede in B Passus III of *Piers Plowman*. See particularly Skeat's note to B III, 188 (*The Vision of William concerning Piers the Plowman*, ed. W. W. Skeat [Oxford, 1866], II, 48–49). The "dim cloud" coming, as it did, immediately after Easter Day, made a very definite impression on Edward. According to Froissart, while the pious Duke of Lancaster was lecturing the King on peace: "il avint à lui et à toutes ses gens ossi, lui estant devant Chartres, un grant miracle qui moult le humilia et brisa son corage, car entrues que cil trettier [franchois] aloient et preeçoient le dit roy et son conseil et encores nulle response agreable n'en avoient, uns orages, uns tempès et uns effoudres si grans et si horribles descendi dou ciel en l'ost le roy d'Engleterre, que il sembla bien proprement à tous ceulx qui là estoient que li siècles deuist finer, car il cheoient de l'air pières si grosses que elles tuoient hommes et chevaus, et en furent li plus hardi tout eshidé. Et adonc regarda li rois d'Engleterre devers l'église Nostre Dame de Chartres, et se voa et rendi devotement à Nostre Dame, et prommist, si com il dist et confessa depuis, que il s'accorderoit à le pais" (Luce, *Froissart*, VI, 4, 5).

26. For a full discussion see R. Delachenal, *Histoire de Charles V* (Paris, 1909), chapters V and VI, pp. 193–265.

27. McKisack, *Fourteenth Century*, p. 140.

28. "J'incline à croire que l'accord était fait *le 3 mai*, et que les jours suivants ont été consacrés à rédiger l'instrument du traité et à résoudre des questions de détail, épineuses peut-être, mais qui n'étaient pas de nature à compromettre le résultat obtenu. Des quittances données par Charles de Montmorency, Ainard de la Tour, Jean de Grolée et Artaut de Beausemblant *le 3 mai 1360*, il ressort que la paix était faite à cette date. Il semble même que ces quatre chevaliers aient quitté Chartres ce jour-là, considérant leur mission de négociateurs comme terminée . . . (II, 198)." See also his remarks on the appearance of May 3 in the treaty itself (*ibid.*, pp. 204–205). Records of the quittances are to be found on p. 194, notes 3, 4, 5, of the work cited, but appear somewhat

more fully in Delachenal's *Chronique des règnes de Jean II et de Charles V* (Paris, 1910), I, 260–261. Quotations are from volume I, p. 260, note 3 of the latter work. It is interesting to compare the "faiz" and the "faiz et a faire" of the quittances with the use of the same formulae in John of Gaunt's grants to Philippa Chaucer (see above, p. 65, note 25, of the present volume).

29. If Chaucer were still in the service of his earliest known patron, Lionel, Earl of Ulster—as it seems certain he was—he would have been in the field in the vicinity of Chartres and hence of nearby Brétigny. Froissart states that Lionel accompanied his father, Edward III, on his arrival at Calais (Delachenal, *Charles V*, II, 148, note 9). At the subsequent ratification of the Treaty of Calais, Lionel was one of those, on the English side, sworn to uphold the treaty (*ibid.*, 256). It was Delachenal's discovery that Chaucer was present at the ratification, and bore letters from Calais to England on behalf of Lionel (*Life Records*, pp. 19–22; p. 20, note 1). Delachenal went so far as to make Chaucer a participant: "Geoffroi Chaucer, alors clerc du roi et attaché à la personne de Lionel, comte d'Ulster, fils du roi d'Angleterre, participa à ce titre aux négociations de Calais" (Delachenal, *Charles V*, II, 241, note 1). That the letters Chaucer bore to England were of a diplomatic nature is highly questionable, but that in his capacity as "clericus" he did not assist Lionel in the ratification of the treaty is almost beyond question (see discussion of the whole matter in *Life Records*, pp. 19–22). Since Chaucer was in the immediate vicinity of Brétigny, where the original draft of the treaty was made up, and was present at Calais "ad tractatum," he could hardly have been unaware of the significance of May 3, since the real deliberations seem to have ended on May 3, and since the treaty which was ratified provided in Item 15 that certain noble prisoners, who were taking the place of King John, should be delivered from their prisons: "s'il n'ont été à accort de certaine raençon, par convenence faite par avant *le tiers jour de may* derrenerement passé ..." (E. Cosneau, *Les grands traités de la Guerre de Cent Ans* (Paris, 1889), pp. 51–52. Cited by Delachenal, *Charles V*, II, 204–205.

30. *Works*, p. 402. Chaucer seems to be engaging in some deliberate ambiguity concerning time. Pandarus has clearly experienced his "tene in love" on May 3 (lines 57–60). Since in the Middle Ages, time was reckoned from sunrise to sunset, and again from sunset to sunrise, the passion of Pandarus has to be computed in a somewhat different fashion. (See Robinson's note to *Knight's Tale*, line 2217 [*Works*, p. 169]). At an indeterminate time on May 3, Pandarus's amatory agony has driven him to bed. Before dawn of May 4, he has made "er it was day, ful many a wente" (II, 63). When he is awakened by Progne, the swallow, he arises and is said to remember his undertaking on behalf of Troilus.

> Remembryng hym his erand was to doone
> From Troilus, and ek his grete emprise ... (II, 72–73).

We know that at the end of Book I (1062–1064), Pandarus is already considering what approach he will make to Criseyde. At what time did he make up his mind as to the day he would make his approach? Was it in the course of his sufferings on May 3, when the successful exercise of his powers of amatory persuasion on the relatively simple Criseyde might have appeared a welcome restorative after his evidently disastrous encounter with his very own very-difficult-to-persuade "bele dame sans merci?" The same unclarity is to be found in Chaucer's treatment of his evident source for the scene of Pandarus's awakening. In Dante, Progne, the swallow, sings—as she is accustomed to sing— just before dawn:

> Nell'ora che comincia i tristi lai
> La rondinella presso alla mattina (*Purgatorio* IX, 14).

Chaucer alters this to "Whan morwen com" (II, 65). If Chaucer had followed Dante exactly, Pandarus would have been awakened before dawn, and his decision to visit Criseyde could have been presented as definitely occurring on May 3. Thus the forging of an important link in the chain of causality which leads to Troilus's extinction could have been definitely connected with May 3. However, Chaucer does not choose to do this. He stresses May 3 in a rather inflated Virgilian fashion:

> As I shal synge, on Mayes day the thrydde (56)

and he attaches the date directly to Pandarus in the first lines of the stanza immediately following:

> That Pandarus, for al his wise speche,
> Felt ek his part of loves shotes keene . . . (57–58)

However, through Chaucer's changing of the time of Progne's song, all we know for certain is that Pandarus woke up on the morning of May 4, remembered his errand on behalf of Troilus, and carried it out. We do not know when he arrived at his decision. We are told only that he remembered. Whether he suddenly remembered his obligation to Troilus, which seems unlikely since he has already been shown thinking about it, or whether his "grete emprise" refers to a plan worked out during his sleepless hours on May 3—or at some earlier time—is quite unclear. In any case, no express connection between May 3 and the chain of events which is to end with Troilus's death is ever made. It is quite possible that Chaucer, at this point, had no inclination to sound his tragic note too forcefully.

31. The "locus classicus" for this is the beginning of the *Roman de la rose*, (ed. Ernest Langlois [Paris, 1920]), II, 3, where in seven lines (45–51) May appears three times. Though May songs go back to pagan origins (see Nelli, *Érotique*, pp. 29–40), it was probably the popularity of the *Roman* which made May so prominent a convention in the romance. The actuality of May "observaunces" in Chaucer's day is a subject beyond the scope of the present essay. For an encyclopedic view of Chaucer's use of May, see J. S. P. Tatlock and Arthur G. Kennedy, *A Concordance to the Complete Works of Geoffrey Chaucer* (Washington, 1927), pp. 579–580.

32. John J. O'Connor, "The Astronomical Dating of Chaucer's *'Troilus,'*" *JEGP*, LV (1956), 560.
33. As noted above, in the Celtic calendar the most prominent names for May 3 are all connected with the Invention of the Holy Cross. The same is true of the English calendar. It is difficult to believe that Chaucer's audience could have thought of May 3 without also thinking of the Invention of the Holy Cross, especially since it had become a part of the liturgy of May 3. (See Robertson, *ELH*, xix, (1952), 19).
34. The popularity of Geoffrey of Monmouth's *Historia regum Britanniae*, which not only provided the British people with a fully developed Arthur but also with a Trojan lineage, was immense. The "Brut" became a standard name for "chronicle" because of Geoffrey's attribution of the founding of Britain to the Trojan Brutus, descendant of Aeneas. (See Charles Foulon, "Wace," in *ALMA*, pp. 94–103).
35. An account of the various versions of the Palladium story is conveniently available in the *New Century Classical Handbook*, ed. Catherine B. Avery and Jotham Johnson (New York, 1962), p. 807. The story, as Chaucer knew it, may be read in as little or as full detail as one wishes in the *Historia destructionis Troiae* of Guido de Columnis (ed. N. E. Griffin [Cambridge, Mass., 1936]), pp. 226 ff. The side glosses provide a useful brief account of the history of the Palladium.
36. The problem of chronology here arises, and the present writer finds himself but ill-equipped to deal with it. The date for *Troilus*, which Robinson finds "satisfactory on literary grounds," is 1385. Robinson's reasoning is as follows: "The *Troilus* would then be clearly later than the *House of Fame*, and probably also than the *Palamon and Arcite*; and it would be separated by only a short interval from the Prologue to the *Legend of Good Women*, which there is reason for dating in 1386–1387." The importance of the Prologue to the *Legend of Good Women* is that it contains a list of Chaucer's works up to the time of the composition of the *Legend of Good Women* (1386–1387), a list of some importance because written by Chaucer himself. The relevant lines concern a work involving two of the principal characters of the *Knight's Tale*:

> And al the love of Palamon and Arcite
> Of Thebes, thogh the storye ys knowen lyte . . . (419–420)

There was then, in existence, before the *Legend of Good Women*, a poem in which Palamon and Arcite figured. If this is the *Knight's Tale,* then that tale could have been written before *Troilus and Criseyde*.

Concerning the chronology of Chaucer's works, there exists an infinitude of arguments. I should like simply to accept as "satisfactory on literary grounds" (p. 811) Robinson's feeling that a little-known poem by Chaucer, concerning "al the love of Palamon and Arcite" anteceded *Troilus and Criseyde*, and that ultimately a known and finished poem, adapted to the personality of the Knight, took its place as the first of the *Canterbury Tales*. I emphasize Robinson's phrase "on literary grounds," because, for reasons I trust will become clear, the *Knight's Tale* seems to me a natural evolution in thought from

Troilus and Criseyde. The reversal of this process I should find very difficult to understand. Robinson's summation of the arguments concerning chronology are to be found on pp. 810–811 (*Troilus and Criseyde*) and p. 669 (*Knight's Tale*) of his edition. [A.L.K.]

37. In Dante (*Paradiso*, xx, 106–117) is recounted the miracle granted to Gregory the Great in his admiration for the justice of Trajan. The supreme example is his turning back from a fully prepared military expedition on the march to do justice upon the murderers of the son of a widow who pleads with him on his departing, much as do the widows of Thebes at Theseus' returning (*Purgatorio*, x, 73–79; *Paradiso*, xx, 43–88). In both the *Teseida* and the *Knight's Tale*, Theseus puts all other affairs aside to make war upon Creon. However, the motivation of the two conquerors is somewhat different. In the version of Boccaccio, like Chaucer an avid reader of Dante, glory seems to have assumed a position superior to justice (*Teseida*, ii, stanzas 33, 49), (ed. Salvatore Battaglia [Florence, 1938], pp. 58–59, 62). In Chaucer, however, Theseus is not in search of glory, but of exerting retributive justice in a fashion which should never be forgotten:

> He wolde doon so ferforthly his myght
> Upon the tiraunt Creon hem to wreke,
> That al the peple of Grece sholde speke
> How Creon was of Theseus yserved
> As he that hadde his deeth ful wel deserved. (960–964)

38. Another indication that Theseus is to be taken as a figure of justice is contained in his reaction or lack of reaction to the capture of Palemon and Arcite. After the battle, the heralds recognize them by their coat-armor as of the royal blood of Thebes. The "pilours," therefore, instead of cutting their throats and removing everything of value, carry them "softe" unto the tent of Theseus (1009–1022). In this act, one is probably not to detect on the part of the "pilours" a sudden tenderness of heart—a quality for which they were not famous—but the recognition of a cash value far in excess of the captured knights' armor and appurtenances. A noble prisoner was a valuable asset—as witness King John of France, whose ransom was set at 3,000,000 crowns (see above, on the *Book of the Duchess*, note 15). Except for the amount involved, there was in the case of King John nothing unusual. A prisoner was an asset, assignable at will, whose value depended on his social rank. Richard I's ransom was another monumental sum, but the king's ransom of both of these notables was probably less present to the English mind of Chaucer's day than the famous Hauley and Shakyl case. Hauley and Shakyl were two squires, who, in 1367, at the battle of Najera, captured Alfonso, Count of Denia, son of the Infante and grandson of the King of Aragon. As was the procedure in the case of King John, the Count was released to collect his ransom, and his sureties were his two sons, Alfonso and Pedro. The younger of these was assigned to the Count of Foix, who made himself responsible for the ransom, and the elder was assigned to the two squires. Ten years later the ransom had still not been collected. At this point,

negotiations between England and Spain made the possession of the elder son, Alfonso, a matter of some moment. Hauley and Shakyl were requested to produce their hostage; they refused, were consigned to the Tower, escaped and took sanctuary in St. Peter's. Hauley was killed on the steps of the altar, and one of the monks who sought to intervene was also killed. As a result, a major confrontation between Church and State took place (see the account by Sydney Armitage-Smith, *John of Gaunt* [London, 1904], pp. 234–237; also G. M. Trevelyan, *England in the Age of Wycliffe* [London, 1909], pp. 87–90). By contrast, when Theseus is presented with the two captured noble kinsmen, he does not treat them as chattel; he sends them off to prison: "he nolde no raunsoun" (1024). When Arcite is later released through the intercession of Perotheus, the point is reinforced: Arcite is released "withouten any raunsoun" (1205). In an age when Chaucer, in the *Parson's Tale*, could point out that a notable feature of the Day of Judgment was that on that day an incorruptible judge would preside, "Ther shul we han a juge that may nat been deceyved ne corrupt (x [I], 167 [*Works*, p. 231]), one can see that Theseus's justice, though influenced more by feeling than by reasoned consideration, is a singularly untainted justice.

39. A further indication of Chaucer's reading of the Middle English romances. "Breme as bare" occurs in the *Morte Arthure*, but is not of so great frequency as one might expect (see *MED*, "bor," 1 [*d*]).

40. Actually by Neptune at the request of Saturn (2685).

41. The earthiness of Arcite's metaphor goes a good way toward differentiating him from Palemon. The passage is evocative of a similar passage in *Piers Plowman* which describes Glutton's ineffectual efforts to depart from the alehouse after a rather prolonged stay:

> He myȝte neither steppe ne stonde   ·   er he his staffe hadde;
> And thanne gan he go   ·   liche a glewmannes bicche
> Somme tyme aside   ·   and somme tyme arere,
> As who-so leyth lynes   ·   forto lacche foules.

(B Passus v, 352–355 [Skeat, *Piers Plowman*, I, 162]). It is possible that Arcite may have spent some time elsewhere than on the battlefield and in the bower.

42. The first three terms are more or less interchangeable in meaning, and their use is primarily a matter of emphasis. "Prescience" is not, as is made very clear in the fifth book of the *Consolation of Philosophy*. The term occurs only once—in Palemon's complaint against the "crueel goddes":

> What governance is in this prescience,
> That giltelees tormenteth innocence? (1313–1314)

Although "prescience" is normally understood to be pure foreknowledge, its use here, in an apparently different fashion, may not be without significance. See note 45, below.

43. For "amphibologie," see Robinson's note to *Troilus and Criseyde*, IV, 1406 (*Works*, p. 831).

44. See p. 166 above. In Boccaccio's version, Arcite, upon his release from Athens, makes a kind of lachrymose tour of the classical Grecian social directory. After finding Thebes laid waste, Penteo, as he now calls himself, proceeds with his entourage—presumably disguised—to enter the service of Menelaus. For a year, unrecognized and in deepening sorrow, he remains with Menelaus, and then leaves Messenia for Aegina, there to serve Peleus, father of Achilles, and perhaps to hear news of Emilia. Arcite's stay with Peleus is of some moment, because events which take place there are to bring about his resolution to return to Athens. In the course of his travels, Arcite's appearance has been changing, and he now realizes that he resembles something unexpectedly released, without due notice, from the infernal regions—all this as a result of his sufferings from love. With changed features and changed name, he comes to Peleus, "in maniera de pover valletto." In search of news of Emilia, he speaks to the master of a ship which has just arrived from Athens, and is about to return. All the master can tell him is: "Whatever goddess in the heavens is most beautiful, she would in comparison with [Emilia], seem lusterless. She [Emilia] is brighter than any star, and—if I say so myself—no such figure as hers has ever been seen." Unfortunately, however, says the master, Emilia's proposed husband has just died.

As might be anticipated, this news is not without its effect on Arcite. He believes his appearance is now so radically changed that even in Athens he cannot be recognized—and the means of returning to Athens is at hand. He therefore returns to Athens, and takes service with Theseus, as he has with Menelaus and Peleus. (*Teseida,* IV, stanzas 1–38 [Battaglia, pp. 101–112]).

Boccaccio's version has been gone into in some detail, because it is important to observe that in all its details there is no real sense of the supernatural. Arcite's tour is calculated to display Boccaccio's classical learning. Thus we are told that Thebes has fallen because of the wrath of Juno, but no real connection has been made between this event and the ultimate fate of Arcite. Arcite cries out against "Fortuna," but his outcries constitute no pattern. We are not even told that the convenient demise of Emilia's "promesso sposo" has anything to do with anything. In Chaucer, the events, if less elaborate, are roughly the same. However, by the substitution of the vision of Mercury for the conversation with the ship's master, Chaucer has very successfully maintained the destinal sense of the poem.

45. As regards earthly affairs, this speech, which comes from the Knight as narrator, is about as deterministic as one is likely to find. It would seem to serve as a very effective method of characterizing the Knight. As a man-of-arms who has spent his whole life in warfare, a deterministic view of what happens on earth would seem a natural one. However, it does not follow that the Knight considers "the sighte above" (1672) as malevolent. Palemon's outcries against the "crueel goddes" (note 42 above) do not turn out to be justified, nor in the conclusion of his tale does the Knight equate a providentially controlled universe with a cruel universe. See p. 179 above.

46. See Robinson's note to 2217.
47. The Knight's sense of humor is, I think, too little appreciated. Cf. lines 2282–2286, 2835–2836. To none of these passages does the *Teseida* offer a parallel.
48. The "nexte houre of Mars" occurs after dawn, and hence Arcite is the last to pray, and his prayer chronologically follows that of Emelye. See note 46 above.
49. In Chaucer's version there is a curious problem in the sequence of events. First the omen occurs, and then Diana appears to Emelye, and declares that the fires will tell what is to be her amatory destiny. In the *Teseida*, Emilia makes a direct request that the fires be made to show what is to be the outcome (*Teseida*, VII, stanza 86 [Battaglia, p. 215]).
50. Here again there arises the question of the extent of Chaucer's knowledge of alliterative verse. Earlier in the *Knight's Tale*, there is evidence of Chaucer's familiarity with alliterative tags (see note 39 above); in *Sir Thopas*, there is the fullest evidence that he knew such tags well enough to parody them effectively; in this passage of the *Knight's Tale*, he demonstrates that he can not only write alliterative verse, but can combine it with rhyming verse.
51. Should any question exist as to the symbolism of the fires, it is answered by Boccaccio himself in what is believed to be his third-person commentary on his own work (see Battaglia, *Teseida*, p. xiv; p. 216, note 91).
52. See note 38 above.
53. It is important to notice that in Boccaccio there is no such pious plan. Emilia was to be given to one Acate, cousin of Theseus, who has perished. Theseus, aware of the nobility of the two aspirants, Arcite and Palemone, finds the tournament simply an easy way to solve the problem of her unmarried state. Whoever can chase his opponent from the field shall have her (*Teseida*, VII, stanza 98; Battaglia, p. 154).
54. Chaucer seems to make Arcite the only one who does die (2708). Hence, Theseus's rules for the tournament have been effective for every combatant except the one Theseus holds most dear (1448).
55. Shakespeare, *King Lear*, iv, i, 36–37 (ed. G. L. Kittredge [Boston, 1940], p. 78).
56. The references are respectively to *Androcles and the Lion* and to *The Devil's Disciple*. See Shaw's postscript to *Androcles* in *Nine Plays* (New York, 1946), p. 977.
57. See *DNB*. A very readable account of his being awarded the youthful Countess of Pembroke is to be found in Amy Kelly, *Eleanor of Aquitaine* (Cambridge, Mass., 1950), p. 248.
58. *Sir Gawain and the Green Knight*, lines 1508–1534, ed. J. R. R. Tolkien and E. V. Gordon, 2nd rev., ed., Norman Davis (Oxford, 1968), p. 42.
59. An extensive and apparently quite factual account of this professional knight-errant of the fifteenth century is given by Georges Chastellain (*Oeuvres*, ed. Kervyn de Lettenhove [Paris, 1866], Vol. VIII).
60. This is a quite selective summary of *Teseida*, IV, 49–91. The stanzas of most importance would seem to be 53, 57, 61, 63, 67, 85 (Battaglia, pp. 114–126).

61. Nelli, *Érotique*, pp. 196–199.

62. *Teseida*, IV, stanza 61.

63. See Beatritz de Dia, "Estat ai en greu cossirier," line 22 (*Anthology of the Provençal Troubadours*, ed. R. T. Hill, and T. G. Bergin [New Haven, 1941], p. 54).

64. It is possible to see in Arcite, the man of war, a later and infinitely more skillfully constructed version of Diomede. Both are primarily interested in war, and only tangentially interested in love. Yet, although Diomede's instantaneous protestations to Criseyde can only be regarded as cynical, and although in Arcite's rhetoric there is no sense of the cynical, the two do have something in common: both instinctively regard love as conquest. As Diomede says of Criseyde, as he takes her from the hand of Troilus to the Grecian camp:

> "whoso myghte wynnen swich a flour
> From hym for whom she morneth nyght and day,
> He myghte seyn he were a conquerour."

(*Troilus and Criseyde*, v, 792–794.)

65. I [A], 1475–1487; 2238–2243; 2325.

66. *Troilus and Criseyde*, v, 1817, 1851. A full study of the incidence of this term and its meaning in the *Troilus* is in progress.

> *Sume* wig fornom,
> ferede in forþwege,   *sumne* fugel oþbaer
> ofer heanne holm,   *sumne* se hara wulf
> deaþe gedaelde,   *sumne* dreorighleor
> in eorþscraefe   eorl gehydde

(*The Wanderer*, lines 80–84, in *Poems in Old English*, ed. Jackson J. Campbell and James L. Rosier [New York, 1962], p. 27. Italics added, phonetic symbols removed, and characters simplified.)

> For God's sake let us sit upon the ground,
> And tell sad stories of the death of kings—
> How *some* have been deposed, *some* slain in war,
> *Some* haunted by the ghosts they have deposed,
> *Some* poisoned by their wives, *some* sleeping killed . . .

(Shakespeare, *Richard II*, III, ii, 155–159, ed. John Dover Wilson [Cambridge, 1939], p. 55. Italics added.)

68. *Chief Modern Poets of England and America*, 3rd ed. (New York, 1946), p. 81.

69. Note that Theseus, listening to the pronouncement by his herald of the restrictions he has devised to prevent fatalities in the tournament, is described as seated by a window "right as he were a god in trone" (2529).

70. See Robinson's note to VII (B²), 3187–3190. Further references to the *Nun's Priest's Tale* will be only by line references.

71. See Robinson's note to 2940, and references there. The *Disticha Catonis* exerted vast influence. It is hoped that an edition of the *Disticha* will be forthcoming in the Chaucer's Library Series. Such an edition, under

the general editorship of R. A. Pratt, has been undertaken by Richard Hazelton, Washington University, St. Louis, Missouri. His *Disticha Catonis* in dissertation form (Rutgers, 1959) is available through University Microfilms.

72. See Pauline Aiken, "Vincent of Beauvais and Dame Pertelote's Knowledge of Medicine," *Speculum*, x (1935), 281–287.

73. "Avisioun," although not completely consistent in meaning, generally carries the idea of supernatural origin. See *MED*, "Avisioun."

74. Rudolph Arbesmann, O.S.A., "Fasting and Prophecy in Pagan and Christian Antiquity," *Traditio*, vii (1949–1951), 31–32.

75. *La divina commedia*, ed. Giuseppe Vandelli (Milan, 1949), pp. 211, 374. See also the commentary of Hermann Gmelin (*Die Göttliche Komödie* [Stuttgart, 1954], ii, 162), and authorities there cited.

76. Chaucer's sympathy with romance *qua* romance is limited. Lancelot receives only one other mention. In the *Squire's Tale*, the narrator rather curiously—given his age and station—despairs of giving a full and adequate account of the amorous intrigues which were in progress. Of such an undertaking who is capable? "No man but Launcelot, and he is deed" (v [F], 287 [*Works*, p. 131]).

77. Bernard L. Jefferson, in his book *Chaucer and the Consolation of Philosophy of Boethius* (Princeton, 1917), has probably made the fullest study of the influence of Boethius on Chaucer. However, in the Nun's Priest's self-contained debate over predestination and free will Jefferson chooses to find three positions: those, respectively, of Bradwardine, St. Augustine, and Boethius (pp. 78–79). This is certainly possible, but are these theological positions not more proximate to the entirely Boethian argument of Troilus in his soliloquy in the temple? (*Troilus and Criseyde*, iv, 946–1078 [*Works*, pp. 451–452].)

78. See p. 157 above.

79. See Robinson's note to line 3347. An English translation of the *Poetria nova* by Margaret F. Nims has recently become available (Toronto, 1967).

80. For a more complex view, see R. E. Kaske, "The Knight's Interruption of the 'Monk's Tale,'" *ELH*, xxiv (1957), 249–268.

81. vii (b²), 3441–3442; x (i), 1083. The reference in both cases is to Romans xv, 9.

11

On the Tradition of Troilus's Vision of the Little Earth

CHAUCER'S MANIFEST INDEBTEDNESS to Boccaccio's *Teseida* (XI, 3–24) for the scene of Troilus's ascent to heaven (*Troilus and Criseyde,* V, 1807–1827) has rather precluded the customary question of Chaucer's sources and has instead focussed attention on Boccaccio's. According to present opinion these sources may be summarized as (1) Macrobius' *Commentary on the "Somnium Scipionis,"* (2) Lucan's *Pharsalia,* and (3) Dante's *Paradiso*[1]—two pagan works with overtones added from a later Christian work. It is the contention of the present essay, however, that the Christian language of Boccaccio's passage is attributable less to Dante than to Boccaccio's use of a previously unnoticed source—commentary on Isaiah XL as incorporated into the *Somme le roi* of Frère Lorens. A possible direct indebtedness of Chaucer to the same source is further suggested.

In Chapter XL of Isaiah, the prophet is instructed to preach the majesty and power of God. The peoples of the earth are to Him as a drop in a bucket, the islands of the sea as dust. He sits upon the vault of the earth, and its inhabitants appear before Him as grasshoppers; He spreads out the heavens as a tent for mankind to dwell in. The youngest and most vigorous of mankind shall fail, but those who hope in the Lord shall renew their strength

Reprinted from *Mediaeval Studies,* XXII (1960), 204–213.

and take wings as eagles.[2] The picture so presented is in essence a kind of visualized sermon on contempt of the world, and St. Jerome, its most authoritative commentator, treats it as such. He points out, for instance, the passing of mighty earthly powers: "Ubi est Xerxis innumerabilis ille exercitus?"[3] and the ridiculous contrast between man's pride and his tiny stature in the universe: "If we consider the various nations in the whole world . . . from ocean to ocean . . . we perceive every race of mankind dwelling in the middle like grasshoppers. *Quid igitur superbit terra et cinis?*" (Ecclesiasticus x, 9).[4] More interesting, however, than his rather conventional treatment of human insignificance is his interpretation of the final verses of Isaiah xl: "They that hope in the Lord shall renew their strength ["mutabunt fortitudinem"]. They shall take wings as eagles." This text St. Jerome associates with Psalm cii, 5: "Thy youth shall be renewed like the eagle's," and points out that the eagle, the only creature able to gaze upon the brilliance of the sun, is able to give new vigor to his old age by changing his feathers. Likewise, he implies, the saints shall be able to gaze upon the spiritual sun and "having put on an immortal body . . . shall be caught up in the clouds to meet Christ."[5]

Subsequent comment on Isaiah xl consists almost entirely of variations upon Jerome's basic interpretation.[6] In the course of this commentary, two tendencies may be observed. The first is to reduce Isaiah's rather complex set of contrasts between God and man to the simple one of size. Thus Haymon of Halberstadt (ninth century) restates Jerome's "grasshopper" passage: "Let us examine all the nations of men, from the east to the west, and from the south to the north . . . and we shall see that in comparison with God . . . they are small and mean."[7] Hervey of Bourg-Dieu (twelfth century) intensifies this contrast: "*quasi locustae, id est minimi.*"[8] The second tendency is to give the final verse a strongly ascetic flavor. Gregory the Great in the *Moralia* begins this line of interpretation by construing the words "mutabunt fortitudinem" in a fashion basically different from Jerome's. "*They who trust in the Lord* . . . change strength, because they who had before been strong in the flesh, seek to be strong in the work of the spirit. They take wings like eagles, because they fly in contemplation."[9] In this new Gregorian interpretation, the emphasis has shifted from the universal problem of human salvation to the more particular problem of the convert who has turned from the world, but is nevertheless being constantly tempted by it. In consequence, the term "fortitudo" has itself undergone a change. It has in some measure lost the more general sense of strength derived from God—which it has in Jerome—and has shifted to something very close to the specific virtue "Fortitudo" by which the Christian, or more particularly the contemplative, resists the temptations of the world. Thus Gregory says: "We change strength, when being converted [by the fire of Divine Love], we flee the present world with as much strength ["virtute"] as before we used to pursue it."[10]

During the late Middle Ages, a work of great popularity, as is attested by the impressive number of existing manuscripts, was the *Somme le roi* of Frère Lorens. This treatise, written in 1279, was widely known not only in France, but also in Italy and England, where it existed both in the French original and in translation. In England it will be remembered as the source of the *Ayenbite of Inwit*, the *Book of the Vices and Virtues*, and Caxton's *Royal Book*.[11] In the *Somme le roi*, Frère Lorens presents an elaborate schematization of the vices and virtues, according to which the Seven Gifts of the Holy Ghost conquer the Seven Deadly Sins and leave in their places the Seven Virtues. Running through this schematization is the theme of contempt of the world, and in connection with it Frère Lorens twice makes use of Isaiah XL. The first occurs in connection with the virtue of Humility. In his treatment of Humility, Frère Lorens follows the established pattern of his work by pointing out that the gift of Fear drives out the sin of Pride and leaves in its place the virtue of Humility. Humility teaches the Christian to flee praise and seek solitude; solitude in turn favors contemplation; and through contemplation the holy soul may attain the vision of Isaiah.[12]

[whan] sche [the holy soul] is rauessched vp to heuene, sche lokeþ aȝen to þe erþe from feer, as Ysaias seiþ, and seeþ it so litle as to regard to þat gret fairenesse and so derk to regard of þilke grete liȝtnesse, so bare and naked to regarde of þilk grete plente of ioye and goodnesse, þan despiseþ he and blameþ hernesfulliche al þat euere is in þe world; richesses, honoure, fairenesse, noblesse . . .[13]

The attainment of this vision is akin to the experience of the Apostles at Pentecost, and means that the Holy Ghost has filled the soul with "grete herte," or Magnanimity, the virtue that "makeþ to despise þe world."[14] Further on, in his discussion of Magnanimity proper, Frère Lorens makes a second allusion to Isaiah XL:

> Who-so haþ þis vertue, he biholdeþ þe world from fer, as seiþ Ysais þe prophete, and hym þingeþ al þe world litel, as a sterre semeþ to vs; þan al þe world and alle þe werkes and alle þe bisynesses, grete and smale, of þe world semeþ to hym as nouȝt or as copwebbes, wher-of Salamon seiþ . . . 'Vanite, vanite, vanite . . .'[15]

From a comparison of the two *Somme le roi* passages with the preceding commentary on Isaiah XL, two principal points emerge. First, although the influence of Jerome may be detected (cf. "rapi in nubibus" and "rauessched vp to heuene"), it is the influence of Gregory that is controlling. Thus the Isaiah vision is attained in contemplation; the virtue through which it is attained is associated with contempt of the world; the virtue itself is bestowed by the Holy Ghost. Second, the vision itself is no longer that of tiny human grasshoppers, as in the earlier commentators, but of the little earth suspended in space. The vision is now expressly "de contemptu mundi."

In the early fourteenth century, contempt of the world reached perhaps its most finished expression in Book XI of Boccaccio's *Teseida*. The soul of the heroic Arcite:

> se ne gì volando
> ver la concavità del cielo ottava,
> degli elementi i convessi lasciando;
> quivi le stelle ratiche ammirava,
> l'ordine loro e la somma bellezza,
> suoni ascoltando pien d'ogni dolcezza.   8
> Quindi si volse in giù a rimirare
> le cose abandonate, e vide il poco
> globo terreno, a cui intorno il mare
> girava e l'aere e di sopra il foco,
> e ogni cosa da nulla stimare
> a rispetto del ciel; ma poi al loco

là dove aveva il suo corpo lasciato
gli occhi fermò alquanto rivoltato;   16
e seco rise de' pianti dolenti
della turba lernea, la vanitate
forte dannando dell' umane genti,
li quai, da tenebrosa cechitate
mattamente oscurati nelle menti,
seguon del mondo la falsa biltate,
lasciando il cielo; e quindi se ne gio
nel loco che Mercurio li sortio.[16]   24

Here well-recognized influences are at work. The heroic soul, viewing from the heavens its own funeral rites, seems to have been suggested by Lucan's *Pharsalia* IX, 1–14, and Arcite's lofty smile of disdain is apparently from the same source, reinforced in all probability by *Paradiso* XXII, 133–135.[17] Most important of the recognized influences is, however, that of the *Somnium Scipionis*. From this Boccaccio clearly derived the general background of his scene: the "stelle ratiche" and the music of the spheres. It has further been supposed that from the *Somnium* Boccaccio also derived the vision of the little world and the idea of contempt connected with it.[18] It is worth while to examine the principal passage on which this supposition rests.

Africanus says to Scipio (Chapter VI):

If the earth seems to thee as small as it really is, keep, then, thine eyes fixed on those heavenly objects; look with contempt on those of mortal life.[19]

Certainly one finds here a strong general resemblance to Arcite's feelings about the world, and in view of other borrowings, Boccaccio might reasonably be supposed to have made use of this passage as well. However, it is also to be borne in mind that the *Somme le roi* was well known in fourteenth-century Italy,[20] and it is likely that the *Somme* possessed for Boccaccio at least two major advantages in his presentation of Arcite's final thoughts. Since the first of these possible advantages involves the much argued question of the location of Arcite's, and after him Troilus's vision,[21] it will be discussed in some detail.

From Frère Lorens's phrase "ravie dusques au ciel," Boccaccio would have understood the Isaiah vision as occurring at the sphere of the moon, the traditional dividing line between things mutable and things eternal.[22] That this location is essential to the moral of worldly vanity Boccaccio intends is made abundantly clear. In the passage of the *Teseida* reproduced above, Arcite perceives the true beauty and order of eternity by contrast to the false beauty and mutability of the world, symbolized by the four elements locked within the "concavità" of the sphere of the moon. According to the standard Aristotelian cosmology, as stated by Vincent of Beauvais, "above the moon there is neither hot nor cold, moist nor dry; their place is beneath the moon. Consequently, there is here (above the moon) no diversity, no *mutability*."[23] Dante makes exactly the same point, contrasting the "corruptibilia," the elements beneath the moon; and the "incorruptibile," the "coelum" or heavens above the moon.[24] It is therefore evident that the sphere of the moon is the optimum—and perhaps the only possible—location for perception of the contrast of mutability and eternity upon which Boccaccio's moral depends. That it is in fact at the sphere of the moon that Arcite's vision occurs is made clear by the details of his flight. He moves upward toward the "cielo ottava" (line 4)—a common way of numbering the sphere of the moon;[25] he leaves behind him the successive "convessi" of the elements[26]—which could exist only beneath the moon; he arrives at a temporary location where he can see both temporal and eternal—which again could be, ideally, only the sphere of the moon; *thence*, "quindi," he departs to his assigned place,[27] guided by the psychopomp Mercury.[28] Both in Boccaccio and in Chaucer flight, vision, and resultant morality require a location at the sphere of the moon.[29] In contrast to his understanding of the Isaiah vision, however, Boccaccio could not have failed to see that the *Somnium* vision occurs at a vast distance from earth—beyond the seven spheres in the Milky Way.[30] From this point Scipio had difficulty in making out the Roman Empire, and it is unlikely that Arcite could have observed those mourning his death.[31] It is perhaps of importance to note in this connection that the vision of Pompey in the *Pharsalia* occurs at the sphere of the moon, and not in the Milky Way.[32]

A second advantage the *Somme* possessed for Boccaccio was that, although similar to the *Somnium* in its contempt of the world, the *Somme* contained Christian rather than pagan reflections, and these Boccaccio seems to have preferred for the autobiographical Arcite. It is precisely here, in the language in which Boccaccio conveys Arcite's reflections, that the influence of the *Somme* becomes most clearly apparent. Boccaccio's "da nulla stimare," "a rispetto del ciel," and "forte dannando" (lines 13, 14, 19) are Frère Lorens's "prise noïent," "au resgard . . . du ciel," and "desprise a certes" (see transcriptions in notes 15, 13); Boccaccio's "vanitate" (line 18) is the *Somme's* "vanité, vanité, vanité." No such close verbal correspondences to the *Somnium*, or indeed to Dante, exist.

Boccaccio's brilliant lines, Chaucer, a judge of good poetry, took over stanza by stanza, but characteristically made them functional to his own poem in a way they can hardly be said to be in Boccaccio's. To reproduce these three stanzas in their entirety would serve no useful purpose, but since it has from time to time been suggested that Chaucer knew Frère Lorens either directly or in translation,[33] it may be relevant to compare a single stanza (lines 1814–1820) with the two passages from the Middle English translation reproduced above. Thus:

Troilus and Criseyde, Book v	*Book of the Vices and Virtues*
"litel spot of erthe" (1815)	"litle" [earth]
"fully gan despise" (1816)	"despiseþ hernisfulliche"
"held al vanite" (1817)	"vanite, vanite, vanite"
"to respect of the pleyn felicite" (1818)	"to regard of þilk grete plente of ioye"

Although the first three extracts from *Troilus and Criseyde* may be paralleled in Boccaccio, the fourth, an exact counterpart of the Middle English translation, may not, and was considered by Root to be Chaucer's "own Boethian addition."[34] The reason for this sudden failure of parallels between *Troilus* and the *Teseida* can of course only be conjectured. However, assuming the earlier part of the present argument to be valid, a possible solution is that Boccaccio's manuscript of the *Somme* simply did not contain the final emptiness-plentitude comparison. Of the eighteen complete manuscripts of the *Somme* I have been able to consult, I find that seven lack the final "si vuide au resgart de cele grant plenté [de ioye]."[35] On the other hand, the readings "greate blisse" (*Ayenbite*)[36] and "grete plente of ioye" (*Book of the Vices and Virtues*) show that the source manuscript or manuscripts of the two English works contained this final comparison with the addition of the bracketed phrase "de ioye." Hence, the evidence, though slight, suggests that when Chaucer was considering models for Troilus's climactic vision of the little earth, he thought of the source of the *Teseida* stanzas as well as of the *Teseida* itself, and supplemented the Italian poem with a full French[37] or English version of the *Somme*. So was incorporated into the *Troilus* the "pleyn felicite" which the *Teseida* lacked.

One other possible indebtedness to the *Somme* remains to be considered. At the conclusion of the first passage reproduced above (p. 201), Frère Lorens provides a kind of catalogue of worldly vanities to be despised: "richesses, honoure, fairenesse, noblesse." Chaucer sums up the consequences of "false worldes brotelnesse":[38]

> Swich fyn hath, lo, this Troilus for love!
> Swich fyn hath al his grete worthynesse!
> Swich fyn hath his estat real above,
> Swich fyn his lust, swich fyn hath his noblesse! (v, 1828–1831)

Allowing for Chaucer's necessary adaptation to Troilus's particular moral character and social status, there is, I think, a fair correspondence between "richesse" and "estat real"; "honoure" and "worthynesse"; "noblesse" and "noblesse."

It is hoped that the above discussion may cast some small additional light on the sources of both Boccaccio and Chaucer. It is also hoped that it may provide a kind of exemplum of the vitality which the Bible possessed for the medieval mind and of the manner in which the biblical text penetrated into literature. Here one can, I think, see something of that process.

NOTES

1. A general treatment of Boccaccio's sources is to be found in H. R. Patch, "Chauceriana," *Englische Studien*, LXV (1930–1931), 357–359. For bibliography, see M. W. Bloomfield, "The Eighth Sphere," *MLR*, LIII (1958), 408, note 1.

2. "Ecce gentes quasi stilla situlae . . . ecce insulae quasi pulvis exiguus./ Qui sedet super gyrum terrae, et habitatores ejus sunt quasi locustae; qui extendit velut nihilum caelos, et expandit eos sicut tabernaculum ad inhabitandum. / Deficient pueri, et laborabunt, et juvenes in infirmitate cadent. / Qui autem sperant in Domino, mutabunt fortitudinem, assument pennas sicut aquilae, current et non laborabunt, ambulabunt, et non deficient" (Isaiah XL, 15, 22, 30, 31).

3. *Commentarium in Isaiam* (*PL*, XXIV, 424).

4. "Si enim in toto orbe consideramus varias nationes . . . ab Oceano usque ad Oceanum . . . omne in medio hominum genus quasi locustas habitare cernimus. *Quid igitur superbit terra et cinis?* (*PL*, XXIV, 423).

5. "Qui autem non in suis viribus, sed in Deo habeant fiduciam . . . audiant: *Renovabitur sicut aquilae juventus tua* (Psalm CII, 5). . . . Crebro diximus, aquilarum senectutem revirescere mutatione pennarum, et solas esse quae jubar solis aspiciant. . . . Itaque et sanctos repuerascere, et assumpto immortali corpore, laborem non sentire mortalium, sed rapi in nubibus obviam Christo" (*PL*, XXIV, 426–427). Cf. I Thessalonians IV, 16.

6. St. Jerome's commentary passed with very little alteration into the *Glossa ordinaria*, where it became in a sense standard (see Nicholas of Lyra, *Biblia sacra cum glossa ordinaria* [Lyons, 1589], or, for a less complete version, *PL*, CXIII, 114). However, not only the *Glossa ordinaria* but all subsequent commentary echoes St. Jerome.

7. "Consideremus ab oriente usque ad occidentem, et a meridie usque ad septentrionem, omnia genera hominum . . . et videbimus quia, ad comparationem Dei . . . parva sunt et modica" (*Commentarium in Isaiam* [*PL*, CXVI, 912]).

8. *Commentarium in Isaiam*, (*PL*, CLXXXI, 386).

9. "Mutant quippe fortitudinem, quia fortes student esse in spiritali opere, qui dudum fuerant fortes in carne. Assumunt autem pennas ut aquilae, quia contemplando volant" (*Moralia*, XIX, xxvii, 50, [*PL*, LXXVI, 131]).

10. "Fortitudinem mutamus, cum conversi tanta virtute praesens saeculum fugimus quanta hoc ante quaerebamus" (*Moralia*, XVIII, xxviii, 45; *PL*, LXXVI, 61).

11. For the above information I am indebted to the excellent introduction by W. Nelson Francis to his edition of the *Book of The Vices and Virtues, EETS O.S.* No. 217 (London, 1942).

12. *Book of the Vices and Virtues*, pp. 126, 140–141.

13. *Ibid.*, p. 141. A transcription of the comparable passage from the *Somme le roi* follows: "quant ele est ravie dusques au ciel, ele resgarde la terre de loins, com dit Ysaies, et la voit si petite au resgart de la grandece du ciel, si leide au resgart de cele grant biauté, si orbe au resgart de cele grant clarté, si vuide au resgart de cele grant plenté [de ioye], lors despit et desprise a certes quanqu'il a au monde de richeces, d'oneurs, de biauté, de noblece" (Bibliothèque Nationale MS Fr 24780, fol. 102ᵃ). The manuscript is fourteenth century and is the most typical, in regard to this passage, of the group of manuscripts I have been able to see. For assistance with this and the following

transcription I am indebted to Professor Alfred L. Foulet of Princeton University. For loan of the necessary microfilms I am indebted to the late Rev. Norman R. Fournier, who, at the time of his death, was preparing a much needed edition of those manuscripts of the *Somme* relevant to the *Ayenbite.*

14. *Book of the Vices and Virtues,* pp. 142, 165.

15. *Ibid.,* p. 164. The comparable passage in the *Somme* reads: "Qui ceste vertu a, il resgarde le monde de loins, comme dit Ysaies li profetes, et ausi li semble le monde comme une estoile feit a nous; donc tous li mons et toutes les cures et les grans besoignes du monde li semblent ausi comme noient, et pour ce les prise noient, nes que toille d'araignes; donc Salemons dit . . . "Vanité, vanité . . . vanité" (MS Fr 24780, fol. 119ᵃ).

16. *Teseida,* XI, 1–24 (ed. Salvatore Battaglia [Florence, 1938], pp. 321–322).

17. See Patch, *Englische Studien,* LXV, 357–359. For an argument that Dante is a major source rather than a contributing source as Professor Patch suggests, see E. J. Dobson, "Some Notes on Middle English Texts," *English and Germanic Studies,* I, (1947–1948), 61–62.

18. R. K. Root (*Book of Troilus and Criseyde* [Princeton, 1926]) regards the contempt of the world idea as also derived from the *Somnium,* and F. N. Robinson apparently follows him in this (*Works,* p. 837).

19. *Parlement of Foules,* ed. T. R. Lounsbury (Boston, 1877), p. 13.

20. Francis points out the existence of three separate translations in Italy during the fourteenth century (*Book of the Vices and Virtues,* "Introduction," pp. xxx–xxxi).

21. Root and Robinson (cited in note 18 above) agree on the sphere of the moon for both Arcite and Troilus. More recent scholars emphatically do not. Jackson I. Cope believes that Chaucer changed Troilus's "resting place" to the sphere of Saturn (*MLN,* LXVII [1952], 245–246); Forrest S. Scott argues that Chaucer transferred him to the sphere of Mercury (*MLR,* LI [1956], 2–5); and Morton W. Bloomfield considers that the tradition of the ogdoad caused both Boccaccio and Chaucer to place their heroes in the eighth sphere, that of the fixed stars ("The Eighth Sphere," *MLR,* LIII [1958], 408–410).

22. Frère Lorens describes the soul as being "ravie dusques au ciel" (see note 13 above). The question then is: What would Boccaccio have understood by the term "ciel"? If he had read the commentators on Isaiah, he would have encountered the following standard interpretation of Isaiah XL, 22: "*qui extendit caelos, et expandit eos sicut tabernaculum ad habitandum.*" It states: "sub eis [caelis] quasi sub tabernaculum habitant homines, supra angeli & sancti" (Nicholas of Lyra, *Biblia sacra,* cited in note 6 above; see also Haymon of Halberstadt, *PL,* CXVI, 912). According then to the *Glossa,* the term "coelum" designates the point of division between mortal and immortal. In the standard cosmology this point of division would be represented by the sphere of the moon. Thus Macrobius: "Infra autem nihil est nisi mortale . . . supra lunam sunt aeterna omnia" (*Somnium Scipionis,* col. 4, in *Macrobii Ambrosii Theodosii opera* [Leipzig, 1848] I, 7). If

Boccaccio had not known the Isaiah commentaries, he would have found exactly the same usage of the word "coelum" in Dante. As summed up by M. A. Orr (*Dante and the Early Astronomers* [London, 1913], p. 441): "The pure region of the spheres, 'il paese sincero,' is immortal as the spirits themselves [*Paradiso* VII, 130–132]; but below the lowest celestial sphere ('la celestial c'ha men salita,' [*Paradiso* IV, 39]) all is mortal and transitory, as the Greeks and Latin poets had said. This is expressed in the Letter to Can Grande, when Dante contrasts the spheres, ('coelum') , and the elements, and says: 'illud incorruptible, illa vero corruptibilia sunt' [*Ep.* X, 435–437].'' Boccaccio would therefore have understood that "ravie dusques au ciel" meant "carried up to a point beyond the elements, that point at which mortal and corruptible things end and immortal begin." This point could only be the sphere of the moon.

23. "supra lunam nec est calor nec frigus, nec humiditas nec siccitas; harum igitur locus est sub luna. Inde nulla ibi est diversitas, nulla mutacio" (Vincent of Beauvais, *Speculum naturale* [Strasbourg, 1473], XVI, xix). The above extract is the opinion of Aristotle as paraphrased by Vincent. Although Vincent later indicates that he disagrees with the conception that mutability does not exist in the realm beyond the moon, he clearly regards the view he is quoting as the prevailing one (see note 22 above).

24. See note 22 above.

25. This number is of course obtained by counting inward from the eighth sphere, or sphere of the fixed stars. It is this system which is followed in the *Somnium Scipionis*, Boccaccio's major source (cf. Root, *Troilus and Criseyde*, p. 561). Both Chaucer (cf. Bloomfield, "The Eighth Sphere," *MLR*, LIII, 409) and Dante (cf. Orr, *Dante*, p. 440) on occasion made use of the inward numbering system as well as the outward.

26. Root quite correctly interprets "degli elementi i convessi lasciando" (line 5) as referring to the elements beneath the sphere of the moon. Miss Orr substantiates his point: "Aristotle seems to have regarded the four elements as flowing into each other, so that these lowly spheres beneath the moon were not sharply divided, but his mediaeval disciples, following the Greek idea to its logical conclusion, conceived them with boundaries as definite as those of the celestial spheres" (*Dante*, p. 442). It is these "convessi" that Arcite is shown leaving behind in his upward flight.

27. It is absolutely essential to observe here that neither Boccaccio nor Chaucer has a word to say about the final resting place of his hero. Each poet describes a flight to the sphere of the moon; from this lofty seat the hero has a vision of the pettiness of earth and the grandeur of heaven. From *that* place—"quindi se ne gio" (line 23) and "forth he wente" (*Troilus and Criseyde*, 1826)—the hero goes to the place assigned him by the psychopomp Mercury. We are never told what that place is, for both Arcite and Troilus are virtuous pagans and, in the fourteenth century, difficult to house authoritatively. The problems of where the vision takes place and what final dwelling place is intended are separate and distinct. As to the latter problem, I think

Bloomfield has found the most likely solution (*MLR*, LIII, 410), although neither Boccaccio nor Chaucer gives us much to go on.

28. For this useful conception, I am indebted to Bloomfield (*ibid.*).

29. If it be granted, as I think it must, that Arcite's vision takes place at the sphere of the moon, it would appear that Troilus's does also. The same contrast of mutable and immutable is made; the same flight is described. The term "eighthe spere" should then obviously be understood as designating the sphere of the moon; i.e., Chaucer has followed Boccaccio's inward numbering as Boccaccio himself followed the inward numbering of the *Somnium*. The reading "seventhe spere" in the majority of the manuscripts seems to be simply an error in the use of Roman numerals (see Root, *Troilus and Criseyde*, p. 561).

30. It is clear from a reading of the *Somnium* that the position of the two Scipios in the Milky Way is outside of the seven spheres. They are obviously looking down through the spheres to the earth (Chaps. 3, 4). Macrobius defines the Milky Way as "unus e circis qui ambiunt celum" (*Macrobii opera*, I, 86), and an illustration of the *Somnium* in Bodleian Library MS Can. Class. Lat. 257 (fol. 1ᵇ) shows the events of the vision transpiring in the Milky Way and shows the Milky Way as a circle cutting across the sphere of the fixed stars (eighth sphere) just inside the *primum mobile*. Dante understood the Milky Way as being a group of fixed stars (eighth sphere) so minute that they are not individually visible from earth (Orr, *Dante*, p. 305).

31. This point, applied to Troilus, is made by Root, *Troilus and Criseyde*, p. 561.

32. *Pharsalia*, IX, 1–14. As Scott points out (*MLR*, LI, 5, note 1), Pompey has essentially the same vision as Arcite. He sees the earth below and the erratic and fixed stars above.

33. Richard Morris in his introduction (n.p.) to the *Ayenbite of Inwit* (London, 1866), *EETS O.S.* No. 23; Wilhelm Eilers, "The *Parson's Tale* and the *Somme de vices et de vertus* of Frère Lorens," *Chaucer Society Essays*, V (1884), 503–610.

34. Root, *Troilus and Criseyde*, p. 562.

35. The following manuscripts lack the comparison indicated: MSS Fr 409 (fourteenth century), fol. 104ᵇ; 942 (1438), fol 66ᵃ; 943 (early fourteenth century), fol. 82ᵃ; 958 (1464), fol. 83ᵃ; 959 (fifteenth century), fol. 74ᵇ–75ᵃ; 9628 (fifteenth century), fol. 42ᵃ; Harvard College Library, MS Fr 123 (fifteenth century), fol. 111ᵃ. The following manuscripts contain the comparison: MSS Fr 938 (1294), fol. 81ᵃ; 939 (1327), fol. 51ᵃ; 940 (fifteenth century), fol. 54ᵃ; 1134 (early fifteenth century), fol. 83ᵃ; 1767 (fourteenth century), fol. 100ᵃ; 1895 (fourteenth century), fol. 84ᵃ; 17098 (fifteenth century), fol. 68ᵇ; 22932 (early fourteenth century), fol. 62ᵃ; 22934 (fifteenth century), fol. 120ᵇ; 22935 (fifteenth century), fol. 104ᵃ; 24780 (early fourteenth century), fol. 102ᵃ. All are Bibliothèque Nationale manuscripts except the Harvard Library manuscript.

36. "zuo emto • to þeziȝþe of þo greate blisse" (*Ayenbite*, p. 143).

37. On the basis of Chaucer's customary practice, one would suppose the source to have been French. If so, the use here suggested of a French

work to supplement Boccaccio's *Teseida* would parallel Professor Pratt's contention that in *Troilus and Criseyde* Chaucer made use of a French translation to supplement the *Filostrato*. See "Chaucer and *Le Roman de Troyle et de Criseida*," *SP*, LIII (1956), 509–539.

38. A single manuscript of the eighteen noted (Bibliothèque Nationale, MS Fr 939 [1327], fol. 51ᵃ) contains a fifth comparison: "si fausse au regard de celle très grant loyauté de paradis ou tout le bien est."

12

Chaucer's Satire of the Pardoner

T HE PRESENT ESSAY IS AN ATTEMPT to demonstrate the institutional nature of Chaucer's satire of the pardoner—to indicate that Chaucer's satire is not directed against false pardoners or against pardoners of any particular establishment, but against the state of institutional decay which made the existence of the pardoner possible. To this end the background of the pardoner will be discussed: his function in the Church, abuses of that function, and legal action to restrain those abuses. Following this, an examination of English collection systems will be made, and finally an application of the foregoing material to the noble ecclesiast of the *Canterbury Tales*.

I

The pardoner is unfortunately so celebrated in literature for the abuses with which he is found associated that his true function within the Church is almost entirely obscured. From the pages of Langland, Chaucer, and Wyclif one could conclude only that the pardoner is a singularly conscienceless salesman of pardons for sin. Yet however true such a conclusion may be in terms of actual practice, in terms of canon law it is completely untrue. Under

Reprinted, with slight revisions, from *PMLA*, LXVI (1951), 251–277.

the law which defined his duties and regulated his activities, the pardoner, or "questor" as he is officially called, had no power to forgive sin or to sell the indulgences he carried about with him. The truth would seem to be that our impressions of the pardoner are derived so completely from representations of his abuses that we are in danger of forgetting that they are abuses—that under canon law very few indeed of the pardoner's actual practices were permitted.

It is necessary first of all to notice that indulgences, as they are called in ecclesiastical documents, or pardons in lay terminology, have nothing at all to do with the forgiveness of sin. Penance involves three acts: contrition, confession, and satisfaction.[1] An indulgence is effective only in regard to the last of these, satisfaction; that is, it is effective in reducing or removing entirely the temporal punishment, or "poena" which remains after the sacrament of confession and absolution has removed the moral guilt, or "culpa."[2] This is made clear in a limiting clause contained in the indulgences themselves. The papal form letter "Si iuxta sententiam," which was employed as a model for indulgences to be communicated by pardoners, provides that indulgences may be granted only to those who are contrite and have confessed their sins.[3] This same phrase is incorporated in so many English indulgences that it may be called general. It is to be found, for instance, in indulgences granted by the Archbishops of Canterbury[4] and York,[5] and by the Bishops of Winchester,[6] Exeter,[7] and Durham.[8] That pardoners frequently if not usually absolved "a poena et a culpa" cannot be doubted, but such absolution was an abuse and occupies an important place in Clement V's catalogue of the abuses practiced by pardoners.[9]

Nor was a pardoner privileged to sell the indulgences he carried with him. An indulgence, as has been said, is granted to one who is properly contrite and confessed. However, an indulgence is a special concession, and the Church may require evidence that such a concession is deserved.[10] No indication seems to have been more acceptable in this respect than the act of almsgiving. Thus Innocent III at the Council of the Lateran (1215) reasserted the doctrine that the work of mercy is a means of laying up treasure in heaven and an act appropriate for the reception of an indulgence. At the same time he prescribed the form "Quoniam, ut ait Apostolus" as the text to be followed in eleemosynary indulgences throughout the Church.[11] From this seems to have developed the more emphatic statement contained in the papal form letter "Si iuxta sententiam,"[12] and echoed, as elsewhere, in an indulgence of Archbishop Melton of York: "Give, therefore, alms that all worlds may be yours, for the giving of alms frees from death, purges sins, and leads the way to eternal life. As water extinguishes a raging fire, so does almsgiving resist sin."[13]

Since the institutions—principally hospitals—for whose support eleemosynary indulgences were granted had an understandable interest in extending the indulgences so granted to the widest circle of beneficiaries, the pardoner became a generally indispensable means to indulgence publication. Yet it must not be forgotten that no matter how indispensable the pardoner's role was, it was in canon law a small and narrowly defined one. The pardoner as instituted was nothing more than a messenger, or "nuntius," who communicated indulgences from the Pope or bishop, who had the power to grant them, to the believer who had fulfilled the conditions necessary to receiving them. As Clement V at the Council of Vienne defined the function of pardoners: "Their sole concern is to communicate to the people the indulgences confided to them and to humbly request alms."[14]

II

It is not surprising that the pardoner refused to accept the limited position assigned him by canon law.[15] He was not interested in the moral aspects of his mission, but in its financial success or failure.[16] Consequently he used every device he knew to assure himself a large and open-handed audience.

The gathering of the audience was a simple matter. His letters contained instructions to the local clergy that he was to be admitted to their churches on Sundays and feast days and permitted to state his business "intra missarum solemnia," generally after the reading of the Gospel.[17] Should the local clergy prove recalcitrant, his letters not infrequently contained a provision empowering him to excommunicate anyone impeding the progress of his collections.[18]

Once his eyes were met with the joyful spectacle of the people gathered together to hear the cause of his pious advent, the pardoner's emotions could scarcely be restrained. With tears streaming from his practiced eyes, he brought forth a multitude of indulgences and preached so moving a sermon on the powers they granted him for cleansing the soul spotted by sin that few could restrain themselves from giving what they had.[19] Upon his numerous fortunate contributors the pardoner conferred sweeping indulgences,[20] nor did he pause in his delivery to question their qualifications for receiving them.[21] He absolved from any sin—perjury, homicide, and others.[22] Legal distinctions were as nothing to him; he absolved "a poena et a culpa."[23] The realms of the dead he likewise declared within his universal jurisdiction, for he could free relatives or friends of contributors from purgatory,[24] or even from hell.[25]

But, alas! he had almost forgotten to mention his relics. Perhaps they were genuine relics,[26] or perhaps, if he were a pardoner of the most abandoned sort, relics of obscure origin—cremated hands and feet,[27] bones of beast or man—which gained in his mouth miraculous powers.[28] The happy mortal, he explained, who kissed these relics should never again feel pain in his teeth, his mouth, or his face.[29]

His address concluded, the pardoner solemnly gathered together his rings, brooches, coins,[30] wheat,[31] and animals,[32] and with a beneficent smile departed in the direction of the nearest tavern.[33]

These practices could not, of course, be carried on without awakening violent and widespread indignation within the Church. In 1215, at the Council of the Lateran, Innocent III promulgated the first general code for the control of pardoners. The canon "Cum ex eo," whose language may be found echoed in canons several hundred years later, provided that no questor, to use the official title of the pardoner, might be admitted who did not possess papal or episcopal letters.[34] Even if duly accredited, he was not to be permitted to preach, but only to read what was contained in his letters,[35] and this was limited to a simple form.[36] Further, questors must amend their lives—they must be discreet and cease living in taverns.[37]

The second major step against the abuses of pardoners was

taken in 1267 by Clement IV in the decretal "Sedis Apostolicae." This pronouncement by Clement stripped the questor of two important privileges often granted him in his letters of authorization: the power to demand shelter and food from the local clergy and the power to command the local clergy to summon the people to hear his commission expounded.[38]

The third and perhaps most important piece of legislation was the "Abusionibus" of Clement V, promulgated at the Council of Vienne (1311–1312). This canon reaffirmed all of the provisions of the Lateran Council and added two new provisions, important because for the first time legal jurisdiction over the questor was clearly defined. The diocesan bishops were empowered to examine the credentials of questors before they were granted the freedom of their dioceses, and to punish them for any unpermitted actions, no matter what immunities they might previously have enjoyed.[39]

Such was the law of the pardoner in England in Chaucer's day. The *Regimen animarum*, a contemporary English handbook for parish priests, gives the following summary of the legislation of Innocent III, Clement IV, and Clement V:

Quid iuris de questoribus qui discurrunt per
ecclesias cum litteris remissionum et predicant
abusiones? Dic quod illi questores vacantes commessationibus et ebrietatibus non debent admitti nisi
exhibeant litteras apostolicas vel litteras episcopi   5
diocesani, et sic preter id quod in ipsis litteris
continebitur nichil proponere populo permittantur.
Forma eorum communis est: "Quoniam, ut ait Apostolus,"
etc. Item debent esse modesti et discreti, nec in
tabernis et aliis locis incongruis hospitari debent,   10
nec inutiles aut sumptuosas facere expensas, nec habitum
false religionis portare. Extravagantibus, De Penitenciis
et Remissionibus, "Cum ex eo." Et addit Clemens IIII
in quadam decreta provulgata in curia que sic incipit,
"Sedis Apostolice," ubi statuitur quod prelati, rectores,   15
et alii clerici curati non tenentur eos recipere in
hospitiis nec eis in necessariis providere, etiam
cuiuscumque religionis sint aut conditionis, nec
tenentur facere convocationem populi ad sermones vel

exhortationes eorum, etiam si de tali convocatione mentio 20
fiat in litteris eorum, quia Papa revocat; et si propter
hoc alia sententia excommunicationis vel interdicti
promulgatur, irrita est et inanis. Et dicit Papa Clemens
Quintus de istis quod questores eleemosinarum non debent
ab aliquo admitti nisi exhibuerint litteras episcopi 25
diocesani, nec licet eis populo predicare nec aliud
exponere quam quod in litteris continebatur predictis;
et debent episcopi diocesani diligenter examinare
litteras apostolicas, ne quicquam fraudis committi
valeant per easdem antequam questores admittantur. Et 30
quia aliqui questores multiplici deceptione animarum
concedunt populo indulgentias motu proprio; de facto
cum votis dispensant; a perjuriis, homicidiis, et
peccatis aliis confitentes absolvunt; mal[e] ablata et
incerta, data sibi aliqua pecunie quantitate, remittunt; 35
tertiam vel quartam partem de penitentiis iniunctis
relaxant; animas parentum vel amicorum illorum qui
eleemosinas eis conferunt, de purgatorio, ut asserunt
mendaciter, extrahunt et ad gaudia paradisi perducunt;
benefactoribus locorum quorum questores existunt 40
remissionem plenariam peccatorum de facto indulgent; et
aliqui ex istis eos a pena et a culpa absolvunt.
Dominus Papa volens huiusmodi abusus abolere per
quos vilescit ecclesiastica censura et auctoritas
clavium ecclesie deducitur in contemptum, expresse 45
revocat omnia et singula privilegia si que sunt premissa
vel eorum aliquo sunt in aliquibus locis, ordinibus, vel
personis questorum huiusmodi quocumque concessa, ne
ipsorum pretextu sit eis materia quam ad premissa
talia auctoritate apostolica ulterius favendi. Qui 50
autem deinceps in premissis vel in aliquo premissorum
delinquirint, vel aliis suis privilegiis abusi fuerint,
per episcopos locorum punientur, privilegio quocumque
nonobstante.[40]

These three pronouncements answered for Chaucer's time the
question, "Quid iuris de questoribus?"[41] The pardoner must bear √
papal or episcopal letters; he must be examined and licensed by
the bishop. If he is permitted to enter the churches of the diocese,
he is forbidden to do more than read his letters and collect con-

tributions. If he errs in his practices or in his mode of life, he is to be punished by the bishop. This was the simple code governing the pardoner.

Enforcement, however, was a very different matter. Churches and bridges were built, the poor fed, the sick healed, all on the proceeds of indulgences. If those proceeds failed, construction of the church stopped,[42] the care of the sick ceased.[43] There was always a temptation on the part of the regular clergy who operated the great hospitals to avoid the regulations that their collectors be brothers "idonei et bone conversationis"[44] and to employ less worthy but more productive brothers.[45] There was likewise pressure to farm out collection rights to groups of professional questors who were willing to pay a good round sum for making unrestricted use of the indulgences granted the hospital.[46]

On the part of the parish clergy also there existed an equally pressing and perhaps equally understandable temptation—to have for their own needs a part of the vast collections drawn from their own parishioners, who might normally be expected to contribute to the support of the parish and the parish priest. It was a painful experience for the parish priest to see the pardoner collect in a day more than he received in months.[47]

Thus the pardoner became to the Church a vice within itself, a vice which even the strongest measures failed somehow to eradicate. An infinity of Church councils might inveigh against his practices,[48] universal suspensions of licenses might be made,[49] requirements that collectors be actual brothers of good reputation emphatically stated,[50] yet aside from a very real limitation upon his most spectacular abuse, that of false relics,[51] the professional collector everywhere continued with little change his indestructible existence.

III

In 1308, the Chapter of St. John of Beverley began construction of the nave of its new minster, having completed the shrine[52] of the saint to whose miraculous offices were attributed the victory of Athelstan at Brunanburh and later that of Henry V at Agincourt.[53] The beginning of the new fabric was signalized by the discharge of the former chief collector, John de Fitling, and the appointment of a new collector, or questor, Elyas de Lumby. Thus we are afforded the rather rare opportunity of observing the setting up and operation of a system for the procurement and publication of indulgences.

On December 18, 1308, a contract was drawn up between Elyas de Lumby and the Chapter. In exchange for his privileges of collection in the province of York and diocese of Lincoln, Elyas promised to post a bond of £20 per year as security for his estimated collections and to remit any amounts received above this sum, deducting only expenses for himself, his horse, his servant, and a robe "with tabard." His duties are worth noting. In addition to collecting, he is to:

1. Procure licenses and indulgences from neighboring bishops and other prelates.
2. Revoke all appointments of questors previously made.
3. Arrest and prosecute all false questors illegally collecting in the name of the Chapter.
4. Substitute questors, with power to revoke the substitution.[54]

Elyas, as "nuntius specialis," apparently enjoyed a position of considerable authority and responsibility.

At the outset of his career Elyas de Lumby faced real difficulties. As the Chapter's chief agent he was expected to maintain or expand the area within which the Chapter collected, and further, to obtain indulgences, the lifeblood of collections.[55] St. John of Beverley had long enjoyed a privileged position in the province of York[56] but had never penetrated farther into the province of Canterbury than the diocese of Lincoln.[57] The Chapter would have liked also to extend its collections into Norwich and Ely,[58] but any such attempt was rendered difficult at this time by a sudden catastrophe which had overtaken all collections in the province of Canterbury. Archbishop Robert Winchelsey, moved by continuing reports of abuses practiced by pardoners within his province, had revoked the licenses of all questors.[59] Even Lincoln was now closed to the Chapter.

To remedy this situation, Elyas set forth on September 12, 1309, with letters to the Archbishop of Canterbury and the Bishop of Lincoln.[60] Apparently his mission was at least partially success-ful, for although he seems to have received no indulgences,[61] collections in Lincoln were later resumed.[62]

From what records of Beverley Minster are available, Elyas de Lumby's success and lack of success as "nuntius specialis" would appear to have been typical. He retained for the Chapter the freedom of the dioceses of York, Durham, Carlisle, and Lin-coln, but was unable, as were those who followed him, to make any substantial headway in the province of Canterbury.[63] Despite earnest efforts, St. John of Beverley remained a local collection system.

Once the areas into which collectors were permitted to go were established, the operation of the system itself was simple and effective. Over each main area was set a chief collector, as John of Stork for the province of York and Richard Monechant for the diocese of Lincoln.[64] Since it was difficult if not impossible to cover all this territory personally, each chief collector possessed the right of substitution.[65] Thus John of Stork delegated to subordinates the deanery of Craven[66] and the archdeaconry of Nottingham.[67] These substituted questors were responsible not only to the Chapter, but to the chief collector who appointed them and set the period of their employment.[68]

If the system of appointments and sub-appointments seems to have been simple enough, the actual sending out of questors was a considerably more complicated matter and involved a double problem. Questors must be duly accredited so that they might be received without incident; they must also be so rigidly controlled that the funds collected could be obtained from them with as little difficulty as possible. Beverley Minster met both of these problems in what one presumes to have been a traditional fashion.

The licensing of the questor as it appears in the Chapter records was almost as complicated a procedure as the arming of Sir Thopas. First came copies of the all-important indulgences, sealed by the Chapter to guarantee their validity[69] and later countersealed by the examining bishop.[70] With his indulgences the questor carried a letter showing his appointment by the Chap-ter, the purpose of which was to provide a check upon his iden-tity.[71] After the bishop had verified the authenticity of the questor and his documents, he would likewise furnish the questor with a sealed letter.[72] This letter was his license to collect within the diocese. It instructed archdeacons, their Officials, and the lesser clergy to receive him, stated the time at which he might be heard,[73] admonished the local clergy to abstain from making deductions from his collection,[74] and limited the validity of the license to a specific period of time.[75] Lastly, the questor might also be provided with a royal writ of protection.[76]

The complicated problem of licensing questors was, however, but a routine matter compared to the problem of assuring the return of the monies and goods collected. The Chapter's solution of this problem, again doubtless a customary one, shows nevertheless considerable energy and ingenuity. Before receiving his credentials, the questor was required to sign a bond guaranteeing payment of the estimated total of his collections.[77] Should he fail, he and all his possessions were declared forfeit, and all legal defenses against the Chapter's claim were waived. Finally, his credentials were handed over to him—for which he likewise signed a bond[78]—and he was sent forth upon his duties with the reminder that the Masters of the Works expected him to appear for an accounting at no very distant date, and should he fail to appear, he would be haled into court.[79] He also possessed the salutary knowledge that the Chapter's intelligence system functioned faultlessly—that should he offer part or all of the contributions he gathered to Venus and Bacchus, the patron saints of pardoners, he would be greeted by letters from the Chapter in the hands of new questors relieving him of his position.[80] This misfortune had befallen numerous gentlemen of his acquaintance.[81]

At first glance the Chapter's administration of its system of collections seems ideal. There were no complaints concerning the behavior of its questors and little diversion of funds. However, the very rigidity of the control exercised indicates the very real danger which lay in the nature of the men Beverley Minster employed. All these questors bear the title "clericus,"[82] so that one supposes that they were in some capacity members of the Chapter. This was not in fact true. In the few instances in which the formula "clericus" is expanded, we find "Patrick Lili of Beverley,"[83] "Thomas Gamell, citizen of Lincoln,"[84] "John of Bristol and John of Stork, citizens of Beverley."[85]

The best example, however, of the kind of connection which

existed between these men and the Chapter is to be found in the records of a brother collector, John de Lincoln. In 1306, John de Lincoln was collector for the fabric of St. Peter of York.[86] During the same year he was also collector in York for the hospitals of St. Anthony of Vienne[87] and of the Holy Ghost in Saxia of Rome.[88] It is more than likely that he did not attempt to fill all these offices in person but substituted questors according to the usual custom. By November, 1312, John de Lincoln had changed positions and was employed by Beverley Minster as its collector in York.[89] In 1313 he was the Chapter's collector in Lincoln,[90] and in 1314 special agent for the Chapter at Canterbury.[91] His name then disappears. Had we comparable records of other churches in Lincoln and York, we should very likely find it again.

In general it may be said that the collectors within the Beverley Minster system of whom we have any record were with rare exceptions[92] professional collectors, hired and fired at the will of the institution employing them, moving about within an area whose inhabitants they knew well enough to make their professional talents appreciated. Something more may be added to the portrait of the professional collector if we notice that the office of collector seems to have run in families,[93] and that the name of the most constantly employed questor, "Monechant" or "Moanchant," suggests a family vocation of professional collecting.[94]

If we turn from the local collection systems, of which Beverley Minster is the best example, to a consideration of the international systems of the great hospitals—St. Anthony of Vienne, St. James of Altopascio, Holy Ghost in Saxia of Rome, St. Mary Roncesvalles, etc.—we note an immediate difference. The materials previously examined concern the relationship between the institution and its collectors and are contained in the records of the institution itself; the records in which the major hospitals appear are all contained in the registers of English bishops and deal in one way or another with the imposition of external controls, those of the Pope, archbishop, or bishop, upon questors for these hospitals. One immediate explanation for this fact is that so far as the present writers are aware, no body of information about the internal affairs of these hospitals comparable to that furnished by Beverley Minster is available.[95] Another less obvious but possibly equally valid explanation is that the local institutions gave less occasion to the appearance of their names in bishops' registers than did the foreign hospitals. The reason for this disparity may perhaps be indicated by following a single collector for a foreign hospital as he goes about his duties.

On June 19, 1310, Brother Bonaventura of the Hospital of St. James of Altopascio in Tuscany, together with a fellow collector, presented his credentials to the Official of the Archbishop of York as was customary.[96] Apparently all was in order, for Brother Bonaventura possessed letters from Leonard Patrasso, Cardinal-Bishop of Albano,[97] and fulfilled, along with his honest friend, the standard provision contained in his letters that the bearers be "confratres . . . vel nuncii idonei et honesti."[98] However, under questioning, Brother Bonaventura turned out to be no brother at all, but merely an ordinary collector, or "procurator substitutus,"[99] while his companion, who is referred to only as "ille Anglicus," was recognized by the Official as a "quaestuarius notorius,"[100] or in more Chaucerian language, a pardoner known from Berwick into Ware.

Since Anglicus has about him some of the lurid atmosphere of Chaucer's pardoner and like him represents a foreign hospital, let us for a moment accept him as a type figure and observe through him the actions of the class he represents.[101]

Anglicus, one may assume, was not usually so unfortunate as at York.[102] A contribution of five marks to the fabric of the cathedral[103] or to the bishop's charity[104] would customarily assure his receipt of a letter of recommendation to the clergy of the diocese.[105] He would then proceed on his way, arriving in due course at the curia of one of the rural archdeaconries into which the diocese was divided. The archdeacon himself would not be in residence (he was characteristically an absentee), but in his stead his Official would be carrying on to the best of his ability the archdeacon's numerous duties—in particular that of guardian of the morals of all within his jurisdiction.[106]

The archdeacon's Official took a kindly interest in pardoners, whether licensed or not. If the pardoner had no valid license— that is, if he were simply in business for himself—the Official was likely to consider this so suspicious a circumstance as to require a deposit of perhaps fifteen marks to re-establish his shaken faith in the pardoner. When this deposit had been duly made, however, the pardoner received the freedom of the archdeaconry,[107] the freedom to enter any church he chose and explain his fictitious business. In addition he received a certain amount of security, for if the bishop heard of his activities, he would address his complaint to the archdeacon or his Official. Records of arrests are not often to be met with.[108]

The authorized pardoner was also welcome at the archdeacon's curia. If the fraudulent pardoner found it necessary to make a deposit, the authorized found it no less necessary to purchase a license,[109] a license the Official had not the slightest legal right to grant.[110] But the Official never demanded something for nothing. Almost all the practices pardoners found most effective in their profession, particularly preaching and absolving, were illegal,[111] and the Official, through the right of inspection within the archdeaconry, possessed the power to summon the pardoner before the court over which he himself presided and to hand him over to the bishop's court.[112]

Anglicus was of course in no position to contest the Official's right to license him. With his new license and without another substantial sum he departed in search of his prey—an audience. This was obtainable with the least difficulty in the church of the parish priest, where Anglicus's original license provided that he was to be heard at the regular sermon time.[113] When Anglicus arrived, the parish priest might not necessarily be happy to see him. In fact, memories of the past Sunday when he had seen the weekly offering disappear into the pockets of pardoners for the Hospital of St. Anthony, the monks of Humberston, and the bridge at Stamford were very likely still with him.[114] If the priest were large and robust or possessed parishioners of that description, Anglicus might find himself cast out of Holy Church in a very real sense. It happened to the best licensed of pardoners—so frequently, in fact, that there was a special papal letter for complaints against just such offenses.[115]

In this predicament there were two general courses open to Anglicus. In concert with brother collectors he could so harass the unfortunate priest as to drive him into submission,[116] or he could take a course more conducive to future friendly relations and divide the proceeds of his mission with the priest. "For the parisch prest and the pardonere · parten the siluer" is Langland's description of this elevating sight.[117]

Now at last he mounted the pulpit and, with lips raised to heaven and tongue sweeping the earth for praise and coins, began his sermon.[118] What his sermon, or more properly his exhortation, was we can gather from a number of contemporary accounts. He came from a hospital so large, as he described it, that all the hospitals in the world put together could easily have been contained within it.[119] He granted more years of pardon than come before doomsday.[120] He confessed and absolved; extracted souls from purgatory and from hell for a modest sum.[121] And in conclusion, with great benevolence, he blessed them all.[122]

And so from the bishop's charity to the grasping fingers of the impoverished parish priest, the trail of corruption spread by the pardoner for St. James of Altopascio, St. Anthony of Vienne, St. Mary Roncesvalles, or any of the distant hospitals was complete—corruption not easily removed, for crime and justice had become inseparable companions. This prostitution of office by which control became assistance we can find expressed in the sober words of Bishop Grandisson addressed to the archdeacons' Officials: "Supported by your wrongful favor and assistance, pardoners travel at will through our diocese seducing the simple and untaught people, and so much as in them lies, deceive their very souls."[123]

The laxity of control which the foreign hospitals exerted on their questors, the opportunities this laxity afforded for the spreading of corruption within the legal framework of the Church —these, it would appear, were the causes for the unenviable reputation which collectors for the foreign hospitals enjoyed. Beverley Minster, operating within four close-lying dioceses, could rule its questors with an iron hand; the foreign hospitals were not in a position to take such action. To seize authorized questors practicing diversion of funds or fraudulent questors possessing no authorization, they found it necessary to appeal to the Pope or to the archbishop, who must in turn take action through his subordinates. Thus we find John XXII sending nuntii to Sweden and Norway to suppress fraudulent collectors purporting to be of the

Hospital of the Holy Ghost in Saxia of Rome,[124] and to Poland and Germany to prosecute fraudulent questors of St. Lazarus of Jerusalem.[125] The same situation is to be found much intensified in the records of St. Anthony of Vienne.[126]

Those foreign hospitals which like St. Mary Roncesvalles had branches in England found themselves in little better plight. Control of these hospitals from outside of England was difficult if not impossible, and their wealth, to which charitable collections were no small contributing factor, made them tempting political prizes.[127] This weakness in the hospital rule seems to have been reflected in a weakened rule of the hospital's questors. The complaints of local English clergy against the unrestrained actions of questors for the Knights of St. John "in Anglia" necessitated the issuance of a bull by Urban V.[128] Wulfran, Bishop of Bethlehem, was so disturbed by his inability to suppress the abuses of collectors for the "Fratres Bethleemitani de Anglia" that he ordered them suspended, and, if they refused to acknowledge the suspension, apprehended and their goods divided.[129]

To the notoriety incident to the uncontrolled activities of these questors may perhaps be added another factor. There is some evidence that the foreign hospitals conducted collections not directly, as did Beverley Minster, but by farming out the collection rights on payment of a fixed fee, after which the purchaser was free to go about his business as his professional instincts dictated.[130]

IV

Having explored with some thoroughness the law of the pardoner and the operation of that law in England, we are prepared to ask the question: What attitude, if any, toward this complex situation is Chaucer expressing in the person of his remarkable artistic creation, the "gentil Pardoner of Rouncivale"?

It is to be noted first of all that Chaucer's Pardoner is precisely an artistic creation. Like all the Canterbury Pilgrims he is constructed upon the principle of what Tatlock has very accurately termed the "vivid type."[131] The Miller's golden thumb, the Knight's love of chivalry, the Friar's generosity to the women within his "haunt"—all are generic characteristics which give to the Pilgrims that suggestion of containing within themselves the whole world of their time which Dryden seems most fully to have apprehended.[132] The Pardoner too is a generic figure. In attitude, practices, and credentials, he is very much what a contemporary who had been in church during sermon time might have expected.

Like the usual professional collector, the Pardoner's interest in his duties is limited to what those duties yield him in cash and negotiable commodities.[133] What he collects he spends in taverns amidst no very spiritual company,[134] yet he is concerned for professional reasons that to the "lewed peple" his life should have the appearance of sanctity.[135] In practices as well as moral principles, he is typical. He preaches at length and with great eloquence;[136] he absolves the folk who kneel beneath his holy bull[137] of any sin at any time.[138] As pious alms anything anyone has to offer is acceptable—coins, brooches, spoons, rings, wool.[139] Even the Pardoner's credentials are standard. Within his wallet reposes a wide variety of indulgences,[140] and his letter of admission, directed to the lower clergy of the diocese, is sealed with the bishop's seal.[141] What at first glance seems most remarkable about his credentials—their presentation to him by the Pope himself—is of course but a common device of pardoners to dazzle their simple contributors.[142] Chaucer's collector of alms is very much like all collectors of alms.

Such are the typical aspects of the Pardoner. Yet, like the other Canterbury Pilgrims, he is something more than a purely generic figure. Aside from the rather striking qualities of person and personality which lie outside the scope of this study, Chaucer has increased the vividness and suggestiveness of his portrait by the addition of two particular characteristics: Roncesvalles and false relics. He has further given definite meaning to his whole presentation by bringing his heightened portrait into ironical juxtaposition with the figure of the Summoner.

It is, of course, difficult to weigh with accuracy the significance of the Pardoner's being "a gentil Pardoner of Rouncivale." Manly believed that the satiric humor to be discovered in the Pardoner lies chiefly in what he took to be a covert allusion to political chicanery in the Hospital of St. Mary Roncevall at Charing Cross.[143] However much truth there may be in this interpretation, it is difficult to believe that the intricate interdevelopment of personality and satire which moves through the General Prologue, Prologue, and Tale exists solely as embellishment for an allusion to the hospital at Charing Cross. It seems more likely that, like Dante,[144] Chaucer was seeking for artistic purposes a particular name for a generic corruption, and chose a name which at a particular point of time possessed the most vivid connotations. It has not previously been observed that at about the time Chaucer was thinking about pardoners, St. Mary Roncesvalles was conducting a building-fund drive for its branch at Charing Cross.[145] But whatever may have been the particular factors which guided Chaucer's choice, it seems certain that that choice would have fallen upon a foreign hospital, for the failure of these hospitals to control the pardoners within their own employ, or within the employ of their branches, had gained them an inescapable notoriety. Whenever there is mention of abuses, it is these hospitals which are specified, both in ecclesiastical documents[146] and in contemporary satire.[147] The name of the foreign hospital in this connection carried a rather clear connotation of corruption and labelled the pardoner who bore that name as of the most ingenious and treacherous sort.

The second particular attribute of the Pardoner, that of false relics, may be said to accomplish the same end from a different point of view. As has been shown, the carrying of false relics was an abuse so rare that no contemporary manual even discusses it, while allusions to the practice are only very infrequently to be met with elsewhere.[148] More luridly than the name of the hospital he represents, the Pardoner's false relics mark him as a dangerous man with souls.

Yet this exemplar of spiritual abuse, the Pardoner, is presented duly licensed,[149] riding in company with the Summoner, the agent of the archdeacon's court, the man who should be putting him behind bars. In this paradox, this ironic portrait of justice and crime singing in close harmony, we reach the center of Chaucer's satire.[150] The satire of the Pardoner is upon the corruption which had permeated a system of justice, corruption which permitted flagrant and undisguised abuse[151] to become the companion of a law enforcement deformed almost beyond recognition. Before our eyes, crime and justice, the Pardoner and the Summoner, amble together in vinous jocularity down the road to Canterbury.

Chaucer's satire of the Pardoner is not upon the Pardoner but upon those who make the Pardoner possible.[152]

V

As a man of his own age, Chaucer looked back upon an earlier age when faith formed the keystone to the whole structure of existence. Though there is for Chaucer a sense of exhilaration in the new—otherwise we should have no Alice of Bath—he is also the medieval man of letters whose artistic creed does not permit open evil to go unchallenged. Implicit in the shift from theocentric universe to egocentric universe is a concern with self which is not necessarily beautiful in those who profess the selfless life of religion. Within the Church of the "newe world" which Chaucer sees taking form everywhere about him, there are those who have no God but personal gain and who, by their practices, render the Church itself suspect.

No force contributed more powerfully to this unhappy situation than did the existence of the pardoner. To men of deep religious feeling everywhere the corruption which the pardoner spread wherever he went, the error he poured into the people, the shadow of ridicule he cast upon the Church were bitter. One finds this feeling iterated and reiterated in Church council after Church council; one finds it also in the utterances of such outspoken bishops as John de Grandisson, Bishop of Exeter, and William Durandus, Bishop of Mende.[153]

What Chaucer has done is simply to present satirically the indignation which earnest men everywhere within the Church were expressing directly. Like Swift's economic proposals,[154] these utterances must be sought out. Like Swift's *Modest Proposal*, the satire of the Pardoner is not easily forgotten.

NOTES

1. Raymundus de Pennaforte, *Summa casuum poenitentiae* (Rome, 1603), p. 442.
2. F. E. Hagedorn, *General Legislation on Indulgences* (Washington, 1924), p. 46.

3. "dummodo de peccatis suis contriti fuerint et ore confessi" (Michael Tangl, *Die päpstlichen Kanzleiordnungen von 1200–1500* [Innsbruck, 1894], p. 281).

4. *Registrum Roberti Winchelsey*, ed. Rose Graham, Canterbury and York Society, LXXVI, 249.

5. *The Register of William Wickwane*, ed. William Brown, Surtees Society, CXIV, 22.

6. *The Register of William of Wykeham*, Part II, ed. T. F. Kirby, Hampshire Record Society, XIII, 123.

7. *The Register of Thomas de Brantyngham*, Part I, ed. F. C. Hingeston-Randolph, Exeter Episcopal Registers, VI, 566.

8. *Richard d'Aungerville of Bury: Fragments of His Register*, Surtees Society, CXIX, 28.

9. ,"et aliqui ex ipsis . . . a poena et a culpa . . . absolvant: nos, abusus huiusmodi . . . aboleri volentes" (*Corpus juris canonici*, ed. Aemilius Friedberg [Leipzig, 1922], II, 1190).

10. Hagedorn, *Legislation on Indulgences*, chap. VI.

11. "Forma litterarum praedicatorum" (J. D. Mansi, *Sacrorum conciliorum nova et amplissima collectio* (Florence, Venice, 1759–1798), XXII, 1050). See also Nikolaus Paulus, "Die Formel: In remissionem peccatorum iniungimus," *Geschichte des Ablasses im Mittelalter* (Paderborn, 1922–1923), I, 120–131.

12. Tangl, *Die päpstlichen Kanzleiordnungen*, p. 282.

13. "[Da]te igitur elemosinam ut omnia munda sint vobis, quia elemosina a morte liberat, peccata purgat, et facit invenire vitam aeternam. Sicut aqua ignem ardentem extinguit, ita elemosina peccato resistit" (*Memorials of the Church of SS. Peter and Wilfrid*, Part II, ed. J. T. Fowler, Surtees Society, LXXVIII, 83).

14. "quum solum ipsis competat indulgentias sibi concessas insinuare populo, et caritativa postulare subsidia suppliciter ab eodem" (Friedberg, *Corpus juris canonici*, II, 1190).

15. In the whole matter of canon law the authors are deeply indebted to the generous personal assistance of Professor Stephan G. Kuttner of Yale University.

16. "peccuniarum questui solum operam impudenter impendunt, et non profectum animarum querunt" (*The Register of John de Grandisson*, Part II, ed. F. C. Hingeston-Randolph, Exeter Episcopal Registers, IV, 1178).

17. See note 73 below.

18. *Bullarium Romanum*, III, 768.

19. "effusis lacrimarum profluviis, ad quas habent oculos eruditos . . . sic motive proponunt, tamque indulgentiarum numerositatem contra statutum generalis Concilii, & relaxationem peccaminum pollicentur, quod vix est aliquis, etiam ipsorum agnoscens nequitias, qui se a subventione eorum valeat continere" (Mansi, *Concilia*, XXIII, 1102).

20. "benefactoribus locorum, quorum quaestores exsistunt, remissionem plenariam peccatorum indulgeant" (this and following citations are derived from Clement V's catalogue of abuses practiced by pardoners [Friedberg, *Corpus juris canonici*, II, 1190]).

21. "indulgentias populo motu suo proprio de facto concedant" (*ibid.*).
22. "a periuriis, homicidiis et peccatis aliis sibi confitentes absolvant" (*ibid.*).
23. "et aliqui ex ipsis eos a poena et a culpa (ut eorum verbis utamur), absolvant" (*ibid.*). The direct effect of this false forgiveness of sin was an erroneous belief on the part of the victim that he was duly confessed and absolved. One of Berthold von Regensburg's numerous indictments of the pardoner reads: "dû verderbest dem almehtigen gote ein michel teil sêlen. Swenne dû ûf stêst unde vergibest einem alle die sünde die er ie getete umb einen einigen helbelinc oder umb einen einigen pfenninc, sô waenet er, er habe gebüezet, unde wil für baz niht mêr büezen" (*Predigten*, ed. Franz Pfeiffer and Joseph Strobl [Vienna, 1862, 1880], I, 117).
24. "animas tres vel plures parentum vel amicorum illorum, qui eleemosynas eis conferunt, de purgatorio (ut asserunt mendaciter), extrahant, et ad gaudia paradisi perducant" (Friedberg, *Corpus juris canonici*, II, 1190).
25. "damnatis in inferno liberationem pro modica pecunia promittentes" (Mansi, *Concilia*, XXIII, 693); "ab inferno, ubi nulla est redemptio. Unde . . . contra iustitiam suam animam patris vel matris vel alicuius se pro certa pecunia extrahere dicunt" ("De helymosinis colligendis: capitulum LXXXVII," *Liber regulae S. Spiritus*, ed. A. Francesco la Cava [Milan, 1947], p. 199).
26. See discussion, note 51 below.
27. "luridis manibus seu pedibus crematorum" (*Bullarium Romanum*, III, 389).
28. "Hi profanissimi, pro reliquiis saepe exponunt ossa profana hominum, seu brutorum, & miracula mentiuntur" (Mansi, *Concilia*, XXIII, 1102).
29. "Et cum forsitan ossa galline deferant secum dicunt: Quicunque illa obsculatus fuerit, in dentibus, ore vel fatie, nunquam dolorem sentiet" (*Liber regulae S. Spiritus*, p. 199). The abuse of false relics is, however, the rarest of the pardoner's abuses; see discussion, note 51 below.
30. "pro uno firmaculo, anulo vel adminus uno denario conferendo" (*Registrum Radulphi Baldock*, etc., ed. R. C. Fowler, Canterbury and York Series, VII, 134).
31. "bladum a simplicibus extorqueant" (*Liber regulae S. Spiritus*, p. 199).
32. "peccuniam, animalia, et cetera queque bona" (Hingeston-Randolph, *Register Grandisson*, I, 444); "pecunia et alia bona" (*Memorials of Beverley Minster: Chapter Act Book*, Part I, ed. A. F. Leach, Surtees Society, XCVIII, 204).
33. "vitae sanctitatem exterius praetendentes . . . eleemosynas . . . postea in ebrietatibus & luxuriis, in omni conspectu prodigaliter consumere non erubescunt" (Mansi, *Concilia*, XXIV, 829); "consumunt in commessationibus, ebrietate, ludis, & luxuriis" (*ibid.*, XXIII, 1102). Examples could be multiplied. The proclivity of the pardoner for the tavern seems to have been one of his best-known characteristics.
34. "Eleemosynarum quoque quaestores . . . admitti, nisi apostolicas vel

diocesani episcopi litteras veras exhibeant, prohibemus" (*ibid.*, XXII, 1050).

35. "Et tunc, praeter id quod in ipsis continebitur litteris, nihil populo proponere permittantur" (*ibid.*). The effect of this provision was to deprive every eleemosynary questor of the right to preach. Abuses in preaching were by no means limited to lay pardoners (see Paulus, *Geschichte des Ablasses*, II, 289), and we have found no basis for J. M. Manly's assertion that "friars and others specially found and declared fit" were permitted to preach eleemosynary indulgences (*Some New Light on Chaucer* [New York, 1926], p. 129). On the contrary, friars or, more properly, hospital brothers engaged in collections are necessarily included because collections for hospitals were presumed to be carried on by members of the order operating the hospital, but that any exception from this rule was made in their favor does not appear. The much used papal form letter "Si iuxta sententiam" specifically prohibits brothers from preaching except as provided by the Lateran Council. This form letter states that questors are to be admitted to churches "ut super elemosinis acquirendis per . . . eosdem fratres, dummodo idonei et bone conversationis existant, verbum exhortationis ad populum proponatur, *salva in omnibus supradictis declaratione concilii generalis*" (Tangl, *Die päpstlichen Kanzleiordnungen*, p. 282). The General Council (Lateran Council of 1215) provided as above that the questor was to preach only insofar as reading the contents of his letters could be considered preaching. The other frequently used papal form letter, "Querelam gravem," contains the same provision (*ibid.*, p. 267). An example of the application of this rule to brothers in England is to be found in the register of John le Romeyn of York: "cum fratres hospitalis predicti [Sancti Jacobi de Alto Passu] vel eorum nuncii ad vos accesserint, fidelium elemosinas petituri, ipsos benigno intuitu admittatis gracius ad petita; *quos, tamen, predicare nolumus ullo modo*" (*The Register of John le Romeyn*, Surtees Society, CXXIII, 7). To this one may add the comments of the canon-law glossators, the clearest of which reads: "questores non sunt permittendi praedicare" (*Clementis Papae V constitutiones* [Rome, 1582], V, ix, 2). On this whole question, see Paulus, II, 289–290, from which the major portion of the above material was taken.

36. "Forma litterarum praedicatorum," which begins, "Quoniam (ut ait Apostolus) omnes stabimus ante tribunal Christi" (Mansi, *Concilia*, XXII, 1049–1050).

37. "Qui autem ad quaerendas eleemosynas destinantur, modesti sint & discreti, nec in tabernis aut locis aliis incongruis hospitentur" (*ibid.*).

38. *Bullarium Romanum*, III, 767–768.

39. Friedberg, *Corpus juris canonici*, II, 1190. On the technical aspects of this canon, see Paulus, *Geschichte des Ablasses*, II, 284–285.

40. "De questoribus," *Regimen animarum* (Harley 2272), fol. 9^b ff. The MS is dated 1343. Through the kind permission of the Trustees of the British Museum, we are enabled to publish in its entirety this valuable summary by an English manualist of the law governing the pardoner in Chaucer's own time. The section has appeared only in

brief extracts in G. R. Owst's *Preaching in Mediaeval England*, (Cambridge, 1926), chap. III. At lines 24–26, "questores . . . diocesani," the text varies from that of the "Abusionibus" (Friedberg, *Corpus juris canonici*, II, 1190) in its insistence on episcopal letters. We have somewhat modernized and corrected the text.

41. To the authority of the *Regimen animarum* on this point, one may add that of a work attributed to Wyclif. In the *Tractatus de blasphemia*, ed. M. H. Dziewicki (London, 1893), p. 272, the author discusses the law of the pardoner and its non-enforcement, noting the "Cum ex eo" and "Abusionibus." The less important "Sedis Apostolicae," however, he does not mention.

42. See letter addressed to collector for fabric of Beverley Minster asking him to turn in his collections immediately, "Quum magister operis ecclesiae nostra[e] pecunia hiis diebus indigeat vehementer" (Leach, *Chapter Act Book*, I, 281.

43. "in hospitali S. Antonii Viennensis diocesis jaceat magna multitudo languencium, cecorum, claudorum, aridorum, et aliorum variis morborum generibus laborancium, expectancium graciam de supernis, quorum corpora et membra sunt de diversis infirmitatibus graviter deformata, ad quorum vite sustentacionem prope dicti hospitalis non suppetunt facultates, nisi devocio Christi fidelium ad illud per elemosinarum largicionem manus porrexerit adjutrices" (Kirby's *Register Wykeham*, XIII, 107).

44. "Si iuxta sententiam" (Tangl, *Die päpstlichen Kanzleiordnungen*, p. 282).

45. See Innocent III's complaint against the Knights of St. John that illiterate lay brothers were being used for collections: "fratres Hospitalis sancti Joannis laici et illiterati" (*PL*, CCXIV, 425).

46. "Quia inverecundi quaestores turpissimos suos quaestus ad firmam emunt" "(*Concilia Magnae Britanniae*, ed. David Wilkins [London, 1737], III, 365); "Nec praedicatio alicujus provinciae eis, vel quibusdam aliis, committatur ad firmam" (Mansi, *Concilia*, XXII, 821).

47. Attempts on the part of the parish clergy to squeeze from the pardoner a part of his receipts seem to have been very general. Typical is the formulary "Querelam gravem," which states, "iidem presbiteri quandam partem elemosinarum pauperum exigunt impudenter" (Tangl, *Die päpstlichen Kanzleiordnungen*, p. 267). Almost all English licenses direct the local clergy to release the collection to the pardoner "absque diminutione qualibet."

48. See Paulus, *Geschichte des Ablasses*, II, 266–287.

49. See, e.g., those by Nicholas IV in 1290 (*Les Registres de Nicholas*, IV, No. 2324–2346) and by Robert Winchelsey, Archbishop of Canterbury, in 1309 (Fowler, *Registrum Baldock*, pp. 103–105).

50. *Jean XXII: Lettres communes*, No. 49814.

51. The carrying of false relics seems to have been the most effectively controlled of all the pardoner's abuses. Genuine relics might legally be carried by the pardoner if the diocesan bishop's permission were obtained (C. Parisiense [1213] in Mansi, *Concilia*, XXII, 821; *Cilium oculi sacerdotis*, cited by Owst, *Preaching* [p. 109, note 1]); but the

sale of such relics was forbidden by the Lateran Council of 1215, and the prohibition, at least insofar as pardoners were concerned, was apparently observed. Traffic in false relics seems also to have been very infrequent. Although one may find the standard abuses of pardoners repeated over and over again, the abuse of false relics does not appear among them. There is no mention of this highly spectacular abuse in any of the manuals which treat of the pardoner, and it is noticed in only a few Church councils: C. Moguntinum, 1261; C. Lugdunense, 1274; C. Trevirense, 1310 (Mansi, *Concilia*, XXIII, 1102; XXIV, 131; XXV, 269). The relative infrequency of the practice of employing false relics is probably to be attributed to a considerably sterner attitude toward this abuse. Thus the Synod of Exeter (1287) provides—without mentioning pardoners—that anyone causing false relics to be venerated be treated as a heretic: "tanquam haereticos censemus graviter puniendos" (Mansi, *Concilia*, XXIV, 830). Only the hardiest of adventurers seem to have been willing to take this risk (for an example of such a group, see *Bullarium romanum*, III, 389).

52. The shrine seems to have been built between 1302 and 1308, and major work upon the nave to have been undertaken immediately after the completion of the shrine (Leach, *Chapter Act Book*, I, xxxiii, xciv–xcv).

53. Leach, *Chapter Act Book*, I, 22; *Acta SS. Bolland.*, xv, 166.

54. Leach, *Chapter Act Book*, I, 229–231.

55. If one catalogues, from the fragmentary existing records, the institutions, all possessing indulgences, which were collecting in the province of York—Beverley Minster's main area of operations—within the same years (1302–1328), the results are impressive. With the exception of St. Mary Roncesvalles, all of the major hospitals are represented—St. Anthony of Vienne (*The Register of William Greenfield*, Part I, ed. William Brown, Surtees Society, CXLV, 107); St. James of Altopascio (*ibid.*, I, 131); Holy Ghost in Saxia of Rome (*ibid.*, I, 107). With them are the major churches of York: the metropolitan church of St. Peter (*ibid.*, I, 4) and the collegiate church of St. Wilfrid (Fowler, *Memorials SS. Peter and Wilfrid*, Part II, Surtees Society, LXXVIII, 82). Somewhat earlier will be found the inevitable perilous bridge and burned monastery.

56. Beverley Minster had received indulgences from Archbishops John le Romeyn for repair of the existing fabric (Leach, *Chapter Act Book*, I, 2) and Thomas Corbridge for the shrine (I, 3). In collections, Chapter questors were allowed to state their business immediately after the privileged metropolitan church of St. Peter, a not inconsiderable advantage (II, 72, in Surtees Society, CVIII).

57. Elyas de Lumby's letter of appointment indicates that collections were customarily made in Lincoln (I, 229). The letter which he carried to the Bishop of Lincoln thanks the Bishop for past favors (I, 253).

58. On June 7, 1314, simultaneous letters were addressed to the Bishops of Norwich and Ely (I, 317). The Bishop of Norwich replied that his diocese was already filled with collectors for recently burned religious buildings within the diocese and with collectors whom he felt obliged

to admit "propter mandata superiorum nostrorum." He could admit no more "absque gravi scandalo" (I, 318). The implication would seem to be clear that by this date (1314) Beverley Minster had still to obtain any further privileges within the province of Canterbury. There is no indication that Beverley Minster was ever licensed to collect in the dioceses of Norwich and Ely.

59. April 11, 1309 (Fowler, *Registrum Baldock*, pp. 103–105).

60. Leach, *Chapter Act Book*, I, 252–253.

61. Elyas's letter to the Archbishop of Canterbury reads: "Vestram paternitatem in Domino requirimus et rogamus quatinus Elye de Lumby, clerico . . . dignemini indulgere, et super hujusmodi indulgentia vestras litteras concedere munere caritatis" (Leach, *Chapter Act Book*, I, 252). This request is principally for permission to collect, but an appeal for the grant of indulgences would seem to be at least implied. If one compares this letter with John of Gaunt's frank request to "ercevesques et evesques" to grant collectors of St. Mary Roncesvalles "pardon et indulgence, et sur ce de granter lettres de mandement a voz obedienters," the parallelism of phrase will be apparent (*John of Gaunt's Register*, I, 45, Camden Society, 3rd Series, xx).

62. On December 23, 1312, three questors were appointed for Lincoln (Leach, *Chapter Act Book*, I, 299). Collections were probably resumed considerably earlier than this record indicates.

63. Beverley Minster tried again in 1314, relying on the influence of William de Melton, in 1309 Provost of Beverley and in 1316 elected Archbishop of York (*DNB*). He is requested to give aid to John de Lincoln, a successor to Elyas de Lumby, who has "quaedam negotia ipsam fabricam et quaestum ejusdem tangentia in curia Domini Cantuariensis Archiepiscopi" (Leach, *Chapter Act Book*, I, 323–324). There is, however, no record of John de Lincoln's having received any indulgences or of collections having been extended into additional dioceses of the province of Canterbury.

64. *Ibid.*, I, 368. Although not early examples (1319–1320), these are among the few which indicate this aspect of the system's operation.

65. See the contract of Elyas de Lumby, p. 219 above. The practice of substitution seems to have been a well-established one. Innocent III in 1198 complains of the ill effects of this delegation of authority: "Quia vero non sufficiunt per se loca omnia circumire, sibi clericos, sacerdotes, laicos, etiam rudes, non religiosos, sed in nequitiis exercitatos assumunt" (*PL*, CCXIV, 425).

66. Leach, *Chapter Act Book*, I, 369.

67. *Ibid.*, I, 382.

68. See Monechant's substitution of John de Claworth. Monechant's appointment by the Chapter reads "praesentibus valituris donec eas duxerimus revocandas." Claworth's appointment by Monechant reads: "praesentibus tantummodo valituris quousque illas duxero revocandas" (*ibid.*, I, 368).

69. Walter de Stamford and Alexander de Derby, questors of Beverley Minster, when sent to Norwich and Ely in June, 1314, were issued "transcriptum duarum bullarum, videlicet Alexandri et Innocentii,

sigillo Capituli consignatum" (Leach, *Chapter Act Book*, I, 317). This is probably a more or less accepted arrangement, since we find Archbishop Robert Winchelsey stating in 1306 that letters may be originals or "eorum tenoribus sub notis et autenticis sigillis contentis" (Fowler, *Registrum Baldock*, p. 39).

70. The seal of the diocesan bishop was the regular guarantee to the clergy of the diocese that the pardoner's credentials were genuine. The inspection of all papal letters was required of the diocesan bishop by the Council of Vienne (see *Regimen animarum*, p. 217 above, lines 28–29). These he seems to have sealed, just as he did indulgences which he himself granted to institutions within his own diocese (*Register Brantyngham*, I, 489, 350). The archbishop also examined and sealed papal letters (Fowler, *Registrum Baldock*, I, 211).

71. Walter de Stamford and Alexander de Derby likewise received from the Chapter letters of appointment or "procuratoria" ("Facta fuerunt duo procuratoria unum Waltero et aliud Alexandro" [Leach, *Chapter Act Book*, I, 317]). Questors were examined by the bishop or his official to make sure that the questor bearing the letter of appointment was the questor named in it (Brown, *Register Greenfield*, I, 131–132).

72. "nostras Literas, vero sigillo nostro munitas, nostrique anuli impressione in dorso sigilli consignatas" (*Register Brantyngham*, I, 320). The practical application of the provision for the episcopal inspection of pardoners' credentials imposed by the Council of Vienne seems to have been that no questor could be admitted without letters from the diocesan bishop. See *Regimen animarum* (p. 217 above, lines 24–26), and note 40.

73. "Proviso quod hujusmodi negotium expediatur sicut decet statim post Evangelium lectum" (Leach, *Chapter Act Book*, II, 72–73). The more usual form is the vaguer "intra missarum solemnia." On this point see Owst, *Preaching*, Appendix I.

74. "absque diminutione qualibet fideliter persolvant et restituant" (Leach, *Chapter Act Book*, II, 72). This provision is of extremely general occurrence.

75. "presentibus post triennium minime valituris" (*Register Wickwane*, p. 22). Most licenses ran for two or three years.

76. The text of this letter of protection does not appear in the *Chapter Act Book*, but it is specified as one of Richard Monechant's credentials in a letter of revocation (II, 27).

77. "juramento corporaliter praestito obligari dicto Capitulo in viginti libris sterlingorum" (Leach, *Chapter Act Book*, I, 230). This bond appears to have been used generally, for the summons addressed to Robert de Pagula, also a questor for Beverley Minster, reminds him to render his accounts "prout juramento corporali a te praestito es astrictus" (*ibid.*, I, 320).

78. "in admissione praefati officii liberata per indenturam" (*ibid.*, I, 298).

79. See citation of Robert de Pagula (*ibid.*, I, 320).

80. *Ibid.*, I, 298.

81. John de Fitling, Elyas de Lumby, John de Bristol, Robert de Pagula,

Richard Monechant, Thomas Gamell, and Thomas Bradele, all were called to a sudden accounting or relieved of their positions at one time or another.

82. The term "clericus" would here seem to indicate that the questor was literate and had possibly received the first tonsure. For a discussion of the whole problem, see Karl Krebs, "Der Bedeutungswandel von M. E. Clerk," *Bonner Studien zur englischen Philologie*, Vol. XXI (1933).

83. Leach, *Chapter Act Book*, I, 369.

84. *Ibid.*, II, 28. He is the only collector to whose name "clericus" is not affixed. However, in other cases the title sometimes is used and sometimes not.

85. "burgenses Beverlaci" (*ibid.*, II, 79).

86. Brown, *Register Greenfield*, I, 4–5. John de Lincoln seems always to have enjoyed a certain distinction. He is here named as collector for the whole province of York, a position he could hardly be expected to fill without substituting additional questors.

87. *Ibid.*, I, 107.

88. *Ibid.* He obtained appointment to all of these offices on the same day, May 21, 1306.

89. Leach, *Chapter Act Book*, I, 298 He must have been employed at some time preceding November, 1312, for the record cited is of his being relieved of his duties by Elyas de Lumby. He was soon re-employed.

90. *Ibid.*, I, 307.

91. *Ibid.*, I, 323–324; see also note 63 above.

92. There are mentions of "dominus Willelmus de Humbleton, capellanus" (*ibid.*, I, 280); "Johannem de Langtoft, capellanum" (I, 298); and "Sir J. Smith" (I, 299). These names occur scarcely more than once each.

93. Brown, *Register Greenfield*, I, 107; Fowler, *Memorials SS. Peter and Wilfrid*, II, 83.

94. Leach, *Chapter Act Book*, I, xcvii. See here editor's remarks on professional collecting.

95. The *Liber regulae S. Spiritus*, ed. la Cava, is an excellent addition to our knowledge of these hospitals, but the rule of such a hospital unfortunately sheds little light on the actual procedures used in the gathering of alms. See "De helymosinis colligendis," pp. 198–199.

96. Brown, *Register Greenfield*, I, 131–132. Some light is shed by this incident on the usual procedure in matters concerning the pardoner. The questors here had come first to the archbishop, who sent them to his Official, because he remembered "quod in domo archiepiscopi non consueverunt negocia hujusmodi expediri set ad officialem omnia mittebantur."

97. *Ibid.*, editor's note. It is difficult to say whether the collectors here mentioned carried an indulgence from Bishop Patrasso, or whether they carried a papal indulgence and an accompanying letter, probably also with indulgence, from the Bishop. The latter is perhaps the more likely. Altopascio was regularly granted papal indulgences and regu-

larly collected in York. One finds such references as early as 1280, when Archbishop William Wickwane admitted questors of this hospital "juxta vires votivas litterarum papalium" (Brown, *Register Wickwane*, p. 212).

98. Brown, *Register Greenfield*, I, 132. This would appear to be one of the commonly used paraphrases of the formulary "Si iuxta sententiam," which provides that collectors be brothers of the Hospital "idonei et bone conversationis" or their nuntii "dummodo non sint questuarii" (Tangl, *Die päpstlichen Kanzleiordnungen*, p. 281). Archbishop John le Romeyn of York in 1287 uses approximately the language of the letters here mentioned in licensing "fratres hospitalis predicti [Sancti Jacobi de Alto Passu] vel eorum nuncii" (*Register Romeyn*, I, 7).

99. "qui videtur procurator substitutus, cum in substitutione nominetur Bonaventura alumpnus et confrater hospitalis" (Brown, *Register Greenfield*, I, 131). The sense of "cum" would here appear to be "although."

100. "Preterea ille Anglicus qui venit cum eo questuarius est notorius, cui in privilegiis committi negocium prohibetur" (*ibid.*, I, 132). The Official refused to permit him to collect because his letters forbade their use by questors of evil repute or "questuarii"; see note 98 above, and Paulus: "Es sollte damit verhindert werden, dass die religiösen Genossenschaften ihre Kollekten durch gedungene Quästoren vornehemen liessen" (*Geschichte des Ablasses*, II, 289).

101. The following examples do not actually concern Anglicus himself. The entry noticed above is the only one mentioning him. All examples used, however, are from records of pardoners for foreign hospitals. Anglicus is employed as a type figure.

102. The rather stern attitude of the Official in this case may in some measure be due to the privileges which the questors were demanding, nothing less than the convocation of all the clergy in the diocese: "Petunt insuper convocacionem cleri vestri per totam vestram diocesim quam sine precepto vestro eciam si nuncius esset idoneus concedere non auderem" (Brown, *Register Greenfield*, I, 132).

103. "Emanavit Litera pro Nunciis negociorum Sancti Antonii, Viennensis Dyocesis, per annum duratura; *et dabunt Fabrice Exoniensi v marcas*" (*The Register of Walter de Stapeldon*, ed. F. C. Hingeston-Randolph, Exeter Episcopal Registers, II, 398). Italics are editor's.

104. "Apud Lawyttone . . . emanarunt quatuor Mandata Archidiaconis et eorum Officialibus, pro subsidio Domus Sancti Antonini; et dabit dicti subsidii Collector ad elemosinam Domini v marcas" (*ibid.*, II, 326). See also the license of John de Wintone to collect in the diocese for the same hospital: "et dabit singulis annis vj marcas" (*ibid.*).

105. On the customary nature of this contribution, Paulus observes: "Es war nämlich vielfach üblich, dass die Sammler sowohl den Bischöfen als den Pfarrgeistlichen eine Abgabe entrichteten" (*Geschichte des Ablasses*, II, 290). This, of course, does not mean that all bishops adopted this procedure.

106. "per se et suos inquirant in parochia in qua officium visitationis impendunt in rebus vel personis aliquid fuerit corrigendum et excessus

si quos ibidem invenerint vel tunc vel in proximo capitulo corrigantur" (W. Lyndwood, *Provinciale* [London, 1529], fol. 5ª).

107. See Bishop Grandisson's citation of Richard de Chuddele, Official of the Archdeacon of Cornwall, for receiving a deposit of fifteen marks sterling "per quosdam ficticios elemosinarum quaestores Sancti Sepulchri" (Hingeston-Randolph, *Register Grandisson*, I, 426–427).

108. Bishops seem to have understood the practices of archdeacons, but rarely to have become explicit as did Bishop Grandisson. Complaints were directed to archdeacons of the regions in which the bishop knew pardoners to be operating without his license, "in . . . jurisdictionis nostrae elusionem manifestam" (*The Register of Richard de Kellawe*, ed. T. D. Hardy, Rerum Britannicarium Medii Aevi Scriptores, Part LXII, iii, 326; cited hereafter as Rolls Series). It is inconceivable that the bishop should know of the activities of these pardoners while the Official, whose profitable business it was to seek out irregularities, did not know of their presence in his own archdeaconry.

109. "Ceterum mirantes audivimus quod quidam inferiores ministri, ut de majoribus ad presens ob eorum reverenciam taceamus, a predictis fratribus et nunciis [Sancti Antonii] pecuniam, pro concedenda eis licencia proponendi negocia pauperum hospitalis predicti et ad opus ipsorum elemosinas colligendi in locis in quibus iidem ministri potestatem habent et jurisdiccionem exercent, extorquere nituntur" (*Register Romeyn*, I, 9). The "inferiores ministri" would appear to be the archdeacons' Official and the "majores ministri" the archdeacons themselves.

110. The diocesan bishop alone was entrusted with examination and licensing. See notes 70 and 72 above.

111. See pp. 214–215 above.

112. The archdeacon is the minister of justice regularly appealed to for the apprehension of pardoners (see note 108 above; Leach, *Chapter Act Book*, II, 27–28). The Council of Vienne, however, placed punishment in the hands of the bishop: "per episcopos locorum punientur" (*Regimen animarum*, line 53).

113. See note 73 above.

114. In York, in the year 1287, for instance, existing records indicate the following institutions were licensed to collect:

Date of License	Institution	Duration
March 19, 1286–1287	St. Anthony of Vienne	1 year
July 31, 1286	Humberston Abbey	5 years
Nov. 10, 1286	St. Cuthbert, Durham	3 years
Oct. 18, 1287	St. James of Altopascio	2 years
April 23, 1286	Bridge at Stamford	3 years
Sept. 10, 1286	Cathedral Whithorn	7 years

115. "Querelam gravem" (Tangl, *Die päpstlichen Kanzleiordnungen*, p. 267).

116. "Urbani V Papae bulla contra quaestores hospital. Jerusalem in Anglia" (David Wilkins, *Concilia Magnae Britanniae*, III, 84; cited

by Jusserand, "Chaucer's Pardoner and the Pope's Pardoners," *Chaucer Society Essays*, v, 432–433).

117. *Piers Plowman*, B Prologue 81. See also Wyclif: "he [the pardoner] schal be sped & resceyved of curatis for to have part of þat he getiþ" (*The English Works of Wyclif Hitherto Unprinted*, ed. F. D. Matthew, EETS O.S. No. 74, p. 154). A more appropriate title would be "English Works Attributed to Wyclif."

118. "Manducemus ergo ut evangelizemus, non evangelizemus et [ut?] manducemus, sicut predicatores conducti, qui ponunt in celum os suum cum bene predicant, set lingua eorum transivit in terra cum laudem vel lucrum captant" (Cava, *Liber regulae S. Spiritus*, p. 198). The figure is from Psalm LXXII, 9 (Vulgate).

119. "et non est ita largum et magnum hospitale in toto mundo . . . si omnes hospitales domus essent in unum congregate" (John Bromyarde, *Summa predicantium* [Basel, 1484], II, Tit. "Mors," cxxxix).

120. "grauntynge mo yeris of pardon than comen before domes day" (Wyclif, *English Works Hitherto Unprinted*, p. 154). See note 117 above.

121. See discussion p. 215 above.

122. *Cilium oculi sacerdotis* (fol. 41ᵃ) reads: "Nec benedictionibus eorum populus se prosternat" (Owst, *Preaching*, p. 109, note 2).

123. "Sicque prefati questores, per nostram Diocesim pervagantes, vestris opere et auxilio et favore suffulti indebito, populum simplicem et indoctum seducunt et, quantum in eis est, fallunt spiritualiter et deceptant" (Hingeston-Randolph, *Register Grandisson*, II, 1179).

124. Paulus, *Geschichte des Ablasses*, II, 287.

125. "se quaestores et fratres militiae S. Lazari Jerosolimitani, licet falso, palam et publice asserunt" (*Jean XXII: Lettres communes*, No. 29656). The military religious order of St. Lazarus, which originated as a hospital for lepers in Jerusalem, had by 1253 transferred its headquarters from Acre to France. By the middle of the fourteenth century, it possessed over three hundred establishments (E. J. King, *The Knights Hospitallers in the Holy Land* [London, 1931], pp. 303–304). The order appeared in England as early as the reign of Stephen (R. M. Clay, *The Mediaeval Hospitals of England* [London, 1909], p. 251).

126. St. Anthony seems to have had the most far-flung collection system of all. Consequently one finds papal letters of complaint in behalf of the order against the operation of false pardoners. (*Les Registres d'Innocent IV*, No. 1411); against refusal to admit collectors to churches (*Les Registres de Clement IV*, No. 1547); against the detention of pigs "nomine Sancti Antonii nutriti" (*Jean XXII: Lettres communes*, No. 49822); etc. The extent of these difficulties would appear to be a measure of the institution's inability to take direct action against distant abuses.

127. The Hospital of St. Mary Roncevall at Charing Cross was a daughter house of St. Mary Roncesvalles in the Pyrenees. From its foundation (*ca.* 1230) to the Black Death (1348–1349) it was the prosperous central house of the order in the British Isles. The effects, however, of

disease, war, and schism made themselves felt, and in 1382, 1390, 1393, and 1396, the king's clerks were wardens of the hospital. It is interesting to note that the king's clerk was not forgetful of collections. False questors were suppressed and a sealed chest containing "bulls, apostolic instruments, and other muniments" was seized (James Galloway, *Historical Sketches of Old Charing* [London, 1914], pp. 1–27, 41; Manly, *Some New Light*, pp. 125–126). The history of the "naturalization" of this alien house corresponds rather closely to that of another, the London house of St. Anthony of Vienne (Clay, *Mediaeval Hospitals*, pp. 208–209).

128. See note 116 above.

129. *Historical Papers and Letters from the Northern Registers*, ed. J. Raine, Rolls Series, Part LXI, 187–188. According to Riant, the "fratres Bethleemitani," an order of hospitallers, arose at the beginning of the thirteenth century (*Études sur l'histoire de l'église de Bethleem* [1888], I, 96). Matthew of Paris seems to regard them as newly arrived in England in 1257, when he comments upon their habit with its distinctive star, and records the gift to them of an establishment in Cambridge (*Chronica majora*, ed. H. R. Luard, Rolls Series, Part LVII, V, 631). It would appear, however, that the Brothers of Bethlehem never were at Cambridge (H. P. Stokes, "Outside Trumpington Gates," Cambridge Antiquarian Society, XLIV [1908], 31) and that the Brothers had arrived in England and established themselves at Bishopsgate in London by 1247 (Dugdale, *Monasticon* [1661], II, 381–383). The famous Hospital of St. Mary of Bethlehem at Bishopsgate was clearly a dependency of the Church of Bethlehem (*Calendar Papal Letters*, XI, 6–8), and was served by the Brothers of Bethlehem, as appears rather definitely from the 1247 grant of the Bishopsgate establishment, where the starred habit of the Brothers is prominently mentioned: "signum stellae deferant publice in Capis, & Mantellis" (*Monasticon*, II, 382). The difficulties which the bishops of Bethlehem experienced in controlling pardoners for their international collection system are indicated by Riant: "À leurs fonctions hospitalières, ils joignaient celles de quêteurs pour l'église de Bethléem; et nos évêques se voient souvent forcés de recourir au S. Siège, soit pour les ramener à l'obéissance, soit pour leur faire restituer le produit de leurs quêtes" (*Études*, I, 97). For assistance with this material, we are deeply indebted to Dr. Richard Emery.

130. In the "Reply of Friar Daw Topias" (*Political Poems and Songs*, ed. Thomas Wright, Rolls Series [London, 1859–1861], II, 78–79), the worthy friar avoids the accusation of farming brought against the friars by saying:

> I trowe thou menys the pardonystres
> of seint Thomas of Acres,
> of Antoun, or of Runcevale,
> that rennen so faste aboute.

The institutions here named are St. Thomas of Acre, St. Anthony of Vienne, and St. Mary Roncesvalles.

131. J. S. P. Tatlock, *Mind and Art of Chaucer* (Syracuse, N.Y., 1950), p. 92.

132. Preface to *Fables, Ancient and Modern*.

133. "For myn entente is nat but for to wynne" (VI [C], 403).

134. "Nay, I wol drynke licour of the vyne / And have a joly wenche in every toun" (VI [C], 452–453). See note 33 above.

135. "Thus spitte I out my venym under hewe / Of hoolynesse, to semen hooly and trewe" (VI [C], 421–422). See note 33 above.

136. See Robinson's note to VI [C] 333 (*Works*, p. 729). Preaching as an abuse is discussed in note 35 above.

137. "Com forth anon, and kneleth heere adoun, / And mekely receyveth my pardoun" (VI [C], 925–926). See note 122 above.

138. VI [C], 913–915; 931–940. See notes 22 and 23 above.

139. VI [C], 906–910. See p. 227 above.

140. "Bulles of popes and of cardynales, / Of patriarkes and bishopes I shewe" VI [C], 342–343; see also I [A], 686–687). All of the prelates here mentioned regularly granted indulgences except cardinals, and cardinals might do so when they possessed jurisdiction. A foreign hospital might conceivably gain indulgences at one time or another from all of them. There is thus no inherent improbability in the source of the credentials. It is, however, difficult to know whether Chaucer is here getting at the much criticized plethora of indulgences "comen from Rome al hoot," or whether he is bringing out a common characteristic of pardoners, the tendency to exaggerate the indulgences they do have: "indulgencias alias quam Literis nostris in ea parte testimonialibus annexas" (Hingeston-Randolph, *Register Grandisson*, II, 1178); "cum veris sibi indultis falsa quedam et subdola miscere dicuntur in suis exortacionibus" (Fowler, *Registrum Baldock*, p. 139).

141. In *Piers Plowman* (B Prologue 68–82), there is an excellent portrait of a pardoner conducting business as usual. He preaches "as he a prest were," (68); displays the bishop's seal as proof of his powers of remitting sin (79); divides his proceeds with the parish priest (81; see p. 225 above, and note 117); and devotes his own portion to the support of the same sins—gluttony and lechery—as Chaucer's Pardoner declares he does (76–77). Langland's central point would seem to be the abuse of the episcopal seal by the pardoner, with the connivance of the local clergy. Chaucer's Pardoner, being the most proficient practitioner in his trade, is rather more pretentious. The "lige lordes seel" is more probably a claim to royal protection (see note 76 above, and Marie Hamilton, "The Credentials of Chaucer's Pardoner," *JEGP*, XL [1941], 70), and hence in accord with his humble admission that the Pope in person presented him with the bulls he displays (see note 142).

142. "Which were me yeven by the popes hond" (VI [C], 922). "Und er giht, er habe von dem bâbeste den gewalt, daz er dir alle dîne sünde abe neme umbe einigen helbelinc odor einen heller" (Berthold von Regensburg, *Predigten*, I, 208).

143. Manly, *Some New Light*, pp. 124–130. See also S. Moore, *MP*, xxv (1927), 59–66.

144. *Paradiso* XXIX, 124 ff. (cited by Paulus, *Geschichte des Ablasses*, II, 282).
It is interesting that Dante chose St. Anthony of Vienne, perhaps the
most widely known of all.

145. In 1393, there is an entry in the *Ely Episcopal Registers*: "Indulg. for
Hosp. B.V.M. of Rouncevall Pampilion' dioc., and for construction
of a branch of it at Charing Cross" (ed. A. Gibbons [Lincoln, 1891],
p. 398). Another reference in Winchester *ca.* 1399 records the granting
of an indulgence by Bishop Wykeham for subscribers to the same
building fund (Kirby, *Register Wykeham*, II, 490). Building funds
were notoriously unending, and we have no reason to suppose that
these two references represent either the beginning or the end.

146. St. Anthony (*Registres d'Innocent* IV, No. 1411; Honorius III, in
Bullarium Romanum III, 389; Jean XXII, *Lettres communes*, No.
49762, etc.); St. James of Altopascio (Brown, *Register Greenfield*, I,
131–132); Holy Sepulcher of Jerusalem (Hingeston-Randolph, *Register Grandisson*, I, 426–427); Holy Ghost in Saxia of Rome (*ibid.*, II,
1178–1179); Knights of St. John (Wilkins, III, 84); Brothers of Bethlehem (Fowler, *Registrum Baldock*, I, 103–105; *Northern Registers*, pp.
187–188). We have not discovered a reference to a purely local institution's being cited in this connection, but the foreign hospitals and
their branches, as indicated above, are frequently cited, and occasionally in a group. Thus Bishop Grandisson specifies as offenders collectors
for the hospitals of the Holy Ghost, St. Anthony, and St. John
(Hingeston-Randolph, *Register Grandisson*, II, 1179).

147. Contemporary satire does not afford a very satisfactory basis for comparison since references to pardoners by the names of the institutions
they represent are not numerous. However, such references as we
have come upon seem to bear out the general pattern. Thus *Piers
Plowman* mentions "Paumpelon" (St. Mary Roncesvalles) and "Rome,"
which may possibly be the Hospital of the Holy Ghost of Saxia in
Rome (C Passus XX, 218), while the "Reply of Friar Daw Topias"
refers to St. Anthony, St. Thomas of Acre, and St. Mary Roncesvalles
(see note 130 above).

148. See note 51 above.

149. See note 140 above. One wonders whether it is not the relics rather
than the credentials which lead Jusserand to the conclusion that the
Pardoner is "false" (*Chaucer Society Essays*, V, 432–433). Jusserand
would have us believe that two separate groups of pardoners existed:
the one a saintly pardoner—who tended rapidly to disappear—and
the other an evil pardoner. Yet in practice no such distinction seems
to have existed. It was quite possible to be a true pardoner one day
and a false one the next—and vice versa. Thomas of the Brothers of
Bethlehem, who preached such abuses as to attain the distinction of
being cited personally by the Archbishop of Canterbury, had in fact
been an accredited pardoner, but had simply refused to accept his
suspension from office (Fowler, *Registrum Baldock*, pp. 103–105; see
also note 129 above). Alexander de Derby, on the other hand, was
apprehended by the Chapter of Beverley Minster and confessed that
he had collected in the Chapter's name without any authorization.

Yet less than two months after the suspension of sentence, he was duly licensed and collecting for Beverley Minster (Leach, *Chapter Act Book*, I, 316–317). The only real distinction between a true and a false pardoner is the possession of a valid license. Jusserand gives us no good reason for considering the Pardoner's credentials invalid.

150. The satiric intention of the Pardoner-Summoner relationship has been recognized by C. R. Sleeth, "The Friendship of Chaucer's Summoner and Pardoner," *MLN*, LVI (1941), 138. However, Sleeth seems to follow Jusserand in considering the Pardoner "false," an oversimplification, as it seems to us (see especially notes 140 and 149 above).

151. In the Council of the Lateran and elsewhere (see *Regimen animarum*, lines 11–12) the wearing of the habit of an order as a kind of camouflage is noted. There is no indication that the Pardoner takes the least trouble to disguise his activities. Although Marie Hamilton has argued skillfully that the Pardoner is an Augustinian canon (*JEGP*, XL, 1–72), there seems to be little of the religious left about him. Whatever he may have been before, and there are definite hints of the apostate about him (VI [C], 439–453), he would seem here to be the strongest example of the "quaestuarius notorius," the professional collector at his worst.

152. The Summoner, the personification of the nonenforcement of law, is here definitely associated with the Archdeacon, but that Chaucer intended to limit the reference of the Summoner to the Archdeacon is doubtful. The location of the Archdeacon's hell, which the Summoner privately reveals to a "good felawe": " 'Purs is the ercedekenes helle,' seyde he" (I [A], 658) is to be found in Gower's *Vox clamantis*. "Torquentur bursa sic reus atque rea" (III, 194) applied to ecclesiastical justice in general. One suspects that Chaucer associated the Summoner with the Archdeacon for the same reason that he associated the Pardoner with a foreign hospital: both seem to have enjoyed unenviable reputations.

153. See Durandus' analysis of the effects of the unrestrained abuses of pardoners. He mentions the deception of the people, the corruption within the Church, and the contempt of the power of the keys which the Church brings upon itself by permitting such abuses (Paulus, *Geschichte des Ablasses*, II, 284). These are almost precisely the aspects of the pardoner which Chaucer places before us.

154. *Proposal for the Universal Use of Irish Manufacture: Proposal that All the Ladies and Women of Ireland Should Appear Constantly in Irish Manufactures*; etc. This is of course not to say that there is no irony in these works.

13

An Augustinian Interpretation of Chaucer's Pardoner

THE PURPOSE OF THE PRESENT ESSAY is to suggest that the Pardoner's Prologue and Tale constitute an integrated study in Augustinian terms of the secret punishment of evil. According to St. Augustine, the soul which turns in pride from God, the supreme good, to seek its satisfactions in a lesser good cuts itself off from grace and, like an organ deprived of the blood which nourishes it, begins to corrupt and decay. The struggle of the degenerating nature with this parasitic evil growing within itself produces an earthly hell whose principal characteristics are burning, insatiable longings—"concupiscence"—and a darkened, perverted mentality. To escape this intolerable struggle of the created nature and corruption, of good and evil, the proud sinner seeks to give himself up entirely to evil, but finds no relief from the good within him; he seeks to laugh at and pervert, if he can, the good he sees about him, but still finds neither rest nor relief. The present essay suggests that the portrait of the Pardoner, so often appreciated for its consistency of dramatic development, may be viewed as possessing another and deeper consistency— that of a spiritual degeneration conceived in Augustinian terms, the history of a mind averted from God, suffering and struggling against the penalty of its own evil. The essay further suggests

Reprinted from *Speculum*, XXVI (1951), 465–481.

that the Augustinian doctrine of the punishment of sin, and the additions made to it by Gregory the Great, were not only available to Chaucer, but to some extent appear in his *Parson's Tale*.

I. *Est enim hic quaedam poena occulta*

In the teaching of Augustine,[1] all sin is by the judgment of God punished, and, if we look deeper, self-punished. Even the sin which to mortal eyes escapes punishment is overtaken by a secret penalty, and that penalty is the progressive mental deformity and suffering which sin itself inflicts upon its perpetrator —the "secreta mentis poena." To understand this doctrine of the punishment of sin by sin, it is necessary first to examine certain assumptions on which the doctrine proceeds—the nature of the human soul, the effect on the human soul of original sin—and then to present against this background the progressive punishment of the spirit which defies God and gives itself up to sin.

To St. Augustine the human soul is at its creation good, the product of a good Creator. The created nature,[2] however, is not a part of God, but was created out of nothing. Hence, while God remains the perfect and immutable good, the creature, possessing an imperfect nature, is a mutable and lesser good. From this imperfection follows the possibility of sin. The will, like the intellect a part and function of the mutable nature, is free to adhere to God, the supreme good, or to avert itself from God to seek its own satisfactions in lesser goods. A lesser good is anything except God.

At the Fall the human will did in fact avert itself from God, preferring the created to the Creator. From this aversion, this separation from God which is the act of sin, followed the two penalties of the Fall: ignorance and concupiscence. Because it departed willfully from the light of God, the mind became darkened and weakened in its ability to know the truth. Because it separated itself from the source of its being, the nature, which was created good, began to revert to the nothingness from which it came; it began to corrupt and decay. The disease and division of the nature, which afflicts the mind with ignorance, afflicts the will with concupiscence. The good nature lusts ("concupiscit") against the evil flaw within itself, striving to remove it utterly; the destructive, corrupting evil lusts against the nature, striving to consume it and to reduce it to nothing. This state of "infirmitas," of opposing lusts struggling against each other for domination of the will, is concupiscence—and concupiscence every man inherited from Adam.[3]

It is against this background of a vitiated nature—darkened and divided—that the Augustinian doctrine of the punishment of sin by sin proceeds. The first step in this progress is the aversion of the now divided will from God. As St. Augustine envisions it, the will is, through its division, faced by two alternatives—the way of humility and the way of pride. The good nature, created by God, urges the will to recognize its infirmity, to turn to God as the source of its being, and with divine aid to resist the evil lusts within it. This is the way of humility. Concupiscence, the lust of the parasitic evil, urges the will to turn from God, to regard the rebellious desires it experiences not as the penalty of a just God, but as a world of pleasure to be exploited to the full. This is the way of pride. If the will follows humility and turns to God, the grace of God restores in some measure the nature corrupted by the Fall. If, despite its knowledge of the existence of God, the will follows pride, it averts itself from God in full awareness of its act, and in that aversion launches itself upon the career of progressive punishment which it is the business of the present section to explore.[4] That punishment may perhaps be summarized as the immediate judgment of God, the struggle against that judgment, and the ultimate judgment of God.

The immediate judgment of God upon the aversion of the will is misery, the misery of mental anguish and mental deformity. Primarily the punishment is an intensification of the two penalties of original sin: ignorance and concupiscence. The intellect is further darkened; concupiscence is increased. The conception of concupiscence is here of extreme importance, for through concupiscence sin and suffering become synonymous. When the will yields to the concupiscence it inherited from the Fall, the good nature is diminished and suffers; the parasitic evil which consumes the nature increases and gains in power. The more one sins, the more concupiscence, the lust of the parasitic evil against the created nature, increases—and with it the darkness of moral ignorance. The more concupiscence and ignorance increase, the more one sins. Concupiscence and ignorance generate sin and sin concupiscence and ignorance in an endless progression. At each step the destruction and suffering of the created nature increase. Thus through concupiscence sin becomes the penalty of sin.[5] In the *Enarratio in Psalmum* LVII St. Augustine gives perhaps his most vivid account of these sufferings. "Evil concupiscence," he says, "is like a burning and a flame." "He who disdains to conquer that concupiscence with which, through the contagion of sin, he is born, and excites and foments further lusts, shall not easily conquer these lusts, but divided against himself, shall be consumed in his own fire." But, as St. Augustine further informs us, the flame which falls as a judgment upon sin has nothing in common with light; it is darkness as well as fire, an "ignis fumosus" in which the sinner loses the sight of God.[6] One may gain a somewhat clearer insight into these punishments if he notes that, according to Gregory the Great, ignorance and concupiscence together constitute an earthly counterpart to the black flame of hell.[7] But the mind in sin is not simply tormented and stultified; it is altered in more subtle ways closely connected with ignorance and concupiscence but less frequently mentioned by Augustine: it is both perverted and embittered. The mind is perverted because the act of sin is perversion in that it prefers what is less—the creature or created thing—to what is supreme, the Creator.[8] The mind is embittered because it has shut itself off from God, losing thereby sweetness and light and gaining shadows and bitterness.[9] Thus, as St. Augustine conceives of him, the man who defies God is no exalted being, but the pain-racked, mentally deformed captive of an earthly hell.

The struggles of the captive to escape this hell are like those of a fish with the hook in his jaws. He seeks to plunge to depths where the pain and inescapable attraction he feels will somehow be lost—to find in love of the creature and created thing compensation for his lack of internal happiness.[10] He likewise seeks cunningly to fight back, to gain relief from his pain by venting the hatred his embittered mind bears toward the sense of God he feels to be bound up with that pain. He hates the peace of God that binds together creation; he hates those who serve God. Like

Satan, his vengeance takes the pattern of his perverted mind, and he attempts to pervert those who enjoy a state to which he himself cannot attain.[11] Alternately fleeing and attacking, his life is given up to evil and his spirit to progressive degeneration. It is extremely important to note in this connection that the Augustinian conceptions of the punishment of sin by sin, and of pride as the first of the sins, were formalized by Gregory the Great—perhaps the most notable transmitter of the Augustianian tradition to the Middle Ages—into a progress of the seven deadly sins. This progress of sin punishing sin originates in pride, moves through the sins of the spirit, and ends in the more material sins—avarice, gluttony, and lechery. Gregory, like Augustine, considers misery the effect of this progress. At least one commentator speaks of the effect as a kind of hell.[12]

At the end of his progress, the rebel has experienced nothing but pain and frustration. He has solved nothing. The good he finds offensive he is powerless to pervert unless God for His own purposes wills it.[13] The pain he would be rid of he can never escape, for the good nature, the work of God within him which experiences the pain, can never be destroyed no matter how deeply he sins.[14] At the end of his progress, as at every point in it, the rebel is still torn by the same struggle of good and evil, confronted by the same two alternatives—humility and pride. He may still return to God, although the difficulty of such a return has been immensely increased by the damage will and intellect have suffered from sin; or he may, despite his misery, still prefer himself to God, his own diseased will to the will of God, the painful pleasures he feverishly pursues to the peace of God. If pride is his choice, the way is opened to the most terrible judgment of God—to be permitted success in his sins, to be abandoned to the lusts of his own heart, "in concupiscentias cordis sui." Upon this text of Paul (Romans I, 24) St. Augustine relies heavily, especially in the influential expositions of Psalms xxxv and lvii. They who knew God, says Augustine in the *Enarratio in Psalmum* xxxv, but spurned Him with the foot of pride and yielded Him neither worship nor thanks are handed over to concupiscence to suffer the pangs of their own lusts.[15] And in the *Enarratio in Psalmum* lvii he says further of the punishment of the proud: "Upon this earth there is a secret punishment. . . .

'Like wax before the flame,' as the Psalmist declares, 'they shall be dissolved and carried away.' Through the lusts of their own hearts, as I have said, shall this be accomplished. . . . But these punishments few see, and therefore are they most highly commended of the Spirit of God. Hear the words of the Apostle: 'God has yielded them up to the lusts of their own hearts.' "[16] Thus, in Augustine's view, the ultimate judgment of God upon pride is to permit it to go its successful way into a kind of fiery bath of its own lusts—a penalty few see, the beginning and end of which is damnation.[17]

That Chaucer knew or had every opportunity of knowing the Augustinian doctrine of the secret punishment of sin through concupiscence is not difficult to demonstrate. Chaucer, like his contemporaries Langland and Gower, evidently possessed a general knowledge of the doctrine of concupiscence, for he devotes a section of the *Parson's Tale* to a discussion of it.[18] The more specialized doctrine of the punishment of actual sin through concupiscence—which appears in the *Parson's Tale* only in fragmentary form—Chaucer could have encountered in any number of works in any number of connections, for the doctrine had become central to the medieval conception of sin.[19] If, for instance, Chaucer had attempted to "bulte it to the bren" with Bishop Bradwardine, as in the *Nun's Priest's Tale* he intimates he did, he would have found the punishment of sin through concupiscence explained in terms of the two expositions of Augustine (Psalms XXXV, LVII) cited above. Bradwardine says in part:

Every penalty of sin is just . . . as is clearly stated in Romans I concerning those who when they knew God did not glorify Him as God or give thanks. Therefore God yielded them up to the desires of their own hearts—to filth. And of this matter one may read in Augustine on Psalm XXXV. "Hear," he says, "what is the foot of pride: they who when they knew God did not glorify Him as God. Therefore there came unto them the foot of pride, whence they came into the depths of sin" . . . and on Psalm LVII: "Like wax before the flame shall they be carried away," and he says, "These punishments few see, and therefore does the Spirit of God most earnestly commend them to our attention. Hear the Apostle saying, "God has yielded them up, etc."[20]

This same doctrine of concupiscence as suffering and retribution for sin Chaucer could also have come upon in John of Salisbury, to whom he is indebted for illustrative material used in the *Pardoner's Tale* and from whom, it appears, he is most likely to have derived his ideas on Lollius.[21] In Book 1 of the *Policraticus*, John of Salisbury defines the relationship between pride and concupiscence, indicating the punishment which pursues those who through pride not only fail to repress concupiscence, but even stimulate the desire to sin:

Let him who fails to curb this love [pride], fear the leprosy [concupiscence] and the moral blindness which threaten to follow from it. If indeed those who fail to repress concupiscence . . . lose Salvation, what shall be the punishment of those who inflame concupiscence as with the blandishments of flatterers . . . what shall they suffer who . . . practice the excitement of all the senses?[22]

The *De contemptu mundi* of Innocent III, which Chaucer translated and from which he seems to have borrowed in the *Pardoner's Tale*,[23] expresses much the same idea from a more striking point of view. Discussing the torments of hell, Innocent points out in highly Augustinian language that hell is not the sole place of torment, for the sinner can never in any place be apart from the flame of concupiscence which torments him. Hell he carries with him:

To him who has rejected God every place is a place of punishment, for he bears with him ceaselessly his own punishment, and wherever he turns encounters torment. "I will produce," says God, "from within you the flame which shall devour you" (Ezechiel XXVIII, 18).[24]

The same punishment, expressed in terms of the progress of the seven deadly sins into which Gregory had recast the Augustinian doctrine of the punishment of sin by sin, Chaucer could very easily have known, for he himself uses this progress in his discussion of the seven deadly sins in the *Parson's Tale*.[25] The idea of an earthly hell as the effect of progressive sin would have been available to him in a manual of the type he used as the source of this same tale. The *Compendium theologicae veritatis* describes the progress of the seven deadly sins and declares that the effect of sin "creates of man Hell, for within the sinner is the flame of avarice, the stench of lechery, the shadows of ignorance, the worm of conscience, the thirst of concupiscence."[26]

Chaucer, then, must have known something about the "secreta mentis poena" which overtakes the proud sinner in his aversion from God. He understood concupiscence in general; he knew, or had every opportunity of knowing, the doctrine of the punishment of sin by sin; he had come into contact with the progress of the seven deadly sins into which the conception of the hell produced by sin had been transmuted.

If we would see with the eyes of St. Augustine—or with the eyes of one who, like Chaucer, lived in a world impregnated with Augustinian ideas and attitudes—evil which proudly struts before the world and defying God rejoices in its own power and success, is only a hollow shell concealing torments which are a kind of prefiguration of those of hell. Such men are not to be feared or envied, for they are filled with the secret judgments of God: "even they who rejoice in evil are secretly wretched, for God has yielded them up to the lusts of their own hearts."[27]

II. SED ISTAS POENAS PAUCI VIDENT

The previous section has attempted to trace the career of the proud apostate from God and to indicate Chaucer's knowledge of the punishment which attends upon that career. It has shown the beginning of this progress in the aversion of the will from God; the immediate judgment of God which is misery; the human attempt to avoid that misery; the ultimate judgment of God. What evidences of this universal pattern, alike inevitable to angel or man, are to be discovered in Chaucer's treatment of the Pardoner? In reply it may perhaps be said—if one is willing to admit the psychology of Augustinian theology as well as the psychology of dramatic presentation—that beneath the surface of dramatic narrative a fairly consistent line of development in terms of this pattern is to be observed. In the Prologue one finds a concentrated study of the evil, destructive side of the Pardoner: his aversion from God through pride, his defiance of the judgment of God. In the tale, which is told as a continuation of this defiance of Divine Providence, there is conveyed paradoxically the power of Divine Providence: one begins to see emerging through the Pardoner's defiance the inevitable judgment of God, the tormenting struggle of good and evil, of humility and pride, to which his aversion has made him heir. In the final confession (lines 915–918) there springs forth suddenly, fully disclosed, the side of the Pardoner's being he has been striving so feverishly to conceal—the nature, created good, suffering, indestructible, whose very presence makes the Pardoner's existence a hidden torment and his whole way of life folly. Of the final judgment of God, Chaucer tells us nothing.

At the end of the Prologue, in the speech with which the Pardoner climaxes his cynical disclosures, Chaucer gives us simply and directly the key to the Pardoner's personality:

> "What, trowe ye, that whiles I may preche,
> And wynne gold and silver for I teche,
> That I *wol* lyve in poverte *wilfully?*
> Nay, nay, I thoghte it nevere, trewely!
> For I *wol* preche and begge in sondry landes;
> I *wol* nat do no labour with myne handes,
> Ne make baskettes, and lyve therby,
> By cause I *wol* nat beggen ydelly.
> I *wol* noon of the apostles countrefete;
> I *wol* have moneie, wolle, chese, and whete,
> Al were it yeven of the povereste page,
> Or of the povereste wydwe in a village,
> Al sholde hir children sterve for famyne.
> Nay, I *wol* drynke licour of the vyne,
> And have a joly wenche in every toun." (439–453)

In this speech upon his will the Pardoner demonstrates not only the aversion of the will from God which is common to all sin, but the pure refusal of the will to serve God which is the sin of pride. The Pardoner sets himself up as his own principle in place of God. In the full knowledge of the existence of God upon which St. Augustine lays so much emphasis, he refuses to serve God. A more completely satisfactory fulfillment of the Augustinian definition of pride would be difficult to find.[28] But this speech is only the climax. If we review what the Pardoner has told us about himself, we find that all the unamiable qualities upon which he congratulates himself: his contempt for his fellow human beings, his refusal to admit correction, his hypocrisy, his shamelessness, his boasting of the harm he does, all are to be found in Chaucer's discussion of the sin of pride in the *Parson's Tale*.[29] It is worth noting that Chaucer's description of the pride of the Pardoner, who *will* not "lyve in poverte *wilfully*," is the exact antithesis of his description of the humility of Christ, who "In *wilful* poverte *chees* to lyve his lyf," (III [D], 1179).

The judgment of God, the inescapable hell within which is the penalty of that pride, the Pardoner is extremely interested in concealing, for he is a man, as he eagerly informs us, whom justice cannot touch. Yet in the Prologue one senses his punishment in certain typical actions of the sinner defying the penalty of his sin—the attempt to escape where pain cannot follow, the attempt to pervert and destroy the offending good.

The Pardoner's attempted escape from the pains of thought is shrewdly calculated by Chaucer. We find that the objects among which the Pardoner revels are money, wine, and women—at least one in every town.[30] These pleasures are not without a plan. They are simultaneously the typical sins of all pardoners: *avaricia, gula, luxuria*,[31] and a very significant pattern in the progressive degeneration of the human spirit. These three sins in the order stated constitute a progression within the seven deadly sins—the final three—and suggest thereby the final resort of the creature which has lost its happiness in the sins of the spirit and now seeks to lose its misery in the more physical sins. In discussing this progression, Gregory the Great says of avarice: "Because within itself the troubled heart has lost the good of happiness, it seeks consolation outside itself; the less internal happiness it has to return to, the more it seeks to obtain external goods." And he adds that to avarice are joined the two carnal sins of gluttony and lechery. It is to be noted that in the *Parson's Tale* these words of Gregory are quoted in the context of this very progression.[32] Thus, since Chaucer indicates in the *Parson's Tale* his familiarity with the significance of this progression and in the Pardoner's speech on his will presents these sins in their conventional order,[33] one may suppose that Chaucer is here suggesting the loss of happiness which begins with the initial sin of pride as the impelling force behind the Pardoner's progress through avarice, gluttony, and lechery. It is indicative of Chaucer's skill as a literary artist at all levels that he is able so effortlessly to fuse the theological pattern with the realistic pattern of the recognized sins of the institutional pardoner.

The second typical action of the defiant apostate is the attempt to pervert, to overthrow, to render ridiculous the order of the universe so painfully opposite to the disorder of his own soul. The Prologue also shows us this aspect of the Pardoner's mind in some detail. Like Satan and Iago he delights in evil:

> "Myne handes and my tonge goon so yerne
> That it is joye to se my bisynesse." (398–399)

but unlike Satan and Iago, his perversion takes an essentially comic form. Under his perverted comic genius everything turns from its proper nature. A sermon against avarice and her followers, gluttony and lechery—the Pardoner's cherished sins—becomes a sermon in financial support of them;[34] the essential regulation which forbade pardoners to grant indulgences to any who were not properly confessed becomes subtly intermingled with his false relics and emerges as a selling device which earns him a hundred marks a year;[35] a supposed holy relic becomes the means by which adultery may be committed with impunity;[36] moist and corny ale becomes an aid to holy meditation. As the Pardoner puts it:

> "... I moot thynke
> Upon som honest thyng while that I drynke." (327–328)

Irony, the humor of inversion, is the appropriate expression of the mind whose values sin has inverted.[37]

The perversion of Christian doctrine, the incongruity he is able to effect, is not only a reflection of the Pardoner's perverted mind, but a source of necessary gratification to it. The Pardoner has within himself a dark unhappy bitterness and malice which claims its pound of flesh. The ironic note of triumph is rather distinct, for instance, in the Pardoner's description of his credentials:

> "Oure lige lordes seel on my patente,
> That shewe I first, my body to warente,
> That no man be so boold, ne preest ne clerk,
> Me to destourbe of Cristes hooly werk." (337–340)

In these lines the Pardoner proclaims the complete superiority of his evil will to God or man. He laughs at human law because it protects him; at the parish priest because he is powerless; at the "lewed peple" because they cannot see behind his hypocrisy; at God because he, a miserable mortal, parodies Christian doctrine with complete impunity. Order is turned upside down. But the Pardoner's jokes are all in one way or another directed at the idea of God, and in this constant attempt to turn "up-so-doun" we can see his terrible need to ridicule and reduce to absurdity the sense of the presence of God from which he can never escape.

At the end of the Prologue we have examined rather thoroughly the evil of the Pardoner. We have seen the genesis of evil within his soul, his revelling in the physical sins, his delight in overturning the good he sees about him. We have further glimpsed in these typical actions of degeneration and perversion the attempt of the tortured mind to escape the judgment it has brought upon itself.

The tale which the Pardoner tells is of course neatly integrated with his announced theme of avarice. In its immediate dramatic effect it is as delightful as "hende Nicholas's" appeal to John the Carpenter's knowledge of scripture in averting the effects of the second flood. Like the tale of the flood, the story of the three rioters gives the ignorant listener the precious sense of peering into "Goddes pryvetee." Essentially it is a simple device of dramatic irony by which the audience comes gradually to understand that the Old Man is not just an old man but something unimaginably mysterious and terrible,[38] while the three malefactors are denied this superior position and understand nothing of the sort. With fascinated horror the "lewed peple" watch the inevitable movement of divine justice and are overwhelmed at the neatness and simplicity with which the villains are dispatched. The moral is clear to them: evil—and particularly avarice—is self-destructive. The sense of their own wealth becomes oppressive. They press forward to rid themselves of so dangerous a commodity and to receive the absolution of this holy man who has peered so deeply into the ways of Divine Providence.

But the Pardoner's tale contains more than the simple plot necessary to gratify the not particularly elevated intelligence of his imagined typical audience. The meaning of the ingeniously chosen motto of his drama, "Radix malorum est Cupiditas," is not exhausted by its use as an encouragement to contributors; it suggests pride and the evil will more than it does avarice.[39] The protagonists of his drama take on qualities which are not simply dramatic. They are drawn from the core of the Pardoner's being; they are personifications of the two forces which are ever in combat in his mind. The tale is a mirror of that never-ceasing struggle.

The essential contrast of the *Pardoner's Tale* is between living in accordance with "Goddes wille" (726) and living "right at our owene wille" (834), the eternal antithesis of the pride of Satan and the humility of Christ. As in the nearly converse situation which Gower presents in the "Trump of Death," Age represents the earthly functioning of the divine law, and those who fail to reverence in age the divine law, Pride.[40] This contrast is first presented in the meeting of the three gamesters and the Old Man. The latter greets them "ful mekely"; the "proudeste" of the three answers him in a very opposite fashion:

> ". . . What, carl, with sory grace!
> Why artow al forwrapped save thy face?
> Why lyvestow so longe in so greet age?" (717–719)

Once this contrast has been established, the opposing sets of values are presented quite consistently. If we consider the three rioters as a group, we find that this characteristic of pride, of setting oneself up as one's own absolute good, is constant and unvaried. The three set out upon a noble enterprise, to save mankind from the false traitor, Death. Thereupon, in true chivalric fashion, they swear brotherhood:

> Togidres han thise three hir trouthes plight
> To lyve and dyen ech of hem for oother. (702–703)

But once individual profit has appeared, the chivalric bond begins to undergo a strange perversion.[41] Says the first rioter to his remaining companion after the youngest has gone for wine:

> "Thou knowest wel thou art my sworen brother;
> Thy profit wol I telle thee anon." (808–809)

Profit, one immediately discovers, contains a tendency toward oneness. The fact that the removal of one sworn brother should appear a "freendes torn" to the others illustrates some characteristics of this oneness: the moral blindness and perversion of normal values which occupy the hearts of those whose God is self. If we would discover in the youngest some nobler quality, we find instead only a more perfect example of the same singleness of self-devotion.

The Old Man is very different. To the pride of the rioters he opposes humility. Although he is not fond of his grim position as world executioner, he will continue "as longe tyme as it is Goddes wille" (726). To their violence, impatience, and instability he opposes a granite stability and dignity: "I moot go thider as I have to go" (749). The Old Man possesses dignity because he possesses humility. He is at once the symbol of the unassailable might of divine government and the symbol of obedience and humility, of the soul angelic or human which subjects its own will to the will of God.

The revellers dispatched in the midst of appropriate agonies and his moving collection peroration ended, the Pardoner has completed his sermon and with it the brilliant record of his successful defiance of God. Law, sermon, relics, all have been perverted to serve his ends. Even the moral exemplum with its dark tones of divine retribution has fulfilled an altered function. That tale, which preaches the divine punishment of sin, which reflects the futility of his own life and foreshadows his ultimate defeat, the Pardoner has used to demonstrate the superiority of his own will to divine punishment, by the example of his own impunity to render the very idea of retribution laughable. But he has not told us the cost of this defiance. What the tale reveals is precisely the price he has paid: the struggle of good and evil, of humility and pride, in which, as St. Augustine informs us, the nature divided against itself is consumed as by a black flame.[42]

But no one, the Pardoner is sure, has glimpsed the corroding hell which concupiscence has produced within him. He stands before the Pilgrims the complete successful sinner. With satisfaction he pauses: "And lo, sires, thus I preche" (915). Perhaps in the faces he sees before him there is a kind of beauty that makes him ugly.[43] Perhaps behind the grinning mask with which he gleefully goes about his work of damnation he may sense the grinning mask of Satan.[44] Perhaps the futility and suffering which is his life demands more than the sublimation his twisted mind has attempted in the tale of Death and the Three Rioters. But whatever be the impelling force, from the depths of his being comes revulsion, the voice of the created nature, the work of God within him which no evil can ever obliterate—which even in the midst of evil cannot lose its love of the good.[45]

> And Jhesu Crist, that is oure soules leche,
> So graunte yow his pardoun to receyve,
> For that is best; I wol yow nat deceyve. (916–918)[46]

"May God grant you the grace to receive His pardon," he says, "the true pardon I cannot buy or sell. So may you never come where I am."

The creature of God speaks like a creature, in humility, but only for a moment. The whole fiction of his joyous life has vanished and the anguish of his soul is laid bare. In desperation he gambles on one magnificent piece of salesmanship—to make the Pilgrims venerate his relics even though they know them to be false.[47] If this be carried off even in jest, it will more than recoup for him his mastery, for the Pilgrims will then knowingly join him in his own sacrilege, will laugh with him in his heretical pranks.[48] If he can but find one man to begin—perhaps a man of the world—Harry Bailly! But for once the Pardoner's stage sense fails utterly.[49] Harry Bailly replies with a vehemence which spares nothing, and the Pardoner's discomfiture is welcomed with violent laughter. Only the Knight is able to save the situation and bring the two together: "Anon they kiste, and ryden forth hir weye" (968).

Evil which has appeared so formidable and destructive is dissipated in laughter; evil which has seemed so repulsive and inhuman is absorbed into the pattern of existence, and the universe goes on undisturbed.

In this conclusion I think we are very near the heart of Chaucer—the profound faith which enabled him to look upon the existence of evil unperturbed and to portray the perpetrators of evil with love and kindness. Like St. Augustine, Chaucer saw no untamed evil in the universe, but only the will of God fulfilling itself even in the acts of the evil: "Therefore God uses the evil, not according to their own depraved wills, but according to His righteous will. For just as the evil make an evil use of their good nature, that is, of His good creation; so does the good God make a good use even of the works of the evil, that His will be nowhere overcome."[50] Like St. Augustine, Chaucer saw no man who was not worthy of love; he hated with a perfect hatred—he hated the vice and loved the man: "And since no one is evil by nature but only by vice, he who lives according to God owes the evil a perfect hatred: let him not hate the man because of his vice, nor love the vice because of the man, but hate the vice and love the man."[51]

And this, I think, is the unity and diversity in Chaucer's presentation of the Pardoner. In his treatment of the Pardoner's practices we feel his indignation; in his treatment of the Pardoner himself we feel only pity. The evils the Pardoner visits upon the world are worthy of indignation; the Pardoner himself is very pitiable. He is an apostate from God, a pariah amidst society. His life is a wretched and pitiful pretense. Chaucer treats him gently because the Pardoner's vice is its own punishment: "Sed et omnis locus reprobis est poenalis, qui semper secum defert cruciatum, et ubique contra se tormentum incurrit."[52]

Of the ultimate end of the Pardoner, Chaucer, who refused to follow Troilus and Arcite to their last abode, tells us nothing. The Pardoner has fulfilled virtually every requirement for damnation, but like all human beings, he is to Chaucer somehow not quite damnable.[53]

NOTES

1. The ensuing discussion of the Augustinian doctrine, as indeed the whole paper, is much indebted to the generous personal assistance of Professor Emeritus Robert L. Calhoun, of the Yale Divinity School.
2. The term "nature" denotes the whole created being, of which the soul is of course a part.
3. For a general treatment of the Augustinian doctrine, see M. L. Burton, *The Problem of Evil* (Chicago, 1909).

4. Humility is the recognition of man's vitiated nature as the penalty imposed by God at the Fall; it is the submission of the will to God through which the soul receives grace and regeneration becomes possible. Pride is the opposition of the will of the creature to the will of God, the Creator; it is at once the aversion of the will from God to lesser goods by which the soul loses grace, and the perversion of values by which the soul abandons God as the ultimate good and sets itself up as its own principle of action (see note 8 below). Both these aspects can be seen in the definition of pride in the *De civitate Dei*: "Quid est autem superbia, nisi perversae celsitudinis appetitus? Perversa enim celsitudo est, deserto eo cui debet animus inhaerere principio, sibi quodammodo fieri atque esse principium" (*PL*, XLI, 420). It is characteristic of those who follow pride that they regard concupiscence as a source of pleasure and seek to enjoy rather than conquer it (see p. 251 above) and that, though aware of the existence of God, they yield God neither worship nor thanks: "*Qui cum cognovissent Deum, non ut Deum glorificaverunt, aut gratias egerunt*" [Romans I, 21] (*Enarratio in Psalmum* XXXV [*PL*, XXXVI, 349]). On this last aspect, the aversion of the will from God in the full knowledge of the existence of God, St. Augustine lays especial emphasis.

5. The simplest statement by Augustine of this doctrine is to be found in the *Contra Julianum Pelagianum*: "ita concupiscentia carnis . . . et peccatum est . . . et poena peccati . . . et causa peccati" (*PL*, XLIV, 787). The doctrine may be found in detailed form in almost any discussion of sin. One may cite Gregory the Great (*Homiliarum in Ezechielem*, I, xi [*PL*, LXXVI, 915–916]), Peter Lombard (*Sententiarum*, II, XXXVI [*PL*, CXCII, 738]), Thomas Bradwardine (*De causa Dei*, I, xxxiv [London, 1618], 296–297), and the *Compendium theologicae veritatis*, III, vii, in *Beati Alberti Magni opera* (Lyons, 1651), XIII, 55.

6. "Concupiscentia mala quasi ardor est et ignis. . . . Qui autem illam concupiscentiam, cum qua de peccati propagine natus est, contemnit vincere, et multas adhuc excitat exseritque libidines, difficulter eas superat, et adversus se ipse divisus, igne proprio concrematur" (*Enarratio in Psalmum* LVII [*PL*, XXXVI, 687, 689]). "*Supercecidit ignis, et non viderunt solem* . . . ignis superbiae, ignis fumosus, ignis concupiscentiae, ignis iracundiae" (*ibid.*, 688).

7. Gregory the Great seems rather clearly to have extended to the punishments of hell the idea of the double penalty of concupiscence and ignorance expressed by Augustine in the *Enarratio in Psalmum* LVII. In the universally known *Moralia* he explains, very much in Augustinian terms, the simultaneous presence of flame and darkness in hell. Citing Psalm LVII, he says: "Natura vero ignis est, ut ex se ipso et lumen exhibeat, et concremationem; sed transactorum illa ultrix flamma vitiorum concremationem habet, et lumen non habet. . . . Hinc etiam Psalmista ait: *Super eos cecidit ignis et non viderunt solem* [Psalm LVII, 9]. . . . Hic flamma quae succendit illuminat; illic, ut superius verbis Psalmistae docuimus, ignis qui cruciat obscurat" (*Moralium*, IX, [*PL*, LXXV, 912, 914]). Peter Lombard follows Gregory in declaring that the corruption of the nature produced by sin is like the flame of hell (*Sententiarum*,

II, xxxvi [*PL*, CXCII, 738]) , while the *Compendium theologicae veritatis* states that hell is within the sinner (see pp. 251–252 above). That Chaucer was aware of the tradition of the dark flame may be gathered from the *Parson's Tale*: "the derke light that shal come out of the fyr that evere shal brenne" (x [I], 183) . Milton's famous "darkness visible" proceeding from the flames of hell would seem also to be a lineal descendant (*Paradise Lost*, I, 63) .

8. In aversion from God, the act of sin, is implied perversion: "Vivit apud te semper bonum nostrum; et quia inde aversi sumus, perversi sumus" (*Confessionum*, IV, xvi [*PL*, XXXII, 706]) . According to St. Augustine, the perversion and corruption of sin are opposed to the order and existence of creation. Because sin deprives the creature of the source of his being, it causes the created to corrupt. Because it inverts the order of existence by preferring the lesser to the supreme, sin produces within the sinner an inversion or perversion of values. As Chaucer's Parson puts it: "And ye shul understonde that in mannes synne is every manere of ordre or ordinaunce turned up-so-doun" (x [I], 260) . Thus existence and order are aspects of the creation of God, while perversion and corruption degrade existence and order toward nonbeing and disorder: "inordinatio vero non esse; quae perversio etiam nominatur atque corruptio" (*De moribus Manichaeorum*, II, vi [*PL*, XXXII, 1348]) .

9. "a luce relinquitur, a tenebris occupatur; vacuatur dulcedine, impletur amaritudine" (*Sermones de tempore* [*PL*, XXXIX, 1974]) .

10. See *Confessionum*, II, ii [*PL*, XXXII, 675–676]) .

11. To St. Augustine happiness is living in conformity with the order of the universe. Conversely the order of the universe forbids that sin, which is disorder, should effect anything but misery: "si peccata fiant, et desit miseria . . . dehonestat ordinem iniquitas. Cum autem non peccantibus adest beatitudo, perfecta est universitas" (*De libero arbitrio*, III [*PL*, XXXII, 1284]) . Bitterness, itself a penalty of disorder or sin, can be removed only by resuming one's proper relation to God. If the sinner refuses to submit himself to God, his bitterness is increased and expresses itself in hatred of everything connected with God, even in envious hatred of the good man whose happiness, so opposite to his own misery, torments him: "Quid est invidia, nisi odium felicitatis alienae? . . . Quis vero sit invidus, qui non ei malum velit, cujus bono cruciatur?" (*Sermo* CCCLIII [*PL*, XXXIX, 1561]) . The great example of this bitter envy is, of course, Satan, who perverted man through envy of the unfallen state he had himself lost (*De civitate Dei*, XIV, xi) .

12. It is to Augustine that the conception of the seven deadly sins seems ultimately to be indebted. Augustine's principal contribution to the doctrine is the central idea of concupiscence as a force through which sin becomes the penalty of sin in an unending sequence (see pp. 247–248 and note 5 above) . Augustine also establishes in the *Enarratio in Psalmum* LVII that pride is the first of the sins and that all other sins are penalties of this primary one (*PL*, XXXVI, 687–688) . However, he never takes the final step of setting up the order in which the major

sins follow from pride. Gregory the Great, who in a much quoted passage follows Augustine in his definition of the punishment of sin (*Homiliarum in Ezechielam*, I, [*PL*, LXXVI, 915–916]), does in fact go beyond Augustine and establish the first major order of the seven deadly sins. The sins as he there states them in the order of their descent from pride are: vainglory (later assimilated into pride), envy, wrath, sorrow, avarice, gluttony, lechery. Gregory's conception of the effect of this progress is the same as Augustine's. The spirit separated from God loses happiness and gains misery. However, Gregory places avarice, gluttony, and lechery in a special position. The spirit loses its happiness in the sins of the spirit, and thereafter, in avarice, gluttony, and lechery, the more material sins, seeks relief from its sufferings (*Moralium*, XXXI, xlv [*PL*, LXXVI, 620–622]). The *Compendium theologicae veritatis* gives a portion of the definition of Gregory mentioned above, and following it a complete progress of the sins. It observes that the effect of this progress is a kind of hell (see pp. 251–252 below).

13. *De civitate Dei*, XIV, xxvi–xxvii (*PL*, XLI, 434–436).

14. Logically sin, which deprives the created nature of the source of its being, might be expected to cause its complete disintegration. This is not, however, true. Divine Providence forbids any created thing to come to nothing (*De moribus Manichaeorum*, II, vii [*PL*, XXXII, 1349]); there is no vice so strong as to remove all of the created nature (*De civitate Dei*, XIX, xii [*PL*, XLI, 639]). This does not, however, mean that the presence of the residual good nature manifests itself in good deeds. In the evil man, the good nature, diminished by sin, is apparent in pain and punishment. The good nature remains "ad poenam."

15. The above is a synthesis of Augustine's *Enarratio in Psalmum* XXXV, 7, 12 (*PL*, XXXVI, 348–349; 353–354).

16. "Est enim hic quaedam poena occulta. . . . *Sicut cera*, inquit [Psalmista] *liquefacta auferentur*. Dixi per concupiscentias suas hoc eis fieri. . . . Sed istas poenas pauci vident: propterea eas maxime commendat Spiritus Dei. Audi Apostolum dicentem: *Tradidit illos Deus in concupiscentias cordis eorum*" [Romans 1, 24] (*PL*, XXXVI, 686–687).

17. The distinction between the punishment of concupiscence, which is the common penalty of all sin, and the punishment which is given as damnation may perhaps be indicated in terms of degree and permanence. According to Augustine, pride, the greatest of the sins, merits the greatest punishment—abandonment to concupiscence, which is damnation in this world and the next. However, as Augustine also maintains, pride is a vice from which few are free. The question then remains: At what point does pride incur this most severe of all punishments? Such a question is unanswerable, since no one knows the judgment of God. However, Bishop Bradwardine, in commenting on the two expositions of Augustine discussed above, makes it clear that a point does exist at which the sinner is permitted to go his way into further sins without the possibility of return: "Facit e[r]go Deus quosdam peccare, sed in quibus iam talia peccata praecesserunt, ut iusto iudicio eius mereantur in desideriis ire" (*De causa Dei*, p. 297).

18. See William Langland, *Piers Plowman*, C Passus XII, 173 ff. (ed. W. W.

Skeat [Oxford, 1886], I, 311) ; *Parson's Tale*, X [I], 322–349. There are also various allusions in Gower: *Mirour de l'omme*, I, 9124; *Confessio amantis*, VII, 5223; VIII, 293; *Vox clamantis*, III, 1911–1916 (*Complete Works*, ed. G. C. Macaulay [Oxford, 1899–1902], I, 106; III, 380, 394; IV, 159) .

19. See note 5 above.

20. Translated from *De causa Dei*, I, xxxiv (p. 296).

21. See Robinson's note to VI [C], 603. The marginal gloss "Policratici libro I" makes it likely that the material is from the *Policraticus* (see *Text of the Canterbury Tales*, ed. J. M. Manly and Edith Rickert [Chicago, 1940], III, 516) . On Lollius and the *Policraticus*, see R. A. Pratt, "A Note on Chaucer's Lollius," *MLN*, LXV (1950) , 183–187.

22. Translated from the *Policraticus*, III, iii: "Quod superbia radix malorum est, et concupiscentia lepra generalis, quae omnes inficit" (ed. C. C. J. Webb [Oxford, 1909], I, 176–177) .

23. See Prologue to the *Legend of Good Women* ([G] 414–415) . Chaucer seems to have made at least one distinct borrowing in the *Pardoner's Tale* (see VI [C], 537ff., and Robinson's note) .

24. Translated from *De contemptu mundi*, III, vi: *De igne gehennali* (*PL*, CCXVII, 739). Latin text, p. 260 below. According to Augustine, concupiscence remains as a punishment in the sinful dead (*De natura et gratia*, I, liii [*PL*, XLIV, 277]) and is present in the fallen angels (*Enchiridion*, I, xxv [*PL*, XL, 244]) . Compare Innocent on the torment of the damned: "semper secum defert cruciatum," and the *Compendium theologicae veritatis* on the torment of the fallen angels: "semper infernum suum secum portant" (*Alberti Magni opera*, XIII, 34) .

25. X [I], 387–955. The indebtedness to Gregory is apparent in at least two respects. First, the order of sins observed in the *Parson's Tale* is Gregory's and is hence almost exactly opposite to Peraldus' in the *Summa de vitiis*, which has been generally considered the most acceptable parallel to the Parson's sins treatise (see Germaine Dempster, "The Parson's Tale," *Sources and Analogues*, pp. 723–724) . Second, portions of the brief progress of Gregory were employed as prefatory material to the discussion of the individual sins. One may find the best example of this in Chaucer's derivation of "avarice" from "accidia." Chaucer: "After Accidie wol I speke of Avarice. . . . For soothly, whan the herte of a man is confounded in itself and troubled, and that the soule hath lost the confort of God, thanne seketh he an ydel solas of worldly thynges" (X [I], 739–740) . Gregory: "Tristitia quoque ad avaritiam derivatur, quia dum confusum cor bonum laetitiae in semetipso intus amiserit, unde consolari debeat foris quaerit; et tanto magis exteriora bona adipisci desiderat, quanto guadium non habet ad quod intrinsecus recurrat" (*Moralium*, XXXI, xlv [*PL*, LXXVI, 621–622]) . This derivation is not contained in Peraldus. In his very different rationale avarice follows luxury.

26. Translated from the *Compendium theologicae veritatis*, III, vii: "De effectu peccati" (*Alberti Magni opera*, XIII, 55) .

27. "*Et de absconditis tuis adimpletus est venter eorum* [Psalm XVI, 14], quibus verbis occulta Dei judicia significata sunt; occulte quippe sunt

miseri, etiam qui gaudent in malis, quos tradidit Deus in concupiscentias cordis eorum" [Romans I, 24] (*Epistola* CXLIX [*PL*, XXXIII, 632]).

28. All elements of the Augustinian definition are here represented: the
knowledge of God, the setting up of the will against God, the exploi-
tation rather than repression of concupiscence (see note 4 above).

29. See "Inobedient," "Despitous," "Inpacient," "Ypocrite," "Inpudent,"
"Swellynge of herte" (X [I], 392, 395, 401, 394, 397, 398).

30. In his remarks on his will (see p. 253 above) the Pardoner would
seem to indicate at once the aversion of the will from God and the
sins in which he takes refuge from the penalty of that aversion: "I
wol have moneie, wolle, chese, and whete/ . . . I *wol* drynke licour of
the vyne/ And have a joly wenche in every toun." Other than pride,
the sins here indicated are avarice, gluttony, and lechery.

31. The typical activities of pardoners were obtaining funds or commodities
by devious means and spending the wealth so acquired in feasting,
drinking, and "amore carnali." Jacques de Vitry describes them: "Sub
pretextu elemosine querunt divitias. . . . Ea vero que turpiter congre-
gunt quam turpius in commessationibus et ebrietatibus expendunt, et
alia consequentia que in oculto et in tenebris ipsi tenebrosi operantur
. . . pudet tamen nos ad presens recitare" ("Historia occidentalis," in
Statuts d'Hôtels-Dieu, ed. Léon le Grand [Paris, 1901], pp. 3–4). In
terms of the seven deadly sins, these activities represent the same sins
indicated in the Pardoner's speech—avarice, gluttony, and lechery.
See above, "Chaucer's Satire of the Pardoner," note 33.

32. Chaucer's translation, together with Gregory's text, is to be found in
note 25 above.

33. See notes 12 and 30 above.

34. It has been objected that the Pardoner's sermon lacks unity because the
theme of avarice is not related to the so-called sins of the tavern (see
the *Pardoner's Tale*, ed. Carleton Brown [Oxford, 1935], pp. xv–xx).
This objection seems to have doubtful validity. All the sins treated in
the sermon—gluttony, lechery, gaming, blasphemy, homicide—are, in
the pattern of the seven deadly sins, connected with the central theme
of avarice. Gluttony and lechery are linked, as the Pardoner piously
notes (VI [C], 483–484, 549), and in the scheme of the seven deadly
sins they follow in order from avarice (see note 12 above). If we
turn to the discussion of the seven deadly sins in the *Parson's Tale*, we
find that gaming, "hasardrie," is a part of avarice (X [I], 793) and that
"blasphemynge and reneiynge of God" comes from "hasardrie." (See
Robinson's note to VI [C], 590.) "Homycide," which the Pardoner does
not mention by name until his final apostrophe to avarice (VI [C], 896),
is not a major division of avarice, but is twice specified by Peraldus as
a consequence of avarice (*Summa virtutum ac vitiorum* [Paris, 1519],
fols. 39, 41). Avarice, though unobtrusive, is clearly central to the
sermon. The Pardoner's method would seem to be to present the off-
shoots of avarice first, embody them in an evolving drama, and end
with a powerful address to what he would have his audience believe
to be the root of all sin, Avarice herself, at the head of all her de-
pendencies—and at just the moment for his collection:

O cursed synne of alle cursednesse!
O traytours homycide, O wikkednesse!
O glotonye, luxurie, and hasardrye!
Thou blasphemour of Crist with vileynye
And othes grete, of usage and of pride! (vi [c], 895–899)

The proceeds of the sermon against Avarice, her handmaids, Gluttony and Lechery, and her lesser followers support the Pardoner's favorite sins—avarice, gluttony, and lechery.

35. vi [c], 377–388. No eleemosynary pardoner was permitted to grant an indulgence to one who was not properly confessed. (See "Chaucer's Satire of the Pardoner," p. 213 above.) The Pardoner's "gaude," very simply stated, is publicly to shrink in horror from granting his great powers of cleansing the soul to any with hidden sins. He thereby places all who do not rush up to contribute in the position of having committed a sin so horrible that they dare not confess it (see analogues to the trick collected by Germaine Dempster in *Sources and Analogues*, pp. 411–414).

36. vi [c], 366–371. This remarkable relic will heal a husband's jealousy though his wife has taken "prestes two or thre."

37. "And ye shul understonde that in mannes synne is every manere of ordre or ordinaunce turned up-so-doun" (x [i], 260).

38. According to Bushnell and Brown, the Old Man is the Wandering Jew; according to Kittredge and Root, Death personified; according to Mrs. Hamilton, "Old Age as the Harbinger of Death" (See Marie P. Hamilton, "Death and Old Age in the Pardoner's Tale," *SP*, xxxvi [1939], 571–576, where the authorities are collected.) To me it would appear that the Old Man must basically be Death himself; otherwise the ironical point to the tale would be lost.

39. To St. Augustine the root of all evil is not money but the evil will. He therefore carefully explains the Pardoner's text (I Timothy vi, 10): "Avaricia enim . . . non in solo argento. . . . Haec autem avaritia cupiditas est; cupiditas porro improba voluntas est. Ergo improba voluntas, malorum omnium causa est" (*De libero arbitrio*, iii, xvii [*PL*, xxxii, 1294]). The will becomes evil through pride, since all sin involves the idea of the opposition of the individual will to the will of God. Hence, one finds Gregory the Great saying, "Radix cuncti mali superbia est" (*Moralium*, xxxi, xlv [*PL*, lxxvi, 621]), and John of Salisbury, "superbia radix malorum est" (see note 22 above).

40. In Gower's tale, which occurs in his treatment of the various branches of pride, the King of Hungary encounters two aged pilgrims. With "gret humilite" he embraces them and kisses their feet. The King's nobles, in particular his brother, "of here oghne Pride" criticize the King for abasing his royalty. As a lesson, the King causes the trump of death to be blown before his brother's house. To his penitent and fearful brother the King explains that the law of man may be altered and is less to be feared than the law of nature, established by God, which he reverenced in the old men (*Confessio amantis*, i, 2021–2253 [*Complete Works*, ed. Macaulay, ii, 90–96]).

41. The irony of this situation was pointed out by the late Professor R. D. French in his undergraduate Chaucer lectures, which regrettably remain unpublished. I am throughout indebted to Professor French and to C. S. Lewis, *Preface to Paradise Lost* (Oxford, 1942).

42. See p. 248 above.

43. "ecce pulchra sunt cum eis omnia, et ipsi turpes sunt" (*Confessionum*, v, ii [*PL*, xxxii, 706]).

44. The perverter laughs at the perverted. Satan and the demons laugh at the perverter, for by his very act he is bringing himself into their hands (*Confessionum*, iii, iii [*PL*, xxxii, 685]).

45. The created nature cannot be brought to nothingness even by the most destructive of sins (see note 14 above). Likewise, the nature, created good, loves the good: "homo naturaliter bonum appetit" (*Compendium*, iii, i, in *Alberti Magni opera*, xiii, 52) and cannot lose this love even in the midst of evil: "Quae tamen natura in malis suis non potuit amittere beatitudinis appetitum" (*Enchiridion*, i, xxv [*PL*, xl, 244]).

46. This crucial speech furnishes the most difficult problem in the interpretation of the Pardoner. Opinion is almost equally divided as to its sincerity. Kittredge and Sedgwick consider the speech an expression of genuine emotion; Patch, Curry, Lumiansky, and Coghill consider it part of a unified plan of deceit intended to culminate in the Pilgrims' reverencing the Pardoner's false relics. For reasons already adduced, it seems to me the genuine expression of inner suffering. Certain considerations, particularly of tone, also seem to support the argument of sincerity. See G. G. Sedgwick, "The Progress of Chaucer's Pardoner, 1880–1940," *MLQ*, i (1940), 431–458, where a full summary of criticism to the date of the article is to be found; R. M. Lumiansky, "A Conjecture Concerning Chaucer's Pardoner," *Tulane Studies in English*, i (1949), 1–29; and Nevill Coghill, *The Poet Chaucer* (London, 1949), pp. 158–162.

47. The ultimate professional achievement of the Pardoner seems to have been by persuasion to impose his will upon an audience which is already aware of the purpose of his pious utterances. In the Council of Mainz, a certain note of professional envy seems to emerge from the thoroughgoing indictment of the practices of pardoners: "so movingly do they preach . . . that there is hardly anyone, even one aware of their villainous tricks, who can restrain himself from contributing" (Mansi, *Concilia*. xxiii, 1102).

48. The use of false relics seems to have been considered a variety of heresy, and was punished as such. Of the continually repeated offenses of the Pardoner this is not one. In the Council of Exeter (1285), the penalties attached to the use of false relics are stated in a way which indicates a very distinct difference between this abuse and the everyday practices of the pardoner (*ibid.*, xxiv, 829–830).

49. This failure is, I think, the best example of the Pardoner's *ignorantia* (see pp. 246–248 above). He has lost the moral sensitivity to understand the feelings of his fellow Pilgrims toward him.

50. "Utitur ergo [Deus] malis, non secundum eorum pravam, sed secundum

suam rectam voluntatem. Nam sicut mali natura sua bona, hoc est, bono ejus opere male utuntur; sic ipse bonus etiam eorum malis operibus bene utitur, ne omnipotentis voluntas aliqua ex parte vincatur" (*Sermo* CCXIV [*PL*, XXXVIII, 1067]) .

51. "Et quoniam nemo natura, sed quisquis malus est, vitio malus est; perfectum odium debet malis, qui secundum Deum vivit; ut nec propter vitium oderit hominem, nec amet vitium propter hominem; sed oderit vitium, amet hominem" (*De civitate Dei*, XIV, vi [*PL*, XLI, 409]) .

52. See note 24 above.

53. According to the tests of good works (*Epistola* CXLIX [*PL*, XXXIII, 632]) and of pride (see note 17 above) , the Pardoner fares badly. However, there is a third test. Augustine invariably states that sin darkens the soul. In the *Enarratio in Psalmum* LVII, he goes further and says that in the damned this punishment has proceeded so far that their eyes are blinded to future punishment (*PL*, XXXVI, 690) . Though the Pardoner has necessarily become in some measure hardened to his sin, he has by no means lost the sense of guilt and horror at his situation, as is testified to by his final confession (lines 916–918) . There is a considerable measure of undestroyed good within the Pardoner, as I think most readers feel. I am not sure, as Kittredge is, that Chaucer is willing to push the Pardoner beyond the point of no return—to make him the "one lost soul" among the Canterbury Pilgrims (G. L. Kittredge, *Chaucer and His Poetry* [Boston, 1927], p. 180, and note 17 above) .

14

A Reading of the "Friar's Tale," Line 1314

ALTHOUGH FEW WORKS OF LITERATURE have been more fully explicated than the *Canterbury Tales*, a few relatively indomitable lines remain. Among these is "Ther myghte asterte hym no pecunyal peyne," which occurs in the course of the Friar's description of the Archdeacon's administration of justice:

> But certes, lecchours dide he grettest wo;
> They sholde syngen if that they were hent;
> And smale tytheres weren foule yshent,
> If any persoun wolde upon hem pleyne.
> Ther myghte asterte hym no pecunyal peyne. (III [D], 1310–1314)[1]

The line which concludes this brief passage has been misunderstood. Skeat's "No fine could save the accused from punishment"[2] is the opposite of the meaning intended. Robinson is closer with "No fine ever escaped him [the Archdeacon]." It is the contention of the present note that the logical subject of the sentence is not the "fine," as both Skeat and Robinson have it,[3] but a composite sinner made up of the two classes of "lecchours" and "smale tytheres" mentioned immediately above. Hence the sentence may be rendered "He [the sinner] could escape no *pecuniary punishment.*"[4] Four passages drawn from contempo-

Reprinted from *Notes and Queries*, CCIV (1959), 190–192.

rary observations on ecclesiastical justice will, I think, bear this out.

The first occurs in Book III of Gower's *Vox clamantis*, and deals with the punishment of lechery. Although lengthy, the passage may be summarized in a single line: "Torquentur *bursa* sic reus atque rea" (III, 194).[5]

The second passage is found in a treatise entitled *On the Seven Deadly Sins*, at one time attributed to Wyclif. Although not unknown to the editors of Chaucer, it does not seem to have received the attention it deserves, for it not only furnishes the best single illustration of the Summoner's practices, but also points the way to the solution of the meaning of the line under consideration. Wyclif is here discussing the sexual sins of the third estate, the "laboreres":

þo þriddle of þo Chirche is not clene of lecchorie, for þei gone togedir as bestis. And þis is knowen to bischop clerkis, for þei spoylen hom in chapiters, as who wolde spoyle a thef; and for hor feyned sommenyng þei drawen hom fro hor laboure . . . and þen by feyned cursyng þei maken hom paye þis robbyng. Þei seyn, as þei mot nede, þat þis þei done by charite, and putten enplaster of cursyng for heele of monnis soule. Bot þis is open gabbyng, as men may wil knowe, sith be streyt covenaunt þei sellen tyme of synnyng, þat þus longe schal he not be lettid for so myche money. . . . And þis falshed schulden lordes lette, and make þis puple be punischid by opun penaunce in hor body, as fastyng, or schameful beetyng . . .[6]

Here in one passage are to be found the Summoner's intelligence system (III [D], 1338–1344; 1355–1358); his procedure in summoning (1586–1589); his permitting a "good felawe" to have his concubine for a year on payment of a quart of wine (649–651); finally the passage throws light on the line under discussion. What Wyclif is saying is that sinners may easily escape "open penaunce in hor body," for it is seldom imposed; pecuniary penance, however, is inescapable, for it is the prevailing mode of punishment.

Since the statements of a poet and a reformer do not necessarily reflect the actual practice of the day, it is useful to compare their observations with those of orthodox churchmen. Two such statements have come to the notice of the present writer, and in each of these Chaucer's actual phrase "pecunyal peyne" appears. Archbishop Thoresby, in his *Constitutions* of 1367, outlines the procedures to be followed by the parish clergy in reserved cases. Penance is to be imposed by the archbishop himself, or by his Penitentiary, and the penitent sinner returned with a stated penance to the parish priest or vicar, who "poenitentiam a poenitentiario injunctam non remittat . . . nec in *poenam pecuniariam* . . . commutare presumat sub poena suspensionis ab officio."[7] That Archbishop Thoresby is alluding by a well-established term to a well-established practice is testified to by the early thirteenth-century English manual *Summa de officio sacerdotis*, or "Qui bene presunt." In his reproof of abuses within the Church, the author observes that the clergy of his day are interested only in "exacciones et extorciones" and neglect the "debita punicio peccatorum." He sums up: "Sola enim *pena pecuniaria* locum in omni genere delictorum optinet."[8]

All authorities would therefore seem to agree that, as for the sinner,

> Ther myghte asterte hym no *pecunyal peyne*.

NOTES

1. *Works*, p. 89.
2. See Skeat, v, 323.
3. *Works*, p. 705.
4. The difficulty with Skeat's translation is obvious. The difficulty with Robinson's is less so because it accords with the sense of the passage. However, if it matches the general sense of the passage, it misses the particular point involved. Literally the line reads "There might escape [to] him no pecuniary penalty." Who is the "him"? If related to the Archdeacon, the line would read: "There might escape to the Archdeacon no pecuniary penalty"; i.e., the Archdeacon could escape no pecunial penalty. It would therefore be the Archdeacon who would be suffering inescapable purse-pains, which is certainly not the sense of the passage. Robinson's translation would thus appear to be arrived at by a curious conversion of "penalty" into the quite opposite meaning of "benefit." If the "him" be referred, as here proposed, to a kind of composite sinner subject to the Archdeacon's jurisdiction, the line would read: "There might escape to the sinner no pecunial pain"; i.e., "The sinner could escape no pecuniary penalty." If so read, the line not only makes sense, but brings out the particular point to be conveyed. The sinner could escape any physical penance, such as fasting

or beating, but he could not escape a penance in his purse—"pecunial pain."

5. III, 189–226. In *The Complete Works of John Gower*, ed. G. C. Macaulay (Oxford, 1899–1902), IV, 112–113. This passage is commented on by Robinson in his note to I [A], 656.

6. *Select English Works of John Wyclif*, ed. Thomas Arnold (Oxford, 1869–1871), III, 166. The parallels to Chaucer are recognized by Arnold, and the passage is duly noted by Skeat, V, 323. The Wyclifite doctrines on excommunication and the relation of lay power to the Church, evident in the passage cited, are, of course, not adduced as parallels to Chaucer. See H. B. Workman, *John Wyclif* (Oxford, 1926), II, 23–27.

7. David Wilkins, *Concilia Magnae Britanniae* (London, 1737), III, 73.

8. Oxford, MS New College XCIV, fol. 96ᵇ. For a discussion of date and authorship, see below, "St. Augustine and the 'Parson's Tale,'" note 8.

15

The Fraternal Kiss in the "Summoner's Tale"

WHEN THE FRIAR of the *Sommoner's Tale* has received
what monetary contributions he can as a result of his hortatory
sermon, and with his confrere has pried about in various houses
for donations in kind, he proceeds to the dwelling of the bed-
ridden Thomas, where he has for long been "Refresshed moore
than in an hundred placis" (III [D], 1767). There he greets the
sick man "curteisly and softe" (1771),[1] and addresses to him
some wholesome words as to the communicative efficacy of
"glosynge" (1793). When the wife of the good man enters:

> The frere ariseth up ful curteisly,
> And hire embraceth in his armes narwe,
> And kiste hire sweete, and chirketh as a sparwe
> With his lyppes: "Dame," quod he, "right weel,
> As he that is youre servant every deel,
> Thanked be God, that yow yaf soule and lyf!
> Yet saugh I nat this day so fair a wyf
> In al the chirche, God so save me!" (1802–1809)

There has been some controversy about the exact nature of
the kiss which the Friar bestows upon Thomas's wife. Professor
Manly assures us that "The friar's greeting of the goodwife was

Reprinted from *Scriptorium*, VII (1953), 115.

the usual mode of salutation and has no sinister implications."[2] Professor Robinson does not deny that the kiss was a customary form of greeting, but he feels that "the tight embrace and the *chirkyng* are not altogether in keeping with the office and character of the priest."[3] Two unnoticed contemporary comments would seem to bear out completely Professor Robinson's contention.

In a passage of the *Vox clamantis* Gower complains that the untaught people are injured by the "incastis exemplis presbiterorum." This unchastity of life he points out in the abuse of the kiss of peace. The customary kiss, he says, is becoming a new custom, and in this custom no law is more evident than the law of nature.[4] The *Regimen animarum* (1343), an unpublished English handbook for priests, warns in similar fashion that the abuse of the clerical kiss with its attendant familiarities renders the character of the priest vile and contemptible:

Et non debet clericus et maxime episcopus cum talibus habere familiaritatem eas osculando vel caput suum in gremio illius ponendo vel aliquid simile, ne vilis ac contemptibilis habeatur ex hoc.[5]

Professor Robinson's doubts as to the innocent import of the Friar's kiss are further supported by the occurrence of the scene between Thomas's wife and the Friar in the context of the Friar-Summoner quarrel. "Vilis ac contemptibilis" is precisely what the angered Summoner is seeking to make the Friar appear, and the latter's calculated "curteisye" with "worthy wommen of the toun" is a prime target.[6]

NOTES

1. *Works*, p. 94.
2. *Chaucer's Canterbury Tales*, ed. J. M. Manly (New York, 1928), p. 590.
3. *Works*, p. 707.
4. *Vox clamantis*, III, 1623–1646 (*The Complete Works of John Gower*, ed. G. C. Macaulay [Oxford, 1899–1902], IV, 150–151).
5. Harley 2272. I, v: *De cohabitatione clericorum et mulierum et de concubinis eorundem.* The manualist is here considering the problem of the cohabitation of a cleric with a female relative excepted from the general prohibition against cohabitation. He finds the danger of the situation to lie in the female attendants who accompany the relative, and quotes St. Augustine: "Qui cum sorore mea sunt, sorores

meae non sunt." It is familiarity with these attendants against which he warns, but there would seem to be little reason to suppose that he would consider the same familiarity less objectionable in the case of "faire wyves." Harley 2272 is discussed above in "Chaucer's Satire of the Pardoner," note 40.

6. Muriel Bowden (*A Commentary on the General Prologue to the Canterbury Tales* [New York, 1948], p. 128) has very well illustrated Friar Hubert as the "curteis" lover. In the detailed reproduction of Friar Hubert which the Summoner presents as the central figure of his own tale, this quality is stressed: "Seyde this frere, *curteisly* and softe"; 'The frere ariseth up ful *curteisly*" (III [D], 1771, 1802) .

16

The Evolution of the "Clerk's Tale": A Study in Connotation

WHEN THE WIDOWED Knight of La Tour Landry one spring day thought back upon his love for his dead lady and the happiness of their life together, he thought also of his daughters and suddenly realized that he had failed to provide them with what their mother would have—the advice necessary to the conduct of their lives, and in particular their marital lives. He therefore hastily gathered together a group of learned "clerks" to supply his regrettable oversight. The result, completed in 1379, is a unique document, the only surviving medieval handbook of advice for daughters.[1] From the vast number of exempla of which the book is composed, there emerges a quite distinct picture of ideal womanhood. The ideal woman honors Holy Church and is constant in her prayers; she devotes herself to good works, in especial the relief of the needy, not feeding little dogs with what the poor might have. In the company of her husband, she is humble, loving, and patient. Even though her husband keep a concubine, her duty is to win him to her by loving patience and not by violent action. In short, she is, with one notable difference,[2] an exact replica of Griselda; or, perhaps more exactly, she, like Griselda, is an exact replica of that composite of virtues which made up the clerical ideal of womanhood, an ideal which the clerk in turn presented to the secular mind in authoritative form. As Alice of Bath pointedly complains concerning the source of this ideal female image, "Who peyntede the leon, tel me who?"[3]

In support of Alice's claim, it is to be noted that the three greatest literary, and hence clerical, minds of the fourteenth century—Boccaccio, Chaucer, and Petrarch—were all powerfully attracted to the story of the patient Griselda, in whom was to be found perfectly realized this same clerical ideal of womanhood. Yet the story of Griselda was by its very nature fraught with difficulty for any writer of the Christian era. It is generally agreed that the roots of the Griselda story go back deep into pagan antiquity,[4] and herein lies its primary difficulty for the Christian author: in its passage from pagan myth to Christian story, a violent clash of religious attitude was inevitable. The story seems to originate as a variant of the Cupid and Psyche myth, in which, to merit the love of the god, the mere mortal must expect to be put to superhuman temptations to break the taboo which is the binding link between immortal and mortal. But the Christian God is not the pagan god. He does not tempt the human object of His love to break the law which is the covenant between them, nor does He permit temptation beyond the power of the human to resist. His moral code is known, and enticement to break it must come from a demonic source, itself existent under the law and under the power of God.

Pagan myth and Christian morality would thus appear to be entirely at odds. However, this opposition is only partially true. Common to both systems is the absolute acceptance, on the part of the uncomprehending mortal, of the divine will. However, the tests or temptations to which the pagan mortal may be exposed are captious and entirely dependent on the pleasure of the god or of the immortal community he inhabits; those to which the Christian may be exposed must, as noted above, fall within an established system of law. When, therefore, with the passage of time, the god-lover becomes Christian husband, and the human-lover Christian wife,[5] the relationship of erstwhile god and mortal falls inevitably within the law of man and wife established by the Old and New Testaments. Within this law, there is no room for the whimsical tests to which Psyche was subjected.

A second difficulty, perhaps even more pressing, was the established doctrine concerning the nature of woman which had come to be accepted in Christian Europe long before the story of Griselda had ever been written down. St. Augustine's conception of man was that of a flawed human being dependent upon divine grace; St. Jerome's conception of woman was that of an even more flawed human being, whose prime characteristic was her mutability. In Chaucer's *Troilus and Criseyde*, the creature so beautiful she seems sent down from heaven, "in scornynge of nature,"[6] slowly, pitiably, but inevitably—falls. Why? The most precise answer is that provided by the distinguished jurist and philosopher Guido delle Colonne. In his *Historia destructionis Troiae*, he explains Criseyde's mutability as simply natural. That women are what they are is "insitum a natura."[7] Andreas Capellanus shows himself of the same opinion by remarking that no one should wonder about the inconstancy of women "quum de natura procedat."[8] The most interesting comment, however, is to be found in the *Roman de Troie* of Benoit de St. Maure, which served as Guido's prime source and as a lesser source for Chaucer. The unfaithfulness of Criseyde Benoit uses as occasion for a diatribe against the mutability of women, in the course of which he rather abruptly halts. He finds it necessary, somewhat to his embarrassment, to make a dazzling exception of his patroness, presumably Eleanor of Aquitaine. She is that prized being, the rare woman who remains constant and defends herself against temptation.

Solomon, he who was possessed of so wise a spirit, says amongst his writings, "He who could find a strong woman [fort femme] should praise his Creator."[9]

This is an allusion to the "mulier fortis" of Proverbs who is to play so significant a role in the Griselda story. In her industrious care for her husband, the "good woman" is a model of female industry and devotion, but the line which introduces her: "Mulierem fortem quis inveniet?" (Proverbs XXXI, 10) is capable of being read in such a way as to produce a witticism dear to the clerical mind: "A good woman, who can find one?"

However, the Griselda on whom Boccaccio, Petrarch, and

Chaucer in succession lavished their attentions is the exact opposite of Criseyde. She not only seems sent down in "scorning of nature"; her every action does in fact scorn the accepted idea of the nature of woman. But herein arises a further difficulty: Griselda not only scorns nature in excelling all that can be expected in woman; she scorns nature also in an opposite and equally incredible fashion, one hardly appealing to the taste of recent centuries. At her husband's behest, she yields up her children to what she firmly believes to be brutal murder. Such were the materials which possessed so irresistible an attraction for the greatest literary minds of the fourteenth century.

I

Boccaccio, the first to attempt a synthesis of the discrete, if not contradictory, elements of the Griselda story, accorded it the highest dignity—the last tale of the last day of the *Decameron*.[10] That day, it will be remembered, is devoted to stories of magnanimity. Tale VI, for instance, records the enamorment of old King Charles for two young fisher queens—"Ginevra la bella e l'altra Isotta la bionda"—by implication the best in duplicate the Arthurian world has to offer, but unfortunately twin daughters of a trusting old knight. As a result of his awareness of his feudal obligations and his humble acceptance of sage advice, King Charles resolutely conquers his desire to acquire both of them:

Ho, Lord! Twins of his bosom. Lord save us! and ho! Hey? What all men. Hot? His tittering daughters of. Whawk?

After this supreme renunciation, all others pale. However, Tale VII is also a tale of self-sacrifice, albeit of lesser magnitude. It concerns King Peter, who, understanding that a young woman, the daughter of a wealthy bourgeois, has fallen in love with him upon seeing him in a tournament, and is about to die of her love, saves her by becoming her knight, and ever after in tournaments carries only the favors she sends him. Tale V comprises a complex set of self-renunciations by knight, squire, and clerk which forms perhaps the closest analogue to Chaucer's *Franklin's Tale*.[11] However, when at the end of the *Decameron* it becomes the turn of

Dioneo to tell the final tale of magnanimity which will "knytte up wel a greet mateere," he declares he will do no such thing, but will tell the story of the mad bestiality ("matta bestialità") of one Marquis Walter. As Dioneo tells it, the story of Walter is that of a young man who gives all his attentions to the pleasures of the hunt and not the slightest thought to marriage—because of which he was considered a wise man. However, his more serious-minded vassals see the succession unsecured and repeatedly urge him to marry, themselves offering to find him a bride of proper ancestry. Walter replies that there are many difficulties in choosing a bride; as to ancestry, for instance, daughters are often unlike their parents, and furthermore it is a wise daughter who knows her own father. He declares that he alone will be responsible for the choice. Walter then adds, in a tone which could hardly be called less than menacing, that whomever he takes for wife:

. . . if she be not honored by you as your sovereign lady, you will discover to your own great injury how gravely I take being married in accordance with your prayers, and against my own will.[12]

It is immediately evident that Walter is far from being caught unprepared by a request of this sort, and that he has prepared in advance a scheme against the time when, as he has foreseen, he must fulfill his feudal obligation of begetting an heir. In a nearby village, he has observed a girl whose beauty and dutifulness toward her aged father will, he feels, assure him an agreeable enough marriage, but whose extreme poverty and occupation of sheepherder will ensure the perpetual humiliation of the retainers who have forced him to marry. These will now, in accordance with their word, be forced to do homage to the lowest of the low. Walter, therefore, immediately arranges the marriage with Giannuculo, Griselda's father, and assembles the vassals who have been instrumental in his forthcoming marriage. He reminds them first of their promise to honor whomever he chooses as his lady, announces the marriage but not the bride, and orders the most splendid preparations to be carried out. On the day of the marriage, he mounts his horse and leads the company of those who have come to honor their new lady to the house of Griselda, who is returning in haste from the well, bucket in hand, to see who the new bride is to be. Walter enters the house and without undue delay obtains Griselda's consent to marry him. He then asks her, in the presence of her father, whether, if he takes her as his wife, she will make every effort to please him,

and never become disturbed over anything he might say or do, and be obedient, and plenty of like matters.[13]

After this he leads her out of the house, and in the presence of the whole company has her stripped ("spogliare ignuda")[14] and the splendid new clothes he has had secretly prepared put upon her. He then and there marries her in a ceremony which is a model of brevity, takes her home, and presides over a wedding feast which would have befitted the daughter of the King of France.

However, much to Walter's astonishment, Griselda occupies her position with such grace that no one could be found that did not love her more than his very self. Despite the reputation for wisdom Walter has unexpectedly acquired—namely, his perception of virtue beneath rags—the planned humiliation of those who have gone counter to his will never takes place, and Walter's strange, involuted nature remains unsatisfied.[15]

The birth of their first child is to Walter a source of great pleasure, but shortly thereafter a "nuovo pensier" comes to him: to put to intolerable proofs his wife's patience ("con cose intollerabili *provare* la pazienza di lei").[16] This probationary process consists initially in removing her daughter under the pretext that his people are grumbling about his wife's low lineage and the problems now posed by the birth of an heir, albeit a female heir. She replies:

My Lord, do with me what you believe may be most to your honor and your pleasure, for I shall be content with all [you may do], since I know that I am of lesser estate than they [who protest against me], and that I was not worthy of the honor to which, through your courtesy, you brought me.[17]

Her reply delights Walter, because he sees that elevation of position has not brought with it pride of position. Griselda has not been "in alcuna *superbia* levata." When the daughter is taken from her by "un familiare" of Walter's under circumstances which convince Griselda that the child is to be murdered, Griselda's expression remains unchanged, and Walter marvels at her constancy ("*costanza*").[18]

The birth of a second child, a son, again finds Walter delighted and again ultimately unsatisfied. Walter's procedure with the male child is much the same as with the female, but intensified. He intimates that he is about to be chased out of his domains because of resentment over the debased lineage of his wife, Griselda, and the birth of a male child, who will now be his successor. He intimates that in the end he will be forced to take another wife. Griselda hears him out patiently ("con *paziente animo*"), and says merely:

> My Lord, think only to content yourself, and to satisfy your own pleasure [*piacer*], and take no thought of me, for nothing is dear to me, except as I see it please you [a te *piacere*].[19]

When her son is taken from her by the same "familiare," Griselda remains to all appearances unmoved.

As a result of Griselda's constancy in this second proof, Walter's curiosity is the more increased, and he resorts to his final trial, his "ultima pruova."[20] The title is not inappropriate. Under guise of a forged papal dispensation, he announces his intention of taking a new bride. Griselda is to be sent back to her father, and hence very possibly to her previous profession of sheepherder. As planned, the climax of the "ultima pruova" is to be the calling back of Griselda as servant-in-chief to prepare the palace against the arrival of the new bride. To this already adequately complex plot, Walter has added two apparently opposite but quite possibly complementary refinements. The first is, in exchange for the splendid jewels and raiment which he has given her, to tender Griselda back her dowry. Since she was stripped before she came, Griselda has none—which means that she must expect to repass naked and on foot the same route over which she had come splendidly mounted and attired. The second of Walter's refinements is to present as the intended bride Griselda's own daughter, now grown to marriageable age. As the first stage in his consciously or unconsciously evolving plan, Walter had sent the daughter to Bologna, to be raised by Walter's sister, the Countess of Panago. There she has in turn been joined by her infant brother. Hence, an intensification of the "ultima pruova," but should Griselda prove successful, an end of trial, and the return of all she had thought lost.

Having thoroughly prepared for his final test, Walter duly proceeds, but with exactly the results both he and the reader have anticipated. However, in terms of the present study, what is lost in suspense is more than gained in connotation. Earlier, when Griselda had been informed by Walter that he must take another wife in order not to be chased out of his lands, Griselda appeared unmoved. She resolved to bear this blow as she had the other injuries of Fortune ("l'altre ingiurie della *fortuna*").[21] In the actual operation of Walter's painstakingly conceived plan, her resolution does not falter. When Walter announces the arrival of his purported dispensation, Griselda, "beyond the nature of woman, held back her tears," and tells Walter that she has ever regarded her lofty position as his wife "as something lent" ("*prestato*").[22] When Walter returns Griselda to her father in as humiliating a fashion as his kindly heart permits, she takes up her household duties as if she had never been apart from them, with strong spirit ("*forte* animo") sustaining the fierce assault of hostile fortune ("della *nemica fortuna*").[23] When asked to prepare for the new bride, the request is like a knife at Griselda's heart because she has not been able to divest herself of her love for Walter, as she had her (former) good fortune ("come fatto aveva la *buona fortuna*").[24] Walter, finally convinced at the purported marriage feast that Griselda has taken as real all the trials she has been subjected to, declares, "Griselda, it is now time that you tasted the fruit of your long patience," and then proceeds to deliver a pompous speech, sketching out the noble purposes of his plan and pointing out the manifest errors of those who had thought him "crudele . . . e bestiale." Lest anyone doubt, he declares in ringing terms his love for his devoted wife: he loves her best of all, because it is manifestly impossible for anyone to boast that he has a wife the equal of Walter's.

The confused state of Boccaccio's emotions at the time he completed the *Decameron* is reflected in the curious double morality of the tale. The first, although bitter, is Neoplatonic in tone:

What can one say of this, if not that even upon impoverished houses, divine spirits rain down from the heavens, just as upon royal houses [descend] spirits more worthy of pig-keeping than of having lordship over men.[25]

The second is full of righteous indignation, rather strangely expressed in the diction of the fabliau:[26]

Perhaps it would have served him right, if his choice had fallen upon one who, when he had chased her out of his house in her shift, would have had her fur so shaken by another, that out of it would have come a beautiful robe.[27]

II

Boccaccio's troubled morality[28] reached Petrarch only belatedly, but how deep an impression it made is very evident. Petrarch not only accorded it the honor of translation into Latin, the language of the historian, the scholar, and the theologian, but furthermore made two separate versions of it, the second being placed as the final letter of his final work—the *Epistolae seniles*.

It was the last letter that Petrarch ever wrote. . . . Perhaps sensing that the shadow of death might soon fall upon him, [Petrarch] made it his valedictory both to his epistle-writing and to his friends. He had grown weary and intended to write no more. One must believe, therefore, that it was with no common emotion that he put those last few words upon the parchment: "Valete amici. Valete epistolae." (June 8, 1374)[29]

What did Petrarch discover in the Griselda story so profoundly to affect him? Essentially he found in it two distinct stories—the first conveyed by the narrative proper; the second, dependent upon the narrative, but conveyed by a vocabulary, theological in origin, of highly connotative terms. These have in the preceding discussion been italicized. The first concerns a girl of the humblest origins who has unaccountably been snatched up into the highest of positions, and equally unaccountably been plunged into the lowest. Through her incredible endurance of the proofs to which she is put by her playful lord, she again returns to the love of her lord and to her previous high estate. The second is rather more complex. In the high estate of prosperity conferred upon her, Griselda has refused to yield to the temptation proper to that estate. She has not been "in alcuna superbia levata," nor has she ever considered that estate otherwise than as something lent, "prestato." In adversity, she bears with patience, "con paziente animo," the deprivations hostile Fortune visits upon her, nor does she ever cry out against the power which controls the moods of Fortune, the power whose pleasure, "piacer," it is to give and to take away—to raise into complete happiness and to plunge into absolute misery. What Petrarch saw in Boccaccio's final tale of the *Decameron* was not the story of a simple girl and her lord Walter, but the previously alluded to story of the "mulier fortis" of Proverbs,[30] who in her constancy against both prosperity and adversity mirrors the human soul striving to be worthy of the love of her Lord.

Petrarch's contributions to the evolution of the Griselda story are essentially two. The first is the imposition upon Boccaccio's tale of a less mechanical and more organic structure. This structure is only slightly indicated and would seem to depend upon the reader's recognition of a certain analogy between the temptations of Christ in the wilderness and the temptations to which Griselda is to be exposed.[31] It consists simply of "Satis est" at the conclusion of Griselda's marital oath and "Satis . . . mea Griseldis" at the conclusion of the temptations.[32] Although Petrarch is somewhat inconsistent and even queasy in his terminology, it becomes clear that the two appearances of "satis" enclose three temptations—identical in nature but under differing guises. The temptation in each case is to break the marital oath sworn to as a condition of the marriage; the forms the temptations take are in accord with the series of "proofs" to which, in Boccaccio, Griselda is subjected—daughter, son, self.[33] Since the temptations are directly dependent upon this magnificently unilateral oath, it is worth noting the extent to which Petrarch has given it edge and definition. In Boccaccio, the all-important marital oath is amorphous, and rather trails off at the end (see above, p. 281). In Petrarch, however, the oath demanded of Griselda and accepted by her is, to say the least, exact:

Are you prepared, with willing spirit, to agree with me in all things, so that you never, in anything, dissent from what is my will; and that to whatever in the future it is my will to do with you, you will give willing consent—without any [sign of] contradiction, either in manner or in word?[34]

Quite astonishingly, Griselda departs from the accepted pattern of medieval womanhood—perhaps because Petrarch had taken the precaution to insert in her bosom a "virilis senilisque animus"[35] —and holds to her word. Thus within the tale a quite effective tripartite structure is established: the appeal to Walter by his vassals and the consequent marriage (in Chaucer, Parts I and II); the three temptations (in Chaucer, Parts III, IV, V, and VI, 939–1050); and finally the celebration of Griselda's triumph (in Chaucer VI, 1051–1162).[36] There then follows a little personal "meditacioun" by Petrarch on the meaning, in terms of "modern women," of Griselda's triumphant constancy.

However, Petrarch's chief contribution to the Griselda story lies not in structure, but in the connotative language which his structure contains. What he does is to conserve the vocabulary he inherited from Boccaccio, and to add to it allusions, scriptural in nature, with a strong appeal to the visual sense. Since the language applied to Griselda and to Walter differs sharply, it would seem necessary to examine each separately.

Griselda, in her position of sheepherder, is a possible but not necessarily perfect attractive of supernal allusion. Petrarch solves this problem simply and expeditiously by Lilliputianizing the sheep into "pauculas eius oves," hence bringing them as close to lambs as probability allows.[37] Since tending her father's diminutive sheep could be a rather leisurely occupation, Griselda simultaneously busies herself in spinning, to the extent of serious damage to her digital tissue. On her return from the fields, she cooks whatever products of the fields are appropriate to the lowly estate of her father and herself—"fortune congruas."

At times unspecified, she is busy cleaning house. To all her father's needs she is piously obedient. In her ceaseless activity, especially in spinning, she is evocative of the previously noted "good woman" of Proverbs XXXI, 10–31, in whom the scriptural commentator perceived the image of the soul striving to become worthy of the heavenly bridegroom Christ. Idleness, even allegorical idleness, is unknown to her. Thus in her activity of spinning, what she spins is the wool of the Lamb, and out of it she fashions her wedding garment for the marriage feast of the Lamb.[38] To the slight and unpatterned references to Fortune in Boccaccio's depiction of Griselda as the "mulier fortis," Petrarch added several allusions, of which the most striking occurs in the scene of her being stripped immediately before the wedding and immediately before the populace. This is done "lest she carry any remnant of her old fortune into her new home."[39] Coming immediately after the ominous "Satis est" with which Walter confirmed her marital oath, there is more than an indication that even the "good woman" strong against Fortune's "adversa et prospera simul" may need all of her spiritual resources.

However, it is to be remembered that the image of the "mulier fortis" is not simply the image of the soul enduring the temptations of prosperity and adversity, but the image of the soul conquering these temptations to arrive at the marriage feast of the Lamb.[40] The element of love which impels the "mulier fortis" is not consistently stressed by Petrarch, but is nevertheless not neglected. In yielding up her children to what she believes to be their deaths, Griselda either implicitly or explicitly states her love for Walter as the cause of her action. In the most poignant scene of her temptations—that of the taking from her of her son—she says, in Chaucer's translation:

> "Deth may noght make no comparisoun
> Unto youre love." (666–667)[41]

The idea of the love-death had of course become immensely influential through the story of Tristan and Yseult. However, although the likelihood of Petrarch's here alluding to the illicit love of Tristan and Yseult is extremely remote, there was an acceptable religious substitute in the *Omelia de Maria Magdalena* attributed to Origen. There Mary expresses her love for her Lord Christ in the romantic "heart" idiom, and also states the strength of her love in terms of death: "Strong as death is love"—a quite direct allusion to the Song of Songs (VIII, 6).[42] Given the popularity of the love-death theme in romance, and the popularity of the pseudo-Origen *Homily*, the love of Griselda, the personification of the "mulier fortis," for her lord Walter could hardly be more effectively expressed. However, despite the reality of her love, the anguish of the temptations of prosperity and adversity to which Walter has subjected her have been no less real. In her triumph over the same temptations, the scriptural commentator perceived in the "mulier fortis" an analogy with Job, who "in prosperity, flourished incomparably in virtues, and in adversity remained to his enemy (Satan) invincible."[43] The opportunity presented by this association is not lost upon Petrarch. When about to be cast naked out of the palace she has so long inhabited, Griselda says: "Naked came I out of my father's house, and in like manner, naked shall I return.[44] This is of course an allusion to the deeply moving lines in the Book of Job (I, 21–22):

Naked came I out of my mother's womb, and naked shall I return thither. The Lord gave, and the Lord hath taken away. . . . Blessed be the name of the Lord.

In all these things, Job sinned not by his lips; nor spoke he any foolish thing against God.

By the industry of Griselda and the form of that industry— spinning—Petrarch has strengthened Boccaccio's identification of Griselda with the "mulier fortis" of Proverbs. By associating her on the one hand with the love of Mary Magdalene for Christ— and ultimately with the love of the "sponsa" of the Song of Songs —and on the other with the patience of Job, Petrarch has made her a formidable spiritual antagonist. Only one more element is necessary—the source of her strength. This Petrarch meets by changing Boccaccio's "fanticella della casa" to "ancilla."[45] He thereby makes an allusion to the "Ecce ancilla Domini" of the Annunciation (Luke I, 38), and hence to Mary, the supreme example of humility. To the patience of Job is added the humility of Mary. These two virtues—in the words of Petrarch's French translator, "humilité et pacience"[46]—are of some significance in this context, because they were considered specifics against tempta- tion—humility winning from God the gift of grace, and grace in turn conferring patience, the strength to bear adversity.[47]

Although Petrarch has, by successive allusions, created of Griselda an allegorical figure of the soul overcoming the tempta- tions of prosperity and adversity in pursuit of its heavenly goal, Walter presents a far more difficult problem. In the work of his predecessor Boccaccio, Petrarch had available a quite credible—if quite hateful—Walter. However, Petrarch's Walter is introduced as a model youth, noble in spirit and in blood. In accordance

with his nobility of spirit, he suffers progressively over the sufferings he inflicts upon his wife. Yet why does he inflict these sufferings? There is no real answer. In the first temptation, his
motivation is labelled "cupiditas"; in the second "curiositas"; in
the third a kind of continuation of both. In desperation, the
French translator pounces upon "merencolie."[48] It would doubtless be possible to fit all these terms into a pattern of abnormal
medieval psychology, but the truth would seem to be that the
uncertainty in Walter's motivation is attributable essentially to
Petrarch's limited interest in lending verisimilitude to the story
as story.

On the symbolic level, Walter should have fared infinitely
better, but he does not. It may be that Petrarch's inordinate passion for allegorical women affected his treatment of Walter, but
in any case Walter does not emerge much more consistently as a
symbolic figure than as a human one. In regard to Walter,
Petrarch seems to have boxed himself. To make the three temptations meaningful, they must be temptations. Accordingly, Walter
is said to be resolved to tempt Griselda in a rather grand Satanic
manner. His intention is described as "altius et iterum atque
interum retentandi."[49] The stated program of repeated and ever
mounting temptations is very impressive. Since the reader to
whom Petrarch addresses his *Epistola* is evidently expected to be
aware of the text with which Petrarch concludes his story, to the
effect that God tempts no one, "ipse neminem temptat" (James 1,
13), he must anticipate from Walter a superbly demonic per-
formance. However, Petrarch has introduced Walter as a noble
youth, and the language in which he describes Walter seems to
reflect his own uncertainties as to what significance to attach to
him. Boccaccio, despite his harsh words concerning Walter, has
never in his own version introduced him as a demonic figure.
Walter puts his wife to the test ("pruova"), but he is never said
to tempt. Petrarch, however, seems to vacillate between an artistic
concern to make the three "proofs" of Boccaccio actual temptations, and a kind of sentimental concern that his own protagonist
Walter should not exceed the bounds of decency. In consequence,
Petrarch's language varies, and falls into peculiar patterns. In the
first temptation [III], his initial declaration of unlimited temptation is qualified by the acceptable term "prove" ("experiendi").

In the second temptation [IV], his motivation is, as has been noted, described as "curiositas." When, at the end of the second temptation, he resolves once more to press forward, his goal is again described as "experiendi." In the third and last temptation, however, that of Griselda herself, his intention is stated without qualification—"retemptare."[50] At this point, Walter would, in terms of connotation, appear fully diabolic. However, it is in this same temptation that Walter cannot contain himself from weeping copiously.[51] If Walter tempts, he cannot be a God-figure; he can, however, be diabolic, which would accord perfectly with the Job allusion. The difficulty here is that devils don't weep over human suffering. In the extended Job narrative, although no reliable data are available, it would be safe to assume that Satan's laundry expenses were minimal.

As a diabolic figure, therefore, Walter turns out to be unsatisfactory, and this may be due in part to Petrarch's evident wish to give him another symbolic dimension, that of Fortune. As has been previously noted, the idea of Fortune is first introduced in the humble meals, "fortune congruas," which Griselda dutifully prepares for her old father, and which serve as a symbol of their low estate; again, in the scene of her abrupt marriage, when Griselda is, by command of Walter, stripped of her old clothes, the stripping is, as has been noted, connected with the idea of Fortune. Conversely, when, at Walter's command, she is sent back to her old home, she strips herself of everything she possessed in her new home—with the exception of her shift, and that she has to bargain for. As she proceeds on her way, barefoot and semi-naked, the people who in tears accompany her curse Fortune.[52] After she arrives at her father's house, she acts with such humility that "no vestige of her prosperous fortune remained visible."[53] In these two scenes, the two sides of Fortune's wheel are clearly indicated, and Walter, who professes to be acting under the compulsion his great "fortune" imposes upon him, is, in reality, the actuator of Fortune. Whatever prosperity and adversity befall Griselda are entirely of his doing. Furthermore, nakedness, which has had in Boccaccio an implicit relationship to the adversity of Fortune, is suddenly realized in the Job allusion introduced by Petrarch. However, before she returns naked to her father's house, it is important to observe in Griselda's semi-nudity that it is she who strips herself ("coram cunctis sese exuens")[54]—in other words, symbolically she has actively complied with the will of him who governs her fortune.

In comparison, Griselda's third stripping, which takes place in the final scene of the supposed wedding banquet, seems rather bare. For a second time Griselda's antique vestments are removed and replaced by new ones. Yet Walter does not command, nor is Fortune mentioned. There is a quite real scene of human joy, and the reader is informed that the revelry was greater than at the original marriage of Walter and Griselda; moreover, that they lived happily ever afterwards in "ingenti pace"—one of Petrarch's sporadic and not very well integrated[55] allusions to the theme of peace. In the final and supposedly climactic scene, Walter has thus been largely divested of the supernatural. In any case, it is difficult to make of Walter a consistent figure on any level. Sometimes he is Satanic, sometimes a personification of Fortune—or perhaps more properly the power behind Fortune—sometimes a kind of sentimental sadist. The introduction of the James 1, 13, text concerning temptation rules out Walter as a God-figure, but he is also never quite Satanic. In the figure of Walter much of the supernatural has been suggested, but it is as a mortal that he ends up. This is convenient for the *a fortiori* argument with which Petrarch concludes. Addressing his readers, he says: If this woman could suffer the temptations a mortal husband inflicted upon her, how much more should you (my readers) suffer patiently and without murmuring the corrective scourges which God, who tempts no one, inflicts.

There is one further matter to note. Petrarch is addressing himself in particular to his male readership, because he finds it of no avail to urge the "women of our time" to imitate the patience of Griselda.[56] Out of this is to come the Clerk's concluding "song" to Alice of Bath.

I I I

When Harry Bailly calls upon the Clerk to tell a tale, Harry also inadvertently provides something of a clue as to what is to follow:

> "Sire Clerk of Oxenford," oure Hooste sayde,
> "Ye ryde as coy and stille as dooth a mayde . . .
> I trowe ye studie aboute som sophyme . . . (IV [E], 1–5)

Although it may not be precisely a "sophyme" he is meditating, the
Clerk has had much to meditate upon. Alice of Bath's last and
most dramatic triumph was over her fifth husband, who whether
it be "by aventure or caas," was a Clerk of Oxenford. The splendor of her victory, recounted in detail, was equalled only by the
utter degradation of clerk Jankyn's defeat.

> He yaf me al the bridel in myn honde,
> To han the governance of hous and lond,
> And of his tonge, and of his hond also;
> And made hym brenne his book anon right tho. (III [D], 813–816)

That a clerk of Oxford, citadel of antifeminism, should ever
have come to so ignominious a state is, to a clerk of Oxford,
unthinkable. But it is not simply that since each Oxford clerk
hangs with other that the Clerk of Oxenford is thereby being
hanged with Jankyn, there is a deeper source of indignation.
When Alice makes Jankyn burn his book, she causes him to
destroy the very symbol of his profession, and hence to proclaim
the victory of sheer female will over male reason. This is to strike
at all order. Not only, as the Clerk says:

> A wyf, as of hirself, nothing ne sholde
> Wille in effect, but as hir housbonde wolde. (720–721)

but the subjection of female will to male will is of divine ordinance, and a part of the order of the created universe. Moreover,
the ordinance which gave man his superior position was made
necessary by the inability of woman to govern herself.

In the Clerk's view, Alice has squeezed the universe into a
badly flattened ball with the wrong side up. A remedy must be
provided, and it is upon this, during the violent interchange
between the Friar and the Summoner, that the Clerk has been
quietly meditating. What he needs is a story which will assert the
ideal of hierarchical order against the heretical inversion of order
preached by Alice of Bath. Fortunately, there comes to his mind
a tale of "Fraunceys Petrak" concerning one Griselda—a marvel-

lous woman, in every way consonant with the clerical ideal of womanhood—who not only successfully resists the temptation to break down by self-assertion the order of marriage, but who, in her humility and patience, mirrors the soul which, against all impediments, wins its way to heavenly reward. Besides, the Clerk seems to remember that this devout tale contains a possibly useful animadversion upon modern women—a good woman, in these days who shall find one? It sounds delicious. The Clerk has, in his silent way, found his story, and Alice, in a somewhat less quiet way, has found her match. "Clericus est mutus/ Licet ingenio sit acutus."

The tale the Clerk tells[57] is, of course, by "Fraunceys Petrak," but it has been considerably altered for the Clerk's benefit by one Geoffrey Chaucer, a fellow pilgrim on the road to Canterbury. In general, these alterations are not so much changes as clarifications and amplifications of what is to be found in Petrarch. They may perhaps be classified under three headings: theme, structure, and connotative language.

Petrarch's theme is distinct enough, except where he touches upon the Augustinian idea of peace as a symbol of order. As has been observed, this he does in a tentative and unstructured manner,[58] doubtless because his essential concern, inherited from Boccaccio, is the presentation of the movement of the soul toward its desired object—the Celestial Bridegroom. Chaucer, however, thinking in terms of his creation, the Clerk, and of the emotions generated in the Clerk by the inversion of marital order preached by Alice of Bath, takes as his theme order, and order as it ought to exist[59] in the marital relationship. As the Clerk sees it, marriage, possessing its own divinely ordained order, and as such a kind of microcosm of universal order, is a proper theater in which the drama of divine order and human disorder can be played out. Chaucer accepts his judgment. In Parts I and II of the *Clerk's Tale*, order predominates in the separate worlds of the two principals. After their marriage at the end of Part II, they are said to live in "Goddes pees . . . ful esily" (423); in Parts III, IV, V, and half of VI, order is brought under stress by the temptation to disorder; in the second half of Part VI, the triumph of order is celebrated, and at the end Walter and Griselda again live in

"pees and reste" (1132). Walter's son also was fortunate in marriage, and lived in "rest and pees" (1137), but this happy condition was due to his perception that modern women could not
suffer what Griselda did. This caustic observation, derived from
Petrarch, then leads to the Clerk's Envoy directed at Alice of
Bath. The terms "peace" and "reste" are, in the prevailing Augustinian theology of fourteenth-century England, symbolic of
order.[60] At every point in the *Clerk's Tale*, the idea of order is
central.

The structure Chaucer uses is directly dependent upon that
of Petrarch. As has been observed, Petrarch imposes upon the
whole of his work a triple division by the simple but effective use
of "Satis" at the beginning of the three temptations, and "Satis"
at the conclusion.[61] Chaucer observes this general division exactly.
In his version, "This is ynogh, Grisilde myn" (365) occurs at the
beginning of the temptations, and "This is ynogh, Grisilde myn"
(1051) at the end of the temptations. In this there is little to be
observed except that Chaucer translated faithfully, as did the
French translator—"C'est assez" occurs at precisely the same
points.[62] However, Chaucer did what the French translator, who
customarily followed Petrarch word for word, did not. He imposed
upon the three temptations so contained within this general structure an absolutely consistent and formulaic structure.[63] In each
temptation scene, there are three parts. First comes the evolution
of the temptation. Walter is overcome by an ungovernable urge
to tempt his wife; he states the temptation, which invariably
involves a loss to Griselda and purportedly to himself. More
important, it is invariably a loss for which Griselda can in no way
see herself morally responsible—hence an unjust loss calculated to
arouse angered protests. Following this, Walter presents the necessity for the loss in an upside-down argument in which the term
"peace" is prominent. Almost simultaneous with the argument
for the necessity of the loss is an exhortation to accept the loss in
patience, because it is the "lord's" will or pleasure that Griselda
accept what has purportedly been imposed upon him. In two of
the three temptations, both argument and exhortation are so
closely linked as to occur in a single stanza. The second part of
the temptation scene is the reaction of Griselda. There is invari-

ably pain and shock, but the temptation to anger and reproach is conquered, and Griselda's obedience to her husband's will is conveyed in a speech which, with the same invariability as the movement of the temptation, shows her obedience to be motivated purely by love. The third and last part of the temptation scene is the gradual return to the state of order which prevailed before the temptation was made.

This formulaic procedure is at the base of Chaucer's artistic method in the *Clerk's Tale*. By absolute consistency of the formulaic repetition, the pattern of temptation is engraved more deeply on the reader's or auditor's mind; within the pattern so established, by a widening of allusion and by the progressive association of certain highly connotative words and images with each of the principals, their characters gain the meanings intended. As in Petrarch, and to a lesser extent Boccaccio, the characters are not characters in the normal sense, but accretions of the connotative words and allusions associated with them.[64]

What the Clerk initially does is to camouflage his intended hideous revenge upon Alice of Bath by carrying the Pilgrims off to a land strange to them, and to places even stranger—"in special" to "Mount Vesulus" and the "Poo" (47–48)—places with which they could hardly be expected to be very familiar. The author of his story is "Fraunceys Petrak," another strange one, whom the Clerk represents as the victim of mortality and a bad rhetorical style. His diversion completed, the Clerk enters upon his story. The protagonist is the youthful Marquis of Saluzzo, who is loved and feared by noble and commoner alike:

> Therwith he was, to speke as of lynage,
> The gentilleste yborn of Lumbardye,
> A fair persone, and strong, and yong of age,
> And ful of honour and of curteisye;
> Discreet ynogh his contree for to gye,
> Save in somme thynges that he was to blame . . . (71–76)

What he is to blame in is that he gives no thought except to his immediate pleasure, his "lust present," which takes the conventional form of hunting and hawking. To the provision of an heir, he appears to have given no thought whatsoever, and his people are understandably disturbed. Though "obeisant, ay redy to his hond" (66), the very fact of their obedience imposes upon him the reciprocal obligation of securing the succession. With "pitous herte," his people in a group approach him. The argument presented by their spokesman is exquisitely deferential. Marriage would be for a man of Walter's high estate a condition of "soveraynetee, noght of servyse" (114). However, the people are but making a request, and to Walter the spokesman says:

> "And ye, my lord, to doon right as yow leste" (105)

and he continues, "If it be your will

> "That for to been a wedded man yow leste;
> Thanne were youre peple in sovereyn hertes reste." (111–112)

The Marquis's heart is touched by their humble plea:

> Hir meeke preyere and hir pitous cheere
> Made the markys herte han pitee . . . (141–142)

and he immediately grants their request. Whereupon,

> . . . they, with humble entente, buxomly,
> Knelynge upon hir knees ful reverently,
> Hym thonken alle . . . (186–188)

Concerning the wedding, all "to his commandement obeye," and busy themselves "To doon unto the feeste reverence" (194–196). So highly hierarchical a "here on hille/ Hit were now grete nye to neuen."[65]

In this first scene of Walter amongst his retainers, the principal words as regards his vassals are "obeisaunce," "mekenesse," "humilite" (reinforced by "buxomnesse"), and "reverence."[66] Their attitude toward Walter is further conveyed by the symbolic gesture of the bended knee. All of these suggest not only acceptance of authority, but willing acceptance of authority. However, although Marquis Walter, the possessor of authority, is, as in Petrarch, presented in quite standard terms as a noble and virtually blameless youth, he is also presented as being, for his subjects, the object both of love and of fear. Such a balance represented the medieval ideal of the ruler—justice tempered by mercy—and in this first scene Walter acts in a quite irreproachable fashion.

His pity for his people—"myn owene peple deere" (143)—and his ready acknowledgment of their request make him look like the Theseus of the *Knight's Tale*—"For pitee renneth soone in gentil herte" (I [A], 1761). On the other hand, there is about the noble youth something of the ominous. In the very meticulousness of the decorum with which the people approach their "lord," there is more than a suggestion that there is indeed in Walter something to fear. To this may be added the introduction of the highly important word "grucche" into the oath he requires of his people:

> "And forthermoore, this shal ye swere, that ye
> Agayn my choys shul neither grucche ne stryve . . ." (169–170)

To "grucche" is not simply to grumble, but to complain wrongly against higher authority—very often God.[67]

By the end of Part I, the ambivalence of Walter's character has been established. Through his compliance with the will of his people, and through the love and pity he feels for them, he can be viewed as something of an ideal ruler. However, through the connotation of the words associated with him: "lord," and particularly "lust"—whatever may be his pleasure—he is as implicitly threatening as Boccaccio's original protagonist was explicitly threatening.[68]

In Part I, Walter has held the center of the stage. In Part II, however, although the arrogance and captiousness of Walter remain evident—particularly in the irreducible minimum of effort devoted to obtaining a bride and the absolute maximum devoted to the splendor of the wedding feast in honor of the minimal bride—it is nevertheless Griselda who herself holds the stage and upon whom all eyes are constrained to focus. Walter has been eyeing her for a considerable while, but knowing the time for his marriage will inevitably come, it is "in sad wyse" (237) that he observes her, and what he finds inescapably attractive is "rype and sad corage" (220), as evidenced in the reverence with which she devotes herself to the care of her ancient father. It is therefore not entirely astonishing that Walter should have perceived in her the essence of what he wanted from his people, and should have demanded from her that essence—not only obedience, but obedience performed with a willingness which admits of no question as to the ultimate rightness of the thing willed. Thus when Walter advisedly demands of Griselda:

> ". . . be ye redy with good herte
> To al my lust, and that I frely may,
> As me best thynketh, do yow laughe or smerte,
> And nevere ye to *grucche* it, nyght ne day?" (351–354)

her reply is what he expects: "As ye wole youreself, right so wol I" (361).

Although this proclamation of unity of will under other circumstances would appear rather striking, it is as noted only an individual version of the comparable oath demanded by Walter of his subjects as a whole. In Walter's domain, "grucching" against the will of Walter is not an acceptable practice, and Walter's subjects seem to accept this as a primary fact of life. What does, however, distinguish Griselda from the others who kneel to hear what is the lord's will is a sequence of two allusions. The first is to the familiar "mulier fortis," but conveyed in one of the most dizzying passages in literature:

> A fewe sheep, spynnynge, on feeld she kepte;
> She wolde noght been ydel til she slepte. (223–224)

The second is a much more powerful allusion, and one of Chaucer's own creation. This is an allusion to the Nativity. According to Luke (II, 7), Mary had simply laid the Christ child in a manger, there being no room at the inn. However, through the immense influence of the prophetic book of Isaiah, from the verse "The ox has known his owner, and the ass his master's crib" (I, 3), the manger gained two permanent inhabitants—the ox and the ass. They are almost invariably represented as being present together at the Nativity, although the ox tends to be the more prominent, sometimes to the exclusion of the ass. When the Clerk explains Griselda's virtue as an example of God's ability to send "His grace into a litel oxes stalle" (207), and when he describes Griselda as kneeling in an "oxes stalle" to hear "the lordes wille" (291–294), the learned cleric of Oxford has amassed a great deal of connotative language. In the immensely popular pseudo-Bonaventura *Meditations on the Life of Christ*, written toward the end of the thirteenth century and still extant in more than two hundred manuscripts,[69] Gabriel kneels before God on accepting his mission to Mary;[70] after the Angelic Salutation, with its "gratia plena," Mary kneels—but only after she has sufficiently overcome her humility to accept her unique position among women. With the angel Gabriel standing before her,

> . . . sche kneled doun with soueryn deuocioun/ and holdynge up bothe hir hondes/ and liftynge up hir eiȝen to heuen/ seide these wordes: Loo here the handmayden and the seruaunt of my lorde . . .[71]

Following which Christ, presumably in heaven, kneels in accepting his painful mission on earth. In conclusion, both Mary and Gabriel kneel.[72] At the Nativity, as at the Annunciation, Mary kneels, this time before the crèche of the infant Christ, and in an "oxes stalle." The ox and the ass also kneel, and for a very practical purpose:

> And anone the Oxe and the Asse/ knelynge doun/ leyden her mowthes on the cracche/ brethynge at her neses vppon the child/ as they knewen by resoun that in that colde tyme the childe so symply hiled had nede to be hatte in that manere.[73]

Through allusion and symbolic gesture, the "ancilla" allusion of Petrarch has been expanded to encompass both the Annunciation and the Nativity. The humility of Mary reinforces the humility of Griselda and touches upon a higher form of order.

However, the Clerk is, in view of his ultimate goal, not interested in making Griselda symbolic of the celestial to the exclusion of the earthly. Griselda is presented in a quite human context. Although people judge her heaven-sent (440), it is because she applies herself to the "commune profit" (431)—in *Piers Plowman* the subject of the rat and mouse parliament[74]—and so brings her people into "reste and ese" (434). To a much further degree, she devotes herself to the well-being of Walter. Together they live "in Goddes pees . . . ful esily" (423). In the prevailing Augustinian theology of the Clerk's day, "peace" and "rest" are symbols of universal and perfect order,[75] and the Clerk has made effective use of them.

In Part III, the first of the temptations, the earlier ambivalence of Walter's character seems to disappear. He is twice

explicitly said to tempt (452; 458) and the temptation is to anger
—to cause Griselda to "grucche" over the injustice willed by her
lord in having her daughter taken from her and ostensibly put to
death, so that her lord may live in the tranquility to which he is
accustomed. To "grucche" would be to break the marital oath
Walter demanded of her, and to which she assented. The precise
nature of the temptation is, as will be indicated, highly important;
it is, however, hardly less important than the act of temptation
itself.

As has been earlier noted, temptation is no part of God, and
he who tempts thereby gives evidence of membership in the
opposite party. Aside from his activity of tempting, there is at
least one other respect in which Walter is a diabolic figure. A
characteristic of the Satanic psychology is hatred of the order of
God and a constant attempt to invert or pervert—to turn "up-so-
doun" that order.[76] Walter's argument to Griselda as to why her
daughter must be done away with is a kind of model of this
psychology:

> ". . . I desire, as I have doon bifore,
> To lyve my lyf with hem in reste and pees.
> I may nat in this caas be recchelees;
> I moot doon with thy doghter for the beste,
> Nat as I wolde, but as my peple leste." (486–490)

This is indeed order turned upside down. It is precisely in "reste
and pees" that Walter has been living. What the people are purported to "leste" is nothing more than his own "lust." Yet not
everything about him suggests the diabolic. He urges Griselda to
keep her oath, which both equate with "pacience" (495). He is
glad not when she yields to his temptation, but when she rejects
it (512). He also feels a measure of pity over the pain he has
inflicted (579).

At first glance, Griselda would appear to be treated as the
counterpart to Walter as tempter. Her humility is stressed and to
a lesser degree her patience. When exposed to the temptation
posed by the removal of her daughter:

> . . . as a lamb she sitteth meke and stille,
> And leet this crueel sergeant doon his wille. (538–539)

In this there would seem to be a rather clear allusion to Isaiah LIII, 7:

> He shall be led as a sheep to the slaughter and shall be dumb as a lamb before his shearer, and he shall not open his mouth.

Hence in Griselda's endurance of adversity there is more than a suggestion of the Christ figure.[77] However, in the nature of Walter's temptation there is possibly contained a more immediate allusion. Despite the authoritative pronouncement of James (I, 13) that God tempts no man, God is said to have tempted Abraham—"tentavit Deus Abraham" (Genesis XXII, 1)—and in a manner exactly comparable to the temptation of Griselda. Abraham is commanded to offer up his only begotten son, Isaac, as a sacrifice to God. In the very popular play, *The Sacrifice of Isaac*,[78] which is believed to have been current in the fourteenth century,[79] the temptation Abraham suffers seems to have changed from the obvious one of disobedience to God's commandment to something rather more subtle. The audience knew that God would not have Isaac killed and that Abraham would not disobey God's commandment. The temptation in the play therefore is not to disobey God, but to "groche" against the incomprehensible commandment which would take from God's faithful follower that which is dearest to him. Accordingly, Abraham in anguish over the prospect of killing what he loves best in the world, says:

> And yit, my dere Lord, I am sore a-ferd
> To groche ony thyng a-gens yowre wyll.[80]

Isaac, when informed that it is God's commandment that he be killed, serenely remarks to Abraham:

> Now, fader, agens my Lordes wyll
> I wyll never groche, lowd nor styll.
> He [God] mygth a sent me a better desteny
> Yf it had a be hys plecer.[81]

The Doctor who appears at the end of the play declares that this story is presented to show:

> How we schuld kepe, to owr po[we]re
> Goddes commawmentes withowt grochyng.[82]

It is Walter's will that the daughter be slain—"this wol I" (493) —and it is the essential part of Griselda's oath that she will carry out Walter's will, whatever it may be, and "never to grucche it, nyght ne day" (354). Griselda has sworn to accord herself entirely to Walter's "lust" (352); Isaac shows himself in accord with God's "plecer."

In this first temptation scene, both Griselda and Walter have taken on further meaning, but in quite opposite fashions: Griselda has become through allusions to the lamb and to the sacrifice of Isaac a kind of personification of patience, and these allusions are striking because essentially visual. However in terms of sheer verbal weight—repetition—it is actually the antecedent virtue of humility which is given the greater emphasis.[83] However, it is neither patience nor humility which forms her true motivation—it is love, and love expressed in the romantic "heart" idiom.

> "Ther may no thyng, God so my soule save,
> Liken to yow that may displese me;
> Ne I desire no thyng for to have,
> Ne drede for to leese, save oonly yee.
> This wyl is in myn herte, and ay shal be . . ." (505–509)

Griselda is very much the "mulier fortis" updated to modern fourteenth-century standards. However, although Griselda does gain in definition, the scene in its totality has the effect of increasing the ambivalence of Walter. Initially he is explicitly the tempter, yet it is a curious tempter who argues against his own temptations. If the Abraham and Isaac analogy holds, Walter is at the conclusion of Part III an even stranger interrelation of the demonic and the divine.

In the second temptation (Part IV), whatever divinity has previously been glimpsed in Walter seems to disappear. Previously Walter's "lust" has to some degree been balanced by "piteé" and "routhe"; likewise the diabolic has been partially offset by suggestions of the divine. In the second temptation, however, neither "pitee" nor "routhe" is in evidence, but in contrary fashion "lust" has been reinforced by a word of like meaning, "plesaunce," which has scarcely appeared before. These two words are associated with Walter some fourteen times. In three lines they occur together, as when Griselda accedes to Walter's will to have her son taken from her:

> "Dooth youre plesaunce, I wol youre lust obeye." (658)[84]

These words are joined in four instances by a word which never appears in connection with Walter before or after—"crueel."[85] Bunched together within a single section of the poem, "lust," "plesaunce," and "crueel" make of Walter a most forbidding personage. What one here sees is Walter the tyrant, but a bewildered tyrant, whose utter astonishment over Griselda's continued acquiescence in the murder of her children drives him to wonder whether she is not herself of "crueel corage" (692), a doubt which hastens him on to the final temptation, in which it will be seen what Griselda herself is made of. Despite Walter's incredulity, Griselda is in the second temptation very much like what she was in the first temptation. She is as usual associated with humility and patience, but the ratio is reversed. Her humility is hardly mentioned, but her patience increases as the need for it increases.[86] From her language, such as the line quoted above (658), and from her sole distinct use of irony:

> "Naught greveth me at al,
> Though that my doughter and my sone be slayn,—
> At youre commandement, this is to sayn.
> I have noght had no part of children tweyne
> But first siknesse, and after, wo and peyne." (647–651)

it is apparent that she sees Walter possessed by a cruel wilfulness, and believes her children dead as a result of that wilfulness. Only an incredible patience proceeding from an incredible love keeps her from breaking her bond:

> "Deth may noght make no comparisoun
> Unto youre love." (666–667)

One further matter is of importance here. In this second temptation scene, the term "adversity" has become defined. In the previous temptation, Griselda is said to have "endured al adversitee" (565), which would seem to mean the pain she experienced over the loss of her daughter, and future undefined adversity which she seems, not entirely incorrectly, to foresee. In the second temptation, she is resolved "the adversitee of Fortune al t'endure" (756). Since the adversity Griselda suffers has as its source Walter, it would appear that in one way or another Walter is to be associated with Fortune.

It is important at this point to note the peculiarity of the organization accepted or created by Chaucer. Parts I and II each have distinct functions, and each initiates and concludes a definable if limited action: the necessity of marriage is represented to Walter, and he agrees; having already chosen his bride, he marries her. Temptations are conventionally three,[87] and to each of the first two—the son and the daughter—a separate section is devoted (Parts III and IV). The third temptation though double, could have been contained in Part V,[88] and Part VI devoted entirely to Griselda's triumph. Chaucer chose not to do this; instead he assigned the first part of the temptation—Griselda's being cast out—to Part V; and to Part VI both Griselda's victory over the second part of the final temptation—her return to Walter's palace for purposes of utter humiliation (939–1057)—and her reward in the scene of the marriage banquet (1058–1127). The reason Chaucer preferred this order is, I think, that it provides a larger area for the third and last temptation of Griselda—an area in which Chaucer gives final definition to the characters of Walter and Griselda through the employment of what might be called connotational subtraction and addition. As has been pointed out, Parts I through IV are accretive, in that certain key words are constants, and to these key words are added further connotative words and allusions. Each character constantly gains. This is not true, however, of Parts V and VI. In these two sections, subtraction as well as addition is present. By the simultaneous use of both, the pattern of connotation is made to move in conformity with the action of the poem.

At the beginning of Part V, when Walter issues his genial eviction notice, there is immediately evident a change both in his own language and in the language used to describe him. Although this, his third temptation, is said to proceed according to his "wikke usage" (785), the word "cruel," which has appeared so strongly in the previous temptation does not appear. Of the other highly connotative words associated with him—"tempt," "lust," "plesaunce"—the first two receive only a single mention, and the last is used as much to indicate Griselda's concern for Walter's "plesaunce" as it is to indicate Walter's concern for his own "plesaunce,"[89] and yet in the past, due observance of his lordly prerogatives has been for Walter a matter of great moment. Further, he feels real "pitee" (893) at sending his wife forth in her seminaked condition. Griselda has, however, perceived no change in Walter and is herself unchanged. When Griselda departs the palace of Walter, her lord, she is the same in love, in humility, and in patience, and yet the temptation to curse the all too evident source of her deprivations must have been intense. As she returns home, barefoot and in her smock, over the same road she had before passed splendidly clothed and splendidly mounted, the people follow her weeping, "And Fortune ay they cursen as they goon" (898). Griselda's old father, in concert, curses the day he was born (902–904).[90] Like Job, Griselda fails to heed her comforters and curses not at all. At parting, what she has had to say is not the expression of angered reproach, but of an infinite humility and an infinite patience:

> "Naked out of my fadres hous," quod she,
> "I cam, and naked moot I turne agayn." (871–872)

One sees here how perfectly Chaucer has carried out what was implied in Petrarch's identical Job allusion. By making Walter consistently the tempter, a step Petrarch never quite took, the story of Griselda becomes the story of Job: the temptation is the same; the means of temptation are the same—the giving and the taking away of children, possessions, worldly position; the reaction to temptation is the same—refusal to become elated with what has been given, refusal to question the justice behind the suffering inflicted by deprivation. Also, for the first time in Chaucer's version the means by which both Job and Griselda are able to withstand temptation are made clear. The patience of Job is proverbial, but at the end of Part V, he is not his usual patient self: "Men speke of Job, and moost for his humblesse" (932). The making of Job an exemplar of the virtue of humility is not without a plan. When returned in the most ignominious fashion to the greatest poverty, Griselda is able to remain a "flour of wyfly pacience" (919) because, like Job, "Hire goost was evere in pleyn humylitee" (926). Petrarch's French translator puts the matter quite clearly. Because in her father's rude house Griselda dwells in a state of "humilité et pacience," no sign of sorrow over her past "prosperité" is ever permitted to appear. As in Petrarch, implicitly, and his French translator explicitly, humility and patience are the virtues against which temptation finds itself powerless.[91]

However, if the Job allusion serves to define Griselda, it is even more effective in defining the complex confusion—taken in its basic sense—which is Walter. The most readily determinable element in Walter is temptation. At the beginning of each of the three "trials" to which Griselda is put, he is said to tempt.[92] In the weakening number of connotative words which define Walter in Part V, this remains a constant. Almost ironically, he is said to be resolved:

> . . . yet his wyf to tempte moore
> To the outtreste preeve of hir corage . . . (786–787)

If the existence in Walter of a kind of muddled diabolism were in need of further proof, it would be forthcoming from the Job allusion. If Job is a figure for Griselda, it would make no sense if Satan were not an opposite figure for Walter.

If this aspect of Walter has all along been relatively clear, another has not, and this is Fortune. In Part IV, it is said of Griselda that she

> Disposed was, this humble creature,
> The adversitee of Fortune al t'endure . . . (755–756)

In Part V, her being cast out of the castle is, as Walter tells her, a "strook of Fortune" (812). Finally, the people who accompany Griselda from her former palace to her immediate hut curse Fortune (898). What they are actually cursing is, of course, Walter, because in this and in every other case, the power which governs the prosperity or adversity of Fortune, as regards Griselda, is Walter.

Logically, therefore, Fortune must be an aspect of the composite that goes by the name of Walter. Beyond simple association, however, what evidence is there that Fortune is to be understood as an aspect of Walter? The answer would seem to be a further association contained in the word "naked." When Griselda leaves the house of Walter, she leaves stripped of all that she most cherished. The Job image is here as moving and as appropriate a one as could be imagined. However, the very language of the Job allusion would inevitably suggest to the medieval reader an extremely famous passage in an extremely famous book—the *Consolation of Philosophy* of Boethius. In this passage, Boethius, imprisoned for treason, is found by Lady Philosophy bewailing his ill-fortune. In order to demonstrate to Boethius the folly of his complainings—after all, he faces nothing of consequence except having his head squeezed until his eyes pop out —Philosophy assumes the character of Fortune, and demands to know what charge of injustice he can bring against her:

Whan that nature brought the foorth out of thi modir wombe, I resceyved the nakid . . . and I envyrounde the with al the habundaunce and schynynge of alle goodes than ben in my ryght. Now it liketh me to withdrawe myn hand.[93]

The parallels of language to the Job allusion as Chaucer inherited it from Petrarch are striking, but what is more striking are the parallels to the Job text itself:

Naked came I out of my mother's womb, and naked shall I return thither. The Lord gave, and the Lord hath taken away. As it hath pleased the Lord, so is it done. (I, 21)

Taken together, the two texts conform exactly to the pattern of "lord" Walter's actions. He receives her naked, stripped of her worn peasant clothes, apparels her richly, and leads her into a life of great "prosperitee." When it is his "lust" and "plesaunce," he withdraws his hand, and in it, all that he has given. Griselda, having been clothed in shining abundance, is then sent forth into the nakedness of adversity.

From the above, it would seem reasonably clear that the actions of Walter are so closely parallel to those of Fortune that something more than simple association exists between them. In like fashion, something more than simple association exists between Walter and temptation. Walter is explicitly the tempter, and on both sides of Fortune's wheel he has put Griselda to the test.[94] As Walter himself summarizes it in the final scene of the story, "In greet estaat, and povrelich arrayed" (1055). However, neither Fortune nor Satan is a free agent; they are respectively willing and unwilling servants of God. Although nothing godlike about Walter is specifically evident, there are two factors which may indicate a highly latent divinity. The first is his conduct of the temptations. He announces their beginning and their end; he counsels Griselda to take in patience her sufferings as something willed by a higher power; he is filled with joy when she does take her sufferings in patience—when she successfully resists the temptation to break her marital oath, and so keeps intact the bond between them. Second, the adversity to which Walter subjects Griselda is real only to the extent of the pain she experiences, and the accompanying temptation to complain against the injustice suffered. Neither her daughter nor her son has been killed, nor has Walter taken a new wife. All of it is unreal.

In the view of the present writer, Walter is a composite of all the supernatural forces to which medieval man felt himself exposed. He is Fortune, raising aloft and casting down; stripping and clothing. He is Satan, making of the vicissitudes of Fortune appropriate temptations. He is God, the master of both, proving his creature, but always with her, urging against the act which would sever the bond between them, revealing ultimately that the world possesses no reality.

The principal function of Part V is probably the definition in symbolic terms of the characters of Walter and Griselda. By the skillful use of subtraction and addition of connotative terms and allusions, the course of the action has been effectively indicated. Griselda's love, her humility, and her patience have been stressed, primarily her humility. Through her association with the indomitable Job, her moral victory is assured. Walter, though gaining in meaning, has, as indicated at the beginning of the present section, lost in power. The words that made him so menacing a figure—"crueel," "lust," "plesaunce"—have diminished or disappeared, but "lord" he remains.[95] Of Walter's conjectured symbolic triplicity, this one element remains stable throughout—"lord."[96] However, the image of Walter as cruel, self-willed tempter has progressively diminished. Conversely, there is an implication that Fortune, who, for Griselda, has previously covered her face with a cloud, is about to show the bright side of her constantly changing visage. Griselda has endured as much hardship as Fortune has immediately available, and the triumph of Griselda is at hand.

One further indication seems to point in the same direction. Griselda has, in the process of humbling herself to make room for the new bride, unobtrusively acquired a new descriptive term—"glad." When Walter informs her that she must leave and yield her place to the new bride, she replies: "Unto my fader gladly wol I wende . . ./For I wol gladly yelden hire my place" (832; 843). Previously, to remain obedient to Walter's wishes has occasioned excruciating pain; gladness in suffering is, even for Griselda, something new. Of glad obedience, Chaucer's Parson remarks:

Of pacience comth obedience. . . . / And understond wel that obedience is perfit, whan that a man dooth gladly and hastily, with good herte entierly, al that he sholde do. (x [I], 673–674)

What the Parson is here discussing is the obedience normally due one's spiritual and temporal lords. If such obedience be perfect, Griselda's must, in the circumstances imposed upon her, be triumphant.

When, at the beginning of Part VI, the Marquis summons Griselda immediately in advance of the supposed new bride's arrival, she kneels before him with "humble herte and glad visage" (949) and greets him with reverence. Walter announces pompously that since Griselda knows his "lust" and his "plesaunce," it is his will that she prepare the house accordingly. He bids her forthwith do her "devoir" (960–966). Even though this is not a new temptation and the temptation formula has already been observed for the third time at the beginning of Part V, this is for Walter an extremely short and bare speech. Walter has no hortatory address concerning the endurance of adversity.

The Clerk, as narrator, does not describe him as tempter, nor as cruel. All that is left of his panoply of connotation is "lust" and "plesaunce," which sound rather like echoes of the past than new assertions.[97] As a matter of fact, these last words of ill connotation cease to be associated with Walter, but turn up in the company of the folk who, earlier weeping and cursing Fortune, accompanied Griselda back to her humble cottage. Now, however, as they observe the splendor of the wedding procession, they shrewdly remark that Walter was no fool "thogh that hym leste / To chaunge his wyf" (986–987). They find "plesaunce" in viewing the beauty of the two children, and conjecture that more "plesant"[98] will be Walter's offspring, because of his new bride's high lineage (986–993). In one of his few self-revelations, the Clerk comments acidly:

> "O stormy peple! unsad and evere untrewe!
> Ay undiscreet and chaungynge as a fane!
> Delitynge evere in rumbul that is newe,
> For lyk the moone ay wexe ye and wane!
> Ay ful of clappyng, deere ynogh a jane!
> Youre doom is fals, youre constance yvele preeveth;
> A ful greet fool is he that on yow leeveth." (995–1001)

In contrast to the "stormy peple," Griselda reverently receives Walter's command that his pleasure be done, proffers the same devoted labor in behalf of his "lust," and reveals the same selfless love which has enabled her to suffer what she has suffered:

> "Nat oonly, lord, that I am glad," quod she,
> "To doon youre lust, but I desire also
> Yow for to serve and plese in my degree
> Withouten feyntyng, and shal everemo;
> Ne nevere, for no wele ne no wo,
> Ne shal the goost withinne myn herte stente
> To love yow best with al my trewe entente." (967–973)

After expressing her gladness at being offered the opportunity to please her lord, Griselda "with glad cheere" meets the bride at the gate; receives the noble guests with "so glad chiere" and such reverence (1013; 1016; 1021) that they wonder what kind of creature dwells beneath such mean and worn clothing.

Finally, after Griselda's appeal that her successor not be subjected to the "tormentynge"—literally, being put to the torture—which she has experienced, Walter's heart is touched with pity. He sees the "glad chiere" Griselda's patience has assumed and recognizes the "constance" and "stedfastnesse" (two relatively new additions to the Griselda connotative word-box[99]) his tormented wife has shown throughout, and proclaims: "This is ynogh, Grisilde myn." With that, all temptation ceases. Walter takes her in his arms, "and gan hire kesse" (1057). Griselda has triumphed.

As the Clerk describes it, the wedding feast at which Griselda's triumph is celebrated (1058–1127) is unaffectedly affecting. Griselda swoons "for pitous joye," and she who has kept her eyes dry throughout her trials, "pitously wepynge," embraces her children. Her emotive state is such that she almost exceeds in effusiveness Sir Thopas's horse:

> . . . with hire salte teeres
> She bathed bothe hire visage and hire heeres. (1084–1085)

The Clerk is overcome:

> O which a pitous thyng it was to se
> Hire swownyng and hire humble voys to heere! (1086–1087)

Having given final expression to her death-defying love for Walter:

> "Now rekke I nevere to been deed right heere;
> Sith I stonde in youre love and in youre grace . . ." (1090–1091)

she again swoons, with her children clutched to her bosom so tightly that it is only with the greatest difficulty that they can be extricated. The Clerk is again overcome as he describes the almost unbearable emotion of those who witnessed the scene:

> O many a teere on many a pitous face
> Doun ran of hem that stooden hire bisyde;
> Unnethe abouten hire myghte they abyde. (1104–1106)

Here sorrow ends and joy begins. In a complete reversal, it is now Walter who does his wife "plesaunce" (1111); again she is stripped—on this occasion rather more discreetly—and magnificently reclothed:

> Thus hath this pitous day a blisful ende! (1121)

All that has preceded has been only preparation for this final scene of the marriage feast, and the last stage of the preparation has been Griselda's glad obedience. When Griselda performs with "glad cheere" the most humiliating of tasks—as an outcast and in wretched clothes to prepare for and receive the ornately adorned bride who is to supplant her in the love of her lord—one feels that she has attained perfection. In the furnace of temptation whatever inferior alloys were in her soul—and they are difficult to find—have been purged away. She is now the pure gold she seemed. When her antique and worn garments are removed and she is arrayed "in a clooth of gold that brighte shoon" —a rare reference to color in the story—and a "coroune of many a riche stoon" placed upon her head (1117–1119), she is prepared for the supper of the Lamb.

Behind temptation and Fortune, the harsh mask in which Walter presents himself to her, Griselda has all along perceived a loving presence which she herself cannot cease to love; and through the perfecting of her love, her humility, and her patience the mask has become thinner and thinner until at last it is dropped. In the course of her temptations, she has seen as through a glass darkly an incomprehensible image: when Walter's mask falls away and all that had seemed lost is not, she sees face to face Him who is lord of temptation and lord of Fortune. By her triumph, she has entered into the joy of her lord.

Let us be glad and rejoice and give glory to him. For the marriage of the Lamb is come, and his wife hath prepared herself. . . . Blessed are they that are called to the marriage supper of the Lamb.[100]

What the Clerk has done is to present the gradual development of perfection, and to present the final consummation of perfection in a scene so melodramatic and so lachrymose as to ensure him complete possession of the emotions of his audience.

If Griselda's perfection be viewed as a figure of the human spirit struggling through prosperity and adversity to attain union with the heavenly bridegroom, it is her love which drives her on. Humility and patience are only what get her to the wedding. Griselda is the triumphant soul seen at the moment of her attainment of salvation. Yet in the emphasis upon her indestructible love for her husband, and her attainment of his love by humility and patience, she is not very different from the clerical ideal set before his daughters by the Knight of La Tour Landry. That such an ideal woman as a human and immediately available wife would be distasteful does not appear from the agonized outburst of the Merchant. As divine or human, she is perfection. Through the hortatory sentimentalism of the Clerk—whose customary form of speech is short and quick—the Pilgrims have been coerced into participating in the "pitous joye" of her triumph and union with the object of her unconquerable love. Her wondrous human presence, with angelic voices singing above, is everywhere felt.

It is at this, his chosen moment, that the Clerk descends upon the desecratress of clericality—Alice of Bath. He does not plunge down all at once, but rather floats down on dovelike wings. The Pilgrims are not denied the happy ending:

> Ful many a yeer in heigh prosperitee
> Lyven thise two in concord and in reste . . . (1128–1129)

nor the expected continuation of the noble familial line:

> His sone succedeth in his heritage
> In reste and pees, after his fader day,
> And fortunat was eek in mariage . . . (1135–1137)

Up to this point, the *Clerk's Tale* could, as has been suggested, be viewed as a kind of marital saint's legend, but deftly and gradually the tone begins to change. The reason Walter's son lived in "reste and pees" is that he did not follow his father's precedent of putting his wife "in greet assay" (1138). Petrarch therefore does not tell this story with the intent of urging present-day women to imitate Griselda's humility, because it is impossible. Petrarch's story is told simply that every person should be constant in adversity. The Clerk concludes, "Lat us thanne lyve in vertuous suffraunce" (1162).

In the Clerk's pious conclusion of his tale, the few implications that post-Griseldian womanhood might possess certain defects have been quite discreetly covered over. Suddenly, they emerge full-blown.

> But o word, lordynges, herkneth er I go:
> It were ful hard to fynde now-a-dayes
> In al a toun Grisildis thre or two;
> For if that they were put to swiche assayes,
> The gold of hem hath now so badde alayes
> With bras, that thogh the coyne be fair at ye,
> It wolde rather breste a-two than plye. (1163–1169)

The "now-a-dayes" is an echo of the "nostri temporis" of Petrarch,[101] and the difficulty of finding a Griselda an echo of the "Mulierem fortem quis inveniet?" of Proverbs. Good women have existed; there are even records of them. But:

> This world is nat so strong, it is no nay,
> As it hath been in olde tymes yoore . . . (1139–1140)

In its infertile old age, the world is producing perilously few "good women."

The clerical witticism on which the Clerk is drawing is to be found in fully developed form in Boccaccio's *De casibus*:

> I do not really believe . . . all women to be perverse. Who could doubt that in such a huge multitude there should not be found some dutiful, modest, extremely holy and fully worthy of the highest reverence? I grant that there are some Christian women in whom flourish vast integrity of mind, virginity, constancy, and other merits. I concede also that some pagan women merited the highest praise. Such women, who, when and if they can be found, are to be loved, cherished, and their virtues extolled beyond those of men. . . . But since they are extremely rare, lest, while we are seeking a Lucretia, we fall into the hands of a Calpurnia or a Sempronia, it is my opinion that one should flee from all of them.[102]

The pure gold of women's souls is now so full of bad alloys[103] that they could not endure what Griselda did without breaking under the strain. Therefore, since this is what modern women are like, men, being reasonable, should accept the fact. The Clerk then dedicates a song to Alice of Bath, whom God maintain "In heigh maistrie," which he will sing "with lusty herte, fressh and grene" (1172–1173). It begins:

> Grisilde is deed, and eek hire pacience
> And bothe atones buryed in Ytaille,
> For which I crie in open audience,
> No wedded man so hardy be t'assaille
> His wyves pacience in trust to fynde
> Grisildis, for in certain he shall faille.
> O noble wyves, ful of heigh prudence,
> Lat noon humylitee youre tonge naille,
> Ne lat no clerk have cause or diligence
> To write of yow a storie of swich mervaille
> As of Grisildis pacient and kynde,
> Lest Chichevache yow swelwe in hire entraille! (1177–1188)

Chichevache is of course the cow who devours patient wives, and whose sustenance is such that she resembles the ribbed sea sand. When in his song to Alice of Bath the Clerk urges, with superb hyperbolic irony, that all women acquire those virtues which will preserve them from the gaping jaws of Chichevache—impatience, anger, ill-temper, the use of any means to bring their husbands to abject submission—and when these same amiable virtues are those professed by Alice herself—the effectiveness of the Clerk's attack is hardly less apparent than its target. The Clerk has carefully constructed his female ideal Griselda by constant juxtaposition to Walter, the tyrant, who gradually becomes symbolic of the kinds of adversity the medieval human daily faced. Yet Griselda's love pierced the externals of adversity and by humility and patience—not by violence and coercion—conquered. When, in the envoy, Griselda is in turn counterposed to the female tyrant Alice professes herself to be, the result is devastating. All the old ideal is, the new woman is not. The beauty of the old order makes the new disorder something less than appealing. The Clerk's vengeance is complete, nor does the irrepressible Alice ever reply.

IV

The final juxtaposition—that of Alice of Bath and the Clerk—
is a kind of monument to Chaucer's humanism. Alice of Bath, the
new woman, whom the Clerk attacks for her profession of ideas
which would overturn the world of order he accepts, is, as one
learns from the story she tells, deeply rooted in the past. The
Clerk, who professes traditional Augustinian beliefs, is very
much of the future. He is not in humility devoting himself to the
feeding of God's sheep, nor in patience suffering what the Parson
suffers as a result of just such a commitment. He is pure scholar,
living on nothing for the sake of his studies, pursuing Aristotle
whose approach is essentially that of the scientific method—an
approach which is to bring down the whole complex structure he
has so clerically defended against Alice of Bath.

APPENDIX: "The Moral Responsibility of Griselda."

For the present day reader the greatest impediment to accepting Griselda as an ideal of womanhood is her obedience to
her husband's desire that she hand over her children to what she
has every reason to believe is brutal murder. The reaction of the
Pilgrims to the story of Griselda does not, however, seem to reflect horror, but rather the wondrous admiration appropriate to
the saint's legend. Harry Bailly sets the tone when he exclaims
"By Goddes bones,/ Me were levere than a barrel ale/ My wyf at
hoom had herd this legende ones."[1] If this were, as Robinson
suggests, the original ending of the tale,[2] the "legende" impression would appear the stronger.[3] One is forced to conclude that
some sort of idea, very present to the medieval mind, has in the
course of centuries become lost. Harry Bailly would hardly be
willing to yield up a precious barrel of ale[4] in exchange for his
wife's absorption of this tale if it had to do with anything resem-
bling female cruelty, concerning which Harry intimates
Goodelief is not entirely unknowledgeable.[5] The Merchant also
understands the tale in a quite opposite fashion. He sees a "long

and large difference" between Griselde's "grete pacience" and his newly wedded wife's "passyng crueltee."[6]

The missing idea may perhaps be one concerning the relationship of husband and wife which was evidently current in Chaucer's day and was not without a certain vitality in Milton's (see discussion below). In the *Book of the Knight of La Tour Landry*, occurs the following highly moral story. Three merchants become involved in an argument as to who has the most obedient wife. The test agreed on is the simple and efficacious one of the husband's commanding, without explanation, that his wife perform whatever it is his pleasure to command. The first merchant commands that his wife jump into a tub of water. The wife quite inexcusably questions why she should perform this rather unusual act and is appropriately buffeted. The same demand is made at the house of the second merchant, with the same outcome. When the three arrive at the house of the third merchant, dinner is upon the table, and the test is by agreement deferred until after dinner—although the third merchant ominously pronounces in the presence of all that whatever he commands shall be done. At this, his wife, who loves and fears him, is not a little astonished. His pronouncement made, the merchant addresses himself to the more immediate matter of the dinner before him. In so doing, he notices the absence of salt, and says to her "saul sur table." His disturbed wife, believing from what she has just heard, that this is the command darkly referred to, immediately leaps upon the table, and sends food, wine, glasses and dishes flying. It is possible that the merchant's diction had become impaired by his already having begun dinner. What he believes he said was "sel sur table"; what his wife heard was "saul sur table." In any case, the victory was by common consent awarded to the exemplary wife of the third merchant.[7]

The moral to the story is rather more sober than the story itself. In the French version the Chevalier concludes: ". . . and thus should every good woman act—fear and obey her lord, and do as he commands, *be it wrong or be it right*, unless the command be too outrageous; and if the command be culpable, she is exculpated, and the blame, if blame there be, remains with her lord."[8] The Knight's implication that a husband's command may be too outrageous to be obeyed is not followed by his English translator, who renders the passage as follows: ". . . & so aught eueri good woman do the comaundement of her husbonde, be it euel or welle, for yef he bidde her thing that she aught not to do, it is his shame."[9]

The durability of the concept in question may be judged by its appearance in the seventeenth-century "Castlehaven Scandal." In April, 1631, Mervyn Touchet, Lord Audley, the Earl of Castlehaven, was brought to trial and convicted of rape and sodomy. From the testimony adduced at the trial it would appear that his most cherished pleasure was to compel, initially by force, his wife, Lady Audley, and his daughter-in-law, the young Lady Audley, to engage in sexual intercourse with his male servants. As for Lord Audley himself, he evinced a keen interest in the proceedings while more or less simultaneously carrying on a homosexual relationship with various of the same group of servants.[10] All this would be of little relevance, were it not for the form of justification on which Lord Audley, the Earl of Castlehaven, professed to rely. According to the Countess his wife's examination:

"The first or second night after we were married, *Antil* [one of Castlehaven's servants] came to his bed side whilest we were in bed, and the Lord spake lasciviously to her [Lady Audley], and told her, her body was his, and that if she loved him, she must love *Antil*, and if shee lay with any man with his consent, it was not her fault, but his."[11] In the same account occurs Castlehaven's justification: ". . . he [Lord Audley] gives his reason by Scripture, she was now subject to him."[12]

The Earl of Castlehaven was duly executed for his heinous crimes, but some question remains as to whether his possibly exaggerated interpretation of the duty owed by wife to husband was the actual and effective cause of his decapitation.[13]

NOTES

1. *Le Livre du Chevalier de la Tour Landry*, ed. Anatole de Montaiglon (Paris, 1854). The translation followed is that contained in a fifteenth-century manuscript (Harleian, 1764), the work of an anonymous

author (*The Book of the Knight of La Tour–Landry*, ed. Thomas Wright, *EETS O.S.* No. 33). For the popularity of the work and its background, see Wright's Introduction.

2. The exception is, of course, Griselda's consent to what she takes to be the murder of her children. See Appendix to this article.

3. The Wife of Bath's Prologue, III [D], 692, in *Works*. For the fable of the lion, see Robinson's note.

4. See D. D. Griffith, *The Origin of the Griselda Story* (Seattle, 1931), and the discussion by J. Burke Severs in *Sources and Analogues*, p. 288 ff.

5. J. Burke Severs (*The Literary Relationships of Chaucer's "Clerkes Tale"* [New Haven, 1942], pp. 3 ff.) discusses the development of the tale in complete detail.

6. *Troilus and Criseyde*, I, 105 (*Works*, p. 390).

7. *Historia destructionis Troiae* (Cambridge, Mass., 1936), p. 164.

8. The naturalness of woman's mutability is here presented in hyperbolically ironical terms. Her nature is essentially acquisitive, and hence the most munificent bidder—as of the moment—automatically becomes the object of her love. "Nobody ought to wonder at this, because it is natural" (Andreas Capellanus, *The Art of Courtly Love*, trans. and ed. John J. Parry [New York, 1941], p. 200); "nec istud debet aliquis admirari, quum de natura procedat" (Andrea Capellano, *Trattato d'amore*, ed. Salvatore Battaglia [Rome, 1947], 392).

9.
    Salemon dit en son escrit,
    Cil qui tant ot sage esperit:
    "Qui fort femme porreit trover
    Le Criator devreit loër. (13,445–13,448)

(*Le Roman de Troie*, ed. Leopold Constans [Paris, 1906], II, 303.) The allusion is to Proverbs XXXI, 10–31, in which the qualities of the ideal wife are enumerated and praised. The opening line of this praise of ideal womanhood reads: "Mulierem fortem quis inveniet?" The "mulier fortis" means literally a "strong woman," and hence capable of allegorical interpretation as one strong in adversity. On the other hand, her implied rarity became a favorite subject of clerical witticism. Both of these developments will be discussed.

10. Giovanni Boccaccio, *Il Decameron*, ed. Giuseppe Petronio (Rome, 1950), II, 335–352. Since the editor has been kind enough to provide line references on each page, citations will be made accordingly. All references are to this edition.

11. *Sources and Analogues*, pp. 377–383. However, the editors of the *Franklin's Tale* article, Germaine Dempster and J. S. P. Tatlock, believe Boccaccio's *Filocolo* to be closer.

12. "se da voi non fia come donna onorata, voi proverete con gran vostra danno quanto grave mi sia l'aver contra mia voglia presa mogliere a' vostri prieghi" (*Decameron*, p. 336. 10–12).

13. "di niuna cosa che egli dicesse o facesse non turbarsi, e se ella sarebbe obediente e simili altre cose assai" (*ibid.*, p. 337.18–19).

14. *Ibid.*, p. 337.22.

15. The interpretation contained in the preceding paragraph is nowhere explicit in the text, but would seem to fit with what has preceded. It is not enough for Walter to rule; he must be actually exerting his lordship and making his lordship felt. The "nuovo pensier" is obviously related to the perfection of Griselda's behavior, which perfection has deprived him of the pleasure of exerting his lordship on his vassals and on Griselda. Now he can discover just how perfect she is only by carrying his lordship to its extreme.

16. *Ibid.*, p. 338.21.

17. "Signor mio, fa' di me quello che tu credi che piú tuo onore o consolazion sia, ché io sarò di tutto contenta, sí come colei che conosco che io sono da men di loro e che io non era degna di questo onore al quale tu per tua cortesia mi recasti" (*ibid.*, p. 338.27–30).

18. *Ibid.*, p. 339.16.

19. "Signor mio, pensa di contentar te e di sodisfare al piacer tuo, e di me non avere pensiero alcuno, per ciò che niuna cosa m'è cara se non quanto io la veggio a te piacere" (*ibid.*, p. 339.28–30).

20. *Ibid.*, p. 340.9.

21. *Ibid.*, p. 340.19.

22. *Ibid.*, p. 340.35.

23. *Ibid.*, p. 341.21–22.

24. *Ibid.*, p. 341.34.

25. "Che si potrà dir qui, se non che anche nelle povere case piovono dal cielo de' divini spiriti, come nelle reali di quegli che sarien piú degni di guardar porci che d'avere sopra uomini signoria?" (*ibid.*, p. 344.8–10).

26. *Le Jongleur Gautier le Leu: Étude sur les fabliaux*, ed. Charles H. Livingston (Cambridge, Mass., 1951).

27. "Al quale non sarebbe forse stato male investito d'essersi abbattuto ad una che, quando fuor di casa l'avesse in camicia cacciata, s'avesse sí ad uno altro fatto scuotere il pilliccione, che riuscito ne fosse una bella roba" (*ibid.*, p. 344.12–15).

28. The struggle within Boccaccio's mind which seems to be reflected in the Griselda story culminated in Boccaccio's religious conversion in 1361–1362. Edward Hutton writes: "Such then was Boccaccio's mood, 'his state of soul,' between the years 1354–1357." Petrarch evidently perceived this early and with great clarity. On December 20, 1355, he wrote from Milan: "From many letters of yours, I have extracted one thing, that you have a troubled spirit" (*Giovanni Boccaccio* [London, 1909], p. 188). The *Decameron* seems to have been completed about 1353 (*ibid.*, p. 171; Severs, *Literary Relationships*, p. 7, note 15).

29. Severs, *Literary Relationships*, p. 11.

30. See Benoit de St. Maure's allusion, note 9 above.

31. See Matthew IV, 10; Luke IV, 13.

32. *Sources and Analogues*, p. 306, line 62; p. 328, line 44. The slight change in language between the first and the second "Satis" would seem to be intended by Petrarch as an indication of warmth and approval at Griselda's having successfully endured what he now calls "coniugalis amoris experimenta." However, both the French translator and Chaucer seem to have preferred giving Walter's expression a more

formulaic sense. The French translator uses "C'est assez" in both places (*ibid.*, p. 307, line 73; p. 329, line 7) and Chaucer "This is ynogh, Grisilde myn" in both places (*Works*, p. 105, line 365; p. 112, line 1051).

33. A quite definite disparity between the pattern of the story and the pattern of temptation here becomes apparent. Griselda is exposed to both the temptation of prosperity and the temptations of adversity. The first is simple and single—pride. The second, the temptations of adversity, are both complex and dramatic. The first is in all versions barely alluded to (cf. *Clerk's Tale*, line 1055).

34. "an volenti animo parata sis ut de omnibus tecum michi conveniat, ita ut in nulla unquam re a mea voluntate dissencias, et, quicquid tecum agere voluero, sine ulla frontis aut verbi repugnancia te ex animo volente michi liceat" (*Sources and Analogues*, p. 306, lines 53–57). I have translated more freely than I should wish, because I have found the passage a difficult one. For instance, the "volenti animo" of the beginning of the passage would seem much less emphatic than the "te ex animo volente" at the close of the passage.

35. *Sources and Analogues*, p. 302, lines 8–9.

36. Both the Latin of Petrarch and the French of an anonymous French translation are printed by Severs in *Sources and Analogues*, pp. 296–331. Severs believes that these texts were used in combination by Chaucer as he composed the *Clerk's Tale*, and that they are the only sources on which he relied (*ibid.*, p. 289). His procedures in arriving at these texts are described in his admirably thorough *Literary Relationships*. It is important to remember that the divisions of the Latin text which appear in *Sources and Analogues* are those of Professor Severs and do not appear in the manuscript; they are made in conformity with the divisions of the *Clerk's Tale* itself (*ibid.*, p. 292).

37. *Ibid.*, p. 302, line 10. Boccaccio is not notably consistent in his presentation of Griselda's profession. She is initially described as a sheepherder (*Decameron*, p. 338.3); however, in the first of his concluding moralities, she would by analogy seem to have been a keeper of hogs, "porci" (*ibid.*, p. 344.10). Boccaccio seems, at this point, to have little interest in any consistent animal symbolism.

38. *Ibid.*, p. 302.10–11. The *Libellus de muliere forti* of Bede seems to provide the basic commentary (*PL*, XCI, 1039–1051). Citation is unfortunately made difficult because the verse divisions are marked not by number but by letters of the Hebrew alphabet, with the unnumbered verse quoted beneath. Hence quotations will be made from verse or verse-incipits as they appear in the Vulgate, and from column numbers in Vol. XCI of the *Patrologia latina*. The industriousness of the "mulier fortis" is constant throughout, and at times has a rather hortatory monastic ring. For her spinning, see verse 19: "She hath put out her hand to strong things; and her fingers have taken hold of the spindle" (*PL*, XCI, 1045–1046). For Griselda's energetic spinning, see *Sources and Analogues*, p. 302, lines 10–11.

39. "ne quid reliquiarum fortune veteris novam inferret in domum" (*Sources and Analogues*, p. 306, lines 65–66).

40. Bede, *Libellus*, verse 1 (*PL*, XCI, 1039).

41. *Sources and Analogues,* p. 316, line 26. Note "nostro . . . amori." Also "nostre amour" (*ibid.,* p. 317, line 92).

42. The *Homily on Mary Magdalene* is certainly not by Origen, but went under his name for a great while. In the passage alluded to, Mary is meditating upon death as a means of finding Christ whom, alive, she cannot find: "quia forsitan inueniret moriens, quem inuenire non poterat viuens, sine quo tamen viuere non valebat. *Fortis est vt mors dilectio.*" (Italics mine.) I have here used the printed Paris, 1604, edition. The quotation is to be found on p. 292, col. 1, G. For Chaucer's translation of the *Omelia,* and his use of the "heart" rhetoric, see "The Book of the Duchess," above.

43. "Hinc est enim quod beatus Job et in prosperitate virtutibus incomparabiliter floruit, et in adversitatibus insuperabilis hosti permansit" (*PL,* XCI, 1052).

44. "Nuda e domo patris egressa, nuda itidem revertar" (*Sources and Analogues,* p. 322, line 29).

45. *Decameron,* p. 342.4; *Sources and Analogues,* p. 326, lines 16–17.

46. *Sources and Analogues,* p. 325, line 64.

47. See "Malory and Color Symbolism," pp. 12 ff. above.

48. *Sources and Analogues,* p. 310, line 3; p. 314, line 4; p. 318, line 59; p. 319, line 38.

49. *Ibid.,* p. 310, line 4.

50. *Ibid.,* p. 310, lines 3–4; p. 314, line 4; p. 318, line 59; p. 320, line 1.

51. "Abundabant viro lacrime, ut contineri amplius iam non possent" (*ibid.,* p. 322, lines 35–36). Walter has shown signs of emotion before (*ibid.,* p. 314, line 43; p. 316, line 27).

52. "multis ac flentibus fortunamque culpantibus" (*ibid.,* p. 322, line 41).

53. "ita ut . . . nullum vestigium fortune prosperioris extaret" (*ibid.,* p. 324, lines 52–53).

54. *Ibid.,* p. 322, lines 38–39.

55. *Ibid.,* p. 328, line 63. See also p. 310, line 11; p. 316, line 12; p. 318, line 64.

56. *Ibid.,* p. 330, lines 69–81. Possibly no more striking example of the power of female literary patronage exists than the conclusion of Petrarch's French translator. What Petrarch wrote, as paraphrased above, was that he was not addressing his story to the women of his time ("matronas nostri temporis"), because the patience of Griselda seemed scarcely possible of imitation by them. He is addressing it to the "constantibus viris" (*ibid.,* p. 330, lines 70–71, 79). The French translator is careful not to be guilty of such dangerous sentiments. As he translates Petrarch's conclusion, it comes out somewhat as follows. "This story is written not only that I may move the women of today to follow the example of Griselda, but it is addressed especially to constant men, if there are any, that they may endure for their Saviour what this poor little woman endured for her mortal husband" (*ibid.,* p. 331, lines 32–45). It is possibly not without relevance that the Preface to the French translation is addressed to "femmes mariees et toutes autres," and it is the "constance et pacience merveilleuse d'une femme" set down by a reverend poet, "Francois Petrach"—may

whose soul be with God. Amen!—that the ladies married and otherwise are to imitate (*ibid.*, p. 297, lines 1–7).

57. If Chaucer understood the literary delicacy of the last of Petrarch's works as well as he understood the vastness of Petrarch's reputation— and he was obviously thoroughly aware of both—why should he select as narrator for this of all stories an unemployed cleric, who "hadde geten hym yet no benefice" (I [A], 291)—at a time when benefices were literally in search of clerics? By the second half of the fourteenth century, the incursions of the Black Death had so depleted the population that innumerable benefices were vacant. Not only that, but those that had them were not eager to retain them. Langland gives a quite vivid picture of the situation:

> Persones and parisch prestes · pleyned hem to the bischop,
> That here parisshes were pore · sith the pestilence tyme,
> To haue a lycence and a leue · at London to dwelle,
> And syngen there for symonye · for siluer is swete.
>   (B Prologue 83–86).

For the acquisition of a benefice, requirements were not high. How is it that a clerk of Oxford is unable to obtain one?

It is perhaps advisable to review what Chaucer tells us about the Clerk. One thing is eminently clear: he comes from Oxford, where he is a student of philosophy and logic. For him, as for Dante, Aristotle is the master of those who know (*Inferno* IV, 131). Since the Clerk is described as being "unto logyk . . . longe ygo" (I [A], 286), it is apparently Aristotle's logical works which particularly attract him. However, since having at his bed's head

> Twenty bookes, clad in blak or reed,
> Of Aristotle and his philosophie . . . (I [A], 294–295)

seems to him the attainment of something close to perfect felicity, one must imagine the Clerk's attachment to Aristotle as being a rather all-encompassing one. It may be added that the conjunction of Oxford and the Clerk's study of Aristotelian philosophy and logic is not without significance.

By 1268, despite earlier ecclesiastical resistance, the teaching of logic and philosophy had, at Oxford, come to be based on the study of Aristotle. So great was the concentration on philosophy and logic during the thirteenth and fourteenth centuries that it had the effect of conferring upon these studies a kind of primacy over related studies. By a curious coincidence, it was at Merton College, the home of the great fourteenth-century Augustinian, Thomas Bradwardine, that logical and philosophical studies were at their most subtle (A. B. Emden, "Learning and Education," in *Medieval England*, ed. A. L. Poole [Oxford, 1958], II, 530–533, especially p. 533). At Oxford, the Clerk would have been exposed simultaneously to traditional Augustinian theology and to Aristotelian logic. For his professional progress, the latter would have been of extreme usefulness, for at every step in his professional career, the student faced the necessity of displaying his qualifications through disputation. To become a "questionist," the first requirement for becoming a bachelor, one had to dispute. To "determine," the next step, one had to hire one of the Oxford schools, and dispute with students of inferior rank: "Determination over, the student became a 'bachelor.' . . . As such he lectured on certain books of Aristotle. After two or three years he was entitled to incept. This he did by disputing on a subject chosen by himself, a ceremony known as *Quodlibeta*. He then received from the chancellor a licence to incept as master, including the valued '*ius ubique docendi*'" (H. B. Workman, *John Wyclif* [Oxford, 1926], I, 95). By the same process of learning and disputing, the clerk could successively become a master and finally a doctor. The problem was of course funds.

The key term here is "benefice," the ecclesiastical living which the Clerk has not, as yet, obtained. The Clerk's learning and morality have been made eminently clear in the *General Prologue*. The line "Ne was so worldly for to have office" (I [A], 292) clearly indicates that in the King's vast administrative system, there was a position open to him should he wish it. Such positions were much sought after, because they offered opportunity for advancement in social status and in waistline, as witness one Geoffrey Chaucer, whose life was spent in the King's service. If the Clerk is learned, morally irreproachable, and qualified for a desirable administrative position, why has he not gotten himself as yet a benefice? The answer is almost certainly patronage. The "persones and parisch prestes" described by Langland as besieging the bishop to divest themselves of their benefices were required by long-standing ecclesiastical law (Workman, *Wyclif*, I, 154) to substitute for themselves curates, whom they would pay as little as possible, and keep the rest of the income from the parish for themselves—meanwhile supplementing their income and comfort by singing "for symonye • for siluer is swete" (*Piers Plowman*, B Prologue, line 86; see preceding quotation). What these people are doing is not actually seeking to rid themselves of their benefices—they are seeking "a lycence and a leue" to substitute a curate. To accept such a position would mean to the Clerk the sacrifice of his studies. Even though it would afford him the opportunity of exercising his favorite virtue as does his fellow pilgrim the "povre persoun of a toun":

> Benygne he was, and wonder diligent,
> And in adversitee ful pacient . . . (I [A], 483–484)

the Clerk's world is learning and teaching, and no matter how little the latter affords him, this is his life and he has no intention of giving it up.

Since the Clerk's appearance is not such as to suggest that secular patronage is very available to him, the sort of benefice he is patiently awaiting in adversity is of a less common type—the benefice impropriated by a college and granted to a scholar or master for support during the period of his studies. It was precisely such a benefice or prebend or both which supported Wyclif at Oxford. Although Wyclif was already receiving the income from his benefice in Fillingham,

Lincolnshire, the University of Oxford on November 24, 1362, presented his name, contained in its "roll of masters," to Pope Urban V as a candidate for additional financial support—"a canonry and prebend of York." Wyclif's biographer remarks: "The forwarding of these annual 'rolls of masters' was the medieval equivalent of the modern fellowship" (Workman, I, 153). The "Clerk of Oxenford" is a contemporary of Wyclif's but not, at the time of his pilgrimage to Canterbury, a cobeneficiary. The Clerk has simply not, as yet, received a benefice within the gift of a college, nor has his name, as yet, been forwarded to Rome. However, no matter what may be the reason for the Clerk's lack of a benefice, what it is important to see is that he will accept nothing which will interfere with his learning and teaching. Study is his god and Aristotle his prophet. The Clerk is the sharp-witted, highly trained professional scholar and disputant, whose mastery of language has been tested at every step in his progress. In him, Alice of Bath has a formidable opponent.

The above interpretation was suggested to me by a lecture given by Canon Astrik L. Gabriel. Its deficiencies are, of course, not to be attributed to him.

58. See note 55 above.
59. The Clerk's declaration on this theme that a wife should will nothing not in accord with her husband's will has a singularly personal ring (see p. 292 above), yet it is to be found in Bede: "quia nil contra suam voluntatem agere" (*PL*, XCI, 1041), and Petrarch: "uxor enim per se nichil velle" (*Sources and Analogues*, p. 318, line 52).
60. See "Langland and Two Scriptural Texts," above, p. 34.
61. See p. 285 above.
62. *Sources and Analogues*, p. 307, line 73; p. 329, line 7.
63. It is difficult to find in Chaucer's carefully patterned treatment of the temptations any element not already present in Petrarch. The latter, however, does not appear to regard absolute consistency as an absolute necessity. Petrarch tends to make use of those elements he feels most appropriate to the particular situation. In general, the pattern he draws becomes somewhat less distinct with each temptation.
64. It is to be noted that in all versions there is no action in the usual sense, but simply confrontation. What occurs is curiously evocative of the *Psychomachia* of Prudentius and the *De amore* of Andreas Capellanus, presumably rather different works.
65. Distracted in inverted order from *Sir Gawain and the Green Knight*, verses 59 and 58 (ed. Norman Davis [2nd. ed. Oxford, 1968]).
66. "obeisaunce": lines 66, 194; "humilite": lines 141, 186; "buxomnesse": line 186; "reverence": line 196. I have attempted to use the noun form in all cases, and to combine under one listing words of the same meaning.
67. See *MED*.
68. "lord": lines 64, 88, 96, 101, 105, 106, 110, 116, 129; "lust": lines 80, 105, 111, 161, 183.
69. See the excellent illustrated translation by Isa Ragusa and Rosalie B. Green (Princeton, 1961); as to surviving manuscripts, see their Introduction, p. xxiii.

70. *Ibid.*, p. 16.
71. Nicholas Love, *Mirror of the Life of Christ,* ed. L. F. Powell (London, 1908), p. 30. Love's version of the *Meditations* is employed only because in language, and possibly in sentiment, it is closer to Chaucer's readers.
72. *Meditations,* ed. Ragusa and Green, pp. 18, 19.
73. Love, *Mirrour,* p. 47.
74. B Prologue, 146 ff.
75. See "Langland and Two Scriptural Texts," p. 34 above.
76. See "An Augustinian Interpretation of Chaucer's Pardoner," pp. 248–249 above.
77. Cf. the "pauculas . . . oves" of Petrarch (*Sources and Analogues,* p. 302, line 10).
78. *The Sacrifice of Isaac,* in *Chief Pre-Shakesperean Dramas,* ed. J. Q. Adams (Boston, 1924), pp. 117–124.
79. *Ibid.*, p. 117, note 1.
80. *Ibid.*, verses 79–80.
81. *Ibid.*, verses 190–193.
82. *Ibid.*, verses 441–442.
83. See IV [E], 538, 548, 566, 603 (*Works,* p. 107).
84. "lust": lines 619, 658, 660, 662, 716, 717, 742, 757; "plesaunce": lines 658, 663, 665, 672, 717, 757; "lust" and "plesaunce": lines 658, 717, 757.
85. "crueel": lines 692, 723, 734, 740.
86. "humilitee": line 755; "pacience": lines 623, 644, 677, 670, 688.
87. Through the influence of I John II, 16. See "Langland and Two Scriptural Texts," p. 40 above.
88. This is the arrangement of the French translator of Petrarch (*Sources and Analogues,* pp. 321–324).
89. "tempte": line 786; "lust": line 847; "plesaunce": lines 792, 873, 964. Of the last word, "plesaunce," it should be observed that the first and third, spoken by Walter, bear rather little emphasis; the medial, spoken by Griselda, immediately follows the Job allusion and bears very considerable weight.
90. This has strong echoes of Job III, 1–3.
91. The association of Job with the conception of patience and humility is made eminently clear in the exemplum of Job in the Knight of La Tour Landry. What is most interesting about the exemplum is that it is stated in the imagery of Fortune, which has all along been present in discussions involving the "mulier fortis" (see pp. 143 ff. above). The Knight, or his clerical compositor, says: "Ye haue welle herde as upon that as tellithe the Bible, how God wolde and sufferithe Iob, that was an holy man, to be tempted, and to falle from gret highe worshippe and richesse unto lowe astate and thereto pouerte, as he that was as mighti and riche as a kinge; furst, how he lost is .vij. sones and .iij. doughtres, after alle his bestailes and richesses, and alle his faire duellinge places ybrent, so that there belefte hym no thinge saue only hym selff and his wiff." Though urged by his un-Griseldian wife to "blame God of this dissese," he "euer thanked God in gret pacience. . . . And whanne almighti God had so assaied and proued

hym, and his gret humilite and pacience, he redressed alle, and gaue hym as moche honoure, worship, richesse, and prosperite, as he had before in alle manere wise" (*Knight of La Tour–Landry*, p. 103).

92. Part III: lines 452, 458; Part IV: lines 620, 707, 735; Part V: line 786.

93. Book II, Prose 2, in Chaucer's translation (*Works*, pp. 330–331). The original reads: "Cum te matris utero natura produxit, nudum . . . suscepi . . . omnium, quae mei iuris sunt, affluentia et splendore circumdedi. Nunc mihi retrahere manum libet" (Boethius, *Philosophiae consolationis libri quinque*, ed. Karl Buchner [Heidelberg, 1960], pp. 22–23).

94. The entrance of Fortune into the tale vastly expanded, for the medieval reader, the immediacy of the tale. In Boccaccio, Fortune is introduced, but only fleetingly. In Petrarch, Fortune is treated more fully, but still only by allusion which is not followed out (see discussion, p. 145 above). It is, of course, in Petrarch that the association of Job (temptation) and Fortune is made, but it is Chaucer who carries through the relationship. As will be indicated in the following discussion, it is he who gives to Walter the statement that he has tried Griselda in prosperity and adversity. This occurs in neither of his predecessors. What is here obvious is that each of the three writers increased, in sequence, the significance of Fortune in the Griselda story, and with reason. The addition to her story of the concept of Fortune brings her closer to humanity as a whole, for on earth Fortune is God's regent, and hence every earthly being, insofar as his earthly existence is concerned, necessarily lives under her rule. In Dante's *Inferno*, she is a goddess, the agent of God's will upon earth, who cares neither for men's adulation in the upward movement of her wheel—"prosperitee"—nor for their curses in the downward movement of her wheel—"adversitee." In accordance with God's will, she spins her wheel and rejoices in her blessedness "volve sua spera e beata si gode" (VII, 94–96). In Chaucer's *Troilus and Criseyde*, Fortune is described as the agency under whose dominion one kingdom arises and another falls, and power is transferred successively from one people to another to the end of time (Ecclus. x, 8).

> Fortune, which that permutacioun
> Of thynges hath, as it is hire comitted
> Thorough purveyaunce and disposicioun
> Of heighe Jove, as regnes shal be flitted
> Fro folk in folk, or when they shal be smytted,
> Gan pulle awey the fetheres brighte of Troie
> Fro day to day, til they ben bare of joie. (V, 1541–1547)

Although the spinning of Fortune's wheel seems pure mutability and is incomprehensible to man—"Though to us bestes been the causes wrie" (*TC*, III, 620)—her wheel moves only in accordance with the will of God, and hence whether man is elevated to "prosperitee" or brought down to "adversitee," the action of Fortune's wheel is controlled by divine justice. Whatever Fortune does is done in accordance with the divine plan which encompasses not only the present but universal history. For man, who is incapable of comprehending this plan, there is temptation on both sides of Fortune's wheel. On the upward swing, man is subject to self-congratulation and hence pride; on the downward swing, he is subject to the very human urge to question the justice behind his sudden descent—to "grucche" against God as the source of the adversity experienced. In the vicissitudes of Fortune, therefore, temptation lurked; and the vicissitudes of Fortune were the life of every earthly being.

95. "crueel" does not appear; "lust": line 847; "plesaunce": lines 792, 873; "lord": lines 814, 845, 858, 862, 881, 889, 907. As regards "plesaunce," the two occurrences are divided between Walter and Griselda.

96. Part I—"lord": lines 64, 88, 96, 101, 105, 106, 110, 116, 129. Part II—"lord": lines 250, 299, 319, 321. Part III—"lord": lines 501, 523, 570, 575, 579. Part IV—"lord": lines 633, 652. Part V—"lord": lines 814, 845, 858, 862, 881, 889, 907. Part VI—"lord": lines 967, 1032, 1088, 1131.

97. "lust": lines 962, 968, 986; "plesaunce": lines 959, 964, 969, 991, 993, 1036, 1111. It will be observed that of the two words only those in lines 962, and 964 are spoken by Walter of himself. If one compares this with Part IV, the difference is striking.

98. "lust": line 986; "plesaunce": lines 991, 993.

99. "Stedfastnesse" appears once in each of the temptations (lines 564, 699, 789), and becomes affective only when it appears in conjunction with "constance" (lines 1050, 1056); "constance" has appeared only once previous to Part VI, but in Part VI there are three occurrences (lines 1008, 1047, 1146), all more or less in association with "stedfastnesse."

100. Apocalypse XIX, 7, 9.

101. *Sources and Analogues*, p. 330, line 70.

102. "Nec animo teneo, sic omnes peruersas esse: quis dubitet quin in tam maxima multitudine reperiantur aliquae piae, modestae, ac sanctissimae, & dignissime summa reverentia mulieres. Sino Christianas, ex quibus plurimae grandi mentis integritate, virginitate, constantia, aliisque meritis floruere: sed et gentiles aliquae summis praeconiis meruere laudes. Quae et si quando reperiantur, amandae, colendae, et pro uiribus extollendae sunt, ultra quam viri. . . . Sed quoniam rarissimae sunt, ne, dum Lucretiam quaerimus, in Calpurniam, aut Semproniam incidamus, ego omnes fugiendas censeo" (*De casibus virorum illustrium* [1544], p. 30).

103. As in Lussheborwes is a lyther alay · and ȝet loketh he lyke a sterlynge,
The merke of that mone is good · ac the metal is fieble;
And so it fareth by some folke now · thei han a faire speche,
Croune and Crystendome · the kynges merke of heuene,
Ac the metal, that is mannes soule · with synne is foule alayed . . .

(B XV, 342–346 [*Piers Plowman*, I, 458]). The Clerk's coin metaphor is possibly the unkindest cut of all. Since it occurs immediately before his direct address to the Wife of Bath, it is altogether likely that the Clerk remembers the "Allas! allas! that evere love was synne!" of her Prologue (III [D], 614), and the "Thanne am I gentil, whan that I bigynne/ To lyven vertuously and weyve synne" of her Tale (III [D], 1175–1176).

NOTES TO APPENDIX

1. IV (E) 1212^{a-d} (*Works*, p. 114).
2. *Ibid*, p. 892.
3. See Robinson's entry under "legende" in his Glossary (*Works*, p. 960); cf. *Legenda Aurea*, the most popular collection of saints' lives, and Chaucer's *Legend of Good Women*.
4. See also VII (B²) 1889–1923 (*Works*, p. 188). It is of some interest that the "pacience" of Prudence, the heroine of "The Tale of Melibee," evokes from Harry a response virtually identical to that elicited by "The Clerk's Tale."
5. See Robinson's note to VII, 1894 (*ibid.*, p. 745).
6. IV (E) 1223–1225 (*ibid.*, p. 115).
7. Ed. M. Anatole de Montaiglon (Paris, 1854), pp. 41–44.
8. ". . . et ainsi doit toute bonne femme fere, craindre et obeir à son seigneur, et faire son commandement, soit tort soit droit, se le commandement n'est trop oultrageux, et, se il y a vice, elle en est desblasmée, et demoure le blasme, se blasme y a, à son seigneur" (*ibid.*, pp. 43–44).
9. *The Book of the Knight of la Tour-Landry*, ed. Thomas Wright, *EETS O.S.*, No. 33, p. 28.
10. The following material has been entirely derived from the dissertation of Dr. Barbara Breasted (Whitesides), " 'Comus' and the Castlehaven Scandal" (Rutgers, 1969) which argues strongly that Milton's *Comus* (1634) is a deliberate refurbishing of the family reputation on the part of Castlehaven's near relatives, the Bridgewaters. The occasion on which *Comus* was presented was the installation of the Earl of Bridgewater in his new dignity of Lord President of Wales (see " 'Comus' and the Castlehaven Scandal," in especial, pp. 45–46, and the Derby-Castleton-Bridgewater genealogy ["Appendix"]).
11. *The Arraignment and Conviction of Mervin, Lord Audley, Earl of Castlehaven . . . on Monday, April 25, 1631* (London, 1642), p. 8; cited by Breasted, " 'Comus,' " p. 46.
12. Breasted, " 'Comus,' " p. 45. The scriptural authority is evidently Pauline: "Let women be subject to their husbands . . ." (Ephesians v, 22); "Wives, be subject to your husbands . . ." (Colossians, III, 18). See also I Corinthians, XI, 3.
13. More immediate and practical considerations seem to have entered in. See Breasted, " 'Comus,' " notes 40, 58.

17

Susannah and the "Merchant's Tale"

W<small>HEN JANUARY CARRIES</small> off "fresshe May" to his walled
garden, he first sings an amorous invitation composed of lines
freely translated from the Song of Songs: "Rys up, my wyf," etc.
(IV [E], 2138–2148).[1] In his invitation he delicately avoids injury to May's sense of modesty by assuring her that they will not
be seen: "The gardyn is enclosed al aboute" (2143). The allusion
here is generally taken to be to Song of Songs IV, 12, where the
beloved is called an enclosed garden and a sealed fountain:
"hortus conclusus, fons signatus." Although an allusion to the
metaphorical garden of the Song of Songs is surely to be detected
here, there is, nevertheless, a second text which seems to be even
more directly alluded to, for, like the *Merchant's Tale*, it describes a quite actual garden in which senile love addresses itself
to a beautiful young wife with the same purpose as does January, and with the same emphasis upon a privacy obtained
through "clyket" and "wyket." The text is Daniel XIII, 20: "Ecce
ostia pomarii clausa sunt, et nemo nos videt"—the address of
the two lecherous elders to Susannah.

It is of course apparent from a reference in the *Man of Law's
Tale* that Chaucer was quite familiar with the Susannah story.[2]
From what sources this familiarity might have been derived is

Reprinted from *Speculum*, XXXV (1960), 275–279.

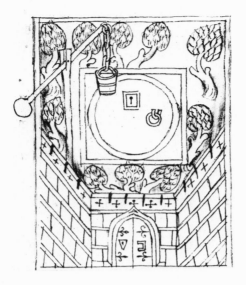

"ORTUS CONCLUSUS"
Yale University Ms. Z 109.073, f. 11ᵃ

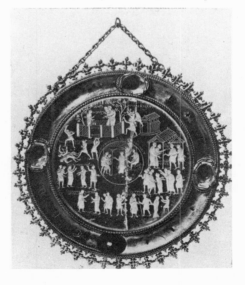

CRYSTAL OF LOTHAIR
In the British Museum, London. Reproduced from *Archaeologia*, LIX (1904)

SUSANNAH AND THE ELDERS

Fifteenth-century painting, Rutgers University Art Museum

uncertain. However, aside from a very probable direct knowledge of the text itself, I would suggest the following: (1) pictorial representations roughly contemporary with Chaucer, (2) a popular fourteenth-century English poem. In medieval art, the story of Susannah seems to have been something of a standard subject. Illustrations as far apart as the ninth and fifteenth centuries show Susannah and her sudden lovers in a garden "enclosed al aboute." The reason for the garden's being represented in this fashion is simply that the reference to "ostia clausa" was understood to mean that the garden, except for these doors, was completely enclosed. Hence, the garden of Susannah became a second "hortus conclusus" and is depicted in the art of the late Middle Ages in much the same fashion as the "hortus conclusus" of the Song of Songs: both are walled gardens with a fountain, trees, and doors.[3] A second path by which information concerning Susannah could have reached Chaucer is a Middle English alliterative-stanzaic poem called *Susannah*, or *Seemly Susan*, or even, perhaps, the *Epistill of Suete Susane* (before 1370).[4] In this poem the anonymous author makes much of the fact that Susannah's is a "pomarium," or fruit garden—an aspect of the story also clearly apparent in pictorial representations of the Susannah story. This "orchard newe," for which Susannah's husband Joachim is famous, contains a vast variety of trees laden with fruit, among them the "pirie" (line 70). The orchard as a whole is arranged in "alees" (line 11) and the delights of the garden are completed by a fountain—the very one in which Susannah took her nearly fatal bath:

> Vndur a lorere ful lowe þat ladi gan leende
> > So sone.
> > By a wynliche welle,
> > Susan caste of hir kelle. (lines 125–128)

If we may assume for a moment that the above sources—text, art, contemporary poem—represent in a general way the forms in which the Susannah story were available to Chaucer, the customary inescapable questions arise: (1) What evidence is there that Chaucer had this material in mind? (2) Assuming that he did, what part does the Susannah allusion play in the *Merchant's Tale*?

To the present writer, the clearest evidence of Chaucer's indebtedness to the Susannah story lies in the virtual identity of statement made in Daniel XIII, 20, and in the line under discussion (IV [E], 2143). This aspect of the problem will be discussed below. In addition, there is the evidence of the Middle English *Susannah*. At least one horticultural detail[5] of this poem was strongly enough imprinted on Chaucer's mind to cause its transplantation into the garden of the *Merchant's Tale*. This is Susannah's laurel-shaded well (see above), which becomes in Chaucer the "welle / That stood under a laurer alwey grene" (2036–2037).[6] So far as I am aware, there is no parallel to this in any of Chaucer's recognized sources.[7] Indeed, it may be suggested that the influence of the *Susannah* garden was not limited to isolated borrowings, but did in fact form a kind of link in the development of the *Merchant's Tale*. If Chaucer knew the poem, as it seems probable he did, and in addition knew something of pictorial representations of the garden, he could have been reminded at once of the "hortus conclusus" of the Song of Songs and of the pear-tree fabliau, for, as has been pointed out, the gardens are in art virtually indistinguishable and in the *Susannah* poem the pear tree luxuriates.[8]

If there is reason to believe that Chaucer had the above material in mind, what is his purpose in alluding to it? Let us, for a moment, consider the steps by which the allusion in question is arrived at. The rankling self-disgust which the Merchant's brief matrimonial experience has engendered within him[9] demands that his surrogate in the tale, old January, be made to look, amongst other things, as disgusting as possible. This end is fully attained in the garden scene, which is itself prepared for by a series of garden references. The questionable character of January's garden is first intimated by its ironical classification as one of his "honest thynges" (2028). Its actual nature begins to become apparent with the allusion to the *Roman de la rose* (2032), and is made more than explicit in the reference to the "god of gardyns," Priapus (2034), an obscene figure in the *Vulgate* of St. Jerome as well as in classical literature.[10] Having fully conveyed the spirit which pervades January's private garden, Chaucer turns to an exposition of the plot by which the garden, far from assisting January in his desire to "lyve ful deliciously," will become the scene of his betrayal (2057–2131). Against this carefully prepared ironic background, January, urged by May, sings his sacrilegious version of the Song of Songs and thereby transforms into comic lasciviousness the holy love the Song of Songs was understood to celebrate.[11] It is in this progressively heightened context of grotesque carnality that the Susannah allusion occurs. January, giddy with expectation, converts "hortus conclusus," an epithet in the Song of Songs descriptive of the chaste "sponsa," into an argument for the undisturbed indulgence of antique lust, and in so doing effectually paraphrases Daniel xiii, 20: "Behold, the doors of the garden are closed [January is never without his silver "clyket"], and no one sees us." With this simultaneous reference to the Song of Songs and Daniel, the series of garden allusions reaches its climax, for here in one brilliant line are juxtaposed the image of supremely chaste love—the "hortus conclusus," with its inescapable Marian overtones[12]—and the image of supremely unchaste love, the doubled unnatural lust of the elders. The series begun with the ironical "honest thynges" has moved through the courtly-love suggestions of the *Roman de la rose*, through the gross symbolism of Priapus, to the violent contrast of chaste and unnatural love contained within January's sacrilegious version of the Song of Songs. As by a series of mirrors, the moral distortion of old January is brought before the reader's eyes, and none reveals him more fully than that which presents a doubled image of January's lust set against the highest love the Middle Ages could conceive.

NOTES

1. *Works*, p. 124.
2. II [B¹], 639–640. It is interesting to observe that Constance's appeal to the example of Susannah is apparently an original Chaucerian addition. Susannah is not cited in this connection either by Trivet (cf. *Sources and Analogues*, p. 171) or by Gower (*Complete Works*, ed. G. C. Macaulay [Oxford, 1899–1902], II, 153–154). See also *Parson's Tale*, line 797.
3. The enclosed garden of the Song of Songs may be seen in the following

representations: (1) *Bible moralisée* (thirteenth century) : MS Paris, Bibliothèque Nationale, Lat. 11560, fol. 79^b; MS Toledo, Biblioteca del Cabildo, II, fol. 79^b, both published in A. Laborde, *Bible moralisée*, II (1912), plate 303; IV (1921), plate 533. Both these illuminations show what appears to be a spear set in the midst of the garden. (2) *Speculum humanae salvationis* (fourteenth century) : MS Paris, Bibliothèque Nationale, Lat. 9584, fol. 14^a; MS New Haven, Yale University Library, Z 109.073, fol. 11^a. The Bibliothèque Nationale illumination is published in *Speculum humanae salvationis*, ed. M. R. James (Oxford, 1926), chap. III. The Yale MS remains unpublished. The garden of Susannah may be seen in the following representations widely spaced in time: (1) Crystal of Lothair (ninth century), British Museum, published in *Archaeologia*, LIX (1904), plate 1; (2) painting (fifteenth century), unknown Central Italian master, Rutgers University Library, unpublished; (3) painting (late fifteenth century), Pinturicchio, Vatican, published in André Michel, *Histoire de l'art* (Paris, 1905–1929), IV, plate 223. Later paintings, though numerous, are too late to have much relevance. For assistance with the above material, I am indebted to Dr. Rosalie B. Green, Director of the Index of Christian Art, Princeton, and to Helmut H. von Erffa, Professor Emeritus, Rutgers University.

4. The poem is contained in the Vernon MS dated 1370–1380. For an account of *Susannah*, see J. E. Wells, *Manual of the Writings in Middle English* (New Haven, 1916), pp. 399–400. The relationship of the poem to the Huchoun controversy is studiously ignored by the present writer. All quotations are from the *Minor Poems of the Vernon Manuscript*, ed. F. J. Furnivall, *EETS O.S.* No. 117, pp. 626–636.

5. Other possible parallels between *Susannah* and the *Merchant's Tale* are that the term "honest" (line 30) is applied to Joachim, husband of Susannah, in connection with his garden (cf. IV [E], 2028) and that the *Susannah* garden is divided (line 11) by "alees" (cf. IV [E], 2324). I am unable to find that these alleys occur in any of Chaucer's known sources; they do, however, appear in *Troilus and Criseyde*, II, 820, and the *Franklin's Tale*, V [F], 1013.

6. The significance of the laurel here may perhaps be explained as follows. Because of the devotion to God which motivated her stalwart resistance to the elders, Susannah was considered a splendid example of the noble warrior against temptation: "tentatori resistere docuit, pugnare docuit" (St. Augustine, *Sermo* CCCXLIII [*PL*, XXXIX, 1508]). Laurel was understood to have been in antiquity the crown awarded the victor; when transformed into Christian terms, it became the unfading crown which is the reward of the triumphant warrior against the vices. Petrus Berchorius, developing a comment by Rabanus Maurus in the *De universo* (*PL*, CXI, 512), says: "Per laurum, quae semper viret, de quo coronabantur dudum victores, intelligo semper virtutem immarcessibilem gloriam paradisi, quae victorum vitiorum, et tribulationum est sine dubio praemium, et corona" (*Reductorium morale*, XII, lxxxiv, in *Opera* [Cologne, 1730–1731], II, 496). It is beneath the laurel that Susannah, in the poem in question, resists the elders (lines

136, 143). In the *Merchant's Tale*, the laurel-shaded fountain is associated with the court of Pluto and Proserpine because, I think, the pear tree rather than the fountain had become for Chaucer the center of dramatic action; also because fountains and the color green were both associated with fairies. See T. P. Cross, "Celtic Elements in Lanval and Graelent," *MP*, xii (1914–1915), 595, note 3; 599.

7. In the *Roman de la rose*, the two opposing earthly and celestial fountains are, respectively, "Une fontaine soz un pin" (line 1427) and a fountain under an olive tree: "une olivete basse/Souz cui toute l'eve s'en passe" (lines 20495–20496). The laurel-shaded fountain is not to be discovered in the *Roman* or in the parallels to the *Merchant's Tale* garden adduced in D. W. Robertson's basic article "The Doctrine of Charity in Mediaeval Gardens," *Speculum*, xxvi (1951), 43–45; or in J. C. McGalliard's "Chaucer's *Merchant's Tale* and Deschamps' *Miroir de mariage*," *Philological Quarterly*, xxv (1946), 204–205.

8. Lines 70, 82, 108.

9. See J. S. P. Tatlock, "Chaucer's *Merchant's Tale*," *MP*, xxxiii (1936), 367–381.

10. Cf. III Kings xv, 13; II Chronicles xv, 16. When St. Jerome came to translate the passages describing the obscene rites observed by Maacha, he found himself in need of a Latin word to render the Hebrew "mifletset" (idol). He used Priapus "pour donner à ses lecteurs latins l'idée de ce qu'était cette sorte d'idole" (F. Vigouroux, *Dictionnaire de la Bible* [Paris, 1912], v [1], 662–663). The *Glossa ordinaria* printed by Migne (*PL*, cxiii, 605, 683) contains no discussion of these passages, but a comment by Nicholas of Lyra using "deus hortorum," Chaucer's exact phrase (cf. iv [E], 2035), is to be found in *Biblia sacra* (Lyons, 1589–1590), ii, 803.

11. The "sponsa" of the Song of Songs was understood variously as the Church, the individual soul, and the Virgin Mary. For a brief and informative discussion of the relationship between these kinds of interpretation, see Paul E. Beichner, C.S.C., "Cantica canticorum B. Mariae," *Marianum*, xxi (1959), fasc. ii, 1–3.

12. It would be difficult to imagine that the Marian connotation of the enclosed garden could have been far from Chaucer's mind. Jerome's *Adversus Jovinianum*, which Chaucer consulted so constantly in connection with the Marriage Group, is perhaps the most important work in the line of interpretation which treated "hortus conclusus" as a figure of the perpetual virginity of the Blessed Virgin (*PL*, xxiii, 254). Twelfth-century hymns make frequent use of this conception. A hymn to the Virgin sometimes attributed to Adam of St. Victor reads:

> Haec est ille fons signatus,
> Hortus clausus

and the same language is used in another twelfth-century hymn to the Virgin:

> Favus stillans, fons signatus,
> Hortus clausus, austri flatus

(Nos. 198.9, 222.13, in *Analecta hymnica*, ed. C. Blume and H. M. Bannister [Leipzig, 1886–1922], LIV, 309, 353.) The continuance of this tradition in the fourteenth century can be observed in the rubric to the *Speculum humanae salvationis* described in note 3 above: "Ortus conclusus et fons signatus significat Beatam Mariam." It is furthermore quite possible that such a hymn as the following furnished the suggestion for January's song to May:

11. Te sponsus
    vocat in meridie:
12. Veni, veni, filia,
    Intra nostra cubilia;
    Surge, surge, propera,
    Fugit hiems, floret vinea.
13. Vox tua vox turturis
    Forma desiderabilis,
 8. Tua sunt ubera,
    vino redolentia
 9. Hortus, in quo
    Deitas latuit . . .

(See No. 224 in *Analecta hymnica*, LIV, 357.) The hymn to the Virgin was of course an artistic form with which Chaucer was familiar (*ABC, Prioress's Tale, Second Nun's Tale*). For a general discussion of Marian symbolism, see F. J. E. Raby, *Christian-Latin Poetry*, 2nd ed. (Oxford, 1953), pp. 363–375.

18

Seith Moyses by the Devel: A Problem in the "Parson's Tale"

In his discussion of how "synne wexeth or encreesseth in man,"[1] Chaucer's Parson makes a rather startling scriptural allusion:

And of this matere seith Moyses by the devel in this manere: "The feend seith, 'I wol chace and pursue the man by wikked suggestioun, and I wol hente hym by moevynge or stirynge of synne. And I wol departe my prise or my praye by deliberacioun, and my lust shal been acompliced in delit. I wol drawe my swerd in consentynge'— / for certes, right as a swerd departeth a thyng in two peces, right so consentynge departeth God fro man—'and thanne wol I sleen hym with myn hand in dede of synne'; thus seith the feend."[2]

Robinson fears that the Parson has here triumphantly vindicated his claim to not being "textueel,"[3] and calls the allusion a "supposed utterance of Moses."[4] However, despite a somewhat apocryphal appearance, the passage does have real scriptural basis. The difficulty would seem to be simply that the Parson has, for reasons not readily apparent, incorporated into the scriptural passage a commentary which transforms it from a rather direct

Reprinted from *Revue Belge de Philologie et d'Histoire*, XXXI (1953), 61–64.

biblical narrative into a figurative progress of sin. In the un-published *Summa de officio sacerdotis* of Richard de Wether-ingsett,[5] the scriptural allusion is accurately stated and the prog-ress of sin carefully distinguished:

Eundem progressum [peccati] facile est assignare in hiis duobus versibus Cantici Exodi, *"Dixit inimicus: Persequar, comprehendam, dividam spolia, implebitur anima mea. Evaginabo gladium meum et interficiet eos manus mea."* [Exodus xv, 9] *Dixit inimicus:* "In sug-gestione, in primis motibus, *persequar;* in delectatione *compre-hendam,* in consensu. *Dividam spolia* in actu. *Implebitur anima mea* in consuetudine. *Evaginabo gladium meum* cum de peccato gloriatur. *Interficiet eos manus mea* in presumptione vel desperatione."[6]

The "Canticum Exodi" is of course the song of triumph of Moses and the Israelites after the submersion of Pharaoh and his army. The particular verse in question (Exodus xv, 9) is a kind of ironic recital of the threats of Pharaoh against the Israelites: "I will pursue, I will overtake, I will divide the spoils," etc. How-ever, the term applied to Pharoah in this verse is not the proper name but "inimicus," a normal equivalent for Satan.[7] Hence to at least one school of scriptural interpretation, the presence of Satan suggested a progress of sin akin to that of the seven deadly sins described by Gregory the Great.[8] Since Moses appears as the narrator of Satan's boasted agency in this progressive degen-eration of the human spirit, it is he who "seith by the devel."

The particular version of the progress stated by the Parson clearly did not come directly from Wetheringsett.[9] One is in-clined therefore to suppose that Chaucer could have derived it virtually from any theological work with a commentary on Exodus. Surprisingly enough, however, the present writer's ex-amination of a rather extensive body of commentary on Exodus reveals nothing comparable to the interpretation advanced in the *Summa.* The standard commentaries treat the "Canticum Exodi" as a symbolic foretelling of the salvation of the followers of Christ and the overthrow of Satan.[10] In this view, the asser-tions of Pharaoh or Satan seem to have been considered uninter-esting. Only three comments which I have seen discuss the passage at all,[11] and none of them discovers in it Richard de Wetheringsett's figurative progress of sin.[12]

Considered in this context, the obscure allusion to Moses and the devil may have some relevance to the even more obscure problem of the source of the *Parson's Tale*. It has previously been supposed that the tale was derived from a continental tradition.[13] Yet here and elsewhere in Richard's *Summa*, there exist parallels which are not present in any continental tradition so far adduced. It would therefore appear possible that the source from which Chaucer drew the Parson's "litel tretys" was not continental at all, but the sort of English manual for parish priests with which the Parson might be expected to be considerably more familiar.

NOTES

1. x (i), 350 (*Works*, p. 237).
2. x (i), 355–356 (*ibid.*, p. 238).
3. Prologue to the *Parson's Tale*, line 57 (*ibid.*, p. 228).
4. See Robinson's note to x (i), 355 (*ibid.*, p. 768).
5. Authorship and date of the *Summa* are discussed below in St. Augustine and the 'Parson's Tale,' see pp. 349–350 below.
6. *Summa de officio sacerdotis*, fol. 45ᵇ. Transcription is from MS New College xciv in the Bodleian Library.
7. See Matthew xiii, 39: "*Inimicus autem . . . est diabolus*," and St. Augustine: "habemus inimicum, diabolum, serpentem antiquum" (*Enarratio in Psalmum* xxx [*PL*, xxxvi, 238]). All commentators on this passage agree that "inimicus" represents Satan. Thus Rabanus Maurus states: "inimicum verum et antiquum hostem . . . id est diabolum" (*Commentaria in Exodum* [*PL*, cviii, 69]). Pharaoh was likewise, though somewhat less prominently, associated with Satan. Origen says: "verum Pharaonem, id est diabolum" (*In Exodum homilia* vi, [*PL*, xii, 332]). See, in this connection, Ezechiel xxix, 3.
8. *Moralia*, xxxi, xlv (*PL*, lxxvi, 621–622). This progress is discussed at fol. 47ᵃ of the *Summa de officio sacerdotis* shortly after the interpretation of Exodus xv, 9. It is interesting to notice that elements of Gregory's progress do in fact appear in the *Parson's Tale* (see above, "An Augustinian Interpretation of Chaucer's Pardoner," note 25). The progress of sin must have been to Chaucer a reasonably familiar conception.
9. It will be observed that Chaucer and Wetheringsett do not agree on the significance of the later steps in the progress. Richard would appear to be directly indebted to the *Summa* of William de Monte (de Montibus), and Chaucer may perhaps be ultimately indebted to the same source. De Monte had gained recognition as a theologian by about 1180, and it is possible that the interpretation of Exodus xv, 9, as a progress of sin began with him (see note 5 above). It would seem clear, however, that Chaucer drew his particular version from a related

work rather than directly from the *Summa of* Wetheringsett or its possible antecedent, the *Summa* of de Montibus.

10. The first and most influential comment is that of Origen. He is followed very closely by Bede, Rabanus Maurus, and Walafrid Strabo. Some additions are made by St. Bruno Astensis and by Rupert, whose version is repeated by Gerhoh (*PG*, xii, 331–340; *PL*, xci, 311–312; cviii, 67–75; cxiii, 226–232; clxiv, 265–266; clxvii, 645–652; cxciv, 1017–1028).

11. Rabanus Maurus, Rupert, Gerhoh (*PL*, cviii, 70; clxii, 648; cxciv, 1022).

12. The only approach to Richard's conception is made by Rupert, who sees in the passage Satan's attempt to overcome regenerate man through direct and indirect attack (*PL*, clxvii, 648–649).

13. See Germaine Dempster, "The Parson's Tale," *Sources and Analogues*, pp. 723–724.

19

St. Augustine and the "Parson's Tale"

In her radcliffe monograph *The Sources of the Parson's Tale*, Miss Kate Petersen concluded that the ultimate sources of the Parson's "litel tretys" were two thirteenth-century Latin works: the *Summa casuum poenitentiae* of St. Raymond of Pennaforte, from which Chaucer drew the material on penance; and the *Summa de vitiis* of Guilielmus Peraldus, from which came the discussion of the seven deadly sins.[1] Because of its highly persuasive parallels and careful construction, Miss Petersen's study has won very general acceptance.[2] In the present writer's opinion, however, there is one aspect of Miss Petersen's work which is perhaps worth some reconsideration, and that is the positiveness of her identifications of the ultimate sources of the tale. Can it be successfully maintained, as Miss Petersen would have us believe, that exactly here and here we may fix the ultimate limits of the sources upon which Chaucer drew in the *Parson's Tale*?

Let us consider first the *Summa de vitiis* of Guilielmus Peraldus. Are the parallels here of such a nature as to indicate that Chaucer must necessarily have drawn his discussion of the seven deadly sins from this particular source? Upon this point the most notable recent student of the *Parson's Tale* observes:

Reprinted from *Traditio*, VIII (1952), 424–430.

"The parallel passages listed by Miss Petersen frequently occur in the two works in such different sequence and surroundings as to make derivation highly doubtful."[3] And for this state of inexact parallelism there is, I think, an excellent reason. The order of the seven deadly sins followed by Chaucer is not that of Peraldus' *Summa* at all, but is, on the contrary, that popularized by Gregory the Great in the *Moralia*.[4] The scattered nature of the parallels between Chaucer and Peraldus is therefore to be explained in terms of the necessity imposed upon Miss Petersen of singling out similarities between two works of rather different organization and content. On the other hand, aside from the matter of order, rather striking similarities are apparent between Gregory and Chaucer. In the *Moralia* the treatment of the sins is not really an order but a progress, and in the *Parson's Tale* definite traces of this progress are discoverable. One finds, for instance, that Chaucer has there translated the statement by which Gregory links *accidia* and *avaritia*, a linking which is quite impossible in the very different order followed by Peraldus.[5] Chaucer's source for the seven deadly sins would seem then to lie in the line of descent from Gregory rather than from Peraldus.[6]

The *Summa casuum poenitentiae*, however, presents a problem very different from that of the *Summa de vitiis*. St. Raymond is known to have exercised throughout the thirteenth and fourteenth centuries, in England as elsewhere, an extremely powerful influence.[7] The probability of Chaucer's use of the *Summa casuum poenitentiae* in one form or another is therefore very great, and this probability is considerably heightened by the numerous parallels of structure and language which Miss Petersen has pointed out. However, even here, can one maintain with complete assurance that Chaucer's discussion of penance must necessarily have come from Raymond of Pennaforte or a follower of his? Actually there appear to have been current in fourteenth-century England compilations by English theologians which treated the problem of penance much as did St. Raymond and were yet quite independent of him. One may cite in this connection the *Summa de officio sacerdotis* of Richard de Wetheringsett, which was written before Raymond's *Summa* had effectively reached England,[8] and which furnishes, nevertheless, accurate parallels to a whole section of the *Parson's Tale* which Miss Petersen has been able to relate only slightly to the *Summa casuum poenitentiae*.[9] The relationship of the *Parson's Tale* to so early a work would seem to suggest either that Chaucer is in fact indebted to more numerous ultimate sources than Miss Petersen has recognized or that the penance material, like the discussion of the seven deadly sins, goes back to a tradition earlier than Raymond or Peraldus.

In the present writer's opinion, the latter possibility offers the better solution. It seems probable that in the rather narrow emphasis which has been placed upon the indebtedness of Chaucer to various individual theological writers, criticism has lost sight of the immense indebtedness of all writers on theology to a great common source, namely St. Augustine. Chaucer's *Parson's Tale* would appear to be no less a part of this tradition than any of the other innumerable tractates on penance which were produced during the thirteenth and fourteenth centuries. In the *Parson's Tale* one finds, for instance, various statements directly attributed to St. Augustine.[10] More frequently one finds the works of Augustine serving quietly and unobtrusively as basic elements in the development of the Parson's argument. The Augustinian phrase and attitude are demonstrably present, but the name has disappeared. St. Augustine has simply become the standard material of the theological writer. Perhaps the most sensible view of the sources of the *Parson's Tale* is merely that of an immense and astonishingly pervasive Augustinian theology, added to by Gregory the Great and others, reworked and transmitted through century after century of compilers to the work or works which Chaucer happened to read.

The purpose of the present paper is to afford some indication of the indebtedness of the *Parson's Tale* to this process of transmission. Through the use of a section of the *Parson's Tale* (lines 322–349), alluded to above, I shall attempt to show the original Augustinian doctrine; a reworking of that doctrine by an English theologian, Richard de Wetheringsett; and Chaucer's use of similar reworked material in the *Parson's Tale*.[11] The Chaucerian text will be found in the left-hand column, extracts from the *Summa de officio sacerdotis* in the right-hand column, and the Augustinian parallels in the Notes.[12]

It is hoped that through a comparison of these passages, the reader will come to regard Chaucer's *Parson's Tale* less as an isolated problem in certain rather specific borrowings than as a very small part of a great tradition.

(322) Of the spryngynge of synnes seith Seint Paul in this wise: that "right as by a man synne entred first into this world, and thurgh that synne deeth, right so thilke deeth entred into alle men that synneden."

Sicut per unum hominem intravit peccatum in hunc mundum et [per] peccatum mors, et in omnes homines mors pertransiit in quo omnes peccaverunt [Romans v, 12] (fol. 44ᵃ).¹³

(323) And this man was Adam, by whom synne entered into this world, whan he brak the comaundementz of God.

Homo iste primus parens est per quem peccatum intravit in hunc mundum cum preceptum domini sui transgressus est (fol. 44ᵃ).¹⁴

(324) And therfore, he that first was so myghty that he sholde nat have dyed, bicam swich oon that he moste nedes dye, wheither he wolde or noon, and al his progenye in this world, that in thilke man synneden.

. . . et sic qui primus fuit immortalis et potens non mori, factus est mortalis . . . mortalitati, i.e., necessitati moriendi, addictus. Ipse, scilicet, et tota eius successio [Romans v]. In omnes homines pertransiit mors in quo . . . omnes peccaverunt, quia omnes in Adam fuerunt carnaliter, materialiter, seminaliter, et essensialiter . . . (fol. 44ᵃ).¹⁵

Lines 325–330

[See Genesis III, 1–7]¹⁶

(331–332) There may ye seen that deedly synne hath first suggestion of the feend, as sheweth heere by the naddre; and afterward, the delit of the flessh, as sheweth heere by Eve; and after that, the consentynge of resoun, as sheweth heere by Adam./ For trust wel, though so were that the feend tempted Eve, that is to seyn, the flessh, and the flessh hadde delit in the beautee of the fruyt

Et sicut in primo peccato serpens primo suasit, mulier delectabatur, vir non repressit sed comedit; sic mistice sensualitas movet, ratio tollerat, consentit homo . . . Inferior pars rationis tanquam mulier delectatur. Ratio vero si consentit . . . mortale peccatum est in anima, et dicitur talis consensus consensus affectionis . . . (fol. 44ᵇ). In corde fit suggestio per dia-

defended, yet certes, til that re-soun, that is to seyn, Adam, con-sented to the etynge of the fruyt, yet stood he in th'estaat of in-nocence.

(333) Of thilke Adam tooke we thilke synne original; for of hym flesshly descended be we alle, and engendred of vile and corrupt mateere.

(334) And whan the soule is put in oure body, right anon is contract original synne; and that that was erst but oonly peyne of concupiscence, is afterward bothe peyne and synne.

(335) And therefore be we alle born sones of wratthe and of dampnacioun perdurable, if it nere baptesme that we receyven, which bynymeth us the culpe. But for sothe, the peyne dwelleth with us, as to temptacioun, which peyne highte concupiscence.

(336) And this concupiscence, whan it is wrongfully disposed or ordeyned in man, it maketh hym coveite, by coveitise of flessh, flesshly synne by sighte of his eyen as to erthely thynges, and eek coveitise of hynesse by pride of herte.

(337) Now, as for to speken of the firste coveitise, that is con-cupiscence, after the lawe of oure

bolum, ut in paradiso serpens suasit. Inde delectatio per carnem, ut ibi delectata est Eva. Postea fit consensus per spiritum, ut ibi Adam consensit . . . (fol. 45ᵃ).[17]

Sed originale peccatum et car-nalis successio ex traduce et pre-iacente materia est. Peccatum vero quod post intravit in mundum, originale dicitur, scilicet, a viciosa origine et corupta et accidit a reatu primi parentis . . . (fol. 44ᵃ).[18]

Sed quam cito anima infundi-tur illi embrioni, originale contra-hitur . . . quod vero ante animae infusionem fuit pena solum, post infusionem est culpa et pena (fol. 44ᵇ).[19]

Sed culpa omnino tollitur in baptismo; pena vero remanet ad pugnam, luctum, et excercicium. Dicitur autem proprie concupissi-bilitas, que facit parvulum con-cupiscibilem et adultum concupis-centem . . . (fol. 44ᵇ).[20]

Concupiscencia carnis est de-siderium omnium que ad volup-tates et delicias corporis pertinent. . . . Concupiscentia oculorum est omnis curiositas . . . in ad-quirendis super vacuis rebus tem-poralibus . . . Superbia vitae est quo quis se iactat in honoribus . . . (fol. 46ᵃ–46ᵇ).[21]

Unde et primam inobedi-enciam in membris virilibus sensit primus parens . . . (fol. 44ᵇ).[22]

membres, that weren lawfulliche ymaked and by rightful jugge-ment of God;

(338) I seye, forasmuche as man is nat obeisaunt to God, that is his lord, therefore is the flessh to hym disobeisaunt thurgh con-cupiscence which yet is cleped norissynge of synne and occasioun of synne.

(339–341) Therefore, al the while that a man hath in hym the peyne of concupiscence, it is im-possible but he be tempted som-time and moeved in his flessh to synne./ And this thyng may nat faille as longe as he lyveth; it may wel wexe fieble and faille by vertu of baptesme, and by the grace of God thurgh penitence;/ but fully ne shal it nevere quenche, that he ne shal som tyme be moeved in hymself, but if he were al refreyed by siknesse, or by malefice of sorcerie, or colde drynkes.

Lines 342–349

. . . quia homo non obedivit suo superiori, nec ei obediat suum inferius, scilicet caro . . . dicitur [concupiscentia] . . . langor nec fomes peccati. Anglice, "Vostringe of sunne" . . . (fol. 44^b).[23]

Est ergo quasi cinis in quo latet igniculus, i.e., fomes peccati frequenter movens sensualitatem . . . (fol. 44^b).[24]

[No parallels in *Summa de officio sacerdotis*][25]

NOTES

1. K. O. Petersen, *The Sources of the Parson's Tale* (Boston, 1901).
2. See Germaine Dempster, "The Parson's Tale," *Sources and Analogues*, pp. 723–760.
3. *Ibid.*, p. 724.
4. *Moralia*, xxxi, xlv (*PL*, LXXVI, 621). The order of Peraldus' *Summa de vitiis* is "gula," "luxuria," "avaritia," "tristitia," "superbia," "in-vidia," "ira," "peccatum linguae." In Gregory the order of the sins in their descent from "superbia" is "inanis gloria" (later assimilated into "superbia"), "invidia," "ira," "tristitia," "avaritia," "ventris ingluvies," "luxuria." This relationship has already been observed by Mrs. Dempster (*Sources and Analogues*, p. 727, note 4). It is interesting to observe that it must also have been well known to Miss Petersen, since the source upon which she principally relies, St. Raymond, ob-

serves: "nota doctrinam quam tradit Gregorius super Job," and lists the sins in the Gregorian order (the passage in question may be found reproduced by Dempster, p. 740). See also Petersen, pp. 26–27.

5. See above, "An Augustinian Interpretation of Chaucer's Pardoner," note 25. One may also observe various other similarities. The divisions of the sins in the *Parson's Tale* are Gregorian, with some expansions. Compare, for instance, "superbia" in Chaucer (*Works*, 2nd ed., p. 239) and "inanis gloria" in Gregory (*PL*, LXXXVI, 621). Various phrases of Gregory, not followed by Peraldus in his rather different rationale, are also present. Chaucer: "Pride the general roote of alle harmes" (line 388). Gregory: "Radix quippe cuncti mali superbia est" (*Works*, p. 239; *PL*, LXXXVI, 621), etc.

6. It is unquestionably true that there are many passages in the *Parson's Tale* to which Peraldus' *Summa de vitiis* offers more accurate correspondences than any other work yet discovered. However, these correspondences may, I think, be explained as Peraldus' partial use of an earlier tradition founded upon the very brief seven deadly sins passage in the *Moralia*. As will be indicated further on in the present essay, treatises of this nature were not created *de novo*, but relied heavily upon earlier sources.

7. See article "Raymond de Penyafort" in *Dictionnaire de théologie catholique*, XIII, 1810. The indebtedness of English manualists to St. Raymond is demonstrated by the author of the *Regimen animarum* (1343), who lists the *Summa summarum Raymundi* as a principal source for his work (G. R. Owst, *Preaching in Mediaeval England* [Cambridge, 1926], p. 297, note 5).

8. About Richard de Wetheringsett not much positive evidence is available. References in the *Summa*, or "Qui bene presunt," indicate that he was a student of William de Montibus, chancellor of Lincoln (d. 1213), and that he was writing probably not later than 1235 (MS Tanner 110, fol. 13ᵃ; MS New College XCIV, fol. 69ᵇ; 94ᵇ). He is variously confused with Richard Grant, Archbishop of Canterbury; William de Montibus, whose *Summa* forms the basis of his own; and Richard de Wetheringsett, chancellor of Cambridge a century later. In respect to the last of these, it is, however, quite possible that the same title, chancellor of Cambridge, applied to the earlier Richard de Wetheringsett may have some basis, since he could have held this office at a time before 1230, when the earliest reference to a chancellor of Cambridge occurs. (H. Rashdall, *The Universities of Europe in the Middle Ages*, ed. Powicke and Emden [Oxford, 1936], III, 278). In any case, the limitation of time references in the "Qui bene presunt" to the first two decades of the thirteenth century, together with the absence of any indebtedness to Raymond of Pennaforte, whose *Summa* was composed after 1222 (date set by Professor Stephan Kuttner; see discussion in *Sources and Analogues*, p. 723, note 3), indicates that the "Qui bene presunt" is one of the very earliest English manuals for parish priests and that it was composed possibly before the *Summa* of St. Raymond, or more probably before its influence had been generally felt in England. On the whole problem of authorship, see J. C. Russell, *Dictionary of Writers of Thirteenth Century England* (London,

1936), 124–125, 196–197. The manuscript extracted in the present article is MS New College XCIV in the Bodleian Library. It is written in a fourteenth-century hand and contains English phrases pointing to west-southwest provenience (see below). For information concerning the dialect area I am indebted to Professor E. Talbot Donaldson, Yale University; concerning problems of the date to the Rev. Leonard E. Boyle, O.P., Pontifical Institute, Toronto. For indispensable assistance with the question of authorship I wish to express my gratitude to Dr. R. W. Hunt, Keeper of Western Manuscripts at the Bodleian Library, Oxford.

9. Lines 322–349. Parallels in the *Summa casuum poenitentiae* are collected by Miss Petersen, *Sources of the Parson's Tale*, p. 34, note 2.

10. The sources of a considerable number of these direct quotations from St. Augustine still remain unidentified. Although it is beyond the scope of the present article to attempt a general tracing of the Augustinian quotations in the *Parson's Tale*, the sources of two definitions of sin may be tentatively identified. At line 368, the Parson says: "Deedly synne, as seith Seint Augustyn, is whan a man turneth his herte fro God, which that is verray sovereyn bountee, that may nat chaunge, and yeveth his herte to thyng that may chaunge and flitte." A close parallel to this is to be discovered in the *De libero arbitrio*, I, xvi: "omnia peccata hoc uno genere contineri, cum quisque avertitur a divinis vereque manentibus, et ad mutabilia atque incerta convertitur" (*PL*, XXXII, 1240). The second definition, at lines 958–959: "Seint Augustyn seith: "Synne is every word and every dede, and al that men coveiten, agayn the lawe of Jhesu Crist" would seem very definitely to come from the much cited statement by Augustine in the *Contra Faustum Manichaeum*, XXII, xxvii: "Ergo peccatum est factum vel dictum vel concupitum aliquid contra aeternam legem" (*PL*, XLII, 418). It is clear that both Augustinian texts have undergone some revision. In the latter (line 958) a whole section "and this is for to synne in herte, in mouth, and in dede," etc., has been added. In a late printed edition like that of Anaclet Reiffenstuel (*Theologia moralis* [1752], p. 71), the Augustinian definition is with very slight change printed in italics and the later commentary: "Dicitur primo, *dictum, factum, vel concupitum*, ad indicandum triplex peccatum, videlicet cogitationis, oris & operis" is distinguished from it. That Chaucer knew where the Augustinian definition ended and the commentary began is not entirely clear. See " 'Seith Moyses by the Devel,' " above.

11. It is not my contention that Chaucer read and followed Richard de Wetheringsett. The *Summa de officio sacerdotis* is used only as an example, doubtless typical, of the reworking of Augustinian material by an English theologian.

12. References to the *Parson's Tale* are from *Works*; to St. Augustine from *Patrologia latina*; and to Richard's *Summa* from MS New College XCIV. To each extract from the *Summa de officio sacerdotis* folio reference is attached. Where dots follow the extract, readings are not consecutive; where no dots follow, the order of Richard is identical with that of Chaucer. The author is indebted to Dr. R. W. Hunt of the Bodleian Library for permission to publish, and to the late Professor Jacob

Hammer and to the Rev. Edwin A. Quain, S.J., for checking the transcription.

13. "Sicut enim Paulus apostolus dixit, *Per unum hominem peccatum intravit in mundum, et per peccatum mors; et ita in omnes homines pertransiit, in quo omnes peccaverunt*" [Romans v, 12] (*Opus imperfectum contra Julianum*, I, cvi [*PL*, XLV, 1120]).

14. "*Per unum hominem peccatum intravit in mundum . . .* Ecce primus homo totam massam damnabilem fecit" (*Sermo* CLXV, VII [*PL*, XXXVIII, 907]).

15. "Alia erat illa immortalitas, ubi homo poterat non mori: alia est ista mortalitas, ubi homo non potest nisi mori" (*Opus imperfectum contra Julianum*, I, lxxi [*PL*, XLV, 1096]; "Omnes enim fuimus in illo uno, quando omnes fuimus ille unus, qui per feminam lapsus est in peccatum" (*De civitate Dei*, XIII, xiv [*PL*, XLI, 386]).

16. The conclusion here of so extended a biblical quotation (story of the Fall) is almost certainly attributable to Chaucer himself. Treatises of this type are generally tightly constructed, and the commentator will very rarely indeed give more than a short quotation with reference. Richard de Wetheringsett, for instance, though dealing with aspects of the same story, gives only fragmentary quotations (fol. 45ᵇ).

17. "Etiam nunc in unoquoque nostrum nihil aliud agitur, cum ad peccatum quisque delabitur, quam tunc actum est in illis tribus, serpente, muliere, et viro. Nam primo fit suggestio sive per cogitationem, sive per sensus corporis . . . quae suggestio cum facta fuerit, si cupiditas nostra non movebitur ad peccandum, excludetur serpentis astutia; si autem mota fuerit, quasi mulieri jam persuasum erit. Sed aliquando ratio viriliter etiam commotam cupiditatem refrenat atque compescit. Quod cum fit, non labimur in peccatum, sed cum aliquanta luctatione coronamur. Si autem ratio consentiat, et quod libido commoverit, faciendum esse decernat, ab omni vita beata tanquam de paradiso expellitur homo" (*De Genesi contra Manicheos*, II, xiv [*PL*, XXXIV, 207]).

18. "Hinc post peccatum [Adam] exsul effectus, stirpem quoque suam, quam peccando in se tanquam in radice vitiaverat, poena mortis et damnationis obstrinxit; ut quicquid prolis ex illo . . . nasceretur, traheret originale peccatum" (*Enchiridion*, I, xxvi [*PL*, XL, 245]); "sed jam natura erat seminalis, ex qua propagaremur: qua scilicet propter peccatum vitiata, et vinculo mortis obstricta, justeque damnata, non alterius conditionis homo ex homine nasceretur" (*De civitate Dei*, XIII, xiv [*PL*, XLI, 386]).

19. I have been able to find no accurate parallel for the statement: "And whan the soule is put in oure body, right anon is contract original synne." However, the latter part of the statement is apparently a development of the Augustinian definition of concupiscence: "ita concupiscentia carnis . . . et peccatum est . . . et poena peccati . . . et causa peccati" (*Contra Julianum Pelagianum*, v, iii [*PL*, XLIV, 787]).

20. "qui nascuntur in mundo, perituri nisi renascantur in Christo" (*Opus imperfectum contra Julianum*, IV, lxxvii [*PL*, XLV, 1383]); "Reatus ejus regeneratione solutus est, conflictus ejus ad agonem relictus est" (*ibid.*, I, lxxi [*PL*, XLV, 1096]).

21. *"omne quod in mundo est,* sicut divinitus dictum est, *concupiscentia carnis est, et concupiscentia oculorum, et ambitio saeculi* [I John II, 16]. Hoc modo tria illa sunt notata: nam concupiscentia carnis voluptatis infimae amatores significat; concupiscentia oculorum, curiosos; ambitio saeculi, superbos" (*De vera religione,* I, xxxviii [*PL,* XXXIV, 153]) .

22. *"Video aliam legem in membris meis, repugnantem legi mentis meae, et captivum me ducentem in lege peccati, quae est in membris meis* [Romans VII, 23]. Ipsa est prima captivitas nostra, qua concupiscit adversus spiritum caro" [Galatians v, 17] (*Enarratio in Psalmum* LXX [*PL,* XXXVI, 891]) . As St. Augustine points out, however, the flesh does not lust without the spirit: "Non enim caro sine anima concupiscit, quamvis caro concupiscere dicatur, quia carnaliter anima concupiscit" (*De perfectione justitiae hominis* [*PL,* XLIV, 301]) . Concupiscence, therefore, is not simply the "firste coveitise" but involves all the appetencies of the spirit divided against itself by original sin at the Fall. "Concupiscence after the lawe of oure membres" was, however, as Richard's *Summa* indicates, the first desire which man experienced after the Fall. Hence it would seem that the comma which Robinson inserts after the word "concupiscence" should be removed to read "concupiscence after the lawe of oure membres." Skeat's reading of this passage appears preferable to Robinson's, although perhaps somewhat overemphatic: "the firste coveitise, that is, concupiscence after the lawe of oure membres" (Skeat, IV, 587) .

23. "Denique, ut breviter dicatur, in illius peccati poena quid inobedientiae nisi inobedientia retributa est? . . . Quid interest unde, dum tamen per justitiam dominantis Dei cui subditi servire noluimus, caro nostra nobis, quae subdita fuerat, non serviendo molesta sit" (*De civitate Dei,* XIV, xv [*PL,* XLI, 423–424]) ; "concupiscentia carnis . . . peccatorum matre multorum" (*De nuptiis et concupiscentia,* I, xxiv [*PL,* XLIV, 429]) . For "occasioun of synne," see note 19 above.

24. It will be observed that up to line 339, parallels to the *Summa* have on the whole been appreciably closer than those to the original St. Augustine. To lines 339–341, however, the *Summa* fails to offer more than a general similarity of idea. Numerous statements by St. Agustine do nevertheless offer correspondences to this section: "Fatigati sunt quodam modo hostes nostri jam etiam per aetatem: sed tamen etiam fatigati non cessant qualibuscumque motibus infestare senectutis quietem" (*Sermo* CXXVIII [*PL,* XXXVIII, 719]) ; "Per Dei gratiam minuitur . . . necessitas nostra" (*Opus imperfectum contra Julianum,* III, lxxi [*PL,* XLV, 1279]) ; "ipsa concupiscentia, cum qua nati sumus, finiri non potest quamdiu vivimus; quotidie minui potest, finiri non potest" (*Sermo* CLI [*PL,* XXXVIII, 817]) .

25. After line 341, there are no further significant parallels in the *Summa* to the section of the *Parson's Tale* under discussion (lines 322–349) . Although St. Augustine makes frequent use of the texts from Paul translated in lines 342–344 (Galatians v, 17; Romans VII, 24) , it has not seemed worth while to reproduce them. The texts in lines 345–349 (St. Jerome; James I, 14; I John I, 8) are not typical of St. Augustine's discussion of concupiscence.

20

Chaucer's Self-Portrait and Dante's

Aɴʏ sᴇᴀʀᴄʜ ꜰᴏʀ ᴛʜᴇ ᴏʀɪɢɪɴᴀʟs of Chaucer's early self-portraits inevitably ends with Dante. Comic self-portrayal, which makes its first appearance with Chaucer's earliest original work, the *Book of the Duchess*, appears in subsequent early works in situations verging upon parodies of comparable scenes in the *Divine Comedy*. One thinks of the Eagle's "Seynte Marye! Thou are noyous for to carye" in the *Hous of Fame*, and, in the *Parlement of Foules*, of Africanus' difficulties in getting the innocent poet through the forbidding gates of the Garden of Love.[1] However, it has not, I think, been observed that Chaucer's self-portrait in the Prologue to *Sir Thopas* offers a further example of the Dantean guide-poet relationship evident in the earlier portraits. Harry Bailly, the self-appointed "gyde" of the Canterbury Pilgrims,[2] addresses Chaucer as follows:

> "What man artow?" quod he;
> "Thou lookest as thou woldest fynde an hare,
> For evere upon the ground I se thee stare."[3]

The source of this passage is, I believe, to be found in *Purgatorio* xix, 40–53. There Dante, weighed down by his vision of the "femmina balba," takes on the appearance of "un mezzo arco di

Reprinted from *Medium Aevum*, xxix (1960), 119–120.

ponte" (42). Virgil, here as elsewhere described by the term "guida" (53), comments, as does Harry Bailly, upon this singular posture:

"Che hai che pur inver la terra guati?" (52)

If one removes the "hare" amplification from Harry Bailly's remarks, the words of the two guides to their respective poets become virtually identical.

The discovery of an immediate relationship between Chaucer's self-portrait and Dante's is perhaps useful in solving a troublesome problem often brought up in connection with the *Sir Thopas* Prologue—the supposed contradiction between the gregarious Chaucer of the *General Prologue* and the aloof Chaucer of *Sir Thopas*.[4] If one compares, in the broadest terms, the artistic methods of Dante and Chaucer, one is struck by their remarkably similar use of what might be called the dual first person singular. In the *Divine Comedy*:

> Dante writes the poem as the record of a journey he once took and now remembers. He writes in the first person; and yet the distinction between Dante speaking as author, and Dante the Pilgrim, is fundamental to the whole structure. The author, when he reminds us of his existence, is outside the fictive world of the poem; the Pilgrim is the protagonist of the drama. . . . The author knows the whole story in advance, the Pilgrim meets everything freshly, for the first time.[5]

A comparable principle has been independently applied to Chaucer with highly rewarding results,[6] and may, I believe, be of service in the present instance. Thus one may suppose that in the gregarious man at the Tabard Inn, Chaucer is introducing to us a fictive creation whose function, like that of Dante's Pilgrim, is to live in the moment and see only the moment. In the "elvyssh" man of *Sir Thopas*, however, the man who "unto no wight dooth . . . daliaunce," Chaucer is, I think, showing himself to us as the artist, the withdrawn intelligence which does not exist from moment to moment, but encompasses the whole fabric of its work. Hence in choosing a model for his final self-portrait, he chose that figure of Dante which most fully suggested to him the distancing and objectification great art requires.

NOTES

1. *Hous of Fame,* lines 573–574, (*Purgatorio* IX, 13–42) ; *Parlement of Foules,* lines 120–154 (*Inferno* III, 1–21). The references to Chaucer are to *Works,* pp. 287, 312. The references to Dante are to *La Divina Commedia,* ed. Giuseppe Vandelli (Milan, 1949), pp. 374–375, 20–21.
2. I [A], 804.
3. VII [B²], 695–697.
4. See Robinson's comment in *Works,* p. 736.
5. Francis Fergusson, *Dante's Drama of the Mind* (Princeton, 1953), pp. 9–10.
6. E. T. Donaldson, "Chaucer the Pilgrim," *PMLA,* LXIX (1954), 928–936; rpt. *Chaucer Criticism,* ed. Richard Schoeck and Jerome Taylor (South Bend, Ind., 1960–1961), I, 1–13. See also *Chaucer's Poetry,* ed. E. T. Donaldson (New York, 1958), pp. 877–881.

Index

Abraham, 301, 302
"Abusionibus" (Clement V), 216, 232n40, 233n41
Acta sanctorum, 114, 121, 139nn29–37, 140nn38–43, 234n53
Adam, 346–47, 351n18
Adam of St. Victor, 337n12
Adèle, countess of Blois, 122, 140n49
Adhemar, Guilhem, 106n87
Adversus Jovinianum (St. Jerome), 337n12
Aegeus, in Chaucer's *Knight's Tale*, 178, 180
Aelfric, 53
Aeneas, 149, 163, 192n34
Africanus, in Chaucer's *Parlement of Foules*, 353
Agincourt, battle of, 127, 133, 218
agriculture, fertility rites and, 109, 110–11, 112, 123, 124, 125, 140n52
Aiken, Pauline, cited, 198n72
Ainard de la Tour, 160, 189n28
Albert of Stade, 149
Albertus Magnus, saint, 251–52, 261nn5, 7, 262n12, 264nn24, 26, 267n45

Alceste, in Chaucer's *Legend of Good Women*, 82
Alcuin, 39, 48n30
Aldhelm, 37–38
Alexander, Bishop of Lincoln, 4
Alfonso, Count of Denia, 193n38
Alfonso el Sabio, 149–50, 151, 153n10
Alice of Bath, in Chaucer's *Canterbury Tales*, 229, 277, 291, 295, 328n103; marital "order" and, 292–93, 294, 313, 315–16
Allegories of the Virtues and Vices in Medieval Art (Katzenellenbogen), 47n19
"Among School Children" (Yeats), 67
Analecta hymnica (Blume and Bannister, eds.), 337n12
Anatomia Mundini (Mondino dei Luzzi), 70–71, 101nn39–41
Andalus: Spain under the Muslims (Hole), 100n34
Anderson, Marjorie, 97n7
Andreas Capellanus, 74–75, 93, 102nn53–54, 103nn55–57; on women, 278, 319n8, 325n64

About the Author

Alfred L. Kellogg has been a professor at Rutgers University since 1947. He received his doctorate from Yale in 1941, and has taught there and at Cornell. He held a Ford Foundation fellowship in 1951–1952, and during this period was a Visiting Fellow at Princeton University and a member of the Institute for Advanced Study. On a Guggenheim Fellowship in 1953–1954, he spent most of his time at Oxford, and in the summer of 1965, which he spent in Cumberland, he was the recipient of an American Philosophical Society Penrose Grant fellowship. He has contributed to numerous scholarly journals and to *Essays in Literary History,* ed. R. Kirk and C. F. Main.